A Champion of the Cross

AMS PRESS
NEW YORK

Y. ob'. serv'. in the Church,

J. H. Hopkins.

A CHAMPION OF THE CROSS

BEING

THE LIFE

OF

JOHN HENRY HOPKINS, S.T.D.

INCLUDING

EXTRACTS AND SELECTIONS

FROM

HIS WRITINGS

BY

REV. CHARLES F. SWEET

NEW YORK

JAMES POTT & CO., PUBLISHERS

1894

Reprinted from the edition of 1894, New York
First AMS EDITION published 1971
Manufactured in the United States of America

International Standard Book Number: 0-404-07202-X

Library of Congress Number: 76-144692

AMS PRESS INC.
NEW YORK, N. Y. 10003

PREFACE.

JOHN HENRY HOPKINS needs no introduction to the American Church. For the last forty years he has been one of the weightiest of the influences which have moulded and directed her thought. Nevertheless, my connection with him is not so clear as to give authenticity to what I have written concerning him. When Dr. Hopkins died two years ago his brother undertook the work of writing the biography. It is to him that a very large degree of credit is due for the material which he afterward handed over to me. I had been one of Dr. Hopkins's students, and to me he had left the task of completing his work on the history and true meaning of the Seventh General Council. Accordingly, when the brother found that he could not complete the biography, it was in a certain sense natural that the materials should be given to me; which was done, and I, with the full approval of all Dr. Hopkins' relatives, undertook the work. The work, then, has been done, as well as it could have been by myself, in such intervals as I could snatch from the work of a parish in a large New England factory city. I have no apologies to make for the carelessness and scrappiness of the work, for I did as well as I could under the circumstances.

I desire to say here just a word or two as to Dr. Hopkins as a *teacher*. I have seen, from the pupils' bench, a good many teachers, in university, and in legal studies, and in theology, and, leaving all question of learning out of consideration (for all know that Dr. Hopkins was a man of genuine erudition), he was simply one of the best that I ever knew. That he was sympathetic will be gathered from the biography. But he was far more. He was simply inspiring. What I am is of little consequence, indeed, but such as I am, after those who gave me life and care and love, I owe to him. This book has been written because I love him, and so have tried to snatch from the maw of Time some relics of his life, whose full beauty will be known of all, as he willed to have it, in God's own day.

CHARLES F. SWEET.

ST. THOMAS' CHURCH, METHUEN, MASS.,
Autumn, 1893.

TABLE OF CONTENTS.

CHAPTER I.

1820–1830.

PAGE

Parents and Early Life 1–10

CHAPTER II.

1831–1842.

Removal from Boston, Mass., to Burlington, Vt.—Graduation from the
University of Vermont—Sonnet-writing in 1838—Interest in Politics, Lithography 11–22

CHAPTER III.

1843.

Life in Savannah, Ga.—Tutor in the Family of Bishop Elliott—Tracts
and Tractarians—Athirst for Love........................... 23–40

CHAPTER IV.

1843–1849.

Goes to Louisiana—Goes to New York City—Reporter on *The Courier
and Enquirer*—Paints Miniatures on Ivory—Prepares "Vermont
Drawing-book of Flowers" and "Vermont Drawing-book of Fig-
ures"—The Print-colorer's Lament—Enters the General Theological Seminary—Chess—*The Church Journal*—Epigrams—Byronic
Collar—His Reading of Hebrew—The Oxford Movement—The New
York Ecclesiological Society—Designs for Stained Glass Windows
—Rood Screen—Needle-work Adornment of Vestments—The First
Alb, Chasuble, and Dalmatic—The First Colored Stole—The First
Pastoral Staff—Designs Altar Plate—Episcopal Seals—Alms Basin
sent by the General Convention to the Church of England—Thanks
by Bishop Wordsworth—Monument to his Father—Pastoral Staff
for First Bishop of Central Pennsylvania—Church Music—Music
Composed and Hymns Written—Carols..................... 41–72

CHAPTER V.

1850-1867.

PAGE

Ordained Deacon—Vigil of Ordination—*The Church Journal*—Six Months' Charge of the Church of the Epiphany, Washington, D. C. —Story of his Public Life—Condition of the Church at this Time —Chanting the Canticles—Calvinism and Catholicity—Tracts for the Times—Reunion of Catholic Christendom—The *terminus ad quem*... 73-81

CHAPTER VI.

1868.

Radicals—Drs. Seymour and De Koven—Staff of *The Church Journal* —St. Stephen's College, Annandale—Revival of the Diaconate— The Beginning of Methodism—The Salvation Army—Lack of Education—Smaller Dioceses—Called a Dreamer, a Doctrinaire—Provinces—Fairness in Distribution of Offices—The General Theological Seminary—Free Churches.—Protestant Episcopal Routine— Flexibility of Practical System—The First Mistake of the Church —Dr. Muhlenberg's *Memorial* 82-104

CHAPTER VII.

1865 and 1866.

Evangelicals—General Convention of 1859—The Church a Haven of Peace—General Convention of 1862—The Highest Political Movement that Rose in the Church—The Southern Church—The Church Completely Reunited—Attitude of *The Church Journal*—Assassination of President Lincoln—Maximilian as Emperor of Mexico— Russia's Sympathy—The Sclavonic Liturgy used in New York— Sale of *The Church Journal*—St. Alban's Church, New York— "The Huckleberry-Pudding Business"—Ceremonial Development —Ritualistic Controversy in England—Ornaments Rubric—Liberty of Ritual—"The Blank Cartridge"—The Oxford Movement —Ritualism—The Thirty Years' War—Dr. Pusey's Eirenicon— Bishop Hopkins' "Law of Ritualism"—The "Declaration"— "The Blank Cartridge" 105-146

CHAPTER VIII.

1867-1872.

The Colenso Affair—The First Lambeth Conference—Journal of the Visit to England and France—Chester Cathedral—Durham Cathedral—York Cathedral—Lincoln Cathedral—Peterborough Cathedral—Norwich Cathedral—Westminster Abbey—St. Alban's, Holborn — St. Paul's Cathedral — Mr. Mackonochie — Archdeacon Wordsworth—Archbishop of Canterbury—Dr. Pusey—Magdalen

PAGE

College—British Museum—Rochester Cathedral—Lambeth Palace
—Meetings of Council—Dieppe—Rouen—Paris—Rheims—Laon—
Amiens—Beauvais—London—All Saints, Margaret Street—Voyage
Home—Death of Bishop Hopkins—Sale of *The Church Journal*—
Began to Write the Life of his Father—Missionary Work—Rector
at Plattsburgh, N. Y.—Reformed Episcopal Church—Use of the
Litany—Early Celebrations—His last Communication for the Pub-
lic Eye... 147–192

CHAPTER IX.

1874–1891.

Rector at Williamsport, Pa.—Parochial Ministration—Proposed Division of the Diocese—An Assistant Bishop Instead—Lecture in
Lock Haven—Life of Rev. James Breck—Proposal to go to Springfield, Ill.—An Appellate Court in Illinois—Trip West—Racine—
Nashotah—Daily Eucharist—Church Congress—Bishop Whitehead's Election to Pittsburgh—Pastoral Staff—Chancellorsville and
the Wilderness—Province of Pennsylvania—Bishop Stevens—Supplemental Deputy to General Convention—Canon on Election of
Bishops—Illuminated Book of Hours—Consecration of Bishop
Walker—Bishop Stevens and the Federate Council—Monsignor
Capel—Order of Corporate Reunion—Deputy to General Convention of 1886—Terms of Union with Religious Bodies—First Elec-
tion to Lectureship on Christian Evidences at the General Theological Seminary—Resigns His Williamsport Rectorship—Visit to
California—Rejected by the Trustees of the General Theological
Seminary when nominated as Lecturer—Gift of Books to the Li-
brary—Knocked down by a Broadway Horse-car—Ordination of
His Nephew—Illness at Troy, N. Y.—Kindness of Dr. Ferguson
—Changes in the Roman Catholic Church—The Iconoclastic Controversy—Defence of Phillips Brooks—The Dream of a Child—He
Marries the Daughter of His Kind Friend—A Few Weeks Afterward He Falls Asleep in Jesus—Buried near His Father in Burling-
ton, Vt.—Tribute from Bishop Thompson.................. 193–237

APPENDIX.

Proportionate Representation—Rain, Light, Heat, and Soil; Sermon
29, S. Mark iv. 28—For Family Prayers, Collects for the
Seven Days of the Week—The Provincial System, American
Church Review, January, 1891—The Lay Element in England and
in America—Three Points, An Essay Read before the Associate
Alumni of the General Theological Seminary, May 31, 1887—De-
cline and Fall of the Low-Church Party, Church and the World,
July, 1872—The Cathedral System in the City, The Regular
Quarterly Paper Read at the Meeting of the New York Ecclesio-
logical Society, January, 1855—Letters.................... 239–372

INDEX 373–374

A CHAMPION OF THE CROSS.

CHAPTER I.

1820–1830.

John Henry Hopkins was born at Pittsburg, October 28, 1820. At the time of his birth his father, who was afterward distinguished in the history of the Church both for his genius and learning, as well as by his position as Bishop of the Diocese of Vermont, was a member of the bar, and already showing in his early manhood the traits which were afterward to make him one of the notable figures that have worn the Episcopal purple ; and no thought had yet come to his mind of any other vocation in life than that in which he was on the beaten road to success.

The elder John Henry Hopkins (born in Dublin of mingled English and Irish blood) was noted for his ready, receptive, strong mind, his independence of character, his moral courage, his unflinching devotion to duty, his pertinacity and hopefulness, and for a general "masculine" type of character. Bishop Hopkins's mind never stopped growing. The principles upon which he based his actions were never forsaken. Some men go on bravely, it may be for a long time, acting upon a certain set of principles, and then seem all at once to be stricken with some mortal panic fear, and, at first wavering, then pausing, then falling from the ranks altogether, they appeal to their old companions to leave like them ; and they denounce those who keep their place "in the ranks hard-pressed" as traitors to the very cause which once engaged *them* heart and soul. This sort of thing happens over and over again in the course of all great movements, and those who take such a course invariably justify themselves by saying that principles are pushed too far. But Bishop Hopkins was no such man. He had clearness of vision to see consequences and the courage to go on whether he liked them or not.

So was it with his son, John Henry, junior. The elements of a character which make it strong, and which are called masculine

1

because men ought to be strong, the son received in full measure
from his father.   But more than this, with the strength of mind
there was also genuine versatility, copying in this, too, from the
father, which was never frittered away in idle accomplishment.
The æsthetic tastes, marked in him by love for art, including its
noblest development, music, which are the sphere of exercise of
what the Germans call the "play impulse" in character, never
sunk into mere recreations or amusements, but were lifted up by
intense personal devotion, and thus made to serve the cause of
religion.

If he received so much from the father there was clearly
enough in him to make him a noteworthy figure in the Church.

It is not often that a man is so happily yoked with one who
harmonizes all the vigorous components of his nature without
weakening them.   She who was the mother of John Henry Hopkins gave to him a rare store of religious enthusiasm, never-fail-
ing zeal, amiability, and extreme tenderness of heart, together
with that peculiar power of fascinating others which some people
possess, and which is called, for lack of a better name, magnetism.   From her, too, came the cheerful patience and sunny good
nature, and the hopefulness worked, like St. Paul's, by experience, and a charity that was never worn out, no matter what
strains were put upon it.   There are different sorts of strength,
and the feminine sort is every whit as worthy of praise as the
more rugged kind.

The father is well known ; the mother, to whom her eldest
son gave as long as he lived a strong, sweet, tender affection, was
not known, except to those who shared her charming society.
Of her influence upon the lives of her children it may here be
said that the dauntless faith and bright hopefulness of her religious life is to be seen in their lives.   She deserves at least a mention in the biography of her best-known child.

Madame Melusina Müller Hopkins was the daughter of Caspar
Otto Müller, a wealthy merchant of Hamburg.   For generations
his family was almost wholly devoted to the German Lutheran
ministry.   He was the first who had broken through the clerical
tradition of the family.   But, adhering strictly to his determination, made in early childhood, not to become a pastor, he had
with varying fortunes followed a mercantile life, and, after some
years in London, settled in Hamburg.   He had married Elizabeth Antoinette Trance, whose family had fled from France in
1685 at the revocation of the Edict of Nantes.

At Hamburg Melusina was born in 1795.   Napoleon's occupation of Hamburg brought ruin upon Caspar Otto Müller, as upon many others.   After seventeen months of fruitless struggle, the effort to retrieve his fallen fortunes was abandoned, and with the few relics of his shattered fortunes and all his family, he set sail for the United States in the last ship that sailed from the Eider before the embargo went into effect.

They landed at Baltimore, after six weeks' voyage, in June, 1808, and soon prosperity gilded the outlook for the future.

But once more war came to blast his hopes, for the British invasion brought the shock of conflict to his door.   The death of General Ross, September, 1814, alone prevented a battle in the very valley of his home.   Once more, therefore, he resolved to quit his home and seek peace and a livelihood further west. Accordingly, in October of that year the Müller family started from Baltimore for New Harmony in Western Pennsylvania. Mr. Müller and his nephew had already, on a prospecting tour, met John H. Hopkins, and were much pleased with him ; but Melusina had never yet seen him, although common friends had felt that they were meant for each other from their extraordinary love of music.

Journeying in big canvas-covered wagons, with the few mementos of happier, peaceful days, they made their way through the mountains, in rainy weather, by frightful roads.   Thus they travelled for three weeks.   After a fortnight the wagons, hub-deep in the clay, were abandoned, and their occupants made their way in Indian file as best they could, when on horseback appeared a solitary traveller, splashed with mud—it was John Henry Hopkins.   This was the meeting of the parents of the younger Hopkins.   Visit after visit to the log-cabin of the Müller family ensued, and there these two accomplished and refined young people learned the lessons of mutual love.   Hopkins was then an iron-master ; but the prospects of success grew less and less promising, and the treaty of peace between the United States and Great Britain, signed at Ghent, December 24, 1814, brought no blessing to the manufacturers of iron.   Enforced idleness revived a former predilection for the law, and he began his studies, being duly entered as a student-at-law.   In May, 1816, John Henry Hopkins and Melusina Müller were married.   The iron-master's business ended in disaster early in 1817 ; and, betaking himself to Pittsburg, to keep the wolf from the door the young couple taught in a fashionable school, the one painting and drawing, and the other music, for piano, harp, and guitar, and singing; while the study of law went on unceasingly.   In April, 1818, he was admitted to practice, and at the time of the birth of his eldest son was reckoned as one of the leaders of the bar.

For nearly fifty-two years—from May, 1816, to January, 1868— Madame Hopkins continued the faithful wife, sympathizing friend, and solace of her husband.   Through his varied and rising career as iron-master, lawyer, priest and Bishop and educator she lived but to reflect his every wish, and to aid him with her unusual energy.   Very much of Bishop Hopkins' career was brilliantly successful, but when his first Vermont Episcopal Institute failed in 1839 many a dark day followed until 1841, when he removed his family from the village of Burlington " out to the woods " of Rock Point.   During these and succeeding years of toil and poverty, when disaster followed upon disaster, Mrs. Hopkins' noble and Christian fortitude, her unstinted and instinctive self-sacrifice, her labors in all domestic cares, and her pious hopefulness stayed up his spirit and refreshed his courage.   When in 1854 that same " Institute " was revived by him and placed on Rock Point, none entered more ardently into the spirit of triumphant thanksgiving for his success in that long effort than she.   They celebrated their golden wedding in 1866.   During their half century of married life thirteen children had been born to them.   Eleven of them lived beyond the age of thirty.   Thirty-seven of their descendants gathered at the old homestead at Rock Point for the golden wedding.   Although all were not there, with thankful joy and pride the loving eyes of both parents welcomed their children to the fourth generation.   And, as other years rolled on, during her sixteen years of widowhood ninety-three instead of thirty-seven greeted their venerable " Mother " and enlarged her heart and deepened her gratitude to God.

Madame Hopkins was gifted with a voice of rare richness, sweetness, and power.   That voice, with perfect truth of intonation combined with sympathetic quality of tone, retained its sweetness and nearly all its range and power until far past three score and ten.   For over thirty years not only did she lead the singing at home in the morning and evening prayers while the Bishop played the accompaniment on the piano to music of his own while all the children sang, but she was her husband's chief reliance in the choir when he was rector of Trinity Church at Pittsburg.   There she was organist; and in Burlington to the very last her chief delight was to sing and play the favorite hymns of her husband's composition, and thus carry herself back in thought to bygone years of unbroken family union.

For the last years of her life her correspondence with her absent children was surprising in its variety and volume. She used to say that she " lived on the United States Mail," so entirely swayed was she to smiles or tears by the letters she received.

The most complete outline of the life of her son would be seen in the letters which he sent her at least every week and related all that he had done or had seen. She held it a sacred privilege to answer each one, and that she did in unfailing clearness of style and penmanship to the very last of her life.

Her religious devotion often amounted to ecstasy, and gave tone to her whole life. One over-mastering passion—no less—swept her soul and moulded her style of daily intercourse with her children. It was the conviction that she was bringing them up for eternity. She died in 1884, in her ninetieth year, and so entered into the rest for which her soul had thirsted during the long years of separation from her earthly partner.

The devotion of such a woman to her children, as well as what she gave them by birth, helps to account for the singular completeness and soundness of her eldest son, John Henry.

When he was but a little child, his father was, at a parish meeting of Trinity Church, Pittsburg, elected rector of the parish, although he was not even a candidate for Orders. Little by little, the desire to work for God in the highest of Christian callings had come to him, and the vanity of laboring for anything except that which shall last throughout eternity made plain to him. Once, when in such a mood, he had gone so far as to write to the Standing Committee of the Diocese as to whether he could be admitted as a candidate for Holy Orders provisionally—not yet seeing his way clear to the abandonment of his profession. He had once casually mentioned these thoughts to a fellow-vestryman of the parish, and he it was who remembered the words. The rector, failing to invigorate the stagnant parish, had departed, and the vestry-man to whom Mr. Hopkins had spoken the year before, resolved, without lisping a syllable to him on the subject, to act upon the information he possessed. On the very day after the departure of the former priest, while Hopkins was attending court in another county, the parish meeting was called. The meeting was fully attended, and the vestry-man brought forward his plan, which was to elect Mr. Hopkins as their future rector, if he would consent to give up the law and proceed to ordination as soon as practicable, serving the parish as lay-reader until duly ordained. The idea of electing as rector a man who was not yet a candidate for Orders drew out some opposition ; but still greater was the reluctance to ask him to resign an income of some $5,000 a year and take instead of it a salary of $800 a year on which to bring up a growing family. After a long and animated discussion the call was unanimously given. At first it did not seem as if this sudden call could possibly be one which God would ratify, because liabilities assumed in business and the needs of an increasing family appeared to forbid peremptorily all thoughts of entering upon the life of a clergyman, with its scanty stipend, and its dependence upon the uncertain favor of congregations, however it might appeal to his heart and imagination. But all these questions were answered for him by one of those interpositions which seem to be the direct sequence of an intelligent will, and which we therefore call Providential ; and, a last obstacle being removed from his way by the noble spirit of heirs of a former partner in business, he accepted the call with the ready obedience which he ever gave to the calls of duty and honor, and, making the long journey from Pittsburg over the mountains to Philadelphia, he was ordained Deacon by Bishop White, December 14, 1823, and on the next Sunday, December 21st, he entered upon his duties in Pittsburg. On the twelfth of the following May he was ordained Priest.

Mr. Hopkins began his parish work with all the vigor of his nature, and, as a first point, no time was lost in settling that a new church was to be built at once. This was but the outward expression of his energy, for, as a result of eighteen months' work in the ministry he presented to Bishop White on his first visit west of the mountains, in June, 1825, a class of nearly one hundred and fifty ; and the parish ranked as *third* in the whole diocese in point of numerical strength.

The church was built after the rector's own designs, with detail in imitation of the perpendicular style of architecture. The flat and plastered ceiling was painted in imitation of fan vaulting, and Mr. Hopkins had to set the workmen a model with his own hands. He used to linger behind, after the church was finished, after a night service, when the sexton was putting out the lamps, and try to fancy that the illusion was complete, and that just before the last light was extinguished he saw indeed one of those vaulted roofs of stone which he regarded as the crowning glory of the art of the architect.

So too in music ; for church music was then in as wretched a condition as church architecture. He began to compose this music himself, until, before he left Pittsburg the whole of the music used in public worship was his own. His style was not, indeed, strictly ecclesiastical, nor had he learned counterpoint. But his taste was formed in the school of Pleyel, Haydn, and Mozart ; and his natural gift was so strong that he produced melodies of striking beauty, which were easily caught by those who had an ear for music, and the simplicity of their structure enabled many to sing an accompanying part without notes, so that singing was general all over the church, and the responses were as hearty as the singing. But the activities of Mr. Hopkins were not confined to these limits. He was the only priest of the Church west of the mountains, and by expeditions to more destitute parts of the State he was the means of establishing no less than seven new parishes during the seven years of his service in Pennsylvania, and he was justly looked upon as the Father of the Church in the whole region which is now known as the Diocese of Pittsburg.

In such an atmosphere of Church ideas young Hopkins was brought up. All things in his father's house centred in the Church, and thus settled his bent for life. To be sure, the conditions of things were then very different from what they are now, and the " highest " Churchman of those days would have trembled with anxiety and fear at the sight of what passes for a matter of course in the most " moderate " sort of Church nowadays. Mr. Hopkins there began his patristic studies ; and he did so with a perseverance and thoroughness of which, at that time, our American Church had given no example. He recognized that the English Reformation was no more nor less than an appeal to the Primitive Church. He understood that the Reformers had no power to originate. They could only restore. They were of no authority whatever unless they restored correctly. He paid little attention comparatively to the Reformation, accepting much too easily the unworthy representations of Burnet. So, one by one as he could afford it, he bought the works of the Fathers, and added collections of the Councils. Thus during eighteen years he read the whole of the ancient Fathers, in the original, down to, and including St. Bernard ; besides carefully plodding through the whole of Hardouin's immense collection of the Councils, which he supplemented by going over the ground again with Mansi. In reading the Greek Fathers he read the Greek as well as the Latin translation, which accompanies the Benedictine edition. From his reading of St. Cyprian, he learned the meaning of the *mixed chalice;* and so throughout his life he always when rector of a parish, mixed water with the wine in the Eucharistic celebration. So, too, he began the custom in Pittsburg of having the bread for the altar made carefully in his own house, and unleavened, in thin cakes, like wafers, deeply indented so as to be easily broken. He reached also, even at that early day, the conviction that many beautiful and " Scriptural " and edifying things had been lost in the Reformation that it would have been better to retain, rich colored vestments, altar lights, and incense.

All these ideas were brought into the boy Hopkins' mind as they came into his father's mental vision ; for he was from the first, with his quick gaze and restless activity, his father's pride and joy, and shared his confidence. In his father's family school he was formed, and repeated in his life the precocity of his father, who had been taught by a mother of great intellectual power, gifted with many accomplishments. His responsive mind even then showed the keenness which made him afterward so dangerous an antagonist.

Mr. Hopkins, although his salary had been increased to $1,200 a year, needed an addition to his income, and at the suggestion of a friend therefore, in the spring of 1826, he took half a dozen young girls into his house to be educated with his own daughters ; and the number was gradually more than doubled. Afterward, as his sons became old enough to need a similar provision, another department was added for boys. The modest frame house was twice enlarged to meet these growing needs, the front, of brick, being last added, and having a touch of collegiate Gothic, with buttresses, pinnacles, and Tudor arches over doors, and hood mouldings over windows. The best room of the house was known as " The Oratory," and was used only for daily morning and evening worship. There was a good parlor organ, its case rising to the ceiling. Along the sides of the room at intervals were little cluster shafts at some distance from the walls, connected by spandrils above, while ribs crossed the flat ceiling diagonally, with pendants at the intersection in the centre. There was always at least one canticle chanted, besides a metrical psalm or hymn ; and all the music was composed by Mr. Hop-

kins, who was usually, when at home, the organist.   On the wall
in the place of honor hung a copy of Raphael's *Madonna della
Seggiola*, made by Mr. Hopkins' own hand.

As the boys' department of the school grew upon Mr. Hopkins' hands, it enabled him to give maintenance to one or more
theological students.

Though dancing was not taught, and even the usual games of
children were mostly dispensed with, and *there were no vacations,*
yet there was no gloom about the school.   Each department had
a garden of its own, and to each pupil was assigned the care of
some specific portion of that garden ; and the old oak grove near
the house was a shadowy delight.   *Our* John Henry early displayed his ability and his entire trustworthiness.   Music, drawing, and painting diversified the more serious branches of study.
There was no competition, and public examinations were not
held.   But twice in each year an evening concert was given in
the large school-room, to which parents and friends from town
were invited ; and joyous festivals they were !   All the per-
formers were teachers or pupils of the school, and every particle
of the music used—overtures, marches, waltzes, solo songs, duets,
vocal choruses—was composed by Mr. Hopkins ; the little orchestra including piano-forte, harp, violins, violoncello, clarionets,
flutes, and French horn.   On a table in the middle of the hall
were placed for inspection specimens of the work of each pupil—
drawings, maps, paintings, or pieces of ornamental writing—the
name and age of the doer being placed in the lower corner.   At
these concerts, and at the daily prayers, and at meals, all the pupils, boys and girls, came together.   But on the two last-men-
tioned occasions the intercourse was only ocular, as they sat on
opposite sides of the oratory, and ate at different tables.   Even
John Henry might not see his own sisters, except when as the
trusted messenger of his father, he carried the drawing and painting patterns and the copy slips from one school-room to the
other.

All the teaching in the school was marked by thoroughness
and accuracy.   Study of the Church Catechism, the learning of
Collect, Epistle, and Gospel of the season and of other parts of
Scriptures, as well as daily prayers, were a marked feature of the
school as became a *Church* school.   Another feature was the recitation of the whole lesson by each scholar.   And no mere facile
recitation of the lesson satisfied the acute mind of the master.
The lesson had to be fixed in the understanding even more firmly

than in the memory before a subject was passed. Here John Henry learned to copy his father's musical manuscript, and later on he learned how to correct it according to the rules of thorough bass.

John Henry here was most deeply, although unconsciously, impressed by all the peculiarities of his father's mind and opinions. Excessively critical as he was by nature and education, he never criticised his father. Following the same line of study and thought he brought to bear upon them a keener perception, more profound study, and a far more disciplined mind, for he was a university graduate, while his father was almost entirely home-taught or self-taught. Consequently, in music, poetry, painting, and style, in theology, in ecclesiology, and in wit, he covered more ground than his father.

But he owed to his father the early direction of his studies and his thoughts. He went only in the path his father pointed out to him, and he followed this to the end.

His father's disposition was austere and dictatorial, whereas in him these elements, without loss of their *strength*, were softened by the warm feelings and sympathetic affection inherited from his mother into gentleness and winning sweetness. He persuaded and converted; that is, in his *personal* intercourse, whereas his father compelled by sheer force of weight. His father never had an intimate friend; but Henry, to give him his home name, was never without his devoted friend, whom he retained his whole life long.

CHAPTER II.

1831–1842.

WHEN Rev. Mr. Hopkins became Assistant Minister in Trinity Church, Boston, he took up, as his chief duty, Seminary work, at Cambridge, not very far from Harvard College. He had also a few private pupils whom he was bringing up with his own sons. This was in 1831. But the progress of time brought about the election of Dr. Hopkins to the office of Bishop of Vermont, and of Dr. Doane as Bishop of New Jersey. They were consecrated along with Drs. McIlvaine and B. B. Smith, October 31, 1832, at St. Paul's Chapel, New York.

In due time, with his family, Bishop Hopkins removed from Cambridge to Burlington, Vt. He felt that Church education was needful in Vermont, which had no Church wealth or strength to begin with, and was losing by every fresh movement of the people toward the great West. So no time was lost in making a beginning for a school. To the house bought for his family were added wings for the school, and in the main building was the Oratory, larger and more beautifully finished than the one in Pittsburg. Henry's precocity made him helpful to his father at a very early age. At fourteen he was a tutor in the school, the first "Vermont Episcopal Institute," which had among its pupils seventy or eighty boys. He heard classes in Latin and French, and had to do his share of the flogging! He was generally active in carrying on the discipline of the school, and in all its work, and was, in short, a trusted coadjutor. Besides his classes in Latin and French, he exercised the trained skill of a born artist in teaching drawing. He was also a member of the school orchestra, playing beautifully on the flute and bugle. His father gave him charge of boating excursions on Lake Champlain. Besides helping in the school, he taught in the Sunday-school and sang in the church choir.

He matriculated at the University of Vermont in 1835, and graduated with honors in 1839. He delivered the Commencement Oration in the presence of Henry Clay, a circumstance which he often recalled with pleasure.*

If it had been possible for him to have received the training of one of the great universities of more recent times, with the varied elective courses showing entrancing visions to the hopeful minds of young men, it is possible that with his sympathetic mind and his natural keenness and thirst for knowledge, he might have been led away into broader fields of knowledge than those upon which he did roam. But here again the early home training in its rather narrow channel, but filled with the sweetness of the humanities, served him in good stead, and the training in the classics and mathematics on the old plan gave him that best and truest culture that means not so much the mere acquaintance with facts as a mastery of their co-ordinating laws, and skill in the art of thinking and the power to attain a knowledge at any time of whatever one needs. He mastered the classics and French and German, and read everything he could lay his hands on. He began to form here the literary style which, seizing the point at

---

* He " proceeded " to his Master's degree in 1845, and presented for that degree a Dissertation on Theories respecting the Site of the Terrestrial Paradise. It lies on the table here now—thirty-six quarto pages long—written in the prettiest and clearest hand imaginable. It is a very amusing composition, and must have made the Professors grin time and again, for it is full of his own quaint, dry humor. The amount of reading its preparation involved was enormous, for it is full of long quotations from such writers as St. Irenæus, St. Athanasius, Philo the Jew, St. Basil, Epiphanius, in *Greek ;* and from Hardouin's Collection of Councils, St. Ambrose, St. Augustine, St. Isidore, St. Gregory, St. Bernard, St. Jerome, Geropius Becanus, " that puffed-up Dutch bladder, one of the most singular compounds of learning, vanity, ingenuity, impudence, and nonsense that ever wrote Latin to prove that Adam spoke Dutch," Ven. Bede, Tertullian, Petavius, Ladovicus Capellus, Salmasius, Cellarius, in Latin, besides a Latin version of St. Chrysostom's words on the subject, and a few lines from St. Thomas Aquinas, and Tostatus, and many other quotations.

He says in the beginning that there are *five theories* as to the site founded on the Mosaic account :

1. Theories celestial, allegorical and mystical ; partly suggested by, and partly confounded with, the celestial Paradise.

2. Those placing Paradise in the Moon, or her vicinity, or the air ; which therefore may be called theories lunatic, or atmospheric.

3. Those placing our first parents in various parts of the world, away from Tigris and Euphrates ; theories mundane at large.

4. Those selecting particular places near Tigris and Euphrates ; theories mundane approximatory.

5. Theories maintaining that the site of Paradise is not now in our Earth, or cannot certainly be established ; to which latter I incline myself ; theories negative.

issue at a jump, revealed it even to the dullest of those to whom, with his intimates, he good-naturedly gave the name of "the stupids," and with all its directness of purpose and its imperturbable good-nature made the *flavor* of his writings worthy of remark. He wrote verses, too, as all men of imagination and feeling do at this time of life, and some of them are well worth reading. One of them is set down here from the collected edition of his "Poems by the Wayside:"

CUPIDON À LA CHASSE.

"From Paphian bowers, where murmuring fountains flow,
  Young Love, all eager to the chase departs.
Life's day is dawning : blithe with hope he starts,
  While Childhood's dreams are not yet flown. But lo !
Where flowers were dreamed of, thorns and thistles grow !
  Soft rosy smiles adorn his youthful face ;
  Before is seen bright Hope and beaming Grace :
The keen darts lurk behind—steeped in sharp woes !
  The fire that forged them lit at woman's eyes ;
  The breath that gave the dead coals life, hot sighs ;
Tempered in tears were they ; their barbèd tips
  Envenomed in the dew of woman's lips ;
The string that wings his shaft is woven of woman's hair :
Is he a god or fiend ? He's both ! My soul, beware ! "

The date of this sonnet is 1838, and it shows not only real poetic fancy and some literary skill in a boy of eighteen dealing with that mighty instrument wherewith "Shakespeare unlocked his heart," but also it reveals the subtle fancy and the sudden spring upon a central idea which appear again and again in after years of controversy.

After his graduation he again assisted his father in the Institute and in parochial work in St. Paul's, Burlington ; and began the study of law in a "little brick office," which is still standing in Main Street, Burlington.

He continued thus during a part of the year 1840, and made good progress ; but the needs of the family induced him to go to New York, and so, in the early summer of that year he removed from Burlington to New York, and worked as a reporter, continuing his law studies.

The financial crisis of 1839 swept away all Bishop Hopkins' investments in the Vermont Episcopal Institute, and the school itself was closed, after futile endeavors to make some arrangement with the creditors. All the domestic expenses were governed by

the most rigid economy. Except for the aid of a washerwom-
an once a week there was no servant kept. Mrs. Hopkins'
health was seriously impaired, and among the children at home
the only daughter was but three years old. The boys, therefore,
divided the work among themselves, and even the Bishop insisted on taking his share also, and for a few mornings came
early and swept and dusted the two principal rooms occupied by
the family. But this was too much even for *their* habits of un-
questioning obedience, and, conspiring for a few days, they
finally flatly rebelled, captured the broom, and established their
domestic revolution ; he yielding at length and agreeing not to
come down till time for prayers, and to let housework alone.

At last the great house became the property of others, and in
May, 1841, no effort, owing to business depression, being made to
procure a parsonage, Bishop Hopkins had to find a house where
he could. The only dwelling then available at a rent within his
means was an aged frame house so dilapidated that his family were
its last tenants.

Young John Henry at this time went through that change
which comes to test most men and proves what their lives are
to be. His mother, ever keen to see the best interests of her
children furthered, had yet the good sense and Christian wisdom
not to follow or question him too closely. But he wrote to his
best loved brother, Edward, then a midshipman on the Brazil
Station, concerning an elder sister—whose letter to himself he
sent to Edward—" I expect you will find it full of all manner of
godly comfort and advice, which will doubtless turn to your
soul's health and salvation. But (not to make a joke of *Religion*,
which is not my intention), seriously, I do think Sister puts a
leetle too much piety in her letters. The first I received from
her after I reached the city was most of it a regular homily on
one of the Scripture Parables, which she thought was peculiarly
applicable to *my particular sins*. I thanked her for the trouble
she was at to bring about my repentance, but thought that if she
had been the parson instead of the parson's *wife*, the *preaching*
would have come from her with a little better grace."

This was during the Log-Cabin and Hard Cider campaign, of
1840 ; and Henry was as much excited as any one. In that
same letter to Edward he wrote : " Excitement is increasing all
over the country. The most immense conventions that ever
were held in this country have responded to the Whig cause.
Among innumerable others there was one at Burlington, Vt., a few

weeks ago where there were present from *fifteen to twenty thou-sand.* . . . The elections are going in our favor all over the country. Louisiana has just been heard from — beat the Locos confoundedly! I have strong hopes that *every State in the Union* will go for old Tip next fall, unless *perhaps,* New Hampshire and, South Carolina, but even they are not desperate. Hurrah for Harrison ! ! !'' This letter was dated New York, July 24, 1840. Soon after he went home for a visit, but finally decided to remain at home, and help his father retrieve his fortunes. Writing to Edward again, August 31, 1840, he says: '' I am such an indispensable article at home. Mother is so un-happy when I am away, and my brothers so uncomfortable, that they will never willingly consent to my going off again. Father's plans, too, in which my co-operation will be required are so inter-esting and various, and will as we so confidently hope be so *money-making,* that the chance of my earning my living at home seems stronger than by going abroad again. We hope by lithog-raphy and school-books to earn in some years enough to save the farm from the general sacrifice of father's property, and then finally live—raising only what we want for our own consump-tion, and keeping *all together*—and when any of us children get married and have families of our own we will build us houses on some part of the farm not very far from the father-house, and shady winding roads will lead radiating from the paternal man-sion to the houses of his children ; and we will still be all like one great family. And there we can carry on our lithography and our book-making, and you can go on with your farming with C—— or E—— or your little E. to carry on the dairy, and have as many sail-boats and as much fishing as you want. Isn't it a glorious plan ? No *tarnation boarding schools* to bother a body eternally with other peoples' children ; and not near enough the village to be curtailed in our liberty of doing whatever we please for fear of other people seeing us. And then we will have an oratory there, as far ahead of this, as this is of every other [for at that time they still lived in the original great house], and all will be peace and happiness, won't it Ned? and won't *you* be *one* of *us ?* Catch me going to law when such a chance as this is in my reach, and catch you in the Navy when you might enjoy it too, that's my notion. *We have not been brought up like other people, and we can never be happy to live like other people.* We may try it, and try it, but we will always sigh for home again, and long to be back there, and *we will come back there at last Ned*—ALL of us—see if we don't, for that is the *only* place where we can *all* be happy. But still we must not be in too great a hurry about all this. We cannot yet call the farm ours, much less dream of building a house on it. We must work and make money, and you must wait till you can retire from the schooner of war *Enterprise* with honor and credit, and without wounding the sensibility of your friends. If possible lay up a little money to fetch you home again. *Above all things* keep out of duels. Because if you get bored through the head or heart by a bullet it is rather improbable that you would ever live with us on the farm, and it would spoil your fun effectually — and to be winged is also disagreeable. What is it after all that a bullying blackguard fool should call you a coward? Is not his abuse more honorable than his praise? Would you have him speak *well* of you, and call you a *whole-souled* fellow? But after all, if by temperate, moderate, forbearing, and gentlemanlike demeanor you cannot keep clear of difficulty with your brutish fellows, and in your profession, I know it is almost impossible to do so, there is one antidote almost infallible—take every opportunity to practise with the pistol till you are a thorough dead shot, and then take care that the fact be generally known and acknowledged, and I'll warrant you won't have duels enough on your hands to trouble you much, and you will not be obliged to keep up that rascally misnomer of honor, to place your dear life, and the *only* one you have, at the risk of every bully that chooses to give himself a little importance by blackguarding or insulting those who are superior to his villainous self. . . . Whiggery is almost everywhere triumphant, and *everywhere gaining.* Indiana, Kentucky, and North Carolina have each given a majority of from ten to twelve thousand for old Tip! To-morrow is election day here, and I will not close this without giving the result in the margin. Even in the States that have gone for Van, his majorities are so wofully slim that it is as good for us as a victory. In B. here we have a log-cabin, and a flag flying all the time. Good-by, *dear* Ned. I dare scarcely hope that we can see you soon, but in the meantime take plenty of hugging and kissing from me in *imagination*, and believe me, as you know me, ever your most loving brother. P. S. —Tuesday evening: Whiggery goes through all the State with a perfect looseness!

J. H. H., JR.

Of this time there is a letter from his mother to Edward, in which she says : " Dear Henry is becoming so nimble about all kinds of housework that he almost seems a substitute for Matilda." Henry wrote again to Edward, November 20, 1840, that " old Tip is certainly elected President of these United States. Three cheers for him, and God bless him ! Thus far only two States have gone for the Kinderhook Dutchman. . . . There has been a grand flag embroidered by the ladies of the West and South which is to be presented to the State giving the largest proportional majority for the hero. Little Rhode Island gave about 2,000 majority out of 8,300 votes—about 24½ per cent.—and she claimed the flag, the saucy little minx ! But *she had not heard from Vermont.* The Green Mountain State fired a big gun that was loaded with 14,500 majority out of over 50,000 votes cast, about 28 per cent., and I'd like to see any State stick a pin above that ! There is not a State in the Union that can come anywhere near it ! The Switzerland of the Union, the topmost rung in the Whig ladder, the only State that never bowed the knee to Baal—*that's little Vermont !* "

He goes on to describe the meetings held in the " log-cabin " built at Burlington for the campaign, and mentions " a very comical song : ' Van, Van, Van is a used-up man ' coming in at the end of each verse." At the last meeting of all, after election, " a resolution to sell the log-cabin and give the proceeds to the poor was passed by *three cheers ;* directions were given about receiving *that flag,* and then they closed with the song, ' Did you ever hear of the Farmer, whose cabin's in the West,' and then they dispersed to meet again for a grand jollification on the 4th of March next."

The poverty of the home is revealed to Edward in this letter :

" We have had a great change in the family lately. We have no ' help ' at all. Mother and Theodore do the cooking, Aunty and Clem. the nursery and chamber-work, Caspar the stable and piggery business, and father and I are sweepers and dusters, and I am the woodman. It takes up, of course, much more of our time, and there is not so much studying as there was, but we are more comfortable. We had a good apple harvest, potatoes tolerable, but the cabbage was almost all eaten up by the cow. We got fifty head, however, from the farm, and made a *barrel of sour-crout,* which is almost fit to eat. There is now a strong probability, if not certainty, that we will begin a plain,

2

substantial stone house out on the farm early in the spring, and move out there about June or July. It takes desperate economy to squeeze out enough money for it—a great deal of the carpenter work in the new house will have to be done by ourselves, *of necessity*, and many parts of it will look rather unfinished for years to come, perhaps. But no matter—we can work it all out by and by, and at last it will be a truly splendid place. The site selected is on the high ledge of rocks commanding a view of the Green Mountains, capped with snow, the college and all Burlington, the bay and the lake north and south, and all the valley of the Onion River, with the mountains in New York besides ; a far more splendid prospect than even the one we have from here. Oh ! it will be glorious ! *but we must work for it !*

" I have begun at lithography, and helped father considerably in making the drawings on stone for the numbers of the Vermont Drawing Book. In the new house I shall have a little workshop with a lithographic printing-press, and carry on a good business, I hope, and help to make money. I have also been reading in law three times a week to Judge Bennett, whom I like very well, and who has been very kind and attentive to me indeed. I shall learn more law at this rate in one year than I could or would in the city in three.

" Caspar has been fattening our pigs for killing for some time past, and yesterday they were slaughtered. The sow weighed nearly two hundred pounds, and the hog two hundred and sixty, all cleaned and cut up, which is pretty good for Cass. To-day we are busy making lard, hogs-head cheese, and all those good things, and even now, while I am writing, I hear the clatter of the sausage-knife downstairs, bringing savory anticipations to my mind, and water to my mouth. Do you ever have first-rate roast pig and sausages in South America ? I hope so ! "

The removal here spoken of to the spot afterward called Rock Point, came about through the boys going there " to cut pea-rods to bush peas in the garden." The excursion was a familiar one, but once when they went over the hill, then just stripped of its timber, the glorious view aroused all Henry's enthusiasm for the beautiful—it was like a revelation. Returning home he inspired the same excitement in his father, and he went the next day with the boys to the same place, and felt the same thrill of rapture, and began to glow with the idea that perhaps means might be contrived to secure the rough-looking spot of rocky ground, and build some sort of homestead there. Bishop Hopkins thought it his duty, for the sake of his boys, to make the attempt, and finally succeeded in making terms for the purchase of the land. And so, the whole family, at least those who could, set to work home-making.

The story of those days reads like the tale of the Swiss Family Robinson on their desert isle. Every day the boys walked out from Burlington, and worked all day blasting and quarrying rocks; clearing away trees, stumps, and bushes; hauling clay, glazing windows, lathing, shingling, flooring, grinding paint, painting, sodding, planting trees, and doing their best to change that wild place, which had been called " Sharp Shins," into a place fit for human habitation. Henry did his full share of all this work, although manual labor was not at all to his taste or according to his training, and at last, on the first of December, the new house was occupied, though the walls were yet very damp, and the finishing and furnishing quite incomplete.

It was dreary at times to see the snow-storms roll over the tops of the young pine forest below the hill, and to find communications with the village shut off by snow-drifts for days together; but the logs were piled only the more cheerily upon the open fireplace, and hard labor and affectionate good humor turned all hardships into happiness. Slowly, the rough place began to put on the beauties of cultivation. All this toil was lightened and brightened by Henry's genial humor. He made himself entertaining to all sorts of people, his life through. A man was a man with him, and he would as willingly sit down by the side of the workman for his noonday meal or to smoke his pipe, while the laughter at his flow of jokes and stories rose on the air, as to be the guest of a' bishop.

This work was done in the summer and autumn of 1841. He writes to Edward from New York, October 20th, of that year :

" Father came down with me to attend General Convention, which has been sitting precisely two weeks and adjourned last night at eleven o'clock, and it has kept father so busy that I have had but little intercourse with him—only catching a glimpse of him, and exchanging a few words once a day. As for myself, I have been at Endicott's Lithographic establishment, where I have made myself master of nearly all the details of business, preparing the stones, drawing, printing, engraving, transferring,

making crayon ink, varnish, etc., etc. ; no small job for the time,
I assure you.   When we left home the new house was all snugly
roofed in, the inside was partitioned and lathed, and nearly all
the first coat of plaster was on.   I had painted the whole, and
puttied more than half the window sash, making the putty myself.   I brought down with me some of my poetry and music,
thinking that, what between magazines and the publishers I
might make enough to buy me some German books and a pair
of pantaloons.   I have walked to and fro about that business between *twenty and thirty miles,* and I don't believe I shall make a
stiver out of the whole lot after all. . . .   I have seen John
and Arthur and Henry Carey since I have been here.   They
are all taller than Caspar !   Such a race of Brobdignagians you
never saw.   John is learning all about the manufacture of iron ;
Arthur is studying theology at the General Theological Seminary,
and is one of the most serious, learned, and estimable characters
of my acquaintance.   Henry is the tallest of the set.   They
used to call him ' Tiny ' you remember ; *they don't now.*"

The Bishop himself wrote to Edward, December 8, 1841, of
having settled in the new house on the first of the month, and
that Henry had attained "all the mechanical skill which the
work of lithography requires.   We purchased a first-rate press
and stock of stones, with all other necessary implements, and he
is now going to work on a plan of the town of Burlington, which
had been suggested as the first of a set of similar plans for all the
towns in the State.   This work will, we trust, be a source of considerable income, and go a great way in due time, to make up for
old losses."   The farm was managed by one after another of the
sons, as they grew older ; Henry being ever the stay of all, and
the trusted counsellor of all, both old and young.   Out of the
most dismal situations his buoyant good-nature found material for
fun.   Incongruities and antitheses he always saw, and his keen
sense of the ridiculous brightened up all about him.   One morning, while he and two of his brothers were at work on the Rock
Point farm, digging potatoes, he caught sight of a wretched old
horse, so lean that Browning's words—

> " One stiff blind horse, his every bone astare,
> Stood stupefied, however came he there !
> Thrust out past service in the devil's stud !
>
> .   .   .   .

> —With that red gaunt and colloped neck a-strain,
> And shut eyes underneath the rusty mane ;
> Seldom went such grotesqueness with such woe,"—

best describe him.   Henry saw the whole thing at a glance, but
ever delighting in an antithesis, he began, suddenly, to recite
Dryden's Alexander's Feast:

> ' 'Twas at the royal feast for Persia won——.'

The other two stopped their work and listened to the beautiful
poetry, which they had never heard before, when Henry, seeing
them completely absorbed and swayed (as Timotheus in the poem
sways the feasters) by the power of the measures, suddenly pointing, cried out, " Look at that horse ! "   The transition was too
much, and all three rolled upon the ground in paroxysms of
laughter.

One morning he and his brother Caspar walked out to Rock
Point in complete silence.   Caspar was moody, because his
father had been scolding him for cutting down a young oak-tree
without getting orders to do so.   He felt outraged that he should
be upbraided when he was doing his best for his father, working
every day and all day to help him, and he had nothing to say,
even to the favorite Henry, while the fit was on.   When the two-
mile walk was done, and as they were about to begin work, Henry
(who had kept complete silence, too), quietly sidled up to him, and
laying his hand on his arm, said, " Cass, if you don't mind, I have
a notion of doing you a great favor."   " What is it ? " growled
Caspar.   " Why," he replied, " I will not repeat to any one a
single word of all you have said this morning."   How could
Caspar keep back a smile which opened the way for a return to
good-humor ?

But such labors brought no return of money, and the Bishop
was heavily involved in debt by the failure of the Institute, and
this burden was increased by the making of the new home, and
the purchase of the new farm and farming tools.   His whole income from all sources amounted to but about fifteen hundred
dollars.   Henry had given up his law studies, and had no means
to support himself as a student.   Within a year, too, a disease of
the throat had arisen which made him lose the natural tone of
his voice.   It was a disease of the windpipe which no medicine
or application could reach, and it was hoped that a change to a
warmer climate might benefit him.   By the time that the family

were in the new house the disease had increased so much that, although he was, as his mother said in a letter of that date, "a son whose sweet society and constant, lovely disposition seems to be the life and comfort of the whole family, especially of his father, who justly calls him 'his companion, his own familiar friend,' and so indispensably useful to us that to make up our minds to part with him was indeed painful, but the only alternative left us." Accordingly he thought of going to the Episcopal Institution in Georgia, which was in charge of his oldest sister, Mrs. Fay; but finally he went to Savannah to be tutor to the son of Bishop Elliott, of Georgia, and to act as the Bishop's private secretary.

From this tutorship he received for two years a thousand dollars per annum, and during those two years he sent his father regularly eight hundred dollars a year to relieve that father of his burden of debt. This sort of generous action never came amiss to him, for he was through life the most unselfish and self-sacrificing of mortals.

CHAPTER III.

1843.

DURING this long absence from home he wrote to his father a series of letters so brilliant, witty, graphic and touching in their sincerity and freshness that they were cherished like heirlooms. It would seem as if no pen could be clearer than his, even in those days of his early manhood, but like the artist he was, since he wrote for the loved ones at home, he put into them pen-and-ink sketches that were used for years in the family school as patterns for drawing lessons. Some of the letters are given here:

"BRIG AUGUSTA, May 15, 1843.

"I spent a very agreeable evening at —— with Mr. B——. He is one of the most amusing men I ever met, and his conversation is quite an intellectual treat. One gets a great deal of information from him, and in a most witty and pungent form, *but very little instruction.* The Rev. Mr. Cook, Dr. Milnor's assistant, was also here; he is a very handsome, pleasant little man, dresses in a clerical cassock, which is very becoming, and seems to be a truly good and pious man. He often tried to temper down the sharpness of Brother B——'s tongue, but only got a little good-natured abuse for his pains. The old gentleman when he is on the subject of popery, or the Tracts, or strict Episcopal government, or the Bishops * *Blunderdonk*, as he calls them, goes it with *a perfect looseness*, to use a cant but expressive phrase. We wound up the evening with some very nice hot whiskey punch, but that was after Brother Cook went away. Wasn't it clerical? I lent Mr. B—— your second letter to Bishop Kenrick and your Miller Sermons to read. But unfortunately he went up to Sing Sing the next day and I haven't heard of them since.

"Another pleasant evening I spent at Mr. Carey's with Mr. Samuel Carey, Arthur, Henry, and the ladies. . . . I think the most delightful day of my visit was spent at the General Theological Seminary with dear Arthur, who is to be ordained

* *I.e.,* the two Bishops Onderdonk—one the Bishop of Pennsylvania, the other of New York.

next June.   I found him with a large folio volume of Cotelerius'
edition of the 'Apostolic Fathers' open before him, and spent
the whole day with him, dining and supping at their common
table.   A good part of the time we passed in the library, where
my bibliomaniacal eyes were refreshed with the sight of a real
Complutensian Polyglott ! and Walton's London Polyglott ! but
unfortunately, without the subsequently inserted dedication to
Charles II.   The first dedication was to Old Noll, who admitted
the paper for it free of duty, but as the Restoration took place
before the edition was fully put out, that was destroyed and a
new one to Charles II. was hastily printed on inferior paper and
inserted in some copies which are very rare.   What is rarest of
all is to find a copy with *both*.   We saw, too, a singular copy of
Law's translation of ' Jacob Behmen ' (the same edition is in the
U. V. M. Library) which had been filled with marginal notes all
through by some enthusiast, about the year 1789, who imagined
he had had direct revelations from the Deity.   The *Acta Sanc-
torum*, too, and many other interesting works I saw there for the
first time.   But after supper came the rarest treat of all.   I attended Evening Prayer in the Chapel, where the psalms for the
day (the 4th, Evening Prayer) were chanted throughout by the
students, in alternate verses, one half of the choir singing one
verse and the other the other (I being one of them, for I could
not help it) and both joining together in the *Gloria Patri*.   It
was delightful ; and the view out of the window, the red sun
sinking behind the flat hills of Jersey, and blinking pensively over
the rippling Hudson added yet another and right welcome charm.
I felt as if I should like never to leave that ugly chapel till I could
go where I could hear the like, or *better*, for the music was not
first-rate.   After service I went up again to Arthur's room, where
we talked about the classics and Latin poetry, and read together
some beautiful odes of Catullus, and some Latin poems, I think
by *Bourne*, which are the prettiest things I ever read not written by
a real Roman.   Between eleven and twelve o'clock Arthur said
he would accompany me as far down as St. Luke's.   We went
several squares further, and then I turned back and walked with
him again as far as St. Luke's, where we parted, God bless him !
   " I called on Dr. Hodges and introduced myself.   I had a
good deal of pleasant chat with him, and sang in St. John's choir
in the afternoon of Sunday.   He asked me to play on the organ
after church, but I was really afraid to try the huge thing.   I was
longing to be at it when nobody was by but myself.   I told him

I would practise hard the next year, and play for him when I came back. I asked him about my being his assistant when the new Trinity is finished, and he seemed to like the idea well. I have little doubt that I could make it go, if I chose. I also called at John Jacob Astor's house and introduced myself to Dr. Cogswell, who resides there, and is Astor's head counsellor about his proposed library. I had a long bibliographical chat with the Doctor, and have no doubt I could make myself one of the assistant librarians there, and probably go with the Doctor to Europe on a book-foraging expedition. That would be nice, wouldn't it? *But I would rather wait a little longer and go with my dear father.* Don't you believe it? Another new acquaintance I made was a Mr. Balmanna, a Scotch virtuoso, to whom I brought a flattering letter of introduction from Mr. Smetz, who has a choice collection of rare books and many engravings in huge folios, and two folios filled with the original drawings. Was not that a treat?

"Here we are now at anchor off the light-house at Savannah, waiting for the tide. The dirty water seems alive with fish. On every side of us the clumsy porpoises rolling their blunt snub snouts up into the sunshine, and with their nimble tails they whisk the muddy tide into a splash of dingy foam, and now and then the back fin of a shark peeps quietly out of the water, and glances in the sun. The air is calm, clear, and deliciously warm, and I wish I was at home.   Ever, your own loving son,

"HENRY."

On the 11th of June he wrote to a relative: "You must not take it amiss if I write to you a little sermon on the text of *Patience*. Patience, dearly beloved, is a virtue rather gotten by practice and forced on by experience than born in us by nature or put on for pleasure, and when the natural parts are lively, the will strong, bodily and mental activity great, the blood young and hot, the temper warm and bold, imagination keen and excursive, and experience and self-command *small*, that lesson of patience is wondrous hard to learn—is easier learnt by rote than by *heart*. But how necessary it is in this world! I may venture to say that there is not one man, not one woman, not one child, that does not desire many things they have not, and cannot have, at least for the present. And yet how few have the sense or the *courage* to be patient; for it takes more cool courage to await an attack than to rush against the enemy. The reason of all this is that our desires and passions are *infinite*, while we live in a world which is to most of us miserably cramped and finite, and we cannot get our full growth here, do what we will.   But while in this cramped condition we often waste our huge force of passion on trifles.   You are a man, and ought to look at things with the reasonable sobriety of a man's judgment. Get *big ideas* into your head, and you will not be so pestered by the little *gnats* of accident—you will not raise a hurricane to blow a fly off your nose, nor cast a thirty-two pounder to kill pismires.   Another thing I want to warn you of is your awful fits of the dumps.   They mostly arise from two sources: selfishness turned sour, or inability in a weak mind to maintain its balance against external circumstances ; to which may be added a third, the idleness of a strong and active mind ; for in such cases it feeds on itself for lack of something else to do.   .   .   .   For my peroration I have two things to recommend : 1st. Accustom yourself to look *only* at the bright side of everything and every-body but yourself, and look at yourself and your own failings on the dark side, *chiefly*, to keep down vanity ; but not *wholly*, to keep down melancholy.   2d.   Learn to think *less about yourself*, and at the same time *set a higher value on yourself*.   I have no room to dilate, but accept the sermon as it was written in the spirit and deep feeling of one who loves you.   .   .   .   Did you ever know that the first Psalm-book published in true blue old Scotland has on the title-page somewhat thus : ' The whole buik of Psaumes in meeter, at the ende whereof will be fund empryntit *ane baudy sang*, etc.'   So at the end of my sermon I give you not a bawdy song, but a little school-boy round which I wrote the other day for my boys when they were grumbling over what they called a hard lesson.''

"SAVANNAH, July 23, 1843.

"MY DEAREST FATHER: This last week has been spent by me in a very pleasant manner. On last Monday morning I began school with little Stephen Elliott alone, who was in a very bad humor because his father would not give him a holiday in the absence of all his schoolfellows. (John Hendrickson has gone north, taking $50 or more from my salary.) The other pupils were all absent because invited by the Mongins to visit them at Dawfasks Island. Ste. was marvellously in the dumps and missed every lesson till about 11 o'clock, when the other two boys came in in high glee, to tell me that Mr. Mongin had invited me and Ste. to spend a week at the island. The Bishop consenting, I sent the two messengers to convey to Mr. Mongin the joyful intelligence that at one o'clock Mr. Hopkins and Stephen would be on the wharf ready to go on board; and so we were, though Ste's supply of clothing, as it could not be gotten ready in time, was left behind to be brought over in the Cockspur boat in the afternoon or on the morrow. The weather was quite warm, but Mr. Mongin's boat had a nice awning, and we enjoyed our pull down the Savannah River very much. There were loads of fruit on board, and a large basket of ice packed up in cotton, and Mr. M—— had his rifle with him, with which he took a couple of shots—one at an alligator, and one at a crane, but both missed. However, just as we came in sight of the house, we saw an alligator with his head just above the water, asleep. We quietly pulled up pretty close, and Mr. M—— shot him in the eyes, he turned on his back, cocked up the white of his tail and his paws, and we rowed up and hauled him in. He was between four and five feet long, and stank awfully.

"It was near four o'clock when we arrived at Bloody Point, the end of the island on which Mr. Mongin's estate is situated. In the old colony times, the government of South Carolina kept up a number of scout boats along the shores, to give notice of the approach of the Spaniards or Indians, who used frequently to make predatory excursions against the southern portion of the colony. These scout boats were once all surprised at this place by the St. Augustine Indians and the crews massacred to a man, and it has been called Bloody Point ever since.

"Here we found a warm welcome and a good dinner. The place is beautifully situated on the narrow end of the island, with the sea before it and New River, an arm of the sea, behind it. There is a great lack of large shade trees, but there is any quantity

of them set out ; and in a few years you will meet in every direction around the house avenues of wild olive, cedar, catalpa, ole-
ander, and other trees, which will not only afford delightful
shade, but some of them will also load the breezes with the most
exquisite perfume. The house is surrounded with flower-gardens,
and all varieties of shrubbery. There are no fences in sight,
but in the immediate vicinity of the house are more than five
miles of hedging. It is not the white thorn, but the casena,
which flourishes near salt water. They clip it carefully twice a
year, and it looks like a solid square wall of green.

"The sea-breeze was delightful and exhilarating, especially to
me, and after dinner we took a pleasant sail in one of Mr.
M——'s sail-boats. The wind was fresh, the waves gave us
now and then a good splashing in our little boat. As we returned the boys said that as they were so wet already they might
as well go in all over with their clothes on. I told them expressly not to do so, as did Mr. M——, but nevertheless they
stayed behind and did it, and after they had dabbled about to
their own satisfaction they came sneaking home after supper,
dripping from top to toe, and with dirty bare feet, and were all
three sent supperless to bed to pay for their fun. The next day,
Tuesday, we kept school in the piazza from nine o'clock till about
four, except that at high tide we took a delightful sea-bath in the
surf, and that at about two o'clock we had dinner—a good dinner, with three or four kinds of meat, fish and fowl, and as a
dessert, water-melon, musk-melons, oranges, pineapples and
bananas were profusely spread before us. These latter we enjoyed two or three times a day besides. After dinner and school
were over, we again repaired to the beach, and Mr. Mongin carried us over in his sail-boat to Cockspur, an island on the Georgia
side of Savannah River (Dawfasks is in South Carolina). It is
on this island the Government is erecting the Fort Pulaski, of
which you have heard me speak. We were introduced to Captain
Mansfield, the engineer in command, and to Lieutenant Alexander, his assistant, who were both very pleasant and obliging to us.
Captain M—— has been there for about twelve years, ever
since the fortification was commenced. . . . He led us all
over the fort, explained to us all the plans of defence, showed us
every part of the works, and I received not only amusement, but
a good deal of instruction from him, as it was the first thing of
the kind I had ever seen. When finished it will mount about
one hundred and thirty guns, and will be sufficient to batter to

pieces any hostile armament that may attempt to pass up Savannah River, or any of the creeks near it.

" On Wednesday we kept school again out in the piazza, and took another delightful bath in the surf. I cut my ' big-toe,' however, on an oyster-shell which was imbedded in the sand, which prevented my enjoying the salt-water again in that way. In the evening we had a fine storm. The wind blew about the house very much as it does at home, and the flashes of lightning from the dense masses of black clouds were truly magnificent. Not very much rain fell, which we regretted, as the plantation was much in need of it. On Thursday morning, before breakfast, I took a sketch of one of the garden walks, with one of those beautiful casena hedges. We kept school in my room on this day, and the day after, for though we kept in the shade of the piazza, yet as the sun would move around we were exposed too much to its heat.

" In another excursion we visited two light-houses, and the Martello Tower. This last is a very curious structure built of tabby with walls ten feet through, only one small door, and no other openings but port-holes.   It is two stories high, with strong magazines and a tank in the basement. It is finished at the top by tabby battlements, which are at present concealed by a corniced roof, to protect the walls from injury by weather. I took a sketch of the light-houses and another of the tower, making four in all that I brought away from the island with me.

" Ever your own son

" HENRY."

" The walks all around are gravelled with oyster-shells, and very bare of shade-trees, and the glare reflected from them was so strong that we all found our faces becoming wofully sunburnt, whereupon took place divers anointings of tallow and cream which were very amusing and comical. I have brought home a fiery snout that has given off four or five coats of ragged skin, and seems to have as many more in reserve. In the evening, after dinner and school, I rode out in the carriage with Mrs. Mongin and Mrs. Elliott, to the seat of Mr. Stoddard; about four miles out by the roads through the fields. We passed a good deal of marsh ground densely timbered, and having an abundance of palmetto in the interior. The variety of forest, marsh, and cotton field made the drive quite pleasing. Mr. Stoddard's house is newer and handsomer than Mr. M——'s, but the situation is not near so healthy nor beautiful, and in the laying out of the grounds cannot compare with it. It looked rather squally overhead just as we arrived there, so without stopping we rode home by the beach. The tide washing the sand makes a fine hard *first-rate* carriage road, better than one macadamized, for it is never dusty. But in parts the driving is a very delicate business, for the beach is literally strowed with stumps of all sorts and sizes. We got home quite safe, however. Our evenings usually passed in this manner : After tea Mr. M——— and I smoked a couple of cigars a piece in the supper-room, while the ladies adjourned to the opposite parlor ; and while smoking, sometimes we chatted together, sometimes the children, all five of them (for little Ellen and Robbie were down there too, with their mothers) would crowd around me, and make me tell them stories. This evening I told them the history of Amadis de Gaul, and promised them one of Buffalmacco's pranks on Calandrino the next time (from Boccaccio's ' Decamerone '). ' Oh ! ' says little Robbie, ' tell it now ! ' ' No,' I said, ' what should I do next time I want to tell you a story ? ' ' Oh ! ' says my little Paddy, ' the next time you need not tell us any at all ! ' So to pay him for such a genuine bull I told him the story. After our smoke I used to go and chat with the ladies, and play for them on the piano or the flute. We had watermelons, bananas, and pineapples again at about ten o'clock ; after that, to bed with what stomach we had left.

"We filled up the last evening with another excursion to Cockspur. The distance is about five miles, and as the wind was not very fair, and the tide against us, we did not sail very rapidly. Mr. M——— himself with one negro went in a light little sailing skiff, which could not well hold more than two. We went in the yawl, that is, the three boys, myself, and three negroes, Henry, Charles, and old Uncle Monday.

"Henry, being the most experienced sailor, was put in command by his ' Massa,' and away we went. Mr. M——— soon outsailed our lumbering craft. The whole river is nearly filled with sandbanks. The tide was now on the ebb, and we ran into the breakers twice before we got over. We left Cockspur at a quarter before seven o'clock, the evening dark and cloudy and the wind pretty fresh, and from such a direction that we had to take a tack to get home. Mr. M———, though he could have outsailed us at once, kept near us, sailing round and round us, and thus we went on unconsciously a great deal farther on the down course than we ought to have done. Mr. M—— found himself in shoal water on a bank which he did not expect and did not recognize, and when once a little boat is among the breakers she has enough to do to look after herself. We too soon found ourselves running upon breakers, which we could see and hear distinctly about us. I told Henry to alter his course, as he would be in them in a minute. But these negroes are perfectly certain of their own presence of mind, and he declared he was just in the right course, and knew where he was going, etc., and hallooed to Charles and Monday to get out their oars, quick! quick!! quick!!! Out they got them after much scolding and confusion, and without changing course rowed us faster into the breakers than ever. We were instantly among them, shipped a good many of them, and, knowing there was no great danger except of a drenching, I was perfectly amused at the terror and vexation of our sables. Henry never would let on that he was frightened, but when we actually got on the bank he ejaculated, 'The Lord have mercy upon us, what shall we do?' in a most pitifully doleful voice. Charles was terrified into dead silence and desperate rowing, so desperate that he soon rowed round old Uncle Monday, and we came out at the other side of the bank (it was not broad) after much scrambling, and with the boat's head turned to Tybee Light instead of Bloody Point. It was now quite dark, we had totally lost sight of Mr. M—— and he of us. He waited for us a long time, to no purpose, and as it threatened to blow too heavily for his little skiff, he sailed home, where in fact he did not arrive more than fifteen minutes before we did.

"After getting through that bank we still held on our original course, and gallantly the rising breeze carried us through the water, which was sparkling and flashing with that beautiful sea-fire. Old Monday now began to growl from the bow that we were going too much to the right, and that Bloody Point was far away t'other side. Henry declared he was right, and thus they jawed away till old Monday's growls were drowned by the noise of another bank of breakers. Here again was the old poling, oars out, and row into the midst of the breakers as fast as possible. Old Monday at every pull gave a mighty hoarse grunt, half from shortness of wind in his old lungs, half from vexation. After getting more wet than ever we at last got through, and then Henry made the grand discovery that we were three miles too far along the shore, and had left Bloody Point far behind us. He then

laid all the blame on old Monday's eyes (though it was all his
own obstinacy), and that made the old fellow more savage than
ever.   Even after this discovery was made they jawed away for a
considerable time before they changed the course, and then we
were so far in shore that with that wind it was impossible to make
Bloody Point.   At last, we ran aground for the last time, but as
we struck a heavy sea capsized the boat, and sent old Uncle
Monday into the surf to cool his rage, and it would have gone
over completely had I not leapt to the windward side of the boat.
The negroes soon carried me out on their backs, and set me
ashore.   Fred and Telfair were not at all frightened, but poor
Ste. was awfully terrified, and clung to my hand with nervous
energy.   We found ourselves only a quarter of a mile from the
house, where our arrival was a great relief to the ladies and to Mr.
M——.   We changed our wet clothes, took a hearty supper, and
talked about our adventure till bed-time.''

In a letter dated August 20, 1843, he relates with great gusto
some of the characteristics of the household of Bishop Elliott.
The whole family were '' great and practical teazers.''   To any
one who ever knew John Henry Hopkins, with his radiant humor
and fondness, nay, his natural proneness to use the weapon of
sarcasm with deadly effect, it seems a very mild thing to say as he
does, that '' as there is always a good deal of wit and humor flying, you will not wonder that I have in some degree fallen in with
the stream, though I am yet so thin-skinned that I would rather
laugh at a joke *not* made at *my* expense.''   From this he goes on to
relate the inception of certain caricatures, sent back and forth between two branches of the family.   So he was set to work at these,
with all his ingenuity and wit on the *qui vive*.   Of one he says:

'' It cost me nine hours of hard work yesterday, has thirty
figures in it, big and little, white, black, and yellow ; the officers
are shining in gold lace, etc., and to see the Bishop and the whole
family laugh at it when it was done was perfectly exhilarating.
The Bishop would look at it, then lay it down, and throw himself
back in his chair and ' haw ! haw ! ' then another look, etc.   I
do all this to exercise myself in designing the human figure, and
in this I am rapidly improving.   It sharpens my faculties of observation famously.   The Bishop says I could make a fortune at
caricaturing, and they all call me another Cruikshank, with too
many other compliments for me to repeat.

" P.S. The Bishop takes no active part in all this. He only laughs heartily at all the jokes in both papers, and now and then suggests a happy thought to be executed by others. All my illustrations are made *to order*, and I sometimes accompany them with epigrams, a style of composition very difficult, but very improving in brevity, neatness, and point, and the Bishop says my poetry is on a par with my prints.

" H. "

When this letter reached his father, the Bishop of Vermont, it did not arouse the glee that was in the mind of the son, for the latter, in a letter dated September 10th, writes :

" It was with great shame and sorrow that I read your last and severe letter of the 30th ult., and discovered how far I had unthinkingly been led astray. But still, dear father, I do not think it quite as bad as you imagined. I determined, however, to break off the whole affair at once, so far as I was concerned, though as I had been hitherto so free with my contributions, and both to our Beaufort and Savannah friends they had become so important a part of the correspondence, that I was puzzled to know how to withdraw without giving offence by my reasons. If I gave the true ones, passing an implied condemnation on others, and thus giving offence, or without giving false excuses (or such as were only partly true), which I could never think of doing.

" I therefore showed Bishop Elliott your letter, and when we were alone he read it all over carefully and slowly, and then told me he agreed with you *entirely*, and that I ought to stop my part of it *instantly*. He said that when he was a young man his mind had taken that bent, and that he was always looking out for the laughable side of everything, and that he had then foolishly sharpened his sense of the ridiculous to such a degree that it still troubled him occasionally at the most solemn moments, and even sometimes in church. He said, too, that he had for some time felt that the thing was going too far, and had often thought he ought to tell me that I was devoting too much time and trouble to trifles, and growing lazy about what was of more importance, but that as finding fault was a disagreeable business he had hitherto delayed it. As to the others, he said that it amounted to little more than a correspondence of mutual pleasantries between brother and sister and immediate relatives on both sides—and even that he would have stopped before now

3

only that he felt he could not exercise the same authority over his brother and sister, who were nearly of his own years, as he could have done over his own children. He assured me repeatedly that in the character of my drawings and in their style of execution I had done nothing calculated to lower me in the esteem of any of my friends here. He gave me a great deal of good advice, and we had a very full and cordial conversation on the subject; and when we bade each other good-night he shook me warmly by the hand, and for the first time in my life I kissed him, which he took very kindly, and promised to explain the matter to the ladies so that I should be tempted by no such requests in the future.

"I am very glad your letter has given me a fair excuse to break off this business. True, I believe I have profited by it in some respects : I have gained a freedom in designing the human figure *with clothes on* which I know I had not before, for I had confined all my little extempore scratches to faces and heads, and before I was put on this business it would have puzzled me to draw a man, woman, or child so as to look natural. It has sharpened my eye too in the observance of nature—and indeed, dear father, I think it was incorrect to call them *caricatures*, as I believe I did. With one exception, I did not at all transgress the modesty of nature, but only tried to *come as close to the life as possible*, and so far did I succeed in this that at least *a dozen striking likenesses* have been discovered when I never meant any, though when I did mean it it could not be mistaken.

"Last Saturday week I saw a notable character among the passengers from Beaufort. I marked him well, and two or three days after I took him down, so that everybody that knew him exclaimed at once: 'That's S—— R——, hat, coat, whiskers, legs, and *all over.*' Yesterday there was a large party, between forty and fifty, came down on an excursion from Beaufort to Savannah, all members and friends of the family connection—and the whole party dined at Mr. Robert Habershaw's. I was there, of course, and from twelve o'clock till half-past three I heard scarcely anything else than thanks for, and compliments about, my drawings, and inquiries eagerly put about my next. I was told over and over what a great sensation they had created in that quiet little city, how they had been sent for, and sent round, till they had been *all over the place.* But with all this, which came entirely too thick for my modesty, I could not but perceive that among some of the thin-skinned ladies there was considerable apprehension lest my attention should be attracted to them, some of them began to teaze others by telling them *they* were to figure in my next, etc. ; and one young lady said : ' Take care, Mr. Hopkins, the Beaufort ladies will quarrel with you.' ' Then I'll stop at once,' said I ; ' I don't know how to quarrel with ladies.' ' Oh, no, no ! ' said she, *avec beaucoup d'empressement,* ' No, don't stop ! we had *rather you would take us all off than stop ;* that would never do.' Besides, what I found very disagreeable, some hints were given me by friends that they wanted me to re-member how such a one looked, etc. So that I became con-vinced every moment, in spite of all their admiration, that you were right and I was wrong. . . . But one thing, dear Father, I have never done ; I have never made the House of God my studio, nor the Sabbath my practising day, for such things, and hereafter it shall be Sunday seven days in the week, as far as caricatures are concerned.

" Forgive me this once, dear Father, for I did not do wrong deliberately, and accept my thanks over and over again for the wise letter that stopped me before I had gone too far, for I should not have had firmness to stop myself.

" P. S. I wish my sorrow could make up for the pain I have given you about this foolish business. Dear Father, may I never again give pleasure to others or to myself at so dear a price as *giving pain to you.*

" A kind of influenza called the Grippe is quite fashionable here now. Several in the house have had it, and my turn may soon come.

" H."

The filial dutifulness showed in these letters never lessened in the least. A gentleman who travelled on the same steamer that brought the Bishop of Vermont and Henry home from the first Lambeth Conference, in 1867, observed once that he had lived long and travelled much, but had never seen anywhere such de-votion to a father as this son showed on that voyage.

In a letter dated October 29, 1843, he says :

" I have just received to-day your interesting letter bringing me the welcome news that the first part of your series on the Tracts has gone to press. But I am sorry, dear father, it was not to be printed in New York by Appleton or the Harpers. I think they would have secured it a larger circulation. As to

Bishop Elliott's order for fifty copies, I think he will renew it ; but as they are meant for general distribution amongst the laity, he prefers waiting till he reads his own copy, to find out whether you have not been *too learned and profound for the comprehension of Georgians in general.* I shall look for it with great eagerness. Your last letter to me on the subject I showed to Bishop Elliott, who asked me to lend it him, to show to some of his friends, and it has created quite a sensation, passing all around the city, and more than one copy having been made ; indeed, I have not got back the original yet ; and everybody feels such glad confidence that now since Bishop Hopkins has taken up the Tractarians, they *will get well dressed* before you are done with them.

" . . . You must not give me too much credit for Hebrew. I only know some of the letters, and could make out all the words I wrote down in that extract, but I have not *studied* the language at all yet, I shall wait for that till I am settled at home.

" Your new French honor will, I suppose, add three more symbolic initials to your name. You are now, I believe, D.D., F.R.S., N.A.—any more ? I think that is a pretty respectably long tail for a comet as far gone in its aphelion as the Bishop of Vermont.

" . . . As to making money, unfortunately such a prominently necessary item in my plans, I am calculating somewhat on the profits of my Goethe, somewhat more on a small work on Ancient Geography for the use of schools, but most of all on your old plan of complete sets of lithographed drawing books, which *all together* ought to make me more than the $500 I remit at present.

[Of this *Goethe* which young Hopkins mentions here, he himself a few years ago wrote to a friend : " As to Goethe, you will find a copy in the See House Library, with ' John Oxenford's ' name on the title-page. The *second* of the four parts of that translation is my work. The other three parts were done by Park Godwin, George Ripley, and Charles A. Dana. The preface states that they had *intended* to reprint the American version, but found that it was too incorrect ! And so they printed it with ' John Oxenford,' on the title-page, stealing our work almost bodily ! I had written the translation of the whole four volumes ; then, after agreeing to go in with the others, taking Vol. II. I revised and rewrote the whole of that volume. I also paid postage (very high then) on the *proofs* of the whole volume.   For all this labor I never received one cent.   But I owed the publishers a small bill for books, amounting to about $26.50, which I steadfastly refused to pay ! "]

" I have some idea of publishing a volume of miscellaneous poems, of which I think I can muster enough to claim a respectable stand amongst the motley crew that crowd the little hillock ycleped the *American Parnassus.*   If I publish poetry at all it will be under my Knickerbocker anagram J. Rheyn Piksohn.   You know, dear Father, our patronymic hath a very proverbial prominence amongst unsuccessful candidates for the bays, and that not only at the time of Sternhold, and the Lord Bishop of Derry's sons (who, by the way, especially Charles, were no bad versifiers), but only a year or two ago some degenerate sprig of the name published in Baltimore a volume of the most contemptible stuff, so as to keep up his antique namesake's unenviable reputation.   My Goethe will appear under my own name, my Geography probably under none—I must not make it too deep or it will be unmarketable.

" Talking about poetry, dear Father, I was yesterday night (the night of my birth-day—I am now twenty-three years old !) smoking my last pipe before going to bed, it was past 12 o'clock, I was forecasting in my own mind my future life, and the way in which it is made so dependent on my throat : I confess my thoughts took rather a pensive turn—when I wrote the following lines, which I think will please you :

" My life is like a freighted barque
   Within a sluggish bay,
Over the smooth inviting main
   Ready to launch away.

" But yet in vain to fill my sails
   The favoring breezes blow ;
In vain to the port of my earthly rest,
   I turn my seaward prow.

" In vain along the other shore
   I see the loved ones stand,
And beckon me over the briny flood,
   Home to my Fatherland

" For bedded deep in solid ground
   At the bottom of ocean hoar,
An anchor cast, still hugs me fast,
   To a flat and dreary shore.

" But my CAPTAIN is on board with me.
  HE sees my longing state :
  Patience, my soul ! HE knoweth best—
  It is for *thee* to wait.

" When at his command the anchor shall rise,
  And I ride the boundless sea,
  May HIS hand guide my little barque
  To the Haven where I would be.

" And when, long tossed on the stormy waves,
  My wanderings all are o'er,
  Let me anchor at last, in the River of Life
  For ever and evermore !

" I have been very industrious of late—week before last I did in five working days forty-five pages of Goethe, and last Friday evening I finished Volume III., and this besides keeping up my daily teaching.

" Best love to all—mother, aunty, brothers, sisters, and all on dear Rock Point, for the architectural adornment of whose noble crags I am constantly building the most magnificent castles in the air.

" I seal this with the new Episcopal seal of Georgia,* which has just arrived from England—a large, heavy carnelian set in heavy gold. It is from my design. How do you like it ?

" Ever your loving son,
                                    " HENRY."

While he was a member of the household of Bishop Elliott, as was natural, he fell in love, and with one whose noble nature, generous heart, and pure soul, made her worthy of himself. But he was bound by his own sense of duty, which was ever the most authoritative voice in the world to him, to think of his father, and the needs of the younger members of the family. Free, he could do something which would not only give himself support, but also enable him to send the major part of his earnings to his parents ; while an engagement of marriage would of necessity force him to save enough to provide a home for his bride, and so cut off a source of revenue which would leave those dear ones at home in need. It was all before him, and although no one could have blamed him if he had simply followed his heart and

* A copy of the Georgia Diocesan Seal could not be obtained.

offered himself, yet he never hesitated, and though, as he wrote in his verses, "Athirst for Love,"

> "——I am athirst for love !
> And yet, for two long years,
> Trembling with smothered hopes and fears,
> Have stood beside a bright inviting stream
>   As if t'were all—a dream.
> Nor ever sank upon my knee, to dip
> Into the wave my parchèd lip ;
> But with a spell-bound eye,
> Stood still and watched that sparkling stream roll by.
> And now I go
> Far from the music of its placid flow ;
>   And bid that yearning love I dare not tell—Farewell ! "

This bitter in the cup of sweetness of those years, years which he always spoke of as the happiest of his life, wrung from him at last a poem, from which the last stanza is quoted. Yet it was as well that he yielded to the call of duty, for she who had unconsciously gained his heart was already promised to another. Years afterward, when the news of her death reached him, he wrote of her this editorial notice in *The Church Journal :* " The sad intelligence brings up before our memory the undimmed recollections of twenty years ago, when it was our happiness to see what she was in that delightful home circle of the sunny South, which looked upon her as its chiefest ornament. It was not so much her beauty, or grace, or her easy and unpretending power in conversation, or her cheerfulness of spirit, flashing forth wit and raillery as the clear evening skies of summer send forth the innocent lightning : nor yet that, in her, *all* these were combined to form a perfect lady. But there was a further attraction —the solidity of her understanding, the depth and earnest strength of her character, which was a latent power in her, shrinking far from the surface, and understood by only a few, though the mysterious magnetism of it was unconsciously *felt* by many who could *see* only the delicately veiled brilliance of her loveliness. All these last were surprised when she devoted herself to the foreign field in China ; but not so the few who knew her best. And those who have been members of that mission can tell how the same wise and patient strength was the central magnet of the work, while nevertheless her name appeared in published letters and reports less frequently than any other. Only as health began to fail, and life to wear away into eternity, the mention began to be more frequent; until now that she has passed beyond the power to hear us, we who knew her best can for the first time speak of her as she deserved. There now lies buried on the desolate shore of the Red Sea [for she died at Suez on her way to this country] one of the noblest, purest, and best of the daughters of South Carolina."

In all these letters, epigrams, sonnets, poems, and translations, we see the shaping of his mind for his life work. His strong, keen mind could not but seek expression for what it was full of, and yet that mind, with all its brilliancy and wit, and readiness for the encounter with like elements opposing it, with all its power of setting down its own thoughts, was not to be exercised in the field of pure literature. We see in these writings the first attempts of the *litterateur;* but in them little of the perfection of written thought with its close-woven web of argument embroidered with its own rich fancies which fairly make the blood tingle with the wit of the writer, or arouse to exasperation at his audacity ; and at last the burst of rollicking laughter as he ran you through and through, that made his writings so interesting in his riper years. That style was the result of careful study in his youth of the best models. He used to revel in South's Sermons, the Letters of Junius, the writings of Addison, Swift, Steele, Dr. Johnson, Burke, Shakespeare, Spenser, and rare Ben Jonson. He was delighted with Boswell's Life of Dr. Johnson, and had always at his tongue's end any number of the sharp sayings and repartees narrated in that book. So, too, the study of the classics had a marked effect upon his style. For the sake of his own style he studied carefully Cicero, Quintilian, Sallust, Cæsar, and Demosthenes. He became a master in the Socratic method of argument, and many and many a time in the wars of words which invariably arise when men of books and talk come together, he wound up an antagonist in the inextricable tangle of his own incautious admissions, and contradictory assertions. From such studies he learned the art of using his own powers which showed themselves in the time of his boyhood.

CHAPTER IV.

1843–1849.

NATURALLY he was looked up to as a Mentor by all the family of children, and all points of scholarship were referred to him. His brother Caspar relates a tale that illustrates his aptness and kindness in using sharp weapons. Caspar had taken it into his head that he could write poetry, and gave himself up during his long vacation to writing a *play* in *blank verse*. When it was done it was submitted to Henry for his criticism. He kept it three days, and made no sign, though of course he knew his brother's consuming curiosity as to his opinion. On the fourth day he brought it to Caspar, saying, " Cass, I have read this paper through carefully three times. I have found *one line* which contains a poetical idea ! *Where did you steal that from ?* " Poor Caspar was struck dumb by such an avalanche; but Henry continued, " Dr. Johnson used to say, if you cannot put fire into your works, better put your works into the fire "—pointing over his shoulder toward the stove. In a rage of mortified vanity and shame Caspar instantly crammed the manuscript into the stove, and watched it till all was burnt. As he turned sadly away he caught a glimpse of his elder brother's sparkling black eye, watching him through the open door ! Not another word was said, and Caspar was radically cured.

After he left Georgia he went to Louisiana, where his sister Emily, Mrs. Charles Fay, had the care of a Church school in her husband's parish. But he did not remain there long, and only one incident of the time was related by his sister. He had whipped one of the boys, whose father, indignant at such an outrage, came in a towering rage with two riding-whips in his hands, and, bursting open the school-room door, thrust one into the grasp of Henry, at the same time dealing him a stinging cut across the face, crying out " defend yourself! " Before a second blow could be dealt Henry had thrown his own whip down, and folding his arms, told his infuriated visitor to strike again, for he should not resist,

because he was a Christian! Henry's reply sounds, it must
be confessed, a little bit affected, but there was never such a
thing as artificiality in his actions.   At any rate the angry South-
ron was soothed, and acknowledged the justice of the punishment given his child, and became a fast friend of young Mr.
Hopkins.

Returning from the South, Mr. Hopkins worked as a reporter
in New York City on the *Courier and Enquirer*.   He also
painted miniatures on ivory, living in a very frugal fashion, and
sending home every cent he could spare.   He reported the debates of the General Convention of 1847, and of various other
meetings of different sorts, political as well as religious.   He
never learned stenography, but wrote down his notes in long
hand, reporting striking sentences as nearly word for word as he
could, and kept the thread of the discourse in his memory by aid
of rapid notes.   Then, writing out his copy, very full and fresh
reports were made, and since he had not only a well-filled, but
also an appreciative mind, his reports probably gave all that was
worth reading of any debate.   During all the years from his
graduation from the University in 1839, till he entered the General Seminary in 1847, he gave his whole powers to the helping
of his father.   It was for him that he taught, painted miniatures, wrote reviews of books, articles for the magazines of those
times (there were then no " literary agencies " to enrich writers
who do not know their own tongue), or songs, both verses and
music.

For, during those years Bishop Hopkins was sorely pressed by
poverty and he made great efforts to earn something by preparing
elementary books for instruction in drawing : and the *Vermont
Drawing-Book of Flowers* and the *Vermont Drawing-Book of Figures* were the result.   These books were, as may be gathered from
their titles, filled with colored plates of Vermont flowers and animals, and it appeared with the name of the younger John Henry
Hopkins upon its title page, and a large part of the work was his.
But much the larger part of the work and the whole of the design
were his father's.   It took those who helped in the work two
whole years to color the prints, but though Henry tried for day
after day to sell the completed books to Young Ladies' Seminaries and such-like schools, it was without avail, and the whole
thing was a dead loss, which it took years to make up.   But although he was so bitterly disappointed he did not lose his good
humor and he wrote, but not for publication :

THE PRINT COLORER'S LAMENT.

When a little boy I was sent to school,
    And after that to college ;
So that my curly pate is full
    Of divers kinds of knowledge.
Yet though for nobler purpose fit
By lore acquired and mother wit,
Dame Fortune, that mad, cross-grained wench,
Has fastened me down to a table and bench,
Where from breakfast time till I go to bed,
Great piles of lithographs, high as your head,
    Before me stand ;
    While, brush in hand,
And surrounded by saucers of various tints,
I must bend to the labor of *coloring prints !*
And since the work drags till it seems, my friend,
As if it had lost its latter end,
I've leisure to brush up my learning never,
Although I've a brush in my hand forever.

E'en mixing the color is no slight job ;
    "Ay ! there's the rub ! "
I've mixed for this everlasting daub,
Enough to fill up a good-sized tub ;
And laid it on, when by my crown,
I'd a great deal rather have laid it down !
Still "paint, paint, paint ! " is the hue and cry,
Until at length, so weary am I,
That at every fresh hue I am ready to cry !

When I began (upon the green)
    I was but green, I own ;
And with a careless hand and tongue
    I let the fact be known.
But with the shadows thick laid on,
    Experience came, and, mark !
When to the deepest shades I came
    I knew how to keep dark.

To rosy tints condemned for weeks
No wonder that my once rosy cheeks
    Quite thin and pale have grown ;
For, putting the pink on the roses' face
    Has taken the red from my own.
From day to day
    I sigh away,
To melancholy thoughts a prey ;
For when toiling for months on the azure hues
    How can I choose
    But get the blues ?

The yellow adds no yellow boys
    To my small stock of pelf ;
And I've been doing browns, until
    I am done brown myself.
So that often to myself I say,
    Through the long day's dreary hours ;
" My path of life is a thorny path,
    Though strewed so thick with flowers."

Our troops, you know
    In Mexico,
Have bravely met and thrashed the foe ;
    Three days they fought at Monterey,
And in the fierce and fatal fray,
    A thousand Mexicans did slay.
Now I my share of the glory crave,
A soldier steady, true, and brave,
For, during this long and desperate fight
I ne'er forsook my colors day nor night.

Now poor Tom Hood tells a pitiful tale
Of a maiden forlorn, and hungry and pale,
Who had no time for gadding about,
    Nor an hour for social chat,
Whose whole life long was but sew-sew
    And bid fair to be short at that ;
And what still worse in a maiden's eyes is,
Although on shirts of all sorts and sizes
She spent so many years of stitches,
She could ne'er have a chance for wearing the breeches.
Yet my predicament is worse,
To all appearances, than hers—
Now this is no joke, indeed it ain't ;
I've too much color for my complaint ;
While for hers no color at all could be seen
(That is provided the shirts were clean).

Nor is it enough that, day by day
I lose my flesh and toil away
    With pockets never fuller—
That close confinement makes me ill,
And with declining health, that still
    My wit grows daily duller—
My vote they mean to take away,
    Because that now, the rascals say,
    I am a man of color !

Now, oh ye stars, look down in pity,
Be melted by my mournful ditty ;
Give me some business suited to my taste,
    Nor let me waste,
    Ye heavenly powers !
The flower of my age on fruitless flowers !

These sacrifices on his part were most freely made, but at last it was decided that, in view of an improvement in the condition of his throat, he should make them no longer, and that he should be free to follow the native inclination of his soul, and complete the dedication of her son to God made by his mother in his childhood, and seek the ministry. Accordingly he entered the General Theological Seminary in 1847, when he was nearly twenty-seven. His age, his experience since leaving the University, and his powers and goodness, made him quite the leading man in all the Seminary, of whatever class.

It was a very different institution from what it is now. The buildings were shabby and mean, even at their best, and quite insufficient for the needs of the school. The library had very inadequate quarters, and in consequence could not be arranged so that full use might be made of the collection of books, which was a very good one. The chapel was a wretched, mean room, and celebrations of the Eucharist were not held except once or twice a year ; such a place as the present dignified, beautiful chapel, with its altar of vari-colored marble, with statues of the saints in the niches of the rere-dos and of the Good Shepherd in the midst, with cross and candles, the pavement of lustrous stones increasing in beauty and costliness as they climb the steps within the sacrarium, the carved stalls of massy oak, the rainbow tints in the windows, filled with saints and angels of the heavenly hosts, the rushing melodies rising daily from the double ranks of the young Levites who fill the seats in the deep, deep choir. All these were never even dreamed of by those who sat on those miserable wooden benches fifty years ago ; yet many of them lived to see this new and better day. The Seminary was poor, and it was also an object of deep suspicion and distrust. There was no ritualism in those days, but there was the soul of it ; and some even of those who were enlisted on the Church side were quite ready to give up the Seminary.

The Faculty was an able one, but the methods of instruction were not such as are approved in these later days, and so long as men recited their lessons, little more was asked from them. The lessons were no task to a practised student like young Hopkins, and he had a great deal of time at his disposal. He supported himself as before. It took but little to satisfy his needs. His life was an ascetic one, for various reasons. In the first place by living simply, he had more money to send home ; in the next place, he had more to give away in charity ; and lastly and above

all, on account of his love of the Cross.   He was an ascetic of
the noblest type—loving, joyous, serene, and cheerful, not in the
least sour or gloomy, or proud or cold.   Therefore he had but
one suit of clothes at a time ; and he lived thus all his life long.
He slept on a plank with a single blanket to cover him, and lived
on Graham crackers, an inch thick, unleavened, and much harder
than pilot-bread, and cold water.

While at the Seminary, he read everything he could.   The extent and variety, accuracy and fulness of his studies were amazing.
The students used to call him, half in jest and yet in earnest,
"Father Hopkins," and the gentleness, sweetness, and consideration with which he met all who came to him, made him loved by
even those who most differed from him.   So, too, though he had
all the fresh hopefulness of youth, yet, his wisdom being beyond
his years, he was a sort of spiritual director to a good many of his
fellows.

He was always ready for an argument, and although he was as
keen as a brier and argued with a rush, and with the pertinacity
of a bull-dog, yet it was always *ad rem* and never *in personam*.
No one was more ready to take sides in the wars of words that
rage so fiercely in all places where students meet, but he was not
pugnacious.   If a head came in sight and seemed to challenge,
nothing ever daunted him ; nevertheless he was not the champion waiting with the chip on his shoulder for the enemy to
knock it off.

The only *game* which the boys and girls of Bishop Hopkins'
schools were allowed to play was chess.   It was the only game
that the Bishop's son ever knew.   He played it with his fellow-
students at the Seminary in a way of his own, marked by completeness of survey of the whole board, subtle and deliberate
development of his attack, unswerving persistence in his plans,
skilful handling of pieces, a strong game with his pawns, and a
sudden unveiling of his aim, and overwhelming advance—very,
very seldom was he beaten.   He gave even strong players odds
of mate by a marked pawn ; or mate on a particular square.
One loved friend, to whom he sometimes gave such heavy odds,
says that once, when he, receiving some odds (no matter what),
played with great care he managed to beat Hopkins.   When the
mate was seen to be inevitable Hopkins was so disconcerted
that his hand trembled with nervousness, and at last completely
lost his wits, though he kept his temper.

He had even then all his great schemes which later on he revealed in the *Church Journal ;*—small dioceses, provinces, the revival of the diaconate, free churches, beautiful worship ; and the whole cycle of Church doctrines and their consequences.

He did not *shave*, and that marked him as one of the " peculiars." We seldom realize that in our daily life we are doing many things that are not in the least natural, so accustomed are we to the conventions of society. Just so we do not realize the pressure of the atmosphere until a part of that pressure is taken off by artifice, as in a cupping-glass. *We* wear full beards, or none, or whiskers or mustaches as we please, and none venture to question the customs of others. Not so in 1847. In those days if a clergyman did not shave other people wrote to the newspapers about it.

Here are two or three of Mr. Hopkins' epigrams on the subject " in answer to Katyn in the *Express* of February 24, 1848," dated by him February 25, 1848 :

I.

A. "The goats have beards, my Friend, and so have you,
Therefore you're one ! "
B. " The goats have beards, I grant ; 'tis also true,
Puppies have none."

II.

If you can single the Puseyites out
By the way they suffer their beards to sprout,
As I believe you say, sir ;
Then true-blue Protestants may be made
By any black Jack in the barbers' trade
With a little soap-suds and a razor.

III.

If the sage inference we must draw
(On the logical plan
Of the smooth-faced man)
That Popery's proved by the style of the jaw ;
John Calvin's creed must have had a flaw,
For his beard was as long as the Moral Law :
While the Pope, an idolatrous sinner,
Who has no more beard than you have wit,
(Being shaved as you know
Both above and below),

Might pass for a Protestant every whit,
Be acknowledged for Puritan company fit
And at the head of the table sit
(Although with laughter his sides might split
Every time he should happen to think of it)
At the next New England dinner !

Mr. Hopkins used to wear in those days an extraordinary Byronic collar, which left his throat quite exposed to view ; in complete contrast with the high collars and swathing neck-cloths then in style. He did this, not to attract attention, but because he believed such a baring of his throat would strengthen it and give him back his voice. Very likely it did help him, and the decrease, since those days, of " clergymen's sore-throat," is likely to have been brought about in part by the use of more sensible collars. Nothing shows more plainly how essentially provincial New York then was, though it had half a million inhabitants, than the story that John Henry Hopkins used to be followed in the streets by people on account of his outlandish collar. He might wear what he pleased *now* and no one would do *more* than turn his eyes toward him. There were a few such things which, on account of his opinions, his boldness and unconventionality in expressing them, and his strong, strange face, made him a noted figure in New York. He was inclined to argue that since his style of dress was his own he might do as he chose, because he did no more than vary from usual customs. But Bishop De Lancey once told him that a public man's exterior belongs not only to himself but to the public also, and that since customs were not *wrong* he would best serve his own interests and the Church's by conforming as closely to them as he could.

When he came up for his final examinations he was especially complimented upon his beautiful reading of Hebrew, and he was considered the head of the school. His reading of Hebrew was beautiful always, as was his reading of all languages, exact articulation, each consonant carefully uttered, but not vocalized ; the most delicate shading of related sounds of words, careful accentuation, not accenting each syllable as is done in the modern ridiculous New England fashion, and a quaint musical modulation made his reading unlike any other reading, and brought out the meaning of Scripture with a rare suggestiveness and devotion.

The Church movement began to show visible effects while Hopkins was at the Seminary. Historically it is known as the *Oxford* movement, because the Tractarians were graduates of that

University.   But in England it began to show itself through the efforts of *Cambridge* men, although Cambridge never has had anything like so strong a Church *tone* as Oxford.   A little coterie of lovers of Church architecture, J. M. Neale, Benjamin Webb (late Vicar of St. Andrew's, Wells Street), Edmund Venables, Precentor of Lincoln ; Harvey Goodwin, late Bishop of Carlisle, and a few others, formed a little society, one of whose rules was to visit some specified church within four miles of St. Mary's Church *weekly.*   This was finally merged into a larger society, which was instituted in May, 1839, and called the Cambridge Camden Society.   Within four years there were among its members or patrons two archbishops and sixteen bishops.   In 1846 the society became the " Ecclesiological (late Cambridge Camden) Society."   From first to last Neale and his friend Webb were the main elements in its success.

These statistics are of interest because they mark almost exactly the beginning of what is called Ritualism.

The New York Ecclesiological Society was founded early in the year 1848, and at the second quarterly meeting the name of John Henry Hopkins, Jr., was placed upon the roll of members.

As in England, the first effort to change the face of the Church was made upon the fabric of churches.   There was no scheming, no deep-laid plan to begin thus and go on toward Ritualism as we see it now ; it was but natural to begin there.   The romantic movement had caused an interest in mediæval architecture, which the sham classicism of the seventeenth and eighteenth centuries had called Gothic, meaning barbaric, and all events united to bring men to the study of those picturesque monuments of the devotion of ages which men fancied as ages of romance and mystery.   In America architects had reared extraordinary edifices on the mistaken principle that Greek buildings could be made to suit our purposes, and had fancied that they could successfully emulate the serene loveliness of Pentelic marble with pine-wood and white paint.   On such or even lower standards American tastes in architecture were formed, and the true Goth was the purblind American.   A soil more destitute of any genuine growth of Church art could not have existed in any other Christian land. There was nothing ready for the hands of those who knew what was good.   Not only were the people to be taught, but they had to learn first of all that there was anything to be taught.   An interest had to be created ; the most elementary principles of art had to be unfolded, enforced, and reiterated..

Mr. Hopkins was a lover of the beautiful in all things from his natural tastes and training, but he had a personal and peculiar interest in the study of pointed architecture, for his father published the first book on the principles of Gothic architecture ever brought out in this country, and lithographed the plates that illustrated it with his own hand.

The Ecclesiological Society did not live more than ten or twelve years, but it gave an impetus to the use of true Church *ornamenta* that has never since died out; and it is almost a pity that instead of the standard of such works, in architecture, the building and arrangement of chancels, altars, mural paintings, stained-glass, and sculpture being in the hands of a number of amateurs it is set for the most part by tradesmen, each with his little stock of patterns stereotyped and commonplace. A long story might easily be made of the part which Mr. Hopkins took in adorning the worship of God, which he said was the best of all good works, and making it more worthy of its object.

Here his remarkable versatility came into play, and the profusion of his art creations, their beauty and variety, and appropriateness and utility, are of themselves remarkable, for he excelled in such works.

He came honestly by his talent. His father was no mean artist, his mother no trifler with art, and their son was full of their spirit, and from his earliest days was taught the craft of the artist. Art was no mere external accomplishment with him, but was one of the springs whence his life flowed; beauty was a trace of the Heavenly Father's love in creation, a relic of the first loveliness and joyful charm of Eden, a smile from the face of God—" whose beauty wakes the world's great hymn." Some of his productions were genuine creations; his imagination was so rich, so true the touch of the poet's hands, so unswerving the sweep of his glance that he dared many things that a man of lesser genius would have made ridiculous. But for that very reason some dull minds, better suited with the commonplaces of mere stock-in-trade, do not care for his works. He knew the rudiments of ecclesiastical art, and its whole grammar, and its higher literature. Symbols, mere dry bones for antiquaries, as most men pretend to use them, were living things in his hands. Yet he never designed an article without providing for its *use* first of all, and for the symbolism afterward. He had studied architecture and knew it well, and was consulted by hundreds of clergymen and building committees. He designed some churches himself, but never if the parish were able to afford an architect by profession, and of these he always recommended the choice of the *best*, and that this architect's plans should not be altered.   But he gave his advice as to arrangements of church and chancel at any time. Their *use* was to be first provided for.   Seats were to be made comfortable, with broad seats to support the legs; heating apparatus to be placed where it would do the most good; altars were to be placed on wide foot-paces, so that "a long-legged priest should not hurt his shins" in kneeling; book-desks were to be at the best angle for easy reading; altars were not to be perched on many steps in a shallow chancel, for that would diminish the breadth of each step, and reduce *to the eye* the depth of the chancel; altars were to be higher than tables, for the book was to be read *standing* and the Blessed Sacrament consecrated standing; and all things to be used were never to have their use taken from them on pretence of beauty.

He designed a large number of stained-glass windows, and supervised the making of the glass.   He was one of the first among us in America to see that a glass window, which is to give light, cannot be treated as if it were a wall or a piece of canvas. The very shadows in painted windows must be translucent.   In churches, too, beauty "for its own sake" was not to be sought. It was to be appropriate, and to tell a story, or illustrate a truth, or set forth some manifestation of grace.

Inside the church there was not to be a hap-hazard collection of beautiful things: in them there was to be harmony, and the unifying power streamed from the Altar, with its Sacrifice.   So all were to tend toward the Altar, and be for it and the Divine Victim immolated thereon.   The chancel speaks of the separateness of God from His creation, the rood-screen marks its division from the nave.   He erected a beautiful oaken screen bearing a great rood, in Christ Church, Williamsport, and it is one of the most striking things in a very dignified church.

He was one of the very first who here taught the art of needle-work for the adornment of the linen for the altar and for the vestments of the priest.   His own surplices were always embroidered in quaint and pretty patterns of leaves or flowers upon the yoke, and they were always the full, long, *mediæval* surplice with ample sleeves, put on over the head, and taking a great quantity of linen.   He never used the short, scanty, little cotta down to the hips, affected by most recent Ritualists, with no credit to their good taste.

He caused to be made the first alb, chasuble, and dalmatic ever made in the American Church. This was in 1850. He knew the time would come when such vestments could be worn for the offering of the Sacrifice of the Altar, and although even after he was ordained priest he did not often use them, it was because scores of priests then wore them regularly with none to hinder. He also made the first colored stole (of violet) ever used in the American Church. This stole had a companion. It was given by Hopkins to a priest who, becoming frightened at the ritual troubles, dyed his *black*. He made the first pastoral staff ever made in America, though not the first one ever used ; Bishop Doane, of New Jersey, having one sent him from England by Mr. Beresford-Hope, made of oak from St. Augustine's, Canterbury.

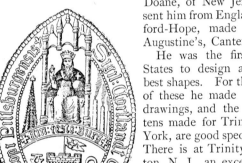

Seal of the Diocese of Pittsburgh, designed by John Henry Hopkins.

He was the first in the United States to design altar plate of the best shapes. For the most elaborate of these he made full-sized colored drawings, and the chalices and patens made for Trinity Chapel, New York, are good specimens of his skill. There is at Trinity Church, Princeton, N. J., an exceedingly rich jewelled chalice made from his designs. All the jewels of a lady of great wealth were devoted to this purpose by her husband, and some hundreds of them are used in this set of altar plate. From first to last Dr. Hopkins made designs for altar plate to the value of nearly half a million !

He made a large number of episcopal seals. In the narrow limits of the vesica piscis he moved with all the freedom and playful spirit of the old Gothic artists. Each design in its own meagre plot has its meaning and *character*, in a double sense. Most such designs are iterations and reiterations of mitres, crossed keys, and crosiers ; not so with his. No two are alike ; they tell a story, and the story is the right one for the place. He is not afraid to take secular objects inside his lines, if they are in the field where the work is to be done. In the seal of the diocese of Pittsburgh one sees the tall chimneys ! For Springfield, deeply

engraven in the superb amethyst given its first Bishop from De-
Koven, are the four streams from the one *spring* parted to water
the *field*—the world—and bring forth the increase, and the
motto " *Deus* dat incrementum ! "

For the first Missionary Bishop of Western Texas, the heroic
Elliott, he made the lion, and the motto, " Vox clamantis in de-
serto." For the first Missionary Bishop to Utah, the home of
the Mormons, he made a seal, which shows the Holy Ghost, as
a dove, descending upon a bee-hive, round which bees are flying. When we recall the fact that the Mormons call their own
region " Deseret, or the land of the honey-bee," the appropriateness of such a design for the seal of a Catholic Bishop is quite
clear. On the coat-of-arms of the State of Maine is a lone star,
with the motto " Dirigo." . For Bishop Neely he designed a
seal showing our Lord walking amid the seven golden candlesticks of the Apocalyptic vision, with an angel holding up this
single star of the state. Sometimes he would make a pun. For
Bishop Starkey he made a *key*, with a *star* in the ring of the
key, and around them the legend, " Qui habet clavem David :
✠ Stella splendens et matutina."

Mr. Henry Wagner, son of " Wagner, of Brighton," in building and adorning a magnificent church at Brighton as a memorial to his father, devised a pictorial representation of the
way colonial, missionary, and American diocesan Churches had
branched from the parent stem. In pursuing his object he asked
from Dr. Hopkins the seals and arms of the American bishops.
He *expected* that these would be poor in design, taste, and
execution ; but on receiving them he was " fearful that their
great superiority would throw the others out of balance, by their
beauty, and their dignity and character, in which most of all the
others were sadly lacking. But, as the result showed, they gave
to the whole a richness and picturesqueness which it had not
possessed before." This was about 1882.

Some of the most noteworthy work he ever did, besides the
designing of so many episcopal seals, are the alms basin which
was sent by the General Convention of 1871 to the Church of
England, as a memorial of the visit of the Bishop of Lichfield
(George Augustus Selwyn) ; the monument to his father, erected
at the Rock Point Cemetery in full view, on the one hand, of the
house built by the Bishop and his sons in 1841, and on the other,
of the Vermont Episcopal Institute ; and the pastoral staff presented by the clergy of the diocese of Central Pennsylvania to

Bishop Howe on the "Golden Jubilee" of his ordination, in 1882. The alms basin is thus described :

The design of the alms basin is meant to be peculiarly appropriate to the occasion. In the centre is the hemisphere, showing the Atlantic Ocean in the midst, with the Old World on the east of it and the New World on the west. The land is matted and slightly raised ; the mountains and rivers being clearly shown. The ocean is burnished, with bright wavy lines engraved on it, indicating the motion of the water. A scroll on the ocean bears the inscription, which expresses the spirit of the gift : ✠ *Orbis veteri novus, Occidens orienti, Filia Matri* ✠ : "The New World to the Old, the West to the East, the Daughter to the Mother." At the South Pole is the date, 1871, of the Bishop's visit. In the upper part of the hemisphere is a circular chased medallion, which covers nearly the whole of Great Britain, and bears a quaint little ship. This is the ship of the Church, having the Cross at its prow, the monogram of the word *Christ* on its sail [the same monogram that was on the famous Labarum or war-standard of Constantine], the Pastoral staff of the Apostolic Episcopate as its mainmast, upheld by two ropes on either side for the other two orders of Priests and Deacons ; and "S. S." on the rudder, for the "Sacred Scriptures." This ship is leaving England, and is headed toward the New World, indicating that our Church received its existence from the Catholic Church through the Church of England.

Outside of this hemisphere is a band about an inch wide, with six words chased in ancient uncial Greek capitals. These are the names of the six undisputed General Councils of the ancient Church, whose definitions of the Catholic Faith are accepted by every orthodox branch of the Apostolic Church throughout the world, and always have been. These six are separated from one another by six hemispheres of *lapis lazuli*, a foreign stone. Its blue tint may well represent the perpetuity of the Catholic faith ; and they are all exactly the same, for all those councils set forth one and the same doctrine, only defending it from different forms of error as they arose at different times. As the word "Catholic" signifies "all the world over," so this band runs all around the globe.

From this band, on the outside, spring twelve oak-leaves, and between them are twelve twigs, each bearing three acorns with burnished kernels. This use of the English oak sets forth the English Church growing outward, and carrying her Catholicity

ALMS BASON SENT BY THE AMERICAN CHURCH
TO THE CHURCH OF ENGLAND
1871-72

[DESIGNED BY REV. J. H. HOPKINS, S.T.D.]

with her wherever she goes, in every direction. The *twelve* is the number of Apostolic fulness and perfection, and the *three* is, of course, a reference to the doctrine of the Trinity, which is the bright and vital point of all Catholicity.

All the parts that have thus far been mentioned are richly gilded, we cheerfully conceding the gold to the Old World, and content to represent ourselves, more modestly, in silver. From behind the oak - leaves and acorns, therefore, spring alternate maple-leaves and palmetto-leaves, the former symbolizing the North and the latter the South, and thus representing the historical truth that both parts of our American Church are the outgrowth of the Church of England. These leaves fill up the hollow of the basin till they touch the rim.

The rim is very broad and nearly flat. It bears the inscription, "It is more blessed to give than to receive." It begins and ends at a jeweled cross, composed of five amethysts, four topazes, eight pearls and eight small garnets, all clustered within a circle, the cross itself thus forming a crown of glory. The words are divided by large stones, more than an inch in diameter, and polished *en cabuchon.* As they refer not to the faith, but to gifts, which are of infinite variety, no two are alike. They are all (with one exception) American stones, agates, moss agates, and jaspers, from Lake Superior, Colorado, Texas, and a piece of gold-bearing quartz from California. The one exception is the first of them, after the word "It," which is a species of *prase* from New Zealand. It was found in a lapidary's shop in Philadelphia, where a large piece of it had been left by a private gentleman who himself brought it from New Zealand. As the Bishop of Lichfield was the world-renowned Selwyn, who, as Bishop of New Zealand, had spent twenty-five years there, doing more than any other one man to organize the synodical system of the Colonial Episcopate of the English Church, and afterward to organize in the same way the Colonial Provincial system, which makes those Colonial Churches as independent of the Mother Churches as our own, a piece of that New Zealand stone was secured at once, as the most appropriate to be placed *first* in the series. The letters are relieved by engraved diagonal lines, termed *shading,* but the lines are cut with a bright tool, so that in the right light they show brilliantly. They signify the shadows or trials of the Church, which, when viewed aright, are always seen to be her chief glories.

Outside the inscription is a very bold cable moulding, the

finish of which shows that it is "a threefold cord, not easily
.broken." This means the three Orders of the Apostolic Ministry ; one strand being burnished bright to represent the Episcopate ; the next under it having *twelve* cross threads representing
the Priesthood ; and the next below that having *seven* longitudinal threads, signifying the Diaconate, the original number of
the deacons being seven. Outside this cable moulding, again, is
a narrow margin of leaves all growing outward, showing the
vigorous outward growth of the Church all the world over.

On the under side of the rim is a plain Latin inscription, more
specifically detailing the circumstances of the occasion which
called forth this gift from the American to the English Church.
It runs thus : "✠ Ecclesiæ Anglicanæ matri, per manus Apos-
tolicas reverendissimi Georgii Augusti Selwyn, Dei gratia, Epis-
copi Lichfieldiensis, pacis et benevolentiæ internuncii, ejusdem-
que auctoris, hoc pietatis testimonium filii Americani dederunt."

This alms basin was solemnly presented in the course of the
celebration of the Eucharist at St. Paul's Cathedral, London.

In the following lines, from the pen of Bishop Wordsworth of
Lincoln, the Church of England is supposed to return thanks for
the late pious offering from the Daughter Church :

> Quod caræ mittis, carissima Filia, Matri
> Accipimus sanctæ pignus amicitiæ.
> Dat dextram veteri novus Orbis ; Nata Parenti ;
> Miscet et Occiduum Sol Oriente jubar.
> Pontus Atlantiaco quamvis interfluat æstu,
> Littora velivolis consociantur aquis ;
> Ecce ! Ratis Christi medium translabitur æquor ;
> Alba ferunt Labarum carbasa ; prora Crucem.
> Funis Apostolico fultum gestamine malum
> Ordinibus binis junctus utrinque tenet ;
> Navem per scopulos Oracula Sancta gubernant ;
> Sic tutam sulcat per maris arva viam :
> Angliacos linquit portus ferturque Carina
> Americæ placido suscipienda sinu.
> Aspice ! qua medium lancis complectitur orbem
> Mystica cælatis clara corona notis !
> Nomina senarum Synodorum pristina cerno,
> Quæ fixam placitis explicuere fidem.
> Germinat hæc circum quercu diadema Britannâ ;
> Donaque fert Trino frons duodena DEO :
> Multicolore nitent diversæ lumine gemmæ ;
> Undique sic radians lucet Amore Fides.
> Crux zonam gemmata aperitque et claudit ; Amoris
> Nam Crux principium est, Crux quoque finis erit,
> Fraternis veluti triplex amplexibus orbis,
> Cuncta Ministerium cingit Apostolicum :

Denique ut externo diffusæ in margine frondes,
   Sic Christi Vitis tendit, in omne solem.
Ergo Te Genitrix, carissima Nata, salutat,
   Et pia de grato pectore vota refert ;
Pacis in æterno constringat fœdere corda
   Cordibus Angliacis Americana DEUS !
Una Fides, unus CHRISTUS, nos SPIRITUS unus,
   Unus et Ipse Suo jungat amore PATER !
Sic, ubi transierint mortalia sæcula, Cœli
   Nos una accipiat non peritura Domus !

An autographic copy of these lines was sent by Bishop Wordsworth to Dr. Hopkins—the acquaintance formed at the time of
the meeting of the first Lambeth Conference (a few instances of
which are mentioned in Dr. Hopkins' Journal) continued by
correspondence as long as the Bishop lived.

Rendered into English prose, the verses read :

" We accept this token of sacred fellowship which you, most
beloved Daughter, send to your beloved Mother.   The New
World gives this pledge of friendship to the Old—the Daughter
to the Parent ; and the Western Sun mingles its splendors with
the Eastern.   Although the Atlantic rolls its tide between us,
our shores are bound together by the sail-covered waters.   And
lo ! here I see pictured the Ship of Christ's Church gliding
across the mid-ocean.   Her snow-white sails bear the Monogram
of the Redeemer and her prow His Cross.   A cord uniting the
two-fold Orders of the Ministry holds firmly on either side a
Mast which bears aloft the token of Apostolic authority.   The
Sacred Scriptures, as the rudder, guide the ship among the rocks.
Thus safely does the Ship plough her way through the furrows of
the sea.   The Bark seems just leaving the shores of England,
soon to be moored in the tranquil harbor of America.

" But look further, where a mystic corona, bright with graven
letters, encircles the central boss of the basin.   I discover upon
it the ancient names of the six General Councils which by their
decrees have determined the everlasting Faith.   And again from
this springs forth a diadem of British oak, of which the twelve-
fold leaves present their fruits to the triune God.   Varied gems
glow with many-colored rays, as Faith radiant with Charity
sheds its light in every direction.   A Cross of clustered gems
fastens the girdle which bears the blessed legend of Charity, for
the Cross is the beginning of Charity as well as its consummation.   A Cable with its triple braided strands, like the Apos-

tolic Priesthood, encircles the whole design.   Finally, as leaves
are pushing forth from the very outer margin, so is the Vine of
Christ still extending itself into every land.

"Therefore, most beloved Daughter, the Mother sends back
her greeting to you, and from her grateful heart utters devout
prayers, that God may knit together American hearts with English in an eternal covenant of Peace!   May the one Faith, the
one Christ, the one Spirit, and the one Father Himself, unite
us all with His own love!   So when earthly scenes shall have
passed away, may the Home in Heaven, which shall never perish,
receive us all together."

The monument to Bishop Hopkins is a great Celtic cross,
which, with its three steps, is fifteen feet high.   It is in itself a
compendium of personal and official history.   One part of it is
particularly interesting.   In the arms of the cross are statuettes
of the twelve Apostles, in groups of three, about a foot high.
Each bears the emblem appropriated to him by the conventional
rules of ecclesiastical art.   No two in the same group look the
same way, and no two figures in the whole number are alike.
Thus they were designed by John Henry Hopkins.   But the
marble carver, with the cartoons before him, could not carry out
the designs.   Whereupon Hopkins took modelling clay, and, although he had never done such a thing before in his life, with
his own hands made every one of the statuettes in clay, and from
these models the carver executed the design !   The Bishop's
Staff, given to the first Bishop of Central Pennsylvania in January, 1882, is a typical example of Dr. Hopkins' rich fancy and
of his characteristic style of teaching by means of symbols.

The staff described by himself in presenting it to the Bishop—
for he was spokesman for the clergy who gave it—though the
description is condensed from the original, is here given.

"The idea of the Pastoral Staff is taken from the shepherd's
crook, because our Lord, who is 'the Good Shepherd,' calls His
ministers to be shepherds.

"It is so constructed as to carry its meaning in its form.   As
the highest function of a Bishop's office is to bring back the
wanderers, so the *crook* of the staff, by which the shepherd caught
and gently drew back the straying sheep, is the highest part of it.
The greater portion of the staff is straight ; for the great bulk of
the Bishop's time is devoted to ruling those who are willing
and obedient.   The lowest part is of baser metal than any of the

rest, and is *pointed*, signifying the coercive power of punishing those who are obstinately bad.   In this particular staff the straight part is divided into three parts.   The lowest of these is of ebony, signifying by its unbroken blackness our state by nature.   The second is of ebony alternated with holly—this last being the whitest of our ornamental woods.   This alternation signifies the conditions of the members of the Church here on earth, where the wicked are mingled with the good.   The upper part, pointing to that future when there shall be ' neither spot nor wrinkle nor any such thing,' is of pure and polished ivory ; and the staff is carried by being grasped by this part of it, for it is our duty to ' lay hold on eternal life.'   But since the recovery of the lost is the chief glory of Christ's work, so the highest adornment of the staff is always expended upon the *crook*.   Here it is of ebony incrusted with jewels : of ebony to remind us of the fallen state from which we have been redeemed ; while the jewels refer to that future glory, when the foundation of the New Jerusalem shall be of precious stones, and God shall make up His jewels—those souls that have been cut and polished by earthly trials and tribulations, so that they may reflect more brilliantly the light of the Sun of Righteousness.

    " As the gift of Episcopal consecration is conveyed with the solemn words ' receive the Holy Ghost for the office and work of a Bishop in the Church of God,' so the number *seven*—the number of the gifts of the Holy Ghost—is seen everywhere.   On the outside of the edge of the crook are *seven* bold crockets, each being of a dark leaf enclosing a golden ball—the gold of the Gospel enclosed in human infirmity.   On the same edge are *seven* stones of *lapis lazuli*, all of the same size, signifying with their deep blue tint the unchanging continuance of God's truth.   On each *side* of the crook are seven jewels, all different, and of different sizes, growing smaller as they go further on.   These signifying the varieties of personal character in God's saints, which are not done away in a future life, but are rather polished to a higher beauty. And the diminishing in size shows that the further progress we make in the spiritual life, the *less* we are disposed to make of ourselves.   Besides these larger stones there are seven groups, each containing seven crystals, and *one* more is added, making the forty-nine up to *fifty*—the full Pentecostal number, the number of the outpouring of the *Holy Ghost* with power—the number of the *Jubilee*.

    " And there is the same number on the opposite side ; so that both together they make up *One hundred*—the mystic number of the Flock of the Good Shepherd : ' What man of you having *an hundred sheep*,' is the sum total He gives us Himself.

" The silver hoop which incloses the centre-piece of the crook gives the same number in another way — for there are fifty scallops cut on the rim of it on each side.

" And what can be more appropriate than the figure of the Good Shepherd Himself standing in the midst of the crook, in the midst of His Flock? And the sheep that are with Him have their meaning also. The one which is standing, and looking up signifies *Europe*, which is the most thoroughly Christianized. On the other side, the one partly rising signifies *Asia*, where the work of evangelization is only partially done. The one lying on the ground at His feet, the darkest of them, is *Africa*, where the work is hardly yet begun. The smallest and youngest is *America*—and this is the lamb in His arms, the dearest place of all. Underneath, before and behind, are the loving commands ' ✠ Feed My Lambs ✠,' ' ✠ Feed My Sheep ✠.'

" In a hollow of the ebony surrounding all this central group there runs in an unbroken circle the three-fold cord of the Apostolic Ministry—the visible evidence of the *unity* of that Church in which Christ is, and with which He has promised to abide until the end of the world.

" Supporting the curve of the crook are two angels, one facing toward the Bishop who carries the pastoral staff, and the other on the opposite side. The one who faces the Bishop bears the *Cross*, for that we all must bear on Earth ; the one who bears the *Crown* is ' on the farther side.'

" All these figures of sheep and angels are of *silver oxidized*, for Churches have their precious metal dulled by the atmosphere of Earth, and He ' chargeth His angels with folly.' But the figure of the Good Shepherd Himself is gilded and burnished, as are also the *Cross*—which is sent by Him—and the *crown*, which will be given by Him ; while the *stars* over the heads of the angels reflect his light, referring as they do to the stars which are the angels of the Churches.

" The largest knop, with six compartments, just above the ivory shaft, is of oak, with reference to the oak of old England, our ecclesiastical Mother. Each compartment bears the name of one of the Bishops who have shepherded the flock in this part of Pennsylvania. First is the name of the venerable White, then in order, Onderdonk, Potter, Bowman, Stevens, and *Howe*.

All these names are cut in strips of sandalwood inlaid in the oak. The sandalwood is one of the most fragrant woods in the world ; and we would thus show that

> " The sweet remembrance of the just
> Shall flourish when he sleeps in dust."

" The entire number of jewels used is one hundred and twenty-seven ; the one hundred of the Flock of God, and *twenty-seven*—being three times three times three—the threefold number of the Ever-Blessed Trinity."

The staff is in two parts, the junction being between the ivory and the mingled ebony and holly portions of the straight part. When thus separated the two pieces fit into places in a case, for convenience of carrying.

Mr. Hopkins was always ready to do such work for any church that asked for his help. He would take long journeys at his own expense in order to make designs suitable to the place. Whatever was done for the Church by anyone he enthusiastically delighted in, and felt personally interested in. He built some lovely little churches of stones gathered on the spot, and when they were finished he went even as far as from New York to Wisconsin or Minnesota to be present at the consecration, and to tell in his own inimitable way the meaning of the whole work, and to fasten the lesson in memory and heart and conscience by a few sentences. He had two or three exquisite sermons on the tabernacle and the temple and the Church which were like living pictures, but these he never wrote out, and only memories remain of his words.

The New York Ecclesiological Society had to make its own footing good in a strong tide of ignorant prejudice, and therefore interested its members in all subjects relating to the worship of the Church.

Consequently the members (among whom were Reverend Doctors Haight, Creighton, John McVickar, Muhlenberg, Francis Vinton, Morgan Dix, Mahan, G. H. Houghton, S. R. Johnson, Forbes, and some bishops as "Patrons") published frequent papers on Church music. Here, too, John Henry Hopkins was *facile princeps*.

His father, as has been noted, had great skill and good taste, and his mother being likewise a skilful performer, and with his Irish and French and German blood and his education from early childhood, he was full of the spirit of melody. The whole

Hopkins family were musicians, and of them Henry was the centre. Church music, bad enough now, and misunderstood, was infinitely worse forty or fifty years ago. There was no knowledge whatever of the true Church style, and the *best* things were but the debased imitations of an untaught secular taste. The English cathedral services were tainted with the same infection. Fioriture and shakes and trills and roulades were looked upon as the climax of operatic singing, and since opera in the florid Italian style was the "best" thing known it was imitated in church. Ordinary hymn tunes were dismal imitations of Protestant-meeting-house tunes, and were as dull as ditch-water. Even they were used but once in the whole service. Good, hearty, congregational singing was not expected, and if lay people tried to sing in church they were looked upon as "queer," or, it may be, as Methodists away from home.

Thus the "solemn order of the service," to use the cant expression of the times, was carried out. Evangelical Churchmen did use hymns, but their heartiness and fervor discredited their use in the true-blue Church parishes, where a freezing, stupid monotony was looked upon as the very climax of orthodox Churchmanship.

The renewed life of the Church breathing from Oxford made all lovely things appear, and the singing birds came, too, in the new spring.

John Henry Hopkins could not but sing. Long before he was in the Seminary he had written hymns and songs. His father had not been trained in the technical part of musical composition, but his son, with a richer and a truer feeling, as was fitting in a later generation, had carefully studied harmony under competent teachers, and had continued his studies. He soon saw that to try to transpose the "devil's songs," or to write words of hymns beneath their notes, was not to improve Church music, but rather to debase it. There are some styles and some themes which are essentially secular, and even profane, and others from association are unworthy of use in the sanctuary. It is not so hard to profane sacred music. One of the most subtle methods of making sacred things ridiculous, and of turning them from their proper use was concocted by John Knox and the other Scottish "Reformers." They heard the melodies of sequences and hymns of the true Church on all sides, and on all sides loved. Accordingly they wrote above the notes other words, sometimes light and trifling and indecorous, and sometimes of the most obscene character, in order to render the music of the Church contemptible.   Some of those melodies are living still, and few or none when they hear " Cauld Kail in Aberdeen," " Comin thro' the rye," or " John Anderson my jo, John," have any idea that those tunes have sunk from the service of the sanctuary into the idle songs of carousers in a tavern.

Following the traces of the best English writers of ecclesiastical music he learned the value and beauty of *two* great schools of Church music all but unknown, except to students of the curious, and entirely unappreciated.   These were the ancient Church modes, and the German chorales, and their kindred, the psalm tunes written by Clement Marot and others for the Huguenot services early in the sixteenth century.   The chorales and French psalm music had more of the Church spirit than contemporary Church music written in Church style.   These last had lost their early simplicity and pure melody.   Their severe outlines were overlaid with all sorts of false ornament, and they were anything but plain song.   The reform effected by Palestrina had not yet been called for.   Mr. Hopkins worked these rich veins with great vigor and devotion.   He mastered the ancient " modes," and was able to use them, not as mere archaisms, but as living things.   Of him W. H. Walter, Mus. Doc., and the organist who probably has done more to form a correct and living Church style here than any other, says that he " always regarded him as a reliable authority in Gregorian music and the ancient tones. He made those a special study."

An incident is related of him, in this connection, which brings out more than one point of his character.

The students of the General Seminary were divided into two antagonistic camps on the subject of Church music.   The forces were marshalled as Gregorians and Anglicans.   Hopkins, at this time not a student, but in Holy Orders, threw himself enthusiastically on the side of Gregorian music, and so excited the wrath of the Anglicanists.   The difference in taste reached the professors, and Dr. Turner, who was passionately fond of music, was an Anglican, while Dr. Mahan was a Gregorian.   In those days the Deanery passed from professor to professor year by year.   This gave each faction one year of triumph, as the respective champions in turn became Dean.

Rev. Mr. Hopkins was the frequent guest of Dr. Mahan, and, more than once filled the place in the chapel of the absent organist during the supremacy of *Anglican* music.   He could

easily have driven his opponents frantic with rage by taking advantage of the situation and playing plain-song for the chants ;
but no, he overwhelmed them with his generosity by playing
Anglican music in the best style, and in a manner far superior
to their own organist.

This incident, trifling in itself, shows the nobility of Hopkins'
soul, his superiority to petty hates, and his magnanimity. As he
was then he ever was, and he showed this greatness of soul in
more weighty causes. Few men who themselves dealt heavy
blows received heavier return than he did from his enemies.
Many cherished their hostility to the end. He never did anything of the kind ; but dropped all settled matters, and forgot
all said or done to his disadvantage.

He published a great many things in the course of years, and
many of them are used in the services of the Church. He generally had some such composition lying on his desk at which he
worked as he could find the opportunity, working it over and
over, and polishing and retouching until it was as good as he
could make it, before allowing it to be published. He wrote a
setting for *Veni Creator* which is in most hymnals, and in
ancient form. It is not so fine as the lovely plain-song melody
which belongs to the hymn, but it is easily taken up by a congregation, and that is more than can be said for the *real* tune. His
tune *Vexilla Regis* for the hymn " The Royal Banners forward
go," and published in one musical edition of the old hymnal is
much better suited to the words than the tune by Lowell Mason
sometimes used for that hymn. He wrote a considerable number of anthems, and settings for the Kyrie Eleison, and all the
parts of a Mass. He published a number of the noblest of the
German *chorales ;* but all these works, owing to the fact that
the one authorized hymnal is used in almost every one of the
Church parishes in the country, are hardly known at all outside
the circle of those personally interested in him, and to a few
musicians.

He wrote some hymns, both words and music, and a few of
them are set down here, although they are all included in the
last edition of his " Carols, Hymns, and Songs," published in
1883.

Of two of these Dr. Muhlenberg said that they were the very
noblest hymns in the English language on their themes ; but they
should be heard sung to their own music to be appreciated.

One of them is for Whitsunday :

Blow on, thou mighty Wind.

FOR WHITSUN DAY.

1. Blow on, Thou mighty Wind! The clov-en tongues de-scend - ing,

Fann'd by Thy dewy Breath, shall blaze and burn, A sacred flame un-end - ing.

Soon shall that Fire be - hold Vile earth transform'd to fine wrought gold;

And gloom of shadowy night That flame shall kindle in - to light:

There - fore, Thou might - y Wind,....... blow on.

5

2. Blow on, Thou mighty Wind,
    And waft to realms unbounded
The notes of Faith and Hope and tender Love
    The Gospel trump hath sounded.
    Those sweetly piercing tones,
That charm all wars and tears and groans,
    Through earth and sea and sky
Upon thy rushing wings shall fly :
Therefore, Thou mighty Wind, blow on.

3. Blow on, Thou mighty Wind ;
    For, tempest-toss'd and lonely,
The Church upon the rolling billows rides,
    And trusts in Thy Breath only.
    She spreads her swelling sails
For Thee to fill with favoring gales,
    Till, through the stormy sea,
Thou bring her home where she would be :
Therefore, Thou mighty Wind, blow on.

4. Blow on, Thou mighty Wind,
    On hearts contrite and broken,
And bring in quickening power the gracious words
    That JESU'S lips have spoken.
    Lo ! then, from death and sleep,
The listening souls to life shall leap ;
    Then Love shall reign below,
And Joy the whole wide world o'erflow :
Therefore, Thou mighty Wind, blow on.

5. To GOD the FATHER, SON,
    By all in earth and heaven,
And to the HOLY SPIRIT, Three in One,
    Eternal praise be given,
    As once triumphant rang
When morning stars together sang ;
    Is now, as aye before ;
And shall be so for evermore,
World without end.   Amen.   Amen.
                —1858.

SONGS OF THE HEART.

[Hexameter and Pentameter.]

Drowned in the thundering roll of the organ's deep diapason,
    All unheard are the songs sung by the lowly of heart.
Soon are the loud tones mute, all dying away in the distance ;
    While those songs of the heart open the portal of Heaven.
                —1849.

The other, " Jerusalem, My Home," is here given, without the music, which, with its plaintive and entreating open phrase, ending in a third, and its modulations into the minor key, well expresses the idea of the hymn—the meditation of the pilgrim on his distant home—and the change of the ending of the last line (the key is C) from E to A, giving the tone of assured possession to the very words of the beginning :

Jerusalem, my Home,
I see thy walls arise ;
Their jasper clear and sardine stone
Flash radiance through the skies.
In clouds of heav'n descending,
With angel train attending
Thy gates of glistering pearl unfold
On streets of glassy gold.
No sun is there, no day or night ;
But, built of sevenfold splendors bright,
Thy Temple is the LIGHT OF LIGHT,
Jerusalem, my Home.

Jerusalem, my Home,
Where shines the royal throne,
Each king casts down his golden crown
Before the Lamb thereon.
Thence flows the crystal River,
And, flowing on forever,
With leaves and fruits, on either hand,
The Tree of Life shall stand.
In blood-washed robes, all white and fair,
The Lamb shall lead His chosen there,
While clouds of incense fill thy air,
Jerusalem, my Home.

Jerusalem, my Home,
Where saints in triumph sing,
While tuned in tones of golden harps
Heaven's boundless arches ring.
No more in tears and sighing
Our weak hosannas dying,
But alleluias loud and high
Roll thundering through the sky.
One chorus thrills their countless throngs ;
Ten thousand times ten thousand tongues
Fill thee with overwhelming songs,
Jerusalem, my Home !

Jerusalem, my Home,
Thou sole, all-glorious Bride,
Creation shouts with joy to see
Thy Bridegroom at thy side ;
The Man yet interceding,
His Hands and Feet yet bleeding,
And Him the billowy hosts adore
LORD GOD for evermore,
And " Holy, Holy, Holy," cry
The choirs that crowd thy courts on high,
Resounding everlastingly,
Jerusalem, my Home !

Jerusalem, my Home,
Where saints in glory reign,
Thy haven safe O when shall I,
Poor storm-tossed pilgrim, gain ?
At distance dark and dreary,
With sin and sorrow weary,
For thee I toil, for thee I pray
For thee I long alway.
And lo ! mine eyes shall see thee, too :
O rend in twain, thou veil of blue,
And let the Golden City through—
Jerusalem, my Home !

—1856.

There are plenty of others worth quoting entire, with their
music, but his own book contains them all.

He wrote several carols also, some of which have the genuine
ring of the true religious folk-song. One of them, " We three
Kings of Orient are," is known everywhere in this country, and
in England, too. He wrote its tune also, which has so strong a
flavor of the antique that not only in England, where the writer
was not known, but in the United States, and in *Church* publications, it has been cited as an "ancient carol." Some others, as
the "Roman Soldier," an Easter carol, and "Gather around
the Christmas Tree," are frequently sung. Others deserve to
be.

Dr. Hopkins was one of the most accomplished hymnologists
in the United States, and he was in this, as in all other things,
an advocate of liberty. No one ever contended more strongly
for the freedom of all parish churches as to the choice of hymns,
and here are some ideas from his book of " Carols, Hymns, and
Songs."

" The only way to *test* a hymn is, not merely to read it silently, or even aloud, but to sing it, over and over again, to *its*

own tune.   .   .   .   The reason why we have so much unsatisfactory material thrust upon the Church, is that, for the most
part, the writers of the words have known little about music, and
the writers of music have had little taste or power in the poetic
field, and therefore there was no *felt organic* connection betwixt
the two.   .   .   .

"It may be asked, 'Why publish any hymns, the words of
which are not in the Hymnal?' This question assumes that the
Church has prohibited the singing of any other hymns besides
those in the Hymnal.   This is altogether incorrect.

"The Church has set forth a Hymnal, which is 'allowed to be
sung,' but there are no words prohibiting the singing of any
others.   When the present Hymnal (superseded in 1892) was
first set forth, it was by 'joint resolution of the two Houses in
General Convention,' and that resolution contained a distinct
prohibition of all hymns except those in the old collection, and
in the new Hymnal.   But, being *only* a 'joint resolution' and
not a *canon*, it was not *law*, and was not binding on anybody.
Since that time, the law of the Church has been put into canonical form—'CANON 23 of Title I. of the *Digest*.'   And in thus
giving it the form of *law* the *prohibition* was deliberately and
totally *omitted*.   Nothing, therefore, can be clearer than that
the singing of other hymns is not a canonical offence; though
no such hymns can claim the same authority as the Hymnal, or
are likely to come into such general use.

"But, if Church hymnody is to grow and improve, this door,
small as it is, *must be left open.*   The singing unto the Lord 'a
new song' is a loving duty of perpetual obligation.   Every generation of Christians feels the impulse, and ought, in some measure, to obey it.   Of the Latin hymns used in mediæval times,
90,000 have already been printed, and innumerable others still
remain in manuscript.   How many of *these* were ever canvassed
by a committee, or voted upon by a Church council?   A German hymn-book, now at my elbow, contains 3,067 hymns, all
equally innocent of conciliar authority.   The writing of hymns,
and the power of composing suitable music to them, are *personal
gifts*, and do not belong to Church councils in *any* sense.   I
should like to see the General Convention go to work to compose
a hymn, or watch one of its committees trying to produce a suitable tune to a hymn!   No; as these are individual gifts, so they
appeal, not to Church councils, which are meant for very different business, but to the *individual consciousness* of other Church

people who share in the same gifts. As spiritual things are spiritually discerned, so the things of poetry are poetically discerned, and musical things are musically discerned. The gifts of God in these departments do not need to be tied up by committees and canons. *At present they are free.* They are likely to remain so. I have conscientiously done my best. Instead of writing *down* to the present general taste in regard to sacred music, the attempt has been made to infuse a little of the older and better and more *distinctly religious* style of earlier times. He who furnishes one good hymn as a permanent part of the devotions of the Church, has done more than he who publishes several volumes of sermons. And if, notwithstanding my best exertions, nothing in this book shall be found worthy to live, no one who believes in the survival of the fittest can witness the result, and see the volume die, more contentedly than ' The Author. ' ''

The last sentence expresses Dr. Hopkins' mind upon everything that he did. No sincerer words were ever uttered by him than these ; when he had done his best he left the future entirely with God.

In his dealings with music and musicians as a parish clergyman it might be thought that his great knowledge of the subject and his own skill as a performer would make him " hard to get along with," or that he would be " cranky " and fussy. Nothing could be further from the fact. He used to say that he knew too much about music to interfere with choir and organist. Furthermore, organist and choir all knew that he had and would express genuine thankfulness and appreciation for their honest efforts, and his presence was a stimulus to hearty endeavor. And where tastes differed, as well they might, he never made his personal taste the law, but entered into the feelings of others so warmly that they usually *offered* him all he asked for.

Thus far, for his connection with the Ecclesiological Society, but his ecclesiological work, as has been shown, continued his whole life.

𝕿𝕳𝕣𝕖𝕖 𝕂𝕚𝕟𝕘𝕤 𝕠𝕗 𝕺𝕣𝕚𝕖𝕟𝕥.

GASPARD.

1. We Three Kings of O - ri - ent are,   Bearing gifts we traverse a -
5. Glorious now be-hold Him a - rise,   KING, and GOD, and SA - CRI -

MELCHIOR.

1. We Three Kings of O - ri - ent are,   Bearing gifts we traverse a -
5. Glorious now be-hold Him a - rise,   KING, and GOD, and SA - CRI -

BALTHAZAR.

- far, Field and fountain, Moor and mountain, Following yon-der Star.
- FICE; Heav'n sings Al-le - lu - ia: Al - le - lu - ia the earth replies.

- far, Field and fountain, Moor and mountain, Following yon-der Star.
- FICE; Heav'n sings Al-le - lu - ia: Al - le - lu - ia the earth replies.

N. B.—Each of verses 2, 3, and 4, is sung as a solo, to the music of Gaspard's part
in the 1st and 5th verses, the accompaniment and chorus being the same throughout.
Only verses 1 and 5 are sung as a trio. Men's voices are best for the parts of the Three
Kings, but the music is set in the G clef for the accommodation of children.

CHORUS.

O Star of Wonder, Star of Night, Star with roy-al beau-ty bright, Westward leading, Still proceeding, Guide us to Thy per-fect Light. *Interlude.*

GASPARD.

2. Born a KING on Bethlehem plain,
  GOLD I bring to crown Him again,
    King for ever,
    Ceasing never
  Over us all to reign.
      Chorus.—O Star, &c.

MELCHIOR.

3. FRANKINCENSE to offer have I,
  Incense owns a Deity nigh:
    Prayer and praising
    All men raising,
  Worship Him GOD on High.
      Chorus.—O Star, &c.

BALTHAZAR.

4. MYRRH is mine; its bitter perfume
  Breathes a life of gathering gloom;—
    Sorrowing, sighing,
    Bleeding, dying,
  Sealed in the stone-cold tomb.
      Chorus.—O Star, &c.

1857.

CHAPTER V.

1850–1867.

HE graduated from the General Seminary in 1850, and was ordained Deacon by Bishop Whittingham, in Trinity Church, June 30th.

The whole of the night before his ordination he passed, alone, in Trinity Church, locked in, and with but one candle to light up the great spaces of the choir and nave. No idle, romantic fancy this, devised by a brain spinning frail and glistening cobwebs, but a long night of prayer, self-examination, meditation, and deep consecration and spiritual communion. Dedicated from his birth, fitted by nature, with his loving heart, his active mind, his zeal and ardor leading to real sacrifice, taught in all ways, and never swerving, except once in early youth, and *that* deviation from morality long and sincerely repented of, and satisfaction made, now at the age of thirty he gave himself anew, by a complete dedication of all his powers to the service of God in the sacred ministry, and knowing no higher call than that which thus knit his heart to God he entered upon his ministry of loving service, constant loyalty, and courage and fidelity.

All his plans were settled. He was to be a Church journalist. He was to be in Deacon's Orders for life, and thus be subject to his Bishop in all canonical obligations, and also, to illustrate the reality of the Order of Deacons.

For nearly three years he made his preparations and arranged for the work of his journal. Once he became discouraged, and went to the house of Bishop Wainwright, intending to ask for Priest's Orders, and to go out to California as a missionary to the Indians ; but on the very steps of the Bishop's residence he made up his mind to try a little longer, and at last he secured the promises of support he needed and the *Church Journal* appeared first of all in February, 1853. During this time he preached in various places ; among others for six months in the

Church of the Epiphany, Washington, where he was in charge
while Dr. French, the Rector, was in Europe.   Those sermons
were first-rate discourses, and bear all the marks which point to
brilliant success as a preacher.   They are clear, direct, in charming style, and forcible in effect.   But he soon gave up the habit
of writing sermons, and his whole stock of written sermons numbered less than forty.   One series on the parable of the sower has
been kept, and one of them is herein given in another place.

So pleased were the Washington people that they gave him a
handsome sum of money over and above what had been promised
to him.   But all this he quietly gave away.   He never dreamed
of saving anything.   God had promised him enough to clothe
and feed him—little enough it took to do that—and that was all
he asked or would have.   He gave away much the greater part of
his income in various ways all his life long.   Yet he was not a
spendthrift, or careless in money matters.   He was an exact and
careful man of business, and kept all his accounts in the most
methodical way.

And now begins the story of his public life.   Henceforth he
was one of the strong forces felt in the Church.   A glance at
some points in the Church may aid the student toward understanding the situation.

In considering the contributions of John Henry Hopkins to
the development of the Church, the past as he saw it, and his own
theories as to its' needs, must be kept in mind.   The time had
come, and he saw it, when the issue between the true principles
of the Church and those of the Puritans within it was to be determined.   Such men, non-conformists in spirit and temper, had
been included in the Church of England for centuries on account
of the needs of the English nation.   The result of their presence,
and of the state alliance, had been a well-nigh stifling of the true
life of the Church.   The highest, truest instinct of the Catholic
Church is directly opposed to the development of national
churches.   The whole world is a sea into which her net is let
down to gather from all sides, of every kind.   And yet there is
a national coloring of the Church in certain regions which makes
her outward appearance and her manner of doing the same things
vary with time and country.   To preserve her union with the
whole Church a national Church must keep unbroken the cord of
government, teaching, and grace; it is no solution of this union
that the national Church shall choose her own pastors in whatever
ways best suit national needs and as she herself may determine;

hold her own local synods or councils, and administer discipline. The English Church in seeking these rights had gone to the very verge of conceding those very rights of freedom.

The tyranny of the state had, and has still, robbed her of all but a formal right of electing her bishops ; it had forbidden the transaction of business in the ancient legislatures of the Church, the two convocations of Canterbury and York, and had prevented the bishops from exercising their canonical rights of discipline. Along with these wrongs had gone a decay of doctrine. At the same time the customs formed in evil times had stiffened into a rigid canon which had been made over into second nature, so that all the unlovely ways of a prosaic and deadly indifferent century had been shaped into the very figure of the Church.   The device of nationalizing the Church had almost cut it off from the great body of the Catholic Church, and, instead of the Church of England being looked upon (as she is if she is anything) as the Catholic Church governing herself in England (ignored though she be by her elder sister) she was to all intents and purposes the bond-slave of the state, and her freedom from the rule of the Roman See had brought a worse evil in causing her to be the subject of an authority, supreme indeed in its own sphere, over the *persons* of her members, but which had no right, by divine delegation, to rule in spirituals.   He is but a careless observer who thinks that such an evil state of things implies a severance from interior Catholic unity.   The evil things brought to light in the long course of the English Reformation have not here been even summarized, but far more abject bondage to the state than now exists in England had been known there *before* the Reformation.   The long residence of the Popes at Avignon did but enslave that very Pontiff whose thunders have ever and anon resounded through the Christian world as if he were the one man free to use the words of God, and it is known as the Babylonish captivity of the Church.

The Gallican Church in the time of Louis XIV. was reduced, under the specious plea of claiming her primitive liberties, to a state of bondage to the crown.

These, and too many others, are examples of royal supremacy in its own sphere encroaching upon the spiritual domain of the Church ; and yet in no cases except of the modern English Church is it asserted that more than the outward bonds of union were severed.

The American Church when she received the Episcopate re-

ceived little more than the seeds of life. Her children had been
denied their birthright as the heirs of the kingdom of God, and
were mere pensioners in halls where they had the rights of
children.

She had received all the dulness, and deadness, and stiffness
of an age which glorified correctness of manner in doing what
was not worth doing at all, as if it were the one thing to be looked
for. But she had the right to freedom, and she was, in theory,
able to assert it. Yet timidity, false humility, mistaken prudence,
dread of precision and of fulness in teaching, over-caution in the
statement of even what was set forth (which last inevitably had
the effect of making people believe that *Church* doctrine was
dangerous if it needed so much guarding) to be believed, all, and
more were blocks along the road to progress.

The Calvinistic evangelicals did indeed warm up the Church
somewhat, but the intuitive perception of the falseness of their
principles only settled the real churchmen back more firmly than
ever upon their assumed manner of rigid coldness.

It is not necessary to suppose that the Oxford Tracts gave the
first impulse here in America toward true Church doctrine. The
leaders of the Church, and even the cautious and gentle White,
had been driven by the needs of their position to lay down
Church principles to justify the existence of the Church here.
Nothing else *could* justify the continuance of the English Church
here. The state connection had been one of the very things
which made bishops dreaded, and the first American bishops
therefore had to disclaim strenuously every intention on their
part to set up such a Church. If the wish of those prelates had
been to set up a more dignified and stately Protestant Church
here they could not have justified themselves for having sought
episcopal consecration with such earnestness ; and sooner or later
the question would have been asked, as it has since been asked in
one form or another, if bishops are no more than protestant ministers in lawn and black satin, what earthly use are they ?

There was no way possible except to plant the germ, at the very
least, of Church, that is Catholic, principles.

They did so. And all those principles can be justified in their
very highest form, and in their most varied development, which
do not, on *Catholic* grounds, include Ultramontane innovations.
They cannot be justified on any narrower basis. On what are
called Low Church principles, the doctrines and discipline of the
system of the Prayer-book are most uncharitable. If there were

no higher ground to take every bitter and every strong phrase used by controversialist, either protestant within, or protestant without, would be fully warranted, and the Church would be the object of their just contempt.

But for a long time there was little show of budding life. The tree seemed to stand in a long winter sleep. Curious are the books which hold the history of those controversies that shrieked and wailed like wintry gales, a century ago, around the question of the lawfulness of the existence of bishops. But, after a while men began to see that a bishop in his essence was no less than a Father in God, and the Church began to grow and show her real life. There was a new thing under the sun. A Catholic Church in the West free, electing its bishops with the concurrent voice of the laity, holding its own councils, ministering the teachings of Christ in the ancient way, and speaking her own tongue. One by one old ways improved, and ways older still were found to be better. Not without question, however : there was as wild a cry of Popery over the very least sign of the new life as has ever set one's teeth on edge in these later days, and it was as futile.

So the frost-bitten limb when the life-blood begins to flow more freely tingles with the torture.

The introduction, for instance, of the custom of chanting the canticles at Morning and Evening Prayer, was hailed as a shameless exhibition of Popery. Seventeen different reasons were set forth for not allowing the chanting of the Psalms.

For a long time the two currents of Calvinism and Catholicity ran in the same channel. The Church slowly broadened and deepened as it went on, and it received accessions from many sides, and exerted an influence far beyond what might have been expected from its members. Here was one source of strength to the Church side that the evangelicals, in their party warfare, did not reckon upon as being against them. When men came into the Church from sectarianism it was because they sought something not to be found whence they came. But the *manifestations* of the evangelicals were one and all of institutions and methods quite natural to those very sects. Men do not leave one series of institutions for another with a far different *ethos*, and then care to see the very customs once discarded on conviction imitated. Coming into the Church they wanted churchmanship, and they did not care for mere imitations of prayer-meetings, and such like. The laity have ever been the great stay of the true sons of the Church. They have reflected the teaching of the clergy with absolute fidelity, and have borne with a large-heartedness that should confound the timid counsels of those who fear where no fear is, a great increase in the variety and richness of true Church life, and have submitted to what is really a considerable tightening of discipline not only with content, but with earnest desire that it should be so. They have learned a thousand things about their true place in Church, and their true rights which, if the " prudent " advice of the men of a few years ago had been heard, they would never have learned, and they have been asked to do, and do with cheerful alacrity, things that, to have suggested half a century ago, would have been considered as madness.

The " Tracts for the Times " were welcomed here, and caused nothing like the alarm they did in England in their later numbers. Some, and it is believed the essential, reasons for this have just been given. Moreover, many who were here ranked as evangelicals in reality were acting from the right point. They were " evangelicals " rather because they were filled with a warm generous love for God and for His glory, and they were repelled from High Churchmen because they could not believe that a barely resuscitated corpse, as yet bound round with swathing bands, was the living, breathing presence of the Bride of Christ.

John Henry Hopkins saw that at last the time had come for the Church to break through this wall of Anglicanism and claim her rights as a national Catholic Church. So he set himself to war against the old conservatism. Few seem to have understood this. But the fact can be shown most clearly, and it explains the animosities he aroused, and why he was called upon to suffer so many slights, and why he was so cruelly and so basely wounded in the end of his days. There was, to be sure, a great war to be waged in the Church before the Low Church party, as a party, could be crushed and scattered, and he was in the thick of the battle. Fortune fought with him in this, and it only needed a few of his Napoleonic strokes to overwhelm them. But, first and last, his great battle was against the old High Church party—the party of stiffened Anglicanism, with its balancing, its unintelligent horror of Rome, its bookish way of looking at the Church between the age of Gregory the Great and the English Reformation, its lack of devotion, from obscuring the teaching of the Cross as a living power demanding sacrifice, its isolation from the great currents of Catholic life, and from the earnest zeal of Methodism, its dread of offending the world, and its ostentatious avoidance of any form of spiritual life that spoke of the need of conversion, and personal devotion and enthusiasm.   His whole life was devoted to obtaining liberty for the Church to live her own life.   To be a Catholic was to be, with him, as free in God's house as Americans are in our commonwealth.   No life had been in the past that might not be again, in its soul and principle of being, in a Catholic American Church.   No life was outside her that was not akin to something within her, or which at worst was not a perversion of her teaching.   No sects existed, except as monuments of sins in her own past life.   Furthermore, he looked upon the Church here as the one destined by the Providence of God for the settling of the problems of the past.   The very slowness toward change, which is so characteristic of the Anglican temper, but made all changes, when made, more solid and enduring.   That he was a controversialist is true, but it was not the essence of his life.   Here the controversies are not detailed except as necessary for the setting forth of the story of his life.   There had to be fightings, and he was a good fighter.   His highest title to the esteem of his fellows is to be found in his self-sacrificing devotion to the Church and his plans for her growth, so that she may be the great missionary force which follows the banner of the King, and seeks but His eternal glory.

In Europe the road to realizing the destiny of a free Catholic Church was hindered on all sides by State interference, and by the struggle of the local Roman. Church for temporal power. Here the way was open for the re-union of Catholic Christendom, and for the adhesion to the Church of all sound, sweet Christian elements now separated from Catholic communion.   *This* is the key to all his efforts toward Christian unity.   No one living in the Church here had, up to the time of his death in 1891, so continuously and so strongly urged upon Christians the need of union.   Others argued as strongly, or as keenly, or appealed with as much earnestness, but for full forty years, at least, he did what he could to learn how others thought and felt, and tried to show how Anglicans look at the matter, and that Catholics alone can invoke authority and love in one.   Furthermore, he never took the mistaken course of minimizing Church doctrines and ways, and thus leading men to accept them in another sense than the usual and Catholic meaning.   His propositions as a basis for negotiating with various religious bodies are far clearer, and we believe more honest, than the now well-known Chicago-

Lambeth Quadrilateral, and they go much further. In saying that he was the "most liberal" in his terms of any offered to the world for agreement it must be understood as meaning from his own standpoint of complete acceptance of the Church.

No mere confederation, or mixture of sects satisfied him. Over and over again he showed the idleness of trying to form a great union Protestant Church, for he saw that it is absolutely impossible to predicate unity of Protestantism, and that unity with Rome is of absolute necessity, as well as with the great Catholic communions of the East. Nothing less than the complete restoration of Catholic communion satisfied him, although it must be with a far different Rome from the one which now endeavors to palm itself off upon the world as representing the only genuine Catholicity.

He saw, too, in this matter that the whole state of Christendom is abnormal ; the Paschal Lamb has no bone broken, but as He hangs upon the Cross all His bones are out of joint.

As long as events shape themselves according to present circumstances, mere treaties and negotiations are preliminary to nearer approach. There are a myriad of old quarrels to be reconciled, and the best that can be done is to hold the old Catholic ground, and wait, listening for the call of God. It may be that this reunion, fondly dreamed of and prayed for, apparently so hopelessly, will yet come, not with Pentecostal fire and breathing, but when, according to the quaint prophecy of Saint Malachi, the last Pope—according to which there are but ten remaining— "In the last persecution of the sacred Roman Church, Peter the Roman shall sit, and feed the flock amid many tribulations, after which the seven-hilled city shall be overthrown, and the tremendous Judge shall judge the people."

No word that he ever wrote, however, can ever be turned into anything like an admission of present anti-Catholic Roman claims, or of her anti-Catholic and unhistorical teachings. As long as they are made terms of communion by Rome they *must* be resisted for the sake of Catholicity. But he was not discouraged in his efforts by the Vatican definitions of 1870, nor by the contempt poured upon the Anglican Bishops' propositions, for he never expected to see any appreciable approach on either side. Herein he showed the disposition of the saints, for he labored from the very highest motive, a desire for the manifestation of our Lord's glory in the coming near of His Kingdom. That he should be allowed to work at all in so great a cause was joy enough for him, and with single-heartedness he did what he could and left the rest without fretfulness or anxiety to God.

Nothing less than this restoration of Catholic communion is the *terminus ad quem* of the Catholic movement in the Anglican communion.

6

CHAPTER VI.

1868.

THE battle against the radical wing of the evangelicals, whose principles were really (at bottom at least) quite different from those of the *old* evangelicals of Simeon's school, was, while it lasted, one for life or death. If the radicals had then triumphed, sooner or later not only the "Catholic party" would have been driven away, but a very large portion indeed of the old High Church party would have been forced out also. A good many of both would have been driven to Rome, a good many more would have sunk into mere liberalism. Nevertheless, even Mr. Hopkins did not intend to force the radicals into a schism, and his optimistic spirit refused to recognize that some of them were so exasperated that nothing else would satisfy them but a Church of their own. Up to the very last, and for some time after the deposition of Dr. Cheney in 1871, he did not see, what was perfectly plain to almost every one else, that there would be a schism. Probably, too, one great reason for the attempts made in 1868 and 1871 to legislate on ritual and ceremonial matters, was that the great body of the Church wished to avert the imminent event. That would account very largely for the sacrifice made of Drs. Seymour and De Koven. It did keep down to virtual insignificance the members of those drawn after Bishop Cummins and Dr. Cheney, and their associates.

In the *Church Journal*, and in many pamphlets, letters, and review articles, Mr. Hopkins contended for the development of the full power of the Church. Of course he took strong "High Church" ground, because in his contention for the right of the Church to exhibit its own life, there was no other ground to take. But he was a churchman, and it was characteristic of him to allow to every other man the *liberty* he claimed for himself. Accordingly, he again and again protested for those rights. And he was never a mere partisan.

Another thing should be considered, and that is, the way in

which he distinguished between persons and their acts.   So far as
can be learnt, even in the case of one controversy where he
dealt a crushing and completely overwhelming blow, he could
never be made to believe that he was not forgiven for it ; although he realized it at the last when the one who for years had
dogged his footsteps, never losing the least chance to assail,
whether openly or in secret by insinuation and innuendo, at last
(aided by cowards) delivered the stroke that well-nigh broke his
stout heart, he never bore any malice nor could understand that
any other could do so.

This habit of identifying an opponent personally with his
cause seems to be a weakness of the clerical mind.   Lawyers and
statesmen understand the distinction, priests hardly ever do.

There were four united on the editorial staff of the *Church
Journal.*   In their editorial capacity all stood on an equality,
though necessarily the greater part of the labor fell to the share of
the one who made it his chief business.   These associates of Mr.
Hopkins were Rev. Drs. Howland, Hobart, and Milo Mahan.
This connection lasted till the outbreak of the Civil War.

Of all the men who influenced John Henry Hopkins, Dr.
Mahan took by far the most important place.   They were men
of just enough likeness and difference to make that rare combination, perfect friendship.   Dr. Mahan was not so versatile
as Hopkins, nor so bright and keen and combative ; but his
mind was deeper, and there can hardly be any question that it
was owing to Mahan's influence upon Hopkins that the latter
was led so quickly into seeing something better, truer, and richer
than a realization of even the standard of the English Reformation.
Dr. Hopkins cherished a very deep affection for his friend and
colleague, and after his death edited all his works, in three volumes, prefixing to the last volume a memoir.   He always spoke
of him with the utmost admiration, and reckoned him as the
very greatest clergyman, whether priest or bishop, that the
American Church had produced.

For some years after the *Journal* was founded there were no
great trials to the Church.   The strain upon its fabric, after the
Gorham case, was lessened, men recovered from their panic, and
the quiet upbuilding of the Temple went on.   There was, to be
sure, some pressure from the evangelicals, and some little trouble
from the founding of their volunteer societies.

There were sneers at " ecclesiologists," and bitter denunciations of very mild changes from the old order as popery, and

the innovation of "preaching in a surplice" was pronounced to be a proof of the real purpose of the "conspirators against the peace of the Church." Great revivals swept over the land, and the evangelical clergymen lost their footing in the rush. But their prayer-meetings and fraternizations with the denominations affected the laity but little. *They* had, many of them, been through *those* experiences before, and wanted none of it repeated in *Church.* Of those clergymen, Bishop Alonzo Potter in 1854 wrote: "I must confess to some vexation and impatience, when I see the golden opportunity for the growth of a truly catholic and evangelical churchmanship endangered by men whose mission in this world seems to be to find fault with the ecclesiastical lot which they inherit from their fathers, or to set their brethren by the ears. Our laymen, as a general rule, will have *churchmanship.* They want that of a generous tolerant type; tolerant toward those within as well as those without. If they can't get it, many of them will take the churchmanship and let the toleration go; and our friends will find themselves where hitherto they always have been, in a minority, which deprives them of the power of directing the legislation or policy of the Church."

But on the whole, the Church movement went on without any serious check, and about as fast as was wholesome.

The course of the *Journal* was to advocate everything that would make strength felt, to concentrate and not to scatter, and to render every organ of the body more efficient. This is illustrated by the words of Bishop Seymour: "On my ordination I was sent by my bishop in 1854 to Annandale, where in the good providence of God I was enabled to found and build up, with a fair prospect of success which has since been achieved, St. Stephen's College, a training school for the sacred ministry. Among those who helped me with sympathy and counsel, after I leave the Bishop of New York, Dr. McVickar, and Mr. John Bard, the first munificent donor of land and money, I must rank next in order Rev. John Henry Hopkins." Its whole plan was constructive; but in order to this it had to wake up the Church, and it did not mince its words, or take a roundabout way. It knew the value of agitation, and when once a matter was started it was not dropped for good as long as there seemed any chance to make anything out of it.

Dr. Hopkins always maintained that the Anglican Church, by insisting so strongly that its clergy should be "gentlemen and scholars," had lost its touch with the great mass of the people.

The revival of the diaconate was advocated by him as a means of remedying this defect, for defect it is. A new canon, allowing the ordination of deacons who had not certain qualifications, was adopted in 1853, and for some time he argued for the full use of the canon. To all intents and purposes the canon is a failure, and only offers a short cut to the priesthood. But his arguments are still valid, and accordingly some of them are herein set down.

" We would have the diaconate and the priesthood stand each on its own bottom. The diaconate, as being more diffusive, miscellaneous, practical, necessarily requires more of ' quantity ' and less of ' quality ' than the priesthood. The priesthood, on the other hand, as being more concentrate, more purely sacerdotal and prophetic, looks more to the quality of its incumbents. One hand can find employment for five fingers. We should deem it a poor parish, very ill provided with ' young, sick, poor, and impotent people ' in which one active priest could not carve out work for at least five *such deacons as are contemplated by the ordinal.*

" The requirement that deacons should be of like ' quality ' with priests tends practically to annihilate the diaconate.

" . . . The most formidable difficulty in the way of the practical efficiency of the canon is the question how far it exposes us to the danger of lowering the style and standard of ministerial qualifications. It may unquestionably tend to lower the standard of *learning* as a qualification for the lowest order of the ministry. The call to preach the Gospel—we speak of course of the ' inward call '—goes forth as of old among the many. This being the case, it is manifestly the duty of the Church to provide some way in which those having such a call may be enabled to obey it without violating Church order. An *unlearned ministry* is, and ever has been, a great power in the world. It is certain that it is useless to forbid such a ministry. In some form or other it will exist in the world.

" If it exists not for us, it will surely exist against us. What we admire in ' the Ordering of Deacons ' is, that the solemn office so clearly defines the limits within which such a ministry may be safely and usefully permitted. It does not follow that there would be any lowering of intellectual qualifications. The fruit of all education is found in good sense, and the ability to use readily and discreetly such talents as God has given. A man may have all these and not know a word of Latin, Greek, or Hebrew.

" As to the second order of the ministry, there need be no lowering of its style and qualifications if only the bishops, standing committees, and others in authority are willing to do their duty.

" The door of the priesthood is guarded by a canon requiring not only good sense but a particular kind of learning. We see no reason why the canon should make examiners less strict than they have been hitherto.   .   .   .   Besides all this, nothing tends more to the preservation of learning than a proper division of labor.   To be a learned man one must give himself mainly to study.   How impossible this is in our present system is pretty generally understood and admitted.   A few thorough scholars in the Church will do more to create a high style of scholarship than a slight tincture of learning equally distributed among all. Our present evil is that everything tends to an average of mediocrity.   We have no unlearned ministers.   We have none, on the other hand, thoroughly learned.   .   .   .   Give us, if possible, educated men ; but if educated men are not to be had, let us have at all events men of zeal and piety and natural ability. With an abundance of these, with strict examinations, we should hope to see learning among our clergy of a higher style and standing than a sparse and overworked ministry can possibly attain.   There will be found in almost every congregation one or more earnest, devout, zealous men whose free labors have been given for years to Sunday-school teaching, visiting, and other duties properly belonging to the diaconate, and who if called by the voice of authority would at once obey the call, though they might never think of offering themselves.   Our bishops have much more power in this matter than they dream of.   We believe that the grace of Holy Orders will be given most fully to such men.   They are already to some extent doing deacon's work : then give them the deacon's commission.   When the deacon's work is again done by a deacon we believe we shall be justified in expecting more of God's blessing upon it than now when it is done by laymen, or women, or not done at all.   In such men the grace of Holy Orders will strengthen and heighten every other grace which they already possess.   What is now a voluntary service will then become a solemn duty.   What is now zeal toward men will then become a responsibility in the sight of God.   What is now the benevolence of human kindness will

then be heightened and ennobled by the stamp of divine authority.''

The latter part of the quotation is a sufficient argument,
although it by no means comes up to all that is said on the
point, to overcome the theory often heard in these latter days
that *laymen's* work is better for the Church than clergymen's
work. Now, as when Hopkins wrote the words, there are no
deacons : deacons are but inchoate priests.

He thus continues as to another point : '' Many of the laity
are now engaged in doing some of the proper and most special
work of the diaconate. And if it were not out of character in
an apostle to make his living with his own hands rather than be
burdensome to some whose faith was yet weak, much more may
our deacons support themselves by similar honest callings until
the faith and zeal of the Church shall be sufficient to support
them in the devotion of their whole life to her service ; a time
not likely to come immediately, for it is hard work as yet to
keep the priests from starving. That feeling of the *sacredness* of
the diaconate is certainly overstrained which practically forbids
the existence of the order amongst us at all. No order of the
ministry was so sacred but that it was meant to be used rather
than to be left alone. Others have so exalted an idea of the dignity of the ministry that they fear lest this may suffer. This is a
mistake, for by giving reality to the diaconate as a distinct order, the priesthood, now practically the lowest order in the ministry, will be *raised* by having a whole order laboring in manifest
subordination to it. And as to deacons themselves, their truest
dignity is to do *deacon's work.*''

The tenth part of the argument is not quoted here, because
the old tradition still masters the field. It *is* set down, because
the making real of deacon's work was one of Dr. Hopkins'
ideas, which he never changed ; and as to his references to a
learned ministry, the very last article he ever wrote, on his
death-bed, has these following words :

'' All the honest learning that can be acquired can be made
useful in the ministry. The true question *here* is, how much
learning ought to be required of every man before he is suffered
to exercise any part of the ministry of the Word ?
'' The Anglican tradition is that every clergyman should be ' a
gentleman and a scholar.' . . . Is it not possible that we

have carried this thing just a little too far ?   Let us look at the fruits of the system in a large way.   How has it been in other countries ?   We answer fearlessly that wherever the bulk of the priesthood has been taken from the bulk of the population, so that social sympathy has not been severed, that the Church has retained her hold upon the bulk of the population, no matter what drawbacks may have existed in any direction whatever. There may have been evils of other sorts—ignorance, superstition, or even immorality—but no other religious organization, on any pretext, has ever been able to get the bulk of the common people out of the hands of the clergy of the Church.

" But how has it been in England ?   There, every schismatical movement, without exception, has been mainly on a lower social level than the bulk of the National Church.   And what is the chief reason of this but the feeling that the clergy were too much ‘ scholars and gentlemen ’ to have real sympathy with the common people.   And the common people do not like to be patronized by those who feel themselves above them.   They are ten times as likely to crowd after those who, as they understand it, do not set up to be better than themselves.

" .   .   .   How did the Methodists arise and rapidly become so powerful ?   Simply because they struck mainly into that stratum of the population which felt (rightly or wrongly) that they had not the sympathy of a ministry who all claimed to be ‘ scholars and gentlemen ! ’   True enough, John Wesley and his brother Charles, and some few others of his chief helpers, were scholars and gentlemen ;   but what shall we say of the great body of preachers who were gathered about them, and by whom, after all, the chief part of the actual work was done ?   They were of the common people.   They were not ‘ scholars.’   They were not ‘ gentlemen.’   They did not pretend to be.   Hardly any one of them could have stood an examination for deacon’s orders.   They did not always talk even grammatical English ;   but their hearts were on fire with zeal.   They had a very respectable familiarity with their English Bibles.   They threw themselves into the work with all their hearts and souls.   They knew how to influence men—careless, hardened, godless men.   They did a wonderful work.   And if the laws of the Church of England had been as free as those of the primitive Church, they, or most of them, might have been in Orders in the Church, and there would have been no schism at all.

" And to come down to our own times, how are we to account

for the wonderful and strange work of the Salvation Army? It is simply the same old story over again. That army draws its officers and its rank and file from those classes which feel that they have no practical sympathy with a Church whose priests are all 'scholars and gentlemen.' Practical, social sympathy is a far more effective weapon among vast masses of men and women than a university degree or the manners of polite and refined society; and in the work of propagating the Gospel among mankind at large, nothing can make up for the want of it. The Church must have a priesthood in practical sympathy with all classes, if she is to do her work among all classes. And as this cannot be done by bringing up all priests to the same social level, the Church must make up her mind to have priests in social sympathy with the different levels among which she is to do her work.

"Some say that the Methodists themselves are aware of their lack of education, and that they have been trying to make up for it, and that there are now among them some men of very respectable learning. All very true. And in proportion as they succeed in this, they are losing precisely that singular force among the common people which was the fountain of their original strength. They are imitating us, and with unhappy luck are imitating our weak points instead of our strong ones. The noblest and holiest revenge we can take will be to learn from them the secret of their original strength. . . .

"Again, it may be objected that all these movements have been on unchurchly lines, and have run into schisms. Certainly. And what does the Lord permit schisms for, except that they may teach His Church, when she will not learn in any other way, what particular part of her own work she has neglected or has performed wrongly. The Church, therefore, has something practically to learn from every sect or schism. And the Church in learning from the sect should be careful to ascertain precisely that one point which originally gave it vitality.

"The great body of the common people will never be reached by any other way than by opening the doors of the ministry wider and wider to that class socially and intellectually which gave to Methodism its earlier and more astonishing successes; only those ministers must be Churchmen and not Methodists.

"But to carry out this great change effectively, other changes also are needed. The bishop, with such a varied ministry, must be clothed with much more of vigorous and personal administrative power. It will not do to leave everything to be regulated solely by written canons. And if the bishops are to have this additional work put upon them two other changes are equally necessary. One is, that dioceses *must* be made smaller, so that the work can be handled by one man, and the mere multiplication of archdeacons and such like will not do. The other is that provinces must be formed. . . . In all this we should simply be returning to the plain and universal practice of the primitive Church.''

John Henry Hopkins was brought up in a very torrent of enthusiasm for the Church—the Catholic Church. There were no hidings in the earth of her life-giving current to his eyes. And he saw with hopefulness for single souls, and deep love for God, that she had the promise of all the workings of the Holy Spirit with His love, His illuminative teaching, and His liberty. He saw that while men might reach single men, that more by far was needed than that. The Church is not a mere assembly of men of like faith and hope and love, but Christ makes the Church; and so Hopkins saw her as the Bride adorned for her Spouse with His own gifts; the new Jerusalem, coming down— the joy of the whole earth revealed from Heaven. It was not enough to create; men must also be kept. Yet the all-glorious, the spotless Church, was not here, but to be hereafter when the chaff had been winnowed from the threshing-floor.

He saw failures in the showing forth of the divine life; great practical corruptions in the Roman Church; equally harmful conservatism in the Anglican of post-reformation ideas. If the Roman corruptions poisoned the stream, the Anglican corruptions restrained it too narrowly, and one worked as much harm as the other. Anglican tradition was keeping things which, in view of far greater and more precious things kept out by it, were not worth keeping. Hopkins in setting about to work practical reforms in the Church had to suffer; and he deliberately chose a track, because he loved the Church, which cut across the way of her teaching at the time; whereas, by his powers, his talents, and goodness and zeal, if he had chosen, without a particle of self-seeking, he might have had any office in her gift.

Men called him a dreamer, a doctrinaire. No words were ever more inappropriately applied to man. Plenty of men before him, and men enough in his own times, taught very much the

same things.   It was because he tried to put his ideas to practice
that men suspected, or feared, or hated him.   Bishop White was
the first American churchman to see that provinces must sooner
or later be formed here ; others saw it after him ; but Hopkins
showed the way practically to set them up, and that was too
much for hide-bound conservatism.

Other Church agitators before him had been content to work in
a narrow track, or by themselves ; they attacked *weak* points.
Hopkins was as fearless as he was lucid in expression.   A strong
point was no more dreaded by him, if he thought he ought to
speak out, than a weak one.   He even dared to point his spear
at Trinity Church herself, and challenged her to a battle *à ou-
trance.**   He pleaded again and again for fairness in the distribution of offices in the gift of the New York Convention.   In those
early days there was " a regency " of High Churchmen in the diocese of New York, and what was done was done by their direction, or concession.   Low Churchmen in those days of bitterness
had little chance of gaining power.   Yet here Hopkins asked for
fair dealing, asserting rightly that power would bring with it the
sense of responsibility, and allay strife, and thus promote better
work.

No man in the Church has ever advocated so constantly, so
powerfully, and so acutely the formation of *small* dioceses.   Here
again it was not his mere argument that made men opposed to
him.   It was because he at once began the work of making his
arguments take concrete form.†   Year after year he kept going the

* In the course of the first half of this century there were several attempts
made to strip Trinity Church of her landed property.   Trinity was the
strong centre of church life and temporal strength.   In some of the latest
attacks Hopkins joined ; and in two pamphlets : " Poor Trinity," and " Rich
Trinity," reminded the trustees of the duties that lay upon them of spending
their income for the good of the whole church in the city.   He carefully examined the records as to every separate parcel of land, set down the times
when leases would fall in, and calculated their values.   There was a concurrent effort in the Legislature of New York State, and one report was prepared by him in the course of a single night, and sent out by the first mail
train to Albany the next morning, reaching there in time for legislative action.

Two significant sequels show the power and justice of his action.   One is
that Trinity *does* now exist for the good of all, and her expenditures are now
far beyond her income from endowments, and the second, that no such attacks have ever since been made, nor any at all, except upon different
grounds.

† He writes to his mother, May 25, 1883, Midnight : " Dearest Mother, before I sleep I must tell you what a wonderful day this has been to me, beyond

movement for dividing the Diocese of New York. When other men dropped the matter, after a defeat, or when interest flagged, he returned again to the charge with the same zest and vigor. At one time Bishop Horatio Potter ceased to use the *Church Journal* as an organ of communication with the diocese. To Dr. Hopkins, more than to any other one man it is due that there are now three dioceses where there was formerly but one; and his influence was felt also in the concurrent division of the Diocese of Western New York. The only wonder is that with the marvellous results of those divisions before the eyes of men—far exceeding his enthusiastic prophecy—no further divisions have taken place for so many years. Long ago he showed how *not less* than *twelve* dioceses should be formed in New York State. Hand in hand with his plans for small dioceses was his plan for the formation of provinces, advocated with like force and pertinacity.

Another institution of the Church in which his interest was deeper and more loving than his interest in others was the General Theological Seminary. In his letter home written en route to Georgia he relates the story of what seems to have been his first visit there. Of it he was an alumnus. Two of its faculty,

any other day of my life. Besides working for division in my own diocese, I have been doing all I could for the movement in the four dioceses of Virginia, North Carolina, Tennessee, and Kentucky. I have been in correspondence with clergy or laity or both, in all these dioceses; and large numbers of my pamphlet on the subject have been circulated in all these dioceses, having been, in some cases, brought prominently forward in the discussions. All the four have held their conventions either this week or last week.

"This morning, just after breakfast, I received a telegram from the secretary of the Kentucky Convention, announcing that division had been *carried* by 19 to 1 of the clergy, and 17 to 3 of the laity! The eleven o'clock mail brought me a long letter from Virginia, showing that though, on the bishop's claim that his health had permanently broken down, they had elected an assistant, they went on the next day to consider division. They knew that, from the difficulty of fixing a *line*, it would not be possible to get it through *this* time; when the motion *was made to lay the subject on the table*, on the ground of the bishop's strong hostility, and their having just elected an assistant, the vote was made a test question of strength as to division; and our friends *carried* the day. They defeated the motion by 3 to 1 of the clergy and 2 to 1 of the laity! And the opponents have given up the game! Just after supper I received another telegram from North Carolina, informing me that division had been *carried* there by a clerical vote of 41 to 12, and a lay vote of 26 to 11, with one parish 'divided!' And at 9.30 P.M., calling on a friend to talk over the good news, he showed me a telegram in a Philadelphia paper, announcing that, in *Tennessee*, the division of the diocese had been carried by an 'overwhelming majority!' This caps the climax, and I go to bed almost too happy to sleep!"

Drs. Mahan and S. R. Johnson, were his warm friends. He gave his services after his graduation as instructor in music. When, long afterward, he was made a trustee, he considered it his sacred duty to be always present at all meetings, unless a higher duty, such as the meeting of a diocesan convention at the same time, made it impossible for him to come.

But that seminary was, as has already been mentioned, suspected of being given over to Puseyism. Some dioceses, although it was a general institution, never contributed the least sum toward its keeping. Some bishops forbade their candidates for Holy Orders to attend it. Other bishops desired schools of their own. All these things tried the seminary severely. But there were other troubles besides. For some time the finances of the seminary had been in an increasingly unsatisfactory condition. The payment of the Kohne legacy of one hundred thousand dollars, anxiously looked forward to for many years as the cure of every stringency, had disappointed these glowing expectations, owing to grievous mismanagement in its investment. There was an entire disinclination on the part of the Board of Trustees to examine into the matter. A large body of men, coming together for only a few hours' session once a year is not likely to manage the work of an investigation willingly or wisely. He was satisfied that an exposure of the facts in the *Church Journal* was the only thing that would lead to any amendment, and was ready to begin the work in 1858. But Professors Mahan and Johnson, who were the most grievous sufferers in income by the then state of affairs, begged him not to do so, and he yielded. The next year he was ready once more, as all the pledges of amendment had remained unfulfilled. But they both, again, so earnestly insisted that he should refrain, that he yielded once more; and they suffered silently one year longer. A third time they attempted the same self-denying intercession, of affirming that the treasurer had made strong promises of amendment: but he was satisfied that he could not keep them, on that system of doing business, and that the sooner the change was effected the better. The war therefore began. And though it did not secure a thorough investigation by a committee of the board, which it *ought* to have done—the laity largely voting for it, and the clergy against it—yet it brought about a very general change in the whole financial management of the institution, including the appointment of H. E. Pierrepont, Esq., as treasurer, who navigated his charge into comparatively clear water.

This is Dr. Hopkins' own account, given in his memoir of Dr. Mahan, but he does not indicate the storm, nor how it raged. It is no part of the purpose which the present writer has, to go into details of past controversy, much less to give them, hardly dying, even now, into embers, any new warmth. But these stories show something besides pugnacity in John Henry Hopkins. They show his hold upon the very points at issue, they show his steadfast zeal, for he never entered a combat lightly, and never withdrew till the campaign was ended, and they show his independence and moral courage. There used to be in school reading books a tale of a Switzer who in the wars for freedom against Austria rushed against the ranks of the enemy, grasped his own strong brand and cleared a way for his companions in arms to follow, but fell himself, receiving the hostile spears into his own breast. Hopkins was a nobler Winkelreid. And he was content to die with all the points of hatred, or distrust, ingratitude or neglect in his heart, if the Church were freer, and stronger in her march.

Some causes advocated by him in the *Church Journal* met with more success. In them he was not so nearly alone.

One of these was the cause of free churches. In these days, even in pewed churches, there is nothing like the exclusiveness of other times. Members of parishes of the Episcopal Church were usually people of social position, refinement, and wealth. The manifold variety of Church work done now was undreamed of then. The Church prided itself upon the standing of its members in society, and the duty of taking the poor, or the people of little means, into the field of Church life was very imperfectly carried out. There are now so many free churches that it seems strange that less than one column in the *Church Journal* contained a list of all the free churches in the country, less than forty years ago. The Church of the Holy Communion, founded by Dr. Muhlenberg, and the Church of the Advent, in Boston, were the most noteworthy of those ventures of faith. But Hopkins did valiant service in this field. He also argued strongly in favor of having service at night instead of the afternoon, as was the usual custom in the Church.

So many services are now held at all sorts of hours, and there is such a variety in the ways of using the Prayer-book, that we often fail to realize the rigid customs of a generation ago, which had almost the force of law, and how strong a current of innovation, as it was thought to be, which should force men to dream of coming to church at any other hour, or for any other services than the old ones.

" ' The Church as it was,' was the favorite watchword with all those who were conservatives. With them the Church was but the most efficient means of keeping things quiet, in the one unvarying routine to which they had themselves been accustomed. For a clergyman to preach in a surplice, or without bands, was quite as much a scandal to them as if he should preach transubstantiation, or impugn an article of the Nicene Creed. To them, a change was a change; all change was bad, and one change was as bad as another. This sort of conservatism abounded among churchmen of both parties, and also among those who disclaimed all connection with either party.

" Others there were who took up the same cry because they held on principle nothing that was distinctive about her.

" Others, once again, there were, who in principle were all they ought to have been, but in feeling had allowed themselves to confound the fashions of the present with the universal truths of all climes and times of Christendom.

" On the other hand there were many whose zeal for the Church had never hardened into any particular school of opinion, or been tied up in the harness of party. Their minds, being honest and free from obstruction, were perhaps *too* ready to go in for anything new, and therefore their zeal needed to be watched and restrained.

" But the hope of the Church was in those heartily, intelligently, and devotedly *hers* in principle, and who wished nothing more than to be hers in practice. Their hearts needed but to beat their way through the crust of obstructive conservatism which stood between them and the work which needed to be done ; the great Ship of the Church rocking

' As idle as a painted ship
Upon a painted ocean,'

only because so many of her crew had a prejudice against hoisting sails to take advantage of the freshening breeze.

" This being the situation as Hopkins shaped it in his mind, for these are his words, he went on to ask : ' Is it in accordance with Catholic antiquity that dioceses should become so immense that the practical influence of the bishops in each parish is reduced to nothing ? Can it be wondered at that a ministry thus cramped in its first Order, and almost destroyed in its third, should be-

come so practically inefficient that it can hardly command its
daily bread without resorting to the arts of professional mendic-
ity? Is it a true conservatism which would reject every plan
for the more efficient organization of the laity in the work of
Church benevolence, when the world and the sects are already
swarming with such societies, and when common sense requires
us to make some such provision among our own people for self-
preservation at least? Is it fulfilling the saying of our Lord that
" to the poor the Gospel is preached " to rest content with the
disgrace of having lost our hold on the middle and lower classes
of society, more wholly than has ever been the case in any other
branch of the Church Catholic in all Christendom? Is it maintaining the faith once delivered to the saints, to be practically elevating the most modern and unimportant portions of our ritual,
into the unbending dignity and indispensable obligation of an
article of the Christian Faith without assenting to which no man
can be permitted even to enter the Church? '

" Communities of men fall into an undiscerning routine and religious communities are subject to the same infirmity. The
Church of England long ago fell into this dry routine method.
We inherited the method, and the spirit that grew up under it.
She is vigorously recovering herself from dulness, dryness, and
barrenness. But we have by no means kept pace with her. We
have peculiarly a Protestant Episcopal routine of our own. It
has been created naturally. It rose out of circumstances. It
is, generally speaking, a very good routine, if recognized as such,
and so regarded by us all. It consists in planting missionary
stations, forming parishes, holding conventions, raising funds,
and keeping the Church machinery going. There is a deal of
work connected with all this: but after all, it is routine work.
It gets to be mechanical. It smoothes the way in parishes and
dioceses so materially that Presbyterial and Episcopal reputations
are made by it, the justness of which we do not question, nor
disparage their worth. But this routine, essential as it is, can be
lifted above the dryness of mere custom only by the definiteness
of purpose with which it is administered, and by a lively sense of
the great object which it promotes.

" We question whether this definiteness of purpose and sensitiveness of spirit exist among us in a degree sufficient to save the
Protestant Episcopal Church from the reproach of discharging its
office in a somewhat unapprehensive way ; living along from year
to year in the work which its natural growth provides for it, and

in its traditional manner, but not seeming to observe, reflect, plan, and execute, with a view as comprehensive as its Apostolic descent and its Catholic relations would lead men to expect, and with a confidence which its conscious possession of principles that were capable of enduring the test of ages, would abundantly justify.

" For what are we organizing dioceses and electing bishops? For what are we training candidates and ordaining them to the ministry? Why is this vast machinery set working wherever the nation extends itself and society presents a surface to work upon?

" ' To save the souls of men,' is, of course, the ready answer. But is it so? We deplore the painful certainty that it is *not* so. Ask the American people to give the answer to the question : Has the Episcopal Church, as a Church, presented itself to you as existing for you all, capable of embracing you *all*, so designed and bound to fulfil its design, ready and anxious and trying to do so, under the constraining love for your souls as being in such a sense her care, that nothing else on earth can fill her place toward you, and be the spiritual mother of you all?

" Does anyone suppose that they would give it any other than one answer? The Episcopal Church is a highly respected denomination among us, and we believe that it is found to be strong and formidable by the sects, in controversy respecting a certain authority which it claims for its bishops. As represented by its public acts, we have not seen the bearing we should look for in a Church that claimed to be the Divinely appointed agent of our salvation. It seems to us, in the main, like one of the Christian sects, though with some striking peculiarities, of which we find it hard to get a consistent and satisfactory view, as the Episcopal Church presents itself to us in its practical working. Now, bishops, priests, and deacons, rites and ceremonies, creeds and sacraments, and all that is distinctive in the Church, exist for the salvation of men of all classes. We can give no other reason for their existence. We could care for them on no other principle. We see not on what other ground they can be zealously maintained as a religious system or effectually administered. And what we have to do is to revive the spirit of such an administration of them. Let us inquire with patient diligence and fidelity what we can do to make all men see and feel the truth and power which we believe are in the Church. Let us go *freshly* to work, escaping from the dulness of usage and the dryness of perfunctory labor, in the consciousness that

7

we seek only to do the work of Christ, and in the assurance that the Church way is the shortest and best to that end.''

He continues concerning impatience for results : '' What shall we say in opposition to a proposed reform, which only desires in *practice*, to our *own professed principles* ?   Would it seem wise to tell such reformers as these that they are, like children, too *impatient of results* ?

'' We of the reformed Church can now look back over a period of three centuries, during which our system, under substantially its present modifications, has been working out its results in various quarters of the world and under every variety of circumstances.   It started with the whole—or nearly the whole—of the people of England and Wales in its bosom.   At one time or other it has been dominant in Ireland and Scotland.   It has had the aid of the Imperial Government, more or less, in some of these United States while they were colonies.

'' It has had that aid in every colony now linked to the mother country.   It has had advantages of wealth, patronage, power, dignity, learning, exclusive control of the universities and schools. It has had the countenance of the noble and the great among a people that bows down to birth and blood.   And none of all these advantages has been possessed in equal degree by any one, or by all put together, of all the sects which have sprung up under her shadow.   All this preponderance of power has been on her side, in addition to the truth of God, the full authority of His Apostolic Church, and the everlasting presence of Christ which, according to His inviolable promise, she has never ceased to enjoy.   Now, in this year of grace 1854, what accounts has the Church of England to give of the results of her stewardship ? Scotland almost wholly Presbyterian.   Ireland five-sixths Romish, Presbyterian, and Unitarian.   Wales so overrun with dissent that the Church is in a fearful minority.   The Church outnumbered, or out-generalled, or both, in nearly every colony over which the British ensign floats.   In this country, the Church, almost strangled in its cradle by the unprincipled policy of the mother country, has ever since been rendered weak and sluggish by inheriting those chronic diseases which so deeply taint the body whence it sprung.   The Church of England, even at home, has lost more and more as time rolled on, until, from owning nearly the whole, she now retains but little more than half of the actively religious portion of her population.   .   .   .

'' Results so steady, so constant, so universal, need some other cure than patience. Three hundred years is long enough. In three hundred years Christianity marched victorious from the manger of Bethlehem to the empire of the world. In three hundred years, England's Church has been more than outnumbered by the spawn of errorists that have crawled forth from her own loins.

" When the results are such as these, let those men be patient who *can*. We can *not*. We have waited long enough. The time is come to see if we cannot do something better than patiently to go on repeating the same fatal blunders for three hundred years longer.

" In the Providence of God, our Mother Church of England has been so closely united with the State that full, free, and independent action in regard to her own affairs has been wholly suspended during about one-half of the time since the Reformation period. That adaptive power by which a living organism so varies its condition in answer to varying circumstances, has been almost wholly paralyzed. The canonical frame-work of the Church of England is really as strange to this age as the city of Ephesus was to the wondering eyes of the Seven Sleepers on awaking from the unbroken repose of well-nigh two hundred years.

" This sameness may seem to some minds like showing great ' tenacity of purpose.'

" The great purpose of the Church should be to preach the Gospel to every creature, baptizing them into the new birth, and feeding them continually with the bread of the new life. And the sure result of a proper tenacity of purpose in this work is that God should add to the Church daily such as are being saved. But the Church will certainly fail, more or less, if she exalts subsidiary purposes to the level of that one great purpose, or suffers them to take precedence of them altogether.

" This is precisely what the Church of England since the Reformation has, to a large extent, done. She has been unable to stretch or adapt her working system in the slightest degree ; and hence every fresh development of life, energy, and zeal within her bosom has invariably resulted in excluding some of the very best working material from among her priests and people.

" This has been the case, too, with a practical toleration of doctrinal differences surely as great as any reasonable man could de-sire. This toleration of doctrinal differences, moreover, detracts from the effect of the supposed ' tenacity of purpose ' in rejecting

change, and reveals the simple truth that the Church has been
ruled in this, her stand-still policy, not by tenacity of purpose,
but by tenacity of practice — a very different thing.   We are
commended to Rome for an example of ' tenacity of purpose ' ;
and rightly, for she exhibits a brilliant specimen of it.   But what
is her *purpose* of which she is tenacious ?   Is it that all varieties
of devotional feeling and religious temperament should be compelled into one monotonous and unvarying formula of expression ?
Is it that offices which exist in her system should be smothered
in practice ?   Is it to discourage all sorts of voluntary associations
of her children, who in one way or another are desirous to aid
the Church in her work ?   Is it to shrink from the probability
of making rapid and extensive conquests from other Christian
bodies, as if *that* were to be regarded as a terrible misfortune ?

" No, none but Protestants so little value the power of the Unity
of the One Body, as to let matters like these stand in her way.
Is Roman tenacity always displayed in requiring the celibacy of
the clergy ?   Or Mass in Latin ?   Or the inviolability of Church
property ?   Or a belief in Purgatory, Transubstantiation and Indulgences ?   Or Communion in only one kind ?   Or complete
independence in spirituals, to say nothing of temporals ?   Or the
existence of Monasteries ?   Or the admission of Jesuits ?   Or
the exclusion of the Bible ?   Or the profession of the whole Tri-
dentine Creed ?   By no means !   None of all these is Rome's
great purpose.   That purpose is the *subjugation of all the world
under the obedience of the Pope.*   Her tenacity she displays in
making all other questions *subordinate* to this.   To secure the recognition of Papal supremacy she has been willing to allow the
marriage of priests, communion in both kinds, and the usage of
the ancient national liturgy to her converts from the Eastern
Churches ; nor have they been required to profess a belief in
purgatory, indulgences, transubstantiation, or the rest of the new
Creed of Trent.   In continental Europe the Papal assent has
been given again and again to the suppression of monasteries ; to
the wholesale confiscation of Church and conventual property ;
to the reconstruction of episcopal sees and the nomination
to ecclesiastical offices by the state ; and the publishing of
no bull from Rome, even in spirituals, without the approbation
of the civil government.   She has tamely pocketed, at one time,
insults and robberies which, at another, she would have resented
with her most sonorous thunders.   She has permitted, or con-
nived at, and sometimes pretends to approve of, the reading

51833

of Holy Scripture in the vernacular by her people.   She has suppressed the Jesuits, and submitted to their expulsion even from Rome itself.

" Rome is willing to tolerate almost every variety of instrument and ordinance, of rite and ceremony, that can co-operate to the one end.   Her clergy are of every grade of intellect and refinement, from the hedge priest to the cardinal prince.   Her rites are of every shade of simplicity and grandeur.   So far is she from any objection to reviving things ancient which may be of present use, that she makes her chief boast of antiquity, and is yet ever ready to adopt any new device that may offer, or drop any ancient usage which may have become superfluous.   Voluntary societies of every kind she permits, uses, cherishes, and multiplies.   She finds room for the meditative silence of La Trappe, and work for the restless intrusiveness and wily intermeddlings of the Jesuit.   She has the extemporary vigor of the revival system, in true Methodist style, with her Passionist and Redemptorist Missions, and the willing confessions of thousands of excited penitents.   She has a constantly growing list of Brotherhoods, Sisterhoods, Confraternities, Sodalities, Conferences, and what not.   Fresh converts, no matter if they come in crowds, she is never afraid of, but is ready to compass sea and land to make them.   And in all the vast variety of her operations, her tenacity of purpose is only made the more brilliantly apparent by the very multitude of the forms in which it appears, and works, and wins.   It is like the tiger, soft and glossy, lithe and springy, nothing rigid about the whole powerful organization—excepting only those great weapons of *tenacity*, the *teeth*, and the *claws*.

" Now, this flexibility of practical system is utterly independent of doctrinal purity.   It is not necessary, to secure freedom from superstition or error, that the Church should be made like the figure of a *stuffed tiger*, rigid all over, constantly *showing* its long white teeth and its protruding claws, but utterly unable to make any use of them, for want of flexibility in the rest of the system.   We are strongly of opinion that there has been no organized secession from the Church which, by a judicious concession involving no yielding of principle, might not have been made from the first a most useful stimulus of increased life and strength *in* the Church ; rather than to be driven out, an indignant and vindictive enemy thirsting for war to the knife against an unnatural mother, who showed herself destitute of all feeling for her most earnest and laborious children.

"In the ages of chivalry the lance was the great knightly weapon, and required long and steady practice before it could be used with force and certainty of aim, from the back of a horse in full gallop.   The knights practised themselves upon the figure of a Turk cut out of wood, turning on a perpendicular pivot, and having a heavy club in its hand.   The whole was so arranged that, if struck on either side of the exact centre, the unlucky marksman, as he dashed by in full career, received a revolving rap from the Turk's club.

"Now, Truth is very much like a wooden Turk ; and the popular mind, borne on that swift but unsteady steed, the Spirit of the Age, is, as might be expected, very little likely to strike the centre the first time, or yet the second.   It may consider itself very lucky if it finds that even ' the *third* time is the charm.'

"The dilemma presented to the *Church* has ever had these two sharp horns : on the one side, ' *Be not conformed to the world*' —' *the friendship of the world is enmity with God;*' and on the other, the plain duty of employing the wisdom of the serpent, and the apostolic example of being ' *all things to all men,*' that by any means ' *she might gain some.*'   The result of the proper balance of these opposite principles was that, while the Apostles and the Church were yet fiercely persecuted by the rulers of the Jews, ' *the* PEOPLE *magnified them.*'   Indeed, the essential popularity of the Christian religion throughout its first and most wonderful three centuries of conquest, is one of the most indisputable facts of history, as well as one of the most active causes of its rapid and complete success.

"After her conquest of Paganism the Church was ready to be all things to all men in matters which did not affect the essentials of the faith ; and accordingly, whatever pleased the people was freely permitted and even encouraged all over Christendom.   But by the sixteenth century it was evident that the compliance which at first was but the kindly condescension of the weak to the strong, had grown into far other and more fatal proportions. The Church had given away her spiritual lordship in order that she might pluck the temporal sceptre from the hands of kings.

"Such was the result to the Church's first experiment in aiming at the mark of popularizing her services.   Her lance struck too far to the right of the centre, and she herself was well-nigh felled to the ground by the inevitable recoil.

"The Reformation has been a second trial of her skill.   With the violent reaction natural to human kind, she has done her ut-

most to rid herself of the dangers of that popular plasticity which
had worked so much mischief.   Her present practical system was
not the result of popular clamor, and has never granted an additional inch to any popular demands for increasing her standard
modicum.

" Apparently hopeless of expansion in the old direction, her
natural and noiseless change has been to sink practically lower and
lower down in the dignity and beauty of celebrating such services
as she has retained ; thus impoverishing the remains of old
energy, while coldly neglecting to provide any practicable out-
let for the new.   She has viewed the *people*, not as her natural
allies, her favorite children, in whose hearts she reigned supreme ;
but rather as secret and sullen foes, whose every additional desire
was construed as an incipient rebellion, whose every yearning
was to be choked down, whose every movement of spontaneous
life was to be visited at once with the inexorable strait-waistcoat.
One popular movement after another has convulsed England and
England's Church, and at times it has seemed as if the day were
lost beyond recovery ; but when the tide has turned the Church
has reappeared from the midst of the chaos, in all her rigid fixity,
not a rubric rubbed out, nor the fold of a surplice ruffled, as if
an indomitable obstinacy of immobility were the highest and
most glorious perfection of that which God ordained to be the
Tabernacle of *life.*

" And what has been the result ?   It took the Church more
than *ten* centuries to feel the recoil of her first mistake.   We can
feel ours plainly enough at the end of *three.*   *Then* she was full of
popular superstitions :   *now* she is empty with popular desertions.
Then she was the centre of the life of the world : now she is like
Art and Science, but one of the accidents of the world's life.
Then she was decked in a gorgeousness which will be popular as
long as human nature remains what it is : now her beauty is departed until she has no heart any longer for even the feast which
she professes to provide for her people.   Except when her congregations listen in silence to the musical performances in an
organ loft, she *reads* her cold praises with a monotonous, muffled,
and melancholy response ; and *preaches* her prayers to unkneel-
ing listeners, who condescend only a mumbled, or smothered, or
a dumb *Amen.*   And *this*, the general standard of her public
worship, is proved by the listless, lazy lounging of too many of
her *great* congregations to be no longer really, *heartily* popular,
even among the bulk of her own people.

" ' Thus ends the second attempt of the Church's lance to touch the centre of truth in this matter. And she is yet suffering from the stunning deadness of the blow with which inexorable and impartial Truth ever punishes those who miss their mark.

" ' But the evil, though great, must not be so exaggerated as to dishearten her children. And there is about her now an abundance of the symptoms of an awakening to greater strength and wisdom than ever before.

" ' *High Church* principles are very respectable principles, provided men will only act them out. If the Church be the Ark in which is the salvation of the world, and if we be the Church, it is high time we cease to live as if the main business for which we were placed in the Ark were to see how many pretexts we could devise to keep other men out of it. If we have any faith whatever in our pretensions, let us rather see how many friendly hands we can reach out, on every side, *to draw other men in.*' "

The offering to the General Convention of Dr. Muhlenberg's famous *Memorial* on the subject of reunion was the cause of the writing of the series of leaders from which the last extracts have been made. It was no fault of either Dr. Muhlenberg, or of Mr. Hopkins and his associates, that the concessions to the sects which they proposed to make failed to meet the approval of the Church at large. The Church itself had not yet learnt how to use her own services with freedom and elasticity. Like the proposals of Bishop Hobart in 1826, they seemed admirable at first view, but on reflection they were rejected. But the spirit of those and similar proposals was taken and used afterward in the Church itself, and thus the freedom and stability of the Prayer Book worship were proved to meet all genuine needs in sectarian bodies.

CHAPTER VII.

1865–1866.

TRUE to its own feelings, the Low Church party felt the thrill of all the popular Protestant agitations. As the anti-slavery movement in the North grew stronger, so the feeling in all religious bodies grew more and more intense. The abolition fever grew hotter and hotter as the fires were fed by the New England philanthropists. Long before the war broke out, some of the Protestant sects were divided upon the point of the lawfulness of slaveholding in Christians. The virus of the wound to the Church's life was deeply felt among the Evangelicals. Yet before the war slavery issues were easily avoided, because the Low Church minority could not afford to divide its forces, and Massachusetts and South Carolina, Virginia and Ohio, were all in that minority together.

The General Convention met at Richmond in 1859, in the midst of the excitement caused by the John Brown raid at Harper's Ferry, and it was like the rising of a rainbow from the angry storm-clouds menacing the nation, to see one great body of Christians, many of whose laymen were in high places in the State, meeting in the centre of disturbance, and not so much as a word spoken in Convention that mentioned the obscene tumult raging all around.

Four Bishops were consecrated at that meeting, and, so great was the popular interest in the Convention, it was at one time planned to have them consecrated in a great tent, to be erected in the Capitol Square !

The Church was, indeed, a haven of peace in those days, but when once the war had come the fever swept everything before it in the denominations, the Methodists going so far as to insert the oath of allegiance in their ordination service. The Low Churchmen as a body went the same way ; and during the war Church interests were nothing to them in comparison with " saving the life of the nation." Hopkins never could see that splitting the

Church with politics would strengthen the life of the nation. With unwavering confidence he anticipated the triumph of the United States and the eventful restoration of the old government, after a longer or shorter period of suffering and trouble. Accordingly he was unflinching in his determination to keep all political questions and issues out of the Church, as far as he could.   By this time the *Church Journal* was altogether the most influential and best supported Church newspaper.   It was quite the strongest utterance in the Church.   If the faith of the Romans in their final triumph in the second Punic war was shown in selling the very ground upon which Hannibal was encamped, surely some note of admiration should be sounded for those true-hearted American Churchmen, Evangelicals as well as High Churchmen who, in the midst of a storm of reproaches and upbraidings, persisted in believing that it was a sin to allow political agitations to enter the Church's councils.   As citizens the Church taught her members their duty to their just rulers.

They felt that armies might bring back the Southern States; but the Church had no armies to operate in bringing back the Southern Dioceses to the General Convention.   If they came back at all, it must be of their own free will, as brothers returning to their own place, to be welcomed once more by brethren.

The General Convention which met in 1862, the darkest time of the whole war for the North, saw the discussion of the whole question in all its bearings.   The first introduction of the question was tabled by a majority of three to one in both Orders.

But, unfortunately, the New York State election was near at hand, and Horatio Seymour, the Democratic candidate for Governor " on the War Platform " was a member of the House of Clerical and Lay Deputies, as a deputy from Western New York. The Democrats were loudly accused of insincerity in putting forth such a platform.   In order to have a favorable effect on that important election, the Democratic members of the House were more willing to do something than they would have been at any other time.   The Republicans being clamorous for action, and the Democrats thus persuaded, the resolutions formerly tabled were sent to a large committee, which reported a series of resolutions which meant next to nothing.   The debate lasted more than a week, hounded on by the daily press of both parties.   In the House Dr. Mead and Dr. Hawks, the Hon. Robert C. Winthrop, Dr. Mahan, and others resisted the effort to pass these resolutions, or to strengthen them, but at last the members of the House of

Bishops began to yield to the strong secular pressure, and the deputies, finding out how the current was setting, passed the mild resolutions by a very scanty majority.

This was the highest political movement that rose in the Church. Loyalty was the great theme of all Protestant pulpits, and resolutions not worth the paper and ink were adopted all over the North ; but, except in the case of three or four dioceses, all similar manifestoes were voted down or tabled *instanter* on their introduction in the Church.

When the war was ended the predominating secular interest was still rampant among the Evangelicals, and one of their organs demanded of the government that some of the leading Southern bishops and clergy should be hanged, on the ground that they had been leaders in the original movement for secession.

The Southern Church has been set up because it was felt that ecclesiastical independence must go along with the civil independence claimed by the seceding States.

When the war was ended it followed that ecclesiastical union must be restored also. Then it was that the value of the influence of the *Church Journal* was seen. Then it was made plain that in resisting political agitation that paper had been expressing the highest patriotism, and, in seeking to restore full relations with the Southern Churchmen, it had confounded all the counsels of bitterness and hatred so freely uttered by Low Churchmen. Some of the Southern bishops resumed their old places the very year of the close of the war, 1865, trusting, in the noble words of the Bishop of New York, "to the love and honor of their brethren ; " the others came back not long after, and in less than a year after the war was over the Church was completely re-united. To no one man is that consummation due so much as to John Henry Hopkins. In his "Life of Bishop Hopkins," at the end of the chapter on the reunion of the Church (from which most of the above account has been gathered, though in piece-meal), he gives a letter to Bishop Hopkins from Bishop Elliott, of Georgia, "the Presiding Bishop of the Protestant Episcopal Church in the Southern Confederacy," wherein these lines occur, in congratulating him upon celebrating his golden wedding—"among those descendants stood my adopted son, John Henry, of whom I feel so proud, whose wise and judicious counsels have done more than almost any human means besides, to bring about the reunion of the children of God at the North and the South."

In writing of the attitude of the *Church Journal* as to the expediency of the *Church* interfering with the affairs of the *nation*,
it must be observed that personally Mr. Hopkins held to the
opinions of the Bishops' Pastoral letter of 1862, and so expressed
himself in the paper.   And a side-light is thrown upon the matter by the following leader written the week after the assassination
of President Lincoln :

" The happy Easter which we were anticipating last week has
been horribly blurred with blood, shed by the hand of an as-
sassin. The whole land was fluttering with flags on Good Friday,
to be draped in universal mourning on Easter Day.   Such overwhelming grief, such an overshadowing sorrow, this country has
never known before.   That so fearful and complicated a plot of
political assassinations should have been deliberately formed, and
so marvellously carried out, shows that demoralization has rotted
down the national character more deeply than any of us dreamed
of.   It is a disgrace as well as a grief.

" To-day, simultaneous services will be held over the whole
land, while the funeral ceremonies of the murdered President are
being celebrated in Washington : and there will be a depth and
an earnestness in them far surpassing anything that has been
known since the war began.

" It is but natural, and yet it is most saddening to see,
that this detestable crime has interrupted, with a sudden black
cloud, the sunshine of good-will that was beginning to gleam
forth warmly and cheerily all over the North, ushering in apparently an era of good feeling, which was encouraged by signs of
corresponding reaction at the South.   Now all is dark again.   No
greater misfortune to that unhappy part of our country could have
happened at this time, than the murder of President Lincoln.

" Political assassination only consecrates in the hearts of a
nation the cause which is thus foully attacked.   And there could
be no greater proof of the safety of the life of the nation, than
that, in the face of so startling a calamity, the reins of power
passed at once to the legal hands, without a shock or even a rip-
ple of disturbance or doubt.   May the Providence of God bring
good out of evil ! "

One incident of the later years of this war may be of interest
for the bearing it has upon objects dear to John Henry Hopkins.
Napoleon III. was maintaining the hopeless Maximilian as Em-

peror of Mexico, and the presence of French troops under Ba-
zaine was felt to be a covert menace to our Government, just
beginning, at the cost of enormous sums of money and of more
precious lives, to have hopes of a favorable ending of the war.
But the administration had its hands full, and could only warn in
a diplomatic way the French Government of the meaning of their
acts in Mexico.   To the immense honor of Russia it should be
remembered that Alexander II., in this hour of our national peril,
when England was barely maintaining officially a cold neutrality
while expressing openly the warmest sympathy with the Southern
cause, and the French Emperor was waiting but for an unfavor-
able turn to our affairs, sent a squadron to New York, and thus
gave us his moral support.

The Russian chaplains of the ships of war were cordially received by the Bishop of New York, and with his full consent and
approval they repeatedly celebrated the Sclavonic Liturgy in
Trinity Chapel.

This caused a great sensation in religious circles, and gave
umbrage anew to the Low Churchmen, who were just then on fire
with the idea of exchanging pulpits with the " evangelical denominations."

The music of the Russian choir quite enraptured Hopkins.
Of it he used to quote Mahan's words describing the music at
the Russo-Greek Chapel in Paris—" O how lovely !   To hear that
sweet and earnest Litany, becoming more and more intense at
every repetition, and seeming at times to be battering the gates
of heaven, the angels the meanwhile answering from within the
closed doors of the sanctuary, it beats all Western uses beyond
comparison ! "   He transcribed the Russian Litany and set it to
the words of our English Litany.   It is far sweeter and more
beautiful than the Tallis setting to which the Litany is usually
sung, and not too difficult for any ordinary choir.

The last years of Hopkins' connection with the *Church
Journal* saw the culmination of its influence.   Whether it would
have kept its place as leader of the journals of the Church if the
alarm over the rise of " Ritualism " had not arisen it is idle to
speculate.

The year 1867 saw victory for the advocates of the division
of the Diocese of New York, after a steady fight on his part for
eight years.   In 1868 he sold the paper in order to give himself
up to writing the life of Bishop Hopkins, and to save his eyesight, seriously weakened by overwork.

The close of the rebellion saw the actual formation of a " Ritual-istic parish " in New York.   Such churches had been in existence some years before that date in England.   There they had been called for by laymen.   The ground lay a little differently here, and accordingly they did not appear quite so soon in America.   But they had been expected.   Long before Ritualism showed itself here the Evangelicals had dubbed the modest revived use of the surplice in the pulpit as a ritualistic abomination.   The eastward position of the celebrant at the altar, to this day a matter of strife in England, and really the key to the whole position of the Cath-olic school as to ceremonial, had been adopted and used even by Evangelicals.   Hopkins had for years advocated the full revival of the Reformation ornaments and ceremonial, and so *he* was ready for them too, and, of course, an unflinching supporter of the men who adopted them.   And yet, he was never, in the vulgar sense of the word, a Ritualist.   For one thing, he was a deacon, and had no rights over ceremonial in any church, and he naturally, as every gentleman will do, followed the customs of the parish priest.   He used to say, " I am not really a Ritualist ; I am a Catholic ; but as long as the word is used as a term of reproach of other men, better than I am, I will never disown it."   To the end of his days as a parish priest his services were the old-fashioned " full morning service."   In his church at Williams-port he introduced the weekly and feast day celebrations, which he always ministered fasting.   At them he wore only the surplice and stole, " taking the eastward position," elevating both the paten and the chalice at the consecration, and inclining pro-foundly after consecrating each kind, and by his whole bearing seemed, especially after consecration, in a sort of ecstasy of devo-tion and adoration.*   He used to do what is so often read of, but seldom seen, bow his head reverently at the holy name of *Jesus wherever it occurs*.   The newer Ritualists content them-selves with turning to the east in the creed, and do not bow at all !

The first apparent result of the ritualistic innovations at St. Alban's was a terrible panic.   The Evangelicals were frightened as a matter of course, and advertised the horrors by every device in their power.   Ritualists were more and less than conspirators,

---

* Let this writer for once speak in his own person, and say that I have seen the greater number of the best known ritualistic churches and their clergy, as well as many others, and I have never seen any man who so im-pressed me with a sense of his profound reverence for the House of God, the sacred altar, and above all, the Blessed Sacrament !

and Jesuits, they were mice, and beasts, and devils; and their churches were menageries, as deadly as hell. Many, too, of the leaders of the advancing wing of the High Church side were swept into line with the Evangelicals. The battle changed front instantly, and all the heavy artillery was brought to bear upon the common ritualistic enemy.

And yet the panic was as senseless as it was wide-spread. The exact changes in the manner of conducting the services had been advocated on various grounds by some of the men who were loudest in their denunciation of them when once they saw them. Furthermore they had not been made lightly or carelessly. In England the Judges Spiritual had pronounced the use of all the ornaments of the second year of Edward VI. to be lawful, in the case of Westerton *v.* Liddell. It is true that since the lawfulness of those ornaments had not been at issue then their favorable judgment on that point was afterward declared to be a mere *obiter dictum*, but, notwithstanding, it was felt that for introducing them in the modern English Church there was abundant authority. And here in America their *lawfulness* had been conceded before they were brought into prominent use. The rector of the new church was no imaginative, romantic priestling, but a man of strong, clear, and cold and dry brain, rigid and unbending in his adherence to a rather narrow Anglican standard, and he was assisted by a young priest of great spirituality and deep piety. But all such considerations went for nothing, if they were noticed at all.

The Evangelicals tried harder than ever to bring such force to bear against the whole High Church life as to effect an entrance for their pet idea of free exchange of ministrations with " other evangelical denominations."

Different clergymen " exchanged pulpits " with ministers, but did not draw out any effectual answer, until one of them invaded the parish of a priest in New Jersey, and preached against his will in a Methodist Church.

For this infraction of a positive canon he was tried by his own Diocesan, and publicly reprimanded. This punishment, which hardly arose to the dignity of " persecution," sufficed to reveal the clear purpose of churchmen that the canons were not to be wantonly broken into shivers, made them hot with anger and shame. They determined to do still more. It was a pity, indeed, that when *High* Churchmen could live up to the Prayer-book *they* could not in peace bring it into open contempt. Still,

their efforts in that particular were so plainly opposed to the
law, which they yet *professed* to love to follow, that but a few of
them ventured, from whatever reason, to keep up that movement.
One of their leaders let a phrase slip from him which Hopkins
seized upon as a cat jumps on a mouse, and made it yield a vast
amount of fun under his skilful treatment.   The *funny* part of
his leader is given here ; more than three times as much, not in
the least degree amusing, followed originally.

" THE ' HUCKLEBERRY-PUDDING BUSINESS.'—Dr. T——, in
his reply to the *Pastoral* of the Bishop of New York, says that
the pamphlet was read by him to ' the Clerical Association of
the Protestant Episcopal Church,' previous to its publication.
But we have been informed, by one who claims to have it on
good authority, that on introducing the subject, before reading
his manuscript, Dr. T—— said : ' Now, brethren, *you know that
I don't like this huckleberry-pudding business myself :* but I have
written this to defend the enlarged interpretation of the canons,
and for the sake of others.'   The story is a very good one, and
carries probability on the face of it.   It has the crisp, clear, and
spicy flavor of Dr. T——'s mind.   It expresses very adequately
the real contempt with which this practical amalgamation with
outsiders is regarded by a great majority of the Low Churchmen
themselves.   And it is in tolerably close consistency with Dr.
T——'s own past career : for, no matter what queer things he
may have said or done on various platforms and in sundry and
divers meeting-houses, Dr. T—— has never, we believe, felt that
there was any ' moral emergency ' for asking a Presbyterian or
a Methodist minister into his pulpit, to preach to his people.
Therefore the story is a good story—a very reasonable and credi-
ble story.   *Si non e vero, e ben trovato.*

" We heartily thank Dr. T—— for the phrases thus happily
coined by him.   It is much better than any that we could have
hit on for ourselves.   The satire is rather broader, indeed, than
we should have thought to be in good taste.   Excepting for the
authentic information on which we receive the story, we should
have felt bound to discuss *au grand sérieux* the question of the
replies to the *Pastoral.*   We should have thought it unseason-
able to treat with even deserved ridicule a controversy in which
the parties who pour out long pamphlet after long pamphlet are
apparently in such dead earnest.   But when we find the chief-
tain and leader of the responsive pamphleteers, whose face is so

sober and stern to the public, cracking such a good joke upon his own friends in private, our sense of propriety relaxes, and we feel perfectly justified in being sensible rather than serious. The phrase is an uncommonly good phrase, even for Dr. T——. And it will not be our fault if it does not stick.

"But what has 'Huckleberry-pudding' got to do with the recognition of non-Episcopal ministers? The spirit of symbolism—which is so much derided by our Evangelical friends, but by which they are so constantly animated without their knowing it—will reveal to us a depth of meaning in this well-chosen epithet.

"Huckleberries are fruits of nature, and not of cultivation: they are therefore fit types of the non-Episcopal denominations, which have indeed many good and pleasant and juicy things about them; but—as denominations—they are the work of nature, not of grace.

"The dough which embraces the huckleberries in the making of the pudding, symbolizes our Low Church friends, who so lovingly embrace these denominations on the ground of ministerial equality. The dough is *not* a work of nature, and those brethren are undoubtedly members of the true Church, children of grace, and leavened with the leaven of righteousness in many *notable* respects.

"But the dough has its chief significance from its unfinished and very pliable condition, and from its accepted meaning as indicating those who are ever ready to yield their position just when they ought to maintain it, and are eager to 'compromise' the very principles which it is their special duty to defend —'dough-faces' is the well-known political term; and the happy epithet of Dr. T—— transfers it, with much greater fitness, to the field of ecclesiastical politics.

"But this is not all. The 'huckleberries' may be lovingly embraced by the 'dough,' yet the 'pudding' is not complete until both parties, thus united, have been plunged into hot water, and kept there a long time—a process so perfectly corresponding to all past ecclesiastical experience on the subject as to need no further elucidation.

"The eating furnishes fresh shades of meaning. 'Huckleberry-pudding' is rather a poor dish. The huckleberries are certainly spoiled; and the dough is very doughy still. The only thing that makes it go down is the sauce—which is furnished from the 'Strong Church' side of the house, and is compounded of

8

sugar, the sweetness of gentle Charity; and butter, the smooth-
ness of good-natured forbearance ; and cinnamon and spice,
which are the wit and humor that always give a pleasant flavor
to the controversy from their side of the question.   But even
with plenty of sauce, it is a dangerous dish, and damaging to
one's good looks.   It stains the tongue ; it stains the teeth ; and
—if one be not an uncommonly nice feeder—it stains even the
lips to such a degree that it makes a man look as if he had kissed
his laundress's indigo bag.   Everybody can see the effect of it,
even afar off ; and everybody that meets such a man on the
street, greets him with, ' So you've been eating huckleberry
pudding, have you ? '   This part of the experience symbolizes
the general blackening that a man is likely to get from the
' huckleberry - pudding business,' and the rather ridiculous
notoriety that it is likely to give him for a long while after ; for it
is always sure to get into the papers, and be copied even into
those that are published afar off, and everybody has his laugh at
the expense of those who have been so free with the ' huckleberry-pudding.'   It is a remarkable thing, moreover, that this
ugly staining quality is developed in huckleberries only by the
' pudding business.'   In their natural uncombined and un-
boiled condition, there is no nicer berry growing, and one may
eat his fill of them, yet they leave no stain at all.   Thus, too,
the proper intercourse with our brethren of the denominations
in their natural condition—in things benevolent, social, literary,
scientific, political, and what not—is very pleasant and juicy,
fresh-flavored and good, and hurts nobody.   It is only an im-
proper mixture in things ecclesiastical that brings out the power
to *stain*.''

It cannot be doubted that such articles, for all their air of
pleasantry, were most exasperating.   Not to take their most
earnest attacks as if they were of any moment was of all things
most likely to arouse the resentment of the struggling Evangelicals.   It was quite another thing when Hopkins attempted to
meet the cross-fire of the old High Churchmen.

It may not be apart from the story to see how he regarded the
ritualistic movement.   It may be questioned whether he ever
planned just such use as was made of the principle he contended
for, when he wrote about elasticity and flexibility in the services,
and about popularizing them.   But the ritual, or to speak more
correctly, the ceremonial development rose naturally from the

Prayer-book, and although it could not be associated so fully as it was in England with charitable and philanthropic work, yet it was, in setting forth the rich beauty of the Prayer-book services, truly a powerful missionary agency, and rather the more so because it was the corporate manifestation of a piety which had too carefully hidden itself in a sort of shamefaced dread of expression. Hopkins never followed it out in his own practice. He was in his ways more like the early Tractarians, very gentle and considerate with others, strict and stern in the discipline of self. He taught the old Evangelical Catholic doctrines of the inspiration and authority of Scripture, the Atonement through the Incarnation, the doctrines of the aversion of the race from God, and of its helplessness apart from grace, the need of repentance, and, in brief, all the doctrines of redemption as they have always been taught in the Catholic Church in all its branches. He kept the fasts of the Church with exactness and severity. His fasts were fasts from meat and drink, and not a mere substitution of one meat for another ; although, indeed, his ordinary table was plainer and scantier than that of any *Religious* House known by experience to the writer. But he defended the Ritualists, and battled manfully for all their rights, with more ardor than if he were writing for his own benefit. He always said he wanted the extremes of Church liberty as far apart as possible, in order that true comprehensiveness and freedom might pervade the Church, so that all the good, which in the sects could only be found by going through them all, might be enjoyed in her in solidarity. He held that all this variety of ceremonial hurts no one, but is *a gradual growth toward something better.* What then was the principle upon which he built his support of the advanced movement ?

It was thus expressed by him at a later period : " When our American branch of the Catholic Church was organized there was an unreasonable fear and jealousy of the tyrannical power of bishops. . . . The entire earlier generation of our American bishops felt and acknowledged the essential position of their Order in this country to be *constitutional :* they were not to be arbitrary rulers whose law was their own discretion. . . . There are some things allowed or required to be done by our American Church legislation. There is no question in regard to *these.*

" There are some things expressly *forbidden ;* there is no question in regard to *these.* The whole difficulty arises in regard to the almost innumerable points in which our American Church legislation has said *nothing.* Now the old and original theory of

American Churchmen is that 'where there is no law there is no
transgression.' The Church of England from the time of the
Reformation has been doing her work under the shackles of *Acts
of Uniformity*, which have been reinforced by a sort of oral tradition that there must be *uniformity* in public worship : and so
there must be some law, by which any one who introduces singu-
larities may be effectively and summarily *put down*. When this
uneasy traditional feeling is brought face to face with the simple
fact that in many branches of ecclesiastical affairs, the American
Church, as far as her own constitution and canons are concerned, has no written law whatsoever.

   " Let us look at two sorts of law, and distinguish them clearly.
Our American constitution and canons are clothed with coercive force beyond question.   But is the case altogether the same
with us in regard to the English canons ?   [The American
Bishops declared in 1808 that the English Table of Prohibited
Degrees was obligatory on this Church.]   So that what the English canon forbids as incestuous the American Church forbids as
incestuous.   But is there a single diocese in which that law has
ever been *enforced* as Church law ?   So that the only conclusion
is this, that unquestioned *coercive* force is to be attributed only
to our American constitution and canons : that coercion based
only on English canon law will not work.   A strong argument
may be based on the binding force of the ancient canons of the
Œcumenical Church—whenever any diocese or Church court
shall think fit to enforce them.   Being œcumenical, they do not
need re-enactment to be binding.   But the probability of a fair
and equitable execution of these canons, by bishops, some of
whom have been *twice* or *thrice married*, is too remote to be
worth discussion.   If *coercive* force cannot be regarded as cloth-
ing the œcumenical canons, then much less does it clothe the
English canons, as such : and if it does not clothe either of these
it certainly does not clothe any other legislation whatsoever outside of our own written American, Church legislation.   .   .   .
The whole ritualistic controversy in England may be said to
rest upon the *Ornaments Rubric* of 1662.   Now, the Puritanical
party refused to wear even the surplice.   And on the organization of the American Church the Puritanical feeling was so
strong and the Church feeling so weak, that it was resolved
to make clean work of this whole business of coercion touching
vestments.   The entire *Ornaments Rubric*, which gave the
maximum [of that which was allowable and which meant the full

system of vestments and ornaments in use at the beginning of the reign of Edward VI.], was struck out.   Not a syllable was left behind.   And when they came to canons, the *minimum*, the ' comely surplice with sleeves,' was struck out also.   There was not a particle of *American* law left by which any bishop could coerce a Low Churchman into wearing anything besides his citizen's dress.   The only exceptions were the rubrics requiring the candidates for Deacons' and Priests' Orders to be at the time of ordination ' decently habited ' ;   and the mention also of the ' rochet,' and ' the rest of the Episcopal habit,' in the Order for the Consecration of a Bishop.   All coercive law (with these exceptions) on the subject of vestments was wiped out.   To make assurance doubly sure, in the vow of canonical obedience the words are, ' Will you reverently obey your Bishop, and other chief Ministers, who, *according to the Canons of the Church*, may have the charge and government over you, etc. ? '   If the bishop wishes obedience under that vow he must point to the canon which gives him express authority to act.   So, too, as to buildings and furniture and arrangements.   The English Rubric, ' the chancels shall remain as they have done in times past,' which has been the law since the reign of Edward VI., and proves that the chancels were to remain *after* the Reformation *the same that they did before*, has no *coercive* force with us at all.   But, though we cannot be *compelled* to follow it if we do not choose so to do, there is *nothing to prevent our making that our guide* if we have a mind to do so.   Thus it is entirely open to our priests and parishes to follow every minute detail of English architecture, arrangement, ritual, adornment, and what not, *if they like*.   If, on the contrary, they don't like any such thing, and prefer to build a church in the style and arrangement of a theatre, or a pagan temple, there is no law to prevent them.   In the same way, whenever our American book has *omitted* anything, without prohibiting what is thus omitted, the difference between our people and the English is this : the English can be compelled to comply with the requirement, and we *cannot ;* but we are free to comply with it if we please.   The English clergyman can be compelled to wear a surplice during the celebration of public worship.   Our clergy cannot be so compelled.   But our clergy are free to wear the surplice if they please ; and almost unanimously they do so please.

    " Now this liberty of ritual is peculiarly in harmony with the characteristics of this American people.   It is a necessary element in giving flexibility to the Church system so that it may more readily work its way in a country cursed with a greater variety of sects and religions than any other country in the world. . . . It is strange how hard it is for some amiable people to understand, that *liberty* means to do as *we* please, and not as somebody else pleases. The propriety, or prudence, or usefulness, of any innovation is not the question here. If a clergyman introduces, unwisely, what his people do not understand, or appreciate, or what they positively dislike or disapprove, he will soon find out that they are as free as he is. That is, at present, all the restrictive legislation we need on the subject." Continuing, Mr. Hopkins wrote upon the contention that " the bishop is authority upon all questions of interpretation of a rubric." " Suppose there is no rubric to interpret ? If the rubric prescribing the vestments of the second year of Edward VI. is omitted, we are told : ' Omission is prohibition—you are prohibited from wearing those vestments.' Very well. Here we come to another omission. The command to go to the Bishop of the Diocese whose discretion shall appease all doubts concerning the meaning of the rubrics, has also been *omitted.* ' Omission is prohibition ' : therefore all who are in doubt as to the meaning of a rubric are *prohibited* from going to the Bishop to resolve it, and *he* is prohibited from exercising his discretion in any such matter. . . . What we object to is that the power to advise should be interpreted to mean the power to command.

" There is another branch of this business—Diocesan legislation. In asking it is a confession that there is no *coercive* law in it at all. And next, all diocesan canons on the subject of ritual are not worth the paper they are written on. The only *binding* legislation is by rubric in the Book of Common Prayer, requiring the approval of two consecutive General Conventions. In securing stability of liberty of ritual in public worship by the constitutional provision that no change can be made short of two General Conventions, our fathers were not quite so stupid as to leave it at the same time in the power of every Diocesan Convention to make fresh changes every year."

This article on " Constitutional Law " was not written till late in the year 1874, but he had made use of the same principle in a more concrete form in 1867, in a series of leaders entitled " The Blank Cartridge."

But at first he took but little notice of St. Alban's Church. He was very far from glorifying it, and, indeed, beyond mentioning it as an item of news when the new services were begun, he took it very much as a matter of course. Some one from the South wrote to ask him " What is Ritualism ? " and he gave the answer, thus :

" As the heavenly bodies move in elliptical orbits, and are constantly drawing nearer to or retiring from the objects from which their distance is measured ; and as the movement of the world's education, though ever onward, is oscillatory in its mode of progression, and none but a fool will suppose that the *clock* goes forward only when the pendulum swings to the right, and goes *backward* whenever the pendulum swings to the left : so is it also with movements within the Church of God, or within the sphere of things spiritual considered on a large scale. And if we would understand fully the meaning of our present position, if we would estimate aright the motion of the pendulum in its present swing before our eyes, we must go back and take our measure on a somewhat extended scale.

" The accumulated abuses and corruptions of the Dark Ages, the horrors of Papal massacres and persecutions, and the incalculable miseries of the wars of religion which accompanied and followed the *necessity* of the Reformation, all intensified by the dread of the Jesuits and the mischiefs wrought by their subtle and marvellously powerful system, led to a steady intensification of the spirit of Protestantism on the one side, and to a similar decay of all true religion on the other, until the sceptical, worldly, and deistical tone of the last century reached its coldest stage among Protestants, and among Romanists culminated in the incomparably worse excesses of the French Revolution.

" In the Church of England, the Wesleys may be said to have begun the reaction toward better things, and the Evangelical party within the Church at length took it up and carried it on. The Oxford movement was, logically, the next step of returning life, keeping everything of Evangelical truth that had been gained, and going onward to revive other important truths that had also been suffered to decay. And, as the Evangelical movement did not need to *invent* or *import* into the Prayer-book and Articles the essential doctrines of Gospel truth, so the Oxford party were equally free from any such necessity. In both cases it was a work of *revival* merely ; revival of what was there, and had been there all along, but which had merely fallen for a long time into practical disuse.

" The whole Oxford movement, therefore, was developed *out of the Prayer-book* and the other standards, and the well-known history, of the Church of England. When this was complete as to doctrine, and when the revival of Church architecture and Church adornment proved that the hearts of the people were ripe for it, the same great principle was carried one step further, and the *Rubrical Law* of the Church of England is now being revived as carefully as the once neglected doctrines of the Gospel, and the once forgotten theory and doctrine of the Church. This rubrical law concerns the outward and visible embodiment or teaching of the doctrine of the Church, the mode of celebrating Divine Service and administering the Sacraments and Ordinances of the Catholic Church, and especially concerns itself with the Holy Eucharist as the highest act of Christian worship, the chief and transcendent means of the Real Presence of our adorable Saviour among His people on earth.

" The majestic and triumphant march of this glorious Church revival has not been wholly confined to our own communion. On the Continent of Europe it has found a response in a strong revival of ancient life among the Lutherans of Germany, a portion of whom once more teach the high sacramental doctrines of their founder ; and also among the Romish churches, where there is a strong, earnest, and growing party, who are struggling to become *true* Catholics, and are steadily working their way toward us, as we are toward them. In the Oriental Communions, also, while there is no sign of their yielding an inch to Papal assumptions, dogmas, or tyranny, yet there is a manifest drawing toward us, as we are feeling our way toward them, with all the hope and love that spring necessarily from a conscious Catholic brotherhood in Christ.

" Nor has the movement been unfelt among the Protestant denominations in England and in this country. Some of our readers may remember a series of articles on *the drift* toward our Church, which has been visible among the denominations in many things for many years past. It has been seen in their mode of conducting worship, in the changed style of their religious edifices, in the efforts to procure liturgies of their own, in their adopting more or less of Church hymns and Church ways, in gradually but rapidly resuming the observance of Christmas, Good Friday, and Easter Day, and such like : and it is going on now more rapidly than ever.

" Now a movement is something that *keeps moving.* Those

who begin it, generally think it ought to stop at the first stage, and are frightened if not hurt when the second generation of thinkers and movers wishes to go further. And these second commonly feel the same toward the third: for individual men are almost invariably more or less narrow or illogical; while the great movements of God's work in the world go on, *through* particular men at the first, *over* them whenever it may become necessary.

" ' Ritualism ' is the name *at present* given to this great Church movement of our age, wherever it is felt outside of the Oriental and Roman communions. At first it was called Oxfordism, or Puseyism; then Tractarianism; now Ritualism; at *all times* it has been denounced as Romanism, or Semi-Romanism, or Romanizing, or Low Popery, or Popery in disguise, or some such thing—all these varieties of abuse having been used so long, so loudly, and so lavishly, that nobody minds them any more. This charging of ' tendencies,' and ' directions ' of movement, is now seen to be the idlest business in the world. A man who is walking down Broadway is walking ' *in the direction* ' of New York Bay, and every step he takes has a ' tendency ' to carry him into salt water where he may be drowned: and that will certainly be his fate—if he don't stop before he gets there. Sometimes, some poor wretch plunges in, and seeks to shuffle off the troubles of a world of which he knows but little, by entering unbidden that other world, of the horrors of which he knows comparatively nothing. But to make the few such incidents the excuse for stopping *all* who are found walking down Broadway, and turning them all round and making them walk *up* Broadway, *for fear* they should walk into the Bay and get drowned, would be a course precisely as sensible as that pursued by Protestants in general in regard to the Church movement: and that is the reason why they, and their mode of argument, and their loud alarums about ' Popery ' and Popish ' tendencies,' have sunk into such utter insignificance and contempt.

" With these very general remarks, nobody can be in any doubt as to what ' Ritualism ' is. In an ' Independent ' Bethel, if the minister begins to wear a black silk gown instead of a dress coat, it is ' Ritualism.' In a Presbyterian congregation, the introduction of chanting is ' Ritualism.' Among the Dutch Reformed, the observance of Lent is a ' Ritualistic abomination.' Among the German Reformed, the new Liturgy which is framed upon the altar idea rather than the pulpit idea, is loudly denounced by its opponents as ' Ritualistic.' In one of our own parishes, which heretofore has had the three-decker arrangement, it is ' Ritualism ' to build out a distinct and properly arranged chancel. Where there has been a table with legs, it is ' Ritualism ' to put an Altar in place of it (though S. Paul's Chapel in this city has had a proper Altar ever since *before* the American Revolution). Where the Altar has been bare, it is ' Ritualism ' to cover it with an Altar-cloth. Where they have had only one Altar-cloth, it is ' Ritualism ' to add one or two more of different colors. Where they have been preaching in the black gown, it is ' Ritualism ' to preach in the surplice. Where they have been preaching in the surplice and black stole, it is ' Ritualism ' to introduce colored vestments or even a colored stole. Where they have not been used to it, it is ' Ritualism ' to bow at the Sacred Name in the Creed. Where they have been used to bow only in the Creed, it is ' Ritualism ' to do it in the *Gloria in Excelsis* or on any other occasion. In some parishes it is ' Ritualism ' to have candlesticks on the Altar, even if the candles are not lighted. In others it is not ' Ritualism ' to have them, but it *is* ' Ritualism ' to light them, unless it be too dark to see to read without them. In some parishes it is ' Ritualistic ' to sing the *Amens;* in others even the full choral service is not ' Ritualism.' Thus we might go on, almost *ad infinitum.* But one short summary covers the whole — Anything; in any particular parish, no matter how slight, that indicates any *movement* toward an *increase of Churchliness*—that is to say, an *increase* in the beauty, dignity, edification, or attractiveness, of public worship, especially if it tend to show increasing honor to our Blessed Lord or the Sacrament of His precious Body and Blood—is *Ritualistic :* and most clearly, if it be something which you don't happen to fancy yourself. Anything which assumes that we American Episcopalians have ' already apprehended,' and are perfect in our mode of doing things, and that our Lord and His service ought *not* to receive any more of time, care, money, and loving reverence than we give them now, and that every parish ought to be crystallized into permanence just where it is at present, every alteration being *necessarily* a change for the *worse :* all such persons will join the cry against ' Ritualism,' and we shall know exactly what they mean by it.

"We hope we have succeeded in making our answer intelligible in all latitudes and longitudes."

He went on to ask "do the people like it?" and he traced the outline of the development of Church life, in this way :

"It is loudly affirmed that any increase in Ritualism is utterly foreign to the tastes of the Anglo-Saxon race in general, and of the American people in particular. And there is a certain amount of foundation for it, in the opposition with which any movement in that direction is sure to be greeted from several quarters. The older people who have been bred up in the present general style of doing things are opposed. The older clergy are generally opposed. The bishops are for the most part opposed. Therefore there is sure to be an outcry over every detail of improvement, however small. Old-fashioned High Churchmen (that is, the great bulk of that party), the whole of the Low Church, and all the Protestant denominations in a body, are ranged in loud and open—even abusive—opposition. And Rome likes it least of all. She tries to make capital out of it indeed, and clamorously insists that it indicates a wholesale movement toward the Papal communion ; and in making this claim, all the Protestant opponents play straight into the hands of the Romanists, reiterating precisely the same charge, at the top of their voices, all the while. Yet Rome really dislikes the movement, knowing that it will *prevent* many persons from resorting to her fold. She knows that where she makes one convert on doctrinal grounds, she makes ten on grounds of æsthetics, of feeling, of impression, and of yearning for something that touches a greater number of points in the complex nature of man. The drier and duller and more cheerless our practical system is, therefore, the more surely will Rome glean a great many loose or dissatisfied people from among us. While the more attractive, the more effective, the more interesting, our services are, the less is she likely to win. All that is left to her, therefore, is, so to speak of the movement from the outside as to increase the suspicion against it inside, and thus if possible choke it off entirely, or so disgust and dishearten those who are engaged in it that they may give up the battle and go over to her, in despair of maintaining a truly Catholic position in the ' Protestant Episcopal Denomination.'

"Now we ask sensible people to say what they can make of the *fact*, that, in spite of this tremendous preponderance of opposition from within and from without, the Church movement—though led by so few—has steadily *won every battle it has fought*

for the past thirty years? Gothic architecture, stained-glass
windows, deep chancels, the removal of the old three-decker arrangement, the revival of the more ancient patterns in vessels of
the Altar, large stone fonts, the placing of the font by the door,
the use of flowers on high festivals, the 'image' of the Cross
outside and inside our churches, the revival of the ancient stole
instead of the scarf, preaching in the surplice, the use of embroidery on both surplice and stole, and now the introduction of
stoles of different colors (which has already made such headway
that in five years or less it will be general), the introduction first
of chanting the Psalter, then boy choirs, and lastly the full
choral service with male choirs in surplices, the slowly but
steadily increasing love for the pure old Gregorian tones, and—
most important of all—the increasing reverence for the Sacraments, the celebration of baptism (to say nothing of marriages
and funerals) in church instead of in private houses, and the
greater frequency of Eucharists, together with a tendency toward
early celebrations: all these things, with many more—such as
the richness of polychromatic decoration—constitute the history
of a great campaign, an ecclesiastical thirty years' war, in which
every point of detail has been a battle-field, fiercely contested at
the time; and every battle-field has brought a fresh victory for
the Church party—a victory, that is to say, for that small, despised, and heartily abused *minority*, against that tremendous,
overwhelming, and loud-denouncing *majority!* Will the majority
be kind enough to chew the cud over that fact, for awhile, and
tell us what they think of it?

"In every case, sooner or later, the minority have been left
in quiet possession of the field of battle—the great fact which,
in all warfare, decides the question of victory or defeat. In a
great many of the points mentioned, the opponents themselves
have come, not only to cease their opposition, but to adopt themselves, with great delight, the very things which, ten years before,
they declared to be 'Popery.' Ten years ago, for instance, the
decoration of the interior of churches with bright colors and gild-
ing was loudly and *universally* denounced by the Evangelical
press as the latest enormity of histrionic display on the part of
the Romanizers; and as being irreconcilable with true views of
the Gospel. And now, St. George's, Stuyvesant Square—the
very centre of Low-Church opposition to 'Ritualism'—is coming out in full strength and brilliancy, so as boldly and successfully to cast into the shade every other building in the country.

"Now it is impossible to account for this thirty years' war of perpetual victories for the minority, except in one way. And that is, by recognizing the truth, that the great Protestant movement, in its eagerness to get away from everything that *looked* like Romanism, had *done a great violence to human nature*, insisting that beauty—whether of architecture, form, color, sweet sounds, vestments, services, flowers, adornment, and what not—that all beauty should be banished from the worship of that God who hath poured out beauty with an infinite profusion over all His works. They committed themselves to the absurd position that no public services *could* be agreeable to God, except such as were so ugly, so dull, so dry, and so repulsive, as to be almost intolerable to man—unless through a miracle of Divine grace. Under the powerful impulse of the Reformation—and there is no greater proof of its power than the length of time that it has prevented the inevitable reaction—the concentrated energies of all Protestant bodies were united in favor of ugliness and baldness : until the Puritan meeting-house of New England in the eighteenth century, and the primitive type of the Methodist Bethel, and the Quaker houses of worship, indicated the point *beyond* which it was impossible for the ugliness of vital piety to go, in manifesting its opposition to the beauty of holiness.

"But human nature is now being revenged upon the ugliness of vital piety. Human nature takes pleasure in beauty of all sorts and kinds. It may try for awhile, under excitement and strong religious prejudice, to pull a long face and persuade itself that drab is the only truly spiritual and delightful color, or that the sight of black suggests all the sweetness and richness of Gospel grace. But the cruel self-torture is sure to break down sooner or later : and that there is a general break down going on all around us now, is as plain as the nose on a man's face.

"For, as human nature is not confined to us Church folks, so the movement is not confined to us, but is felt through every prominent portion of the Protestant denominations. From time to time for years past, we have called attention to *The Drift* among them, showing their increasing disposition toward churchliness in a great variety of points. They move so fast, indeed, that now and then they get ahead even of our own Low Church people, and leave them lagging ludicrously far in the rear.

"For some two or three centuries, God gave the Protestants what they wanted. 'He gave them their desire, and *sent leanness withal into their soul.*' They have at length found it out ;

and by a general and instinctive movement they are now earnestly at work to discover whether all that was really needed or actually gained by the Reformation cannot be fully preserved, while nevertheless restoring the beauty of holiness, in such degree as God Himself has sanctioned in His Word and in His works, and such as was the universal heritage of His Church before the spirit of ambition and usurpation, division and schism, began to cheat her out of her birthright.

" Our readers will now understand the solid basis of that ' audacity ' of which our opponents complain so constantly, and which actually at times almost seems to take their breath away. *Thirty years of unvarying victories on every field of contest,* are a tolerably solid ground for ' audacity ' in any party. Those who have thus conquered against such odds, feel that only the Spirit and power of God working in them and with them could have given them the victory: and in *that* strength they are equally ready for all the conflicts that are yet to come. It is no part of ' the Gospel ' as *they* have learned it, that all beauty of form, color, melody, harmony, fragrance, motion, arrangement, are so entirely consecrated to the world, the flesh, and the devil, that they *cannot* lawfully be used in honor of the God who made them. They find that the noblest, purest, costliest, and best of *all* these were in His Word commanded to be used in His service, and are used in His service in the Court of Heaven ; and they *know* that to come as near as possible to those glorious models, with an honest and faithful heart, is the nearest and the dearest approach that can be made, during our present dispensation, to the realization of a heaven upon earth.''

About this time the different parts of Dr. Pusey's '' Eirenicon '' came out, and this work, coming as it did, when the public heart was softened, and stirred to something very like sympathy by Newman's '' Apologia,'' gave a keener edge to the fear that arose '' like a summer's cloud '' of Rome. Keble was dead, and the memories of churchmen were fresh with the spell of the thrilling voices of the earlier '' Tracts for the Times.'' The movement was daily becoming more powerful in England, and a feebler, but still an harmonious vibration from the same sweeping touch was felt here. When, then, in 1866, at the request of a number of priests, among whom were Dr. Dix, and Drs. (afterward Bishops) Young and Doane, and laymen, the Bishop of Vermont published a thin volume with a smoking censer on the cover, and bearing the title "The Law of Ritualism" it was felt that "something must be done" that would have some effect in stopping the inroads of the two enemies that it was feared were working in concert—Romanism and Ritualism. Accordingly in March, 1867, a Declaration by Twenty-eight Bishops was published, which was noticed in the *Church Journal* by four successive leaders under the title "The Blank Cartridge"—but he shall tell his own story.

"THE BLANK CARTRIDGE.—Thus far we have had less to say editorially concerning '*Ritualism*' than any of our contemporaries. Beyond the giving of the current news from England, and our notices of the Bishop of Vermont's book, a few brief paragraphs are all the *editorial* attention that we have given to the subject : while our contemporaries have some of them given up column after column for months together, to the exciting theme. But silence is no now longer possible. The Bishop of —— has sent to the *Christian Witness* the following document. It has long been expected, and the reasons for its extraordinary delay are not very clearly expressed : yet the date of its appearance in our columns is not altogether inappropriate. There will now be no lack of material for mortification and humiliation during Lent :

"JANUARY 10, 1867.

" The Committee appointed to draft this Declaration, owing to the great distance between the dwelling-places of its members and their frequent absences from their homes, were not able, very speedily, to complete their work.

" It was by the unanimous advice of the Bishops assembled at Detroit, in December, that the Committee resolved to postpone this publication, until the remotest of our Bishops might be heard from ; but, even at this date, it is supposed that several of them have never received the circular of the Committee.

" As in the ' Colenso Case,' several of the Bishops object to this form of meeting an evil which they deeply deplore ; but not one of the Bishops heard from has expressed any sympathy with the Ritualistic movement. The reverse is the fact.

" The Committee think it proper no longer to delay the publication.

—— —— *Secretary.*

" *Whereas*, at a meeting of the House of Bishops, held in the City of New York in the month of October, the subject of

Ritualism was brought to the notice of the House and considered with a great degree of unanimity ; and

" *Whereas*, on account of the absence of a number of the Right Rev. members of the House, and the fact that the House was not sitting as a co-ordinate branch of the General Convention of the Protestant Episcopal Church in the United States of America, it was regarded as inexpedient to proceed to any formal action ; and

" *Whereas*, it was nevertheless regarded as highly desirable that an expression of opinion on the part of the Episcopate of this Church should be given, with respect to ritualistic innovations ; *Therefore*, the undersigned Bishops, reserving each for himself his rights as Ordinary of his own diocese, and also his rights as a member of the House of Bishops sitting in General Convention, do unite in the Declaration following :

" We hold in the language of the XXXIVth Article of Religion, that ' every particular or National Church hath authority to ordain, change and abolish Ceremonies or Rites of the Church, ordained only by man's authority, so that all things be done to edifying ; ' and also in the language of the same Article that : ' it is not necessary that Traditions and Ceremonies be in all places one, or utterly like ; for at all times they have been divers, and may be changed according to the diversity of countries, times and men's manners, so that nothing be ordained against God's Word ; ' and also, that this Church was duly organized as a ' particular and National Church ' in communion with the Universal or Holy Catholic and Apostolic Church of Christ, and that this organization which took place immediately after the American Revolution, was settled under the careful direction and advice, and with the cordial co-operation of godly, well-learned and justly venerated divines, who were well acquainted with the history of the Church of England before and since her blessed Reformation, and who thoroughly understood what was and is still required by the peculiarities of this Country and its people.

" We hold, therefore, that the ceremonies, rites and worship then established, ordained and approved by common authority, as set forth in the Book of Common Prayer of this Church, are the Law of this Church, which every Bishop, Presbyter and Deacon of the same has bound himself by subscription to the Promise of Conformity in Article VII. of the Constitution to obey, observe and follow : and that no strange or foreign usages should be introduced or sanctioned by the private judgment of any member or members of this Church, Clerical or Lay.

"We further hold, that while this Church is 'far from intending to depart from the Church of England in any essential point of doctrine, discipline or worship, or further than local circumstances require,' it yet has its peculiar place, character, and duty as a 'particular and National Church;' and that no Prayer Book of the Church of England, in the reign of whatever Sovereign set forth, and no Laws of the Church of England have any force of Law in this Church such as can be justly cited in defence of any departure from the express Law of this Church, its Liturgy, its discipline, rites and usages.

"And we, therefore, consider that in this particular National Church, any attempt to introduce into the public worship of Almighty GOD, usages that have never been known, such as the use of incense, and the burning of lights in the order for the Holy Communion; reverences to the Holy Table or to the Elements thereon, such as indicate or imply that the Sacrifice of our Divine Lord and Saviour, '*once* offered,' was not a 'full, perfect and sufficient sacrifice, oblation and satisfaction, for the sins of the whole world;' the adoption of clerical habits hitherto unknown, or material alterations of those which have been in use since the establishment of our Episcopate; is an innovation which violates the discipline of the Church, 'offendeth against its common order, and hurteth the authority of the Magistrate, and woundeth the consciences of the weak brethren.'

"Furthermore, that we be not misunderstood, let it be noted that we include in these censures, all departures from the Laws, rubrics and settled order of this Church, as well by defect as by excess of observance, designing to maintain in its integrity the sound Scriptural and Primitive, and therefore the Catholic and Apostolic spirit of the Book of Common Prayer.

"Signed by the following Bishops."

The House of Bishops met on the 5th of October last, and remained in session on the 6th and 7th of that month, and then adjourned. In his little book called ———— publishes, as the last of its contents, a "Letter to a Bishop," dated October, 1866." This letter thus begins:

"I agree with you that the matter of ' Ritualism ' is becoming a serious one for us, as well as for the English. I regarded it

9

as simply absurd, while it was presented in a single instance in New York, where the feebleness and shallowness of a foppish puerility have served the useful purpose of a caricature. But the appearance of the Bishop of Vermont's little book is a serious thing, as it opens the door for experiments which are not unlikely to be made in respectable churches, if not in some of the most important seats of the Church's dignity and strength.''

As this letter is proved by its date to have been written either immediately before (which is very improbable) or within a little while after, the above *Declaration* was sent on the rounds for signatures—and written, too, by the Bishop who has taken the leading part in that work, and who is generally understood to be the writer of the Declaration itself : we can be doing no injustice by interpreting the Declaration in the light thus thrown upon it from ——.

" There were, then, only two causes for the five months' incubation that has produced the above document signed by twenty-eight Bishops. One was, the 'single instance in New York,' to wit, the little church of S. Alban in this city—which is alluded to by the Bishop with his usual dignified amenity of phrase, and is further regarded by him as 'simply absurd.' The other was, 'the Bishop of Vermont's little book,' which was '*a serious thing.*' If the Twenty-eight meant merely to condemn S. Alban's, they were undertaking to bishop it in another man's Diocese ; for the Bishop of New York—notwithstanding the urgent pressure brought to bear on him—is *not* one of the signers. He has never given any express sanction to ' Ritualism ' so called : but while he amiably neglects to put the law of the Church in force against sundry Low Churchmen who openly set it at defiance, he is *not* likely to bring the hand of authority to bear hardly upon the clergy and congregation of S. Alban's, who have broken no law at all.
" The document, then, must be understood chiefly as a demonstration against the Bishop of Vermont's book. Now, at the time of the meeting in October, that book had not been quite *one week* before the public, and many of the Bishops, who were the loudest in denouncing it *had not yet read it.* Moreover, the Bishop of Vermont is the Presiding Bishop, and though it is as allowable to differ in opinion from the Presiding Bishop as from any other Bishop, it is proper that the acknowledged chief of the

Episcopal Order should be treated with a certain degree of respect by his younger brethren.   If he writes an erroneous book, let some one or more of them write a reply which shall disprove and correct the error.   If he have done anything calling for even the lightest form of 'admonition,' the Canons provide for the mode of his trial, when he may have an opportunity to be heard in his own defence: and any combination of his brethren to admonish him in his absence, and in respect to a book which many of them had not even read, would have been a canonical outrage.   To circulate a *Declaration* which shall have the effect of denouncing his book while nevertheless neither his name nor his book are *specifically* alluded to, may be the means of obtaining a larger number of signatures from those who do not understand the real drift of the operation : but it is an act of cowardice in one point of view ; and in another, the signatures thus obtained are obtained practically under false pretences. But both the concealment and the policy of it are of little use, when the "Secretary" himself, while pushing the *Declaration* for signatures, is kind enough to let the cat out of the bag, and inform us that ' the Bishop of Vermont's little book ' was the only 'serious thing' under consideration at the time.   And, moreover, this agrees entirely with what we heard from Bishops themselves during the meeting of the House in October.

" Now, the relation in which we stand to the Presiding Bishop makes it not only our right but our duty to stand up in his defence against this attack from so large a number of his brethren. When so many of those lift up their heel against the venerable hand that was laid upon their heads—when so many of the Fathers turn publicly against the Canonical Chief of their own sacred Order—they must expect as a matter of course that a reverence for that Order will not now be a shield to *them :* for they have themselves beaten it down, or thrown it away.   As we have had occasion to say once before, the Bishops must learn to show due respect to one another, if they are to be properly respected themselves.

" The fact that our own Bishop, the Bishop of New York, has *not* signed the *Declaration*, is only an additional reason, to us, for exercising our rightful freedom in regard to it.   Though, as we have said before, he has not expressed any approval of the so-called ' Ritualism,' nor is likely so to do, yet we are informed that, in the discussion on the subject in the House of Bishops, he ridiculed the Anti-ritualistic crusade as a " Mrs. Partington

kind of business;'' plainly told the Bishops that they could no
more keep down the Ritualistic movement by their " *Declaration* " than they could keep down the rising tide with a broom ;
and that the general average of our parochial services in this
country might yet bear very considerable improvement, with
great gain to the cause of the Church.   The Twenty-eight Bishops
have since then been nearly five months hard at work with their
broom, notwithstanding : and the above *Declaration* is the result.   Ten years, or five years, or even one year hence, we shall
be willing to abide by the confession of any one of the Twenty-
eight as to the comparative height of the tide, and as to the probable effect of their *Declaration* upon its rise.

   " During the months of preparation—though the original Circular was headed ' ☞ *This paper is to be regarded as private
and confidential, until completed by the signatures of Bishops* '—
its coming was heralded, or its appearance demanded—by the
Episcopalian and (we believe) by every other Church paper, as
well as by the *Church Review.*   The *Church Journal* paid
respect to the ' private and confidential ' mark at the head of
it, and made no allusion to the document whatever.   For the
credit of the House of Bishops, we hoped that such a document
would really never appear.   We knew it would do more to advance the cause of Ritualism than anything else could do.   But
all the opponents of Ritualism felt sure that the expected *Declaration* would be a great gun, whose discharge would shatter Ritualism
in pieces.   It has at last been fired off, and turns out to be but a
blank cartridge.   It will make some noise for a short time, and
then be comparatively—for the signers' sakes, would that it could
be *wholly*—forgotten.   And that will be all.

   " We ask our readers to preserve the *Declaration* for a close
comparison with what we shall say of it hereafter, in proving our
position that it is but a ' blank cartridge.'

   " The *Declaration* set forth by the Twenty-eight Bishops is, as
we have said, a mere blank cartridge.   It is—so far as its main
object is concerned—mere sound, with no substance whatever.

   " First of all, the *Whereases* prove that the House of Bishops
itself regarded it as ' inexpedient to proceed to any formal action '
on the subject : which is as much as to say that what is now published by the Twenty-eight does not call for any formal recognition, as binding on any person whatsoever.

   " Next, those *Whereases* prove that the *Declaration* does not
claim to be anything more than ' an expression of opinion ; '

which amounts to nothing with anybody who feels that he has sufficient grounds for a different opinion of his own. The worth of an opinion depends entirely upon the competency of the parties concerned to form and express ' an opinion as *is* an opinion.' At the time when the Bishop of Vermont's book appeared, there were not six men in the House of Bishops who could have told the difference between a chasuble and a cope, without first being informed by somebody else. And the opinion of the Twenty-eight cannot be expected to command any general acquiescence, when the signers of it do *not* include those Bishops who are the highest of their Order in age, or in learning, or in the importance of their Dioceses.

" The *Whereases* contain a still further phrase, which nullifies the whole document, and really turns it into a palpable farce. It is this : ' The undersigned Bishops, *reserving each for himself his rights as Ordinary of his own Diocese,* and also his rights as *a member of the House of Bishops* sitting in General Convention, do unite in the *Declaration* following,' etc. That is to say, the signers of this ' opinion' expressly *repudiate* the idea *that any one of them is to be bound by it,* either in the administration of his own Diocese, or in his votes in General Convention ! Now, if the signers themselves are not to be bound by it, in the name of common sense who else *is ?* Was ever such an *opinion* set forth before ? Do not the signers themselves here invite everybody to treat their opinion with the same contempt which they thus pour upon it themselves ?

" To proceed with the substance of the *Declaration.*

" In the first paragraph, about Article XXXIV., there is nothing to be objected to, except that ' the peculiarities of this country and its people' cannot be regarded as in all respects what they were ' immediately after the American Revolution.' ' Times and men's manners ' have manifested many shades of diversity since then. And this change has been the greatest precisely in those directions which have the closest relation to a practical increase of Ritualism. The XXXIVth Article, therefore, is a much better authority in favor of many and great changes, than it can possibly be for preserving the precise style of celebrating the services which prevailed ' immediately after the American Revolution.' Nay, there is hardly one of the signers who can point to a single church in his Diocese where the ritualistic standard is now *as low* as it was in the days referred to. The Bishops themselves could not endure the baldness, coldness, and poverty of it; and if they tried to force it on their clergy and people, the attempt would be in vain. We have all happily advanced so far, that no Diocese in the land could bear to go back again to *that*. And a paragraph which logically means that, if it means anything, is only a ' blank cartridge.'

" The positive part of the next paragraph, declaring the obligation of the subscription of Conformity required in Article 7 of the Constitution, is well enough meant; but it is so curiously worded as to limit the obligation to ' the ceremonies, rites, and worship *then* established, ordained, and approved by common authority,'—to wit, ' *immediately* after the American Revolution.' Now, inasmuch as the American Revolution took place in 1776, and was completed by the Peace of 1783, this ' immediately ' cannot—even with some stretching—be made to include more than the work of 1789, which set forth the Prayer-Book proper, down to the end of the Psalter (which is therefore the last item in its Table of Contents). The Twenty-eight, there-fore, do actually *exclude* from ' the Law of this Church,' the Ordinal, adopted in 1792—*sixteen years* after the ' American Revolution ; ' and also the Form of Consecration of a church or chapel, adopted in 1799; the Articles of Religion, adopted in 1801 ; and the Institution Office, adopted in 1808 ; which were subsequent to the American Revolution *twenty-three, twenty-five,* and *thirty-two years,* respectively ! And no reference is made to the *Digest* as being any part of ' the Law of this Church ! ' Of course they did not mean this ; but they have actually *said* it ; and we have a right to interpret strictly the language of a document which attempts to impose an intolerable strictness of construction as binding upon other people.

" But the negative part of that same paragraph is equally queer —if it is to be understood as it stands, that (beyond the ' usages ' which prevailed immediately after the American Revolution) ' no strange or foreign *usages* should be introduced or sanctioned by the private judgment of any member or members of this Church, Clerical or Lay.' There is no coherence between this part of the sentence and the positive part that precedes it. The one refers only to *law,* the other only to *usages.* The position is, that whereas certain things were made *law* in 1789, therefore *other* things which were *not* made law at that time, or at any other, ought never to change from what they were in 1789. To state a precisely similar case : The Constitution of the United States, adopted in 1787, forbids the making of sumptuary laws, so that the style of hats to be worn nowaday is not regulated by law. *Therefore*, it was wrong ever to change the style of hats worn in this country, ' no strange or foreign ' styles of hats should ever have been introduced here from Paris or elsewhere ; and all loyal gentlemen should *now* wear only the cocked hats that were in use at the time when the Constitution was adopted in 1787. Verily, ' here is wisdom ! '   The old three-decker arrangement of the chancel ; the duet between parson and clerk ; the total disuse of chanting—all the canticles being *everywhere* read ; the total disuse of the cross as a visible symbol ; the total ignor-ance of Gothic architecture ; the celebration of the Holy Com-munion only three or four times in a year in the most advanced parishes ; the almost universal celebration of baptisms, marriages, and funerals in private houses ;—all these ' usages ' were right, and should never have been changed !   And the changes from time to time made in these and other respects—the altered cut of the surplice so that we have now half a dozen varieties at least ; the change of the old scarf into a fringed stole ; the use of more or less embroidery on both surplice and stole ; the preach-ing in the surplice ; the disuse of that ridiculous and flimsy ap-pendage, the bands ; the dispensing with breeches, and silk stockings, and shoe-buckles ; the chanting of the canticles ; the changes of chancel arrangement by which due prominence was given to the altar ; the introduction of large stone fonts in-stead of baptismal bowls ; the introduction of the lectern for the Bible and the faldstool for the Litany ; the bringing in of Easter flowers, and Christmas-trees, and anthems, and boy choristers, and surpliced choirs, and antiphonal chanting, and choral ser-vices, and daily prayers, and weekly Eucharists, and many other things that might be named—all these are ' strange or foreign usages ' that ought *not* to have been ' introduced or sanctioned by the private judgment of any member or members of this Church, Clerical or Lay ' ; and yet that is precisely the way in which they all *were* introduced, and many other similar changes ; and the process will go on just as rapidly after this *Declaration* as before—if not a little more so.   And what do the Twenty-eight propose to do about it ?   Legislate our present liberty away ?   No : they expressly repudiate that !   Enforce this their present ' opinion,' each in his own Diocese ?   No : they expressly repudiate *that*.   Do they think that those Bish-ops who do *not* sign it will enforce the opinion any better than those who do ?   Hardly !   The ' Secretary ' who circulated the

Declaration for signatures, says expressly: ' For one, I am disposed to vote, in the House of Bishops, that *all* questions about ' blue and purple and scarlet ' should *lie on the table*, to be called up only when ' the beauty of holiness ' shall be more visible among us. This is just what the Ritualistic party want, and *all* that they want in this matter. The Church of America *now leaves to her children a larger liberty on all these subjects than is at present to be found in any other branch of the Catholic Church.* The Ritualists are determined to *use* that liberty for the restoration of ' the beauty of holiness,' to the utmost of their power. And the ringleader in getting up this implied censure upon the Presiding Bishop and the Bishop of New York —himself kindly assures the Ritualists that until " ' the beauty of holiness ' shall be more visible among us "—that is to say, *until the Ritualists shall have done their work—he* will vote for *laying on the table* all measures which would tend to abridge the present liberty which is now left to them by the law. Was there ever, then, a *blanker* cartridge than this *Declaration ?* "

But there is more, and stranger, yet to come !

" The third paragraph of the *Declaration* of the Twenty-eight begins with reaffirming the assertion in the Preface of the Prayer-Book, that ' this Church is far from intending to depart from the Church of England in any essential point of doctrine, discipline, or worship ; or further than local circumstances require ; ' and asserting that we are ' a particular and National Church ' : which is right enough. They then go on to say, ' that no Prayer-Book of the Church of England, in the reign of whatever sovereign set forth, and no Laws of the Church of England, have any force of Law in this Church such as can be justly cited in defence of any *departure from the express Law of this Church*, its Liturgy, its discipline, rites, and usages.' The whole pith of this lies in the vague word ' usages ' at the end of it. The ' express Law of this Church ' does not recognize mere ' usages ' as being subject to ' law ' at all. The insertion of the word in this connection is equivalent to sending the gentlemen of the present day back to the cocked hats of their great-grandfathers in the year 1787. Yet, if that word be omitted, the whole paragraph, with all its formidable sound, hits nobody, and nothing. Nobody claims the right, from merely English Law, to make ' any departure from *the express Law* of this Church.' The *only* question is in regard to cases where there is *no* ' express Law of this Church.' Blank cartridge again !

"We might easily dismiss this point here, but we cannot consent that the Twenty-eight Bishops shall attempt, by an informal opinion, to stultify the action of their own House *as a House*, in times when the true principles of the changes made 'immediately after the American Revolution' were much better understood, and that by the very men who made them.

"The whole question turns, not on 'the express Law' of the Church of America, but on matters which *are not mentioned* in the 'express Law' of the Church of America, though they *are* mentioned in the 'express Law' of the Church of England. And the House of Bishops has expressed itself at least *twice* on the subject, once as touching the question of the English *Canons*, and once as touching the question of *Rubrics* dropped from the American Book.

"First as to the Canons :—In 1808, the question of the Prohibited Degrees came before the House of Bishops on a message from the Lower House. This is a subject on which our American Church legislation is totally silent, but on which the English Canon law speaks with perfect distinctness, setting forth the table of *thirty* degrees which are prohibited 'by the law of God.' Some have thought that the 'Law of God' does not so clearly forbid *all* the degrees there enumerated : and it is evident that the House of Bishops thought that *possibly* some alterations might be made in it '*without* departing from the law of God.' This makes the case still stronger, for it proves that the 'obligatory' character of that English Canon was derived simply from the fact that it *was* English Canon, which the Church of America had not yet seen fit to '*alter.*' We quote from the Journal of 1808 :

"The House of Bishops, having taken into consideration the message sent to them by the House of Clerical and Lay Deputies, relative to the subject of marriage, as connected with the Table of Degrees within which, according to the Canons of the Church of England, marriage cannot be celebrated, observe as follows :

"'Agreeably to the sentiment entertained by them *in relation to the whole ecclesiastical system*, they consider *that Table* as *now obligatory on this Church*, and *as what will remain so ; unless* there should *hereafter* appear cause to *alter* it, without departing from the Word of God, or endangering the peace and good order of this Church.'

"This decision was sent down to the Lower House, and was ac-

cepted without one word of opposition there. So that we have
the distinct authority of the whole General Convention (Bishop
White presiding in the Upper House at the time), declaring that
English Canons, *when not expressly altered* by our own Church,
are ' *now obligatory* ' upon ' this Church,' and ' will remain so '
until we *do* ' alter ' them ; and that this is the principle upon
which our ' *whole ecclesiastical system* ' rests.   So much for
Canons.

" Now for *Rubrics.*—The English Prayer-Book has a Rubric
after the third Collect, in both Morning and Evening Prayer, as
follows : ' ¶ *In Quires and Places where they sing, here fol-
loweth the Anthem.*' This Rubric is entirely *omitted* in our
American Book. According to the principles of the *Declaration,*
the singing of Anthems not provided for by ' express law ' immediately thenceforward became ' an innovation which violates
the discipline of the Church, offendeth against its common order, and hurteth the authority of the Magistrate, and woundeth
the consciences of the weak brethren.' But is that what *the
House of Bishops* thought about Anthems in the year 1814,
when Bishop White again was presiding, and Bishop Hobart sat
with him ? Let us consult once more the Journal of the House
of Bishops, and see what was their ' resolve,' when it was *supposed* that the ' express law ' of the American Church was needed
in order to *sanction* the acting upon a Rubric which had been
dropped :

" ' *Resolved,* That it is not expedient, during this Convention,
to go into a review, either in whole or in part, of the Book of Common Prayer. It could not, however, but give satisfaction to the
Bishops to recollect, that Anthems taken from Scripture, and
judiciously arranged, may, according to the known allowance of
this Church, be sung in congregations at the discretion of their
respective ministers.'

" This too, like the other, was formally sent down to the Lower
House, and was there received without one word of remonstrance.
Now, this decision touching Anthems could not have rested upon
what was then the American *usage,* for it is notorious that at that
time they had only just begun to chant some of the Canticles
(an innovation which then created a greater outcry of ' Popery '
than the Choral Service does now), and Anthems had as yet
been introduced *nowhere* on this side of the water. Therefore it
is undeniable that we here have the House of Bishops declaring,
and the Lower House accepting, the position that a practice

which rested solely on an English Rubric *dropped from the American* Book, might still be *continued* as being ' *according to the known allowance of this Church;* ' and that, although the practice itself had thus far *never* been known on this side of the water.

" These resolutions explain fully the true meaning of the phrase in the Preface of the Prayer-Book, ' this Church is far from in- ending to depart from the Church of England in any essential point of doctrine, discipline, or worship, *or* further than local circumstances require.' The true meaning of this is evidently, that this Church is not only far from intending to depart from the Church of England *in essentials*, but is also *far from intending* to depart from the Church of England in *any* respect ' further than local circumstances require.' The ' local circumstance ' that Bishop Seabury had received consecration from the Scottish Bishops, signing a *Concordat* in regard to the Scottish Communion Office, *required* that certain additions from the Scottish Book should be made in our Eucharistical Canon. The local circumstance that we had been for 150 years without Bishops here, until Church feeling had so nearly died out that it was hopeless to dream of *enforcing* the old Rubrics in all their minuteness and stringency, *required* that those Rubrics should be *dropped*, so that those who disliked their operation *might be under no fear of compulsion* in that direction by the discipline of the Church. Where a Rubric has been *dropped*, Bishops and Ecclesiastical courts cannot *compel* their observance. But where the observance has not been *prohibited*, and where nothing has been *put in the place* of a dropped Rubric, there the Clergy and Congregations are left free to practise the old Rubric, or not, just as they please ; and no Bishop has power to *compel* them either to do it or to let it alone. The observance of such a dropped Rubric is, not ' the express Law,' but ' *the known allowance of this Church.*'

" Now, what the House of Bishops thus term ' *the known allowance* ' of still acting upon a *dropped Rubric*, is the exact principle on which the whole Ritualistic controversy turns. In the English Book, just before Morning Prayer, we have the following Rubric :

" ' The Morning and Evening Prayer shall be used in the accustomed place of the Church, Chapel, or Chancel ; Except it shall be otherwise determined by the Ordinary of the place. And the Chancels shall remain as they have done in times past.'

" And here it is to be noted, that such Ornaments of the

Church and of the ministers thereof at all times of their Ministration, shall be retained and be in use as were in this Church of England by the Authority of Parliament, in the second year of the Reign of King Edward the Sixth.

" Now, we have not *altered* this Rubric in the American Book. We have not put something else in place of it. We have simply *omitted it altogether*, just as was done with the Rubric about Anthems. At that time, *Anthems* were practically as completely unknown in America as Albes and Chasubles and Copes. Now, if one part of the above dropped Rubric is illegal in America it is all illegal : and therefore the American clergyman has no right to say the Morning and Evening Prayer from the Chancel, nor have we any right to arrange the Chancel itself as we do. There is absolutely not the scrape of a pen in the shape of *American* legislation to justify what is our universal practice. The Twenty-eight bishops would sweep away the lawfulness of our present custom with the besom of destruction. But happily, their position, which is as untenable in regard to the ' Ornaments of the Church and of the Ministers thereof at all times of their Ministration,' as in regard to all the rest—is a mere *innovation*, unknown to the Fathers of the American Church, who have left on record their deliberate and unanimous judgment to the contrary, both as to Canons and Rubrics. There is no doubt that the venerable Bishop White wrote with his own hand both the Resolutions which we have quoted above from the old Journals of the House of Bishops : Resolutions which have been the basis on which *all* the improvements of the past half-century in our mode of celebrating divine service have been quietly and steadily builded up. They embody the principle upon which ' our whole ecclesiastical system ' rests. They cannot be expunged now by the *innovations* of Bishops who seem totally to forget the past, in their anxiety to arrest the progress of the present, and block all further advance in the future.

" As rockets reserve their most brilliant coruscations for the last, and shine the brightest just before leaving nothing of their glory but the stick : so the *Declaration* of the Twenty-eight Bishops reserves its most extraordinary features for the closing paragraphs. With a ' therefore '—based upon the foundation which we have totally destroyed with the Resolutions of the House of Bishops in 1808 and 1814—they go on to denounce certain ' usages ' which (as they say) ' have *never been known* ' (*sic*) ! What *can* the Twenty-eight Fathers mean ? If these things ' have never been known,' how happened *they* to have heard of them, and to have come out so strongly against them? And as if once using this strange word was not enough, they afterwards condemn also ' the adoption of clerical habits *hitherto unknown !* ' Now as this language is perfectly plain, we have a right to conclude that the Twenty-eight Fathers mean to condemn only such things as ' *have never been known,*' and such habits as are ' *unknown hitherto* ' : and of course—except by some non-natural interpretation—they cannot mean the doings of the Ritualistic party, for *they* have been known by the most general newspaper clamor of our day—in English papers and American, High-Church, Low-Church, Broad-Church, and No-Church—for some years past. How the Bishops could describe such doings as things ' that have *never* been *known,*' is beyond our comprehension, unless they were determined that their *Declaration* should be laughed at. And they actually specify, as things that have ' never been known,' the use of incense and lights during the Holy Communion —things that are notoriously almost as ancient and as universal as the Episcopate itself ; and much *more* ancient and universal than such Bishops as these Twenty-eight.

" But, as if this were not enough, they next condemn such ' reverences to the Holy Table or to the elements thereon ' as ' indicate or imply that the Sacrifice of our Divine Lord and Saviour, " *once* offered," was *not* a full, perfect, and sufficient sacrifice, oblation and satisfaction, for the sins of the whole world.' When we first read this, we could hardly believe our eyes. But, concluding—as we are forced to do—that the simple historical fact on the subject is one of the things ' that have *never been known* ' to the Twenty-eight, we do assure them, upon the honor of one who happens to know what he is talking about, that there is not now, and there never has been in any age any branch of the Catholic Church in any land, that has held that ' the Sacrifice of our Divine Lord and Saviour " *once* offered," was *not* a full, perfect, and sufficient sacrifice, oblation and satisfaction, for the sins of the whole world : ' and therefore that it is a simple *impossibility* that any reverences or other acts or gestures whatsoever *could* ' indicate or imply ' a doctrine which no Catholic Christian has ever held. The knowledge of theology indicated by this most extraordinary phrase of the *Declaration* is such as we should not have been surprised at in Dr. Cumming or Mr. Spurgeon : but in our own Bishops, and *Twenty-eight* of *them !* Oh!

" But perhaps this was only another device to insure that the 'big gun' should prove a blank cartridge after all. As only those 'reverences' are condemned which 'indicate or imply' an impossibility, of course no censure is expressed against any 'reverences' which are *actually in use* anywhere in Christendom. Is that it? Certainly nothing else can be made of it!

"But no! All the above, together with 'material alterations' of the clerical habits 'which have been in use since the establishment of our Episcopate' are in a lump, condemned in the language of the XXXIVth Article. To introduce any one of all the above enumerated 'abominations' is declared by the Twenty-eight to be 'an innovation which violates the discipline of the Church, offendeth against its common order, and hurteth the authority of the Magistrate, and woundeth the consciences of the weak brethren.' What is here declared to be a thing that 'violates the discipline of the Church,' we have already proved, *by the House of Bishops,* to be 'according to the *known allowance* of this Church.' It cannot 'offend against its common order,' because it is a matter upon which the Church hath made no 'order' at all. And as to 'hurting the Authority of the Magistrate,' what *can* the Twenty-eight Fathers mean? Is the *Mayor of New York* to send a squad of police to stop the singing of Anthems in Trinity Church? Or is *Governor Fenton* to interfere to compel the clergy of St. Alban's to put out the lights on the altar, to give up a violet chasuble, to preach in a black gown, and *not* to bow at the Sacred Name? What *can* the Twenty-eight have been thinking of when they thus referred, in this connection, to the 'authority of *the Magistrate?*' We give it up in despair!

" But is there any sufficient reason for them to speak of their '*consciences?*' They use, in quotation marks, the language of the XXXIVth Article, *as if it applied to the case.* That case, be it remembered, is in regard to things of which our American ecclesiastical law says *nothing at all.* Now read the language as it occurs in the Article in its proper connection:

" ' . . . Whosoever through his private judgment, willingly and purposely, doth openly break the traditions and ceremonies of the Church, which be not repugnant to the Word of God, and *be ordained and approved by common authority*, ought to be rebuked openly, (that others may fear to do the like,) as he that offendeth against the common order of the Church, and hurteth the authority of the Magistrate, and woundeth the consciences of the weak brethren.'

"Here it is as clear as daylight, that the language quoted by the Twenty-eight from the Article applies only to those who ' break ' what *has been* ' *ordained and approved by common authority.*' And the Twenty-eight, without one word of qualification, apply it solely to the case of things which have *not* been ' ordained and approved by common authority,' nor even so much as *mentioned* in the legislation of the Church! Is that *honesty ?* Is it a fair specimen of the Episcopal ' *conscience ?* ' Why, it entirely beats anything to be found in Tract No. 90, or the ' Eirenicon ! ' But ' peradventure it was an oversight.'

" Two other proofs of the utter emptiness of this ' blank cartridge ' yet remain to be noticed.

" The last paragraph of all is devoted to Low-Church irregularities ; by way of trimming the boat, we suppose, and to give an impression of fairness and impartiality. The proportion of Episcopal attentions is, indeed, rather unequal. It is a proportion of *thirteen* lines belaboring and denouncing those whose only object is to render more glorious the service of God, to one line bearing upon those who have set at defiance the fundamental prerogative of the whole Episcopal Order, and recognize Presbyterian ordination as valid, and get Presbyterians to assist in consecrating the Holy Communion in our own churches. This proportion of thirteen to one puts us in mind of Falstaff's tavern bill : ' What, only one ha'penny-worth of bread to this intolerable deal of *sack ?* ' However, the Twenty-eight ' include in these censures *all departures* from *the Laws, rubrics and settled order of this Church, as well by defect* as by excess of observance, designing to maintain in its integrity the sound Scriptural and Primitive, and therefore the Catholic and Apostolic, spirit of the Book of Common Prayer.' And this is signed by all the Low-Church Bishops in the House. The Declaration is *unanimously* signed by *their* Bishops ; yet how much will *they* mind it ? Does not everybody know that *that part* of it will be treated by the Low-Church party as a farce ? And is it to be supposed that those of the other party, whose Bishops are *not* unanimous, will treat it with any greater respect on *their* side ? And yet, without this transparent farce at the end, the *Declaration* would hardly have received signatures enough to bear publication at all.

" Once more: In the original circular of the *Declaration* sent out by the Committee for the signatures of Bishops, there was the following address from the Committee to each individual Bishop :

" ' Rt. Rev. Brother—The following draught of a paper to be signed by such of the Bishops as may approve of its purport, was made by the undersigned committee, appointed at the late meeting of the House of Bishops, and is now sent in order that you may, if you desire to do so, subscribe your name, and return it to the Secretary of the Committee. He will then send to each Bishop the document, with all its signatures printed, leaving to each Diocesan his own course as to its publication, or reception, in his own Diocese.'

" It is thus kindly provided, by the getters up of the *Declaration* themselves, that it shall not be considered as either ' published ' or ' received ' in any Diocese whose Bishop does not choose that it *shall* be published and received. It is thus certain that—whatever be its fate elsewhere—it is a perfectly ' blank cartridge ' in the Dioceses of Vermont, New York, Pennsylvania, Maryland, and others—sixteen Dioceses, and among them the most powerful on the list. Indeed, as it is left to ' each Diocesan ' to take ' his own course as to its publication, or reception, in his own Diocese,' we have a right to conclude that where it has not been specially published by the Bishop of a Diocese, his merely having signed it is to go for nothing. Except the Dioceses of Massachusetts, Ohio, and Iowa, then, and two or three more, the *Declaration* may be considered, in all the Dioceses of the United States, as one of the ' things that *never were known.*'

" But that original circular (which is no longer ' private and confidential ' now, being ' completed by the signatures of Bishops ') concludes with a notable proof of the fatality of style which makes this *Declaration* read in some parts so much like a broad joke. Not content with censuring ' usages that have *never been known,*' and condemning ' clerical habits *hitherto unknown,*' and talking of a doctrine concerning the sacrifice of Christ that was never held anywhere, and quoting the language of the Article for the precise *opposite* of its real bearing, and the refusal to be bound by an opinion which they set forth expressly to influence others, and the talk about ' the authority of the *Magistrate* ' as having anything to do with Ritualism in this country, not content with all this, we say, that *Circular*, with singular felicity, closed with the following request :

"☞ *Further delay is not desirable, and as this may fail to reach many Bishops in due course of mail, telegraphic answers are requested in such cases.*

" What could be a better cap-sheaf for such a *Declaration* than such a request?   It is as much as to say—*If you do not receive this letter, please answer immediately by telegraph !*   Nothing else can be made of it.   Perhaps we can now guess the reason why so many Bishops did not reply.   How could they answer a letter which they *never received*, about things which ' were *never known* ' ?

" With this last shout of laughter, let us part with our curious *Declaration* in all good humor.   It has been but a blank cartridge all the while—a little loud and startling to weak nerves at first, perhaps, but doing nobody any harm except the signers. And we bear such good-will to them, that—if they will let us— we shall forget all about it as soon as possible.   We know they did not mean to do it ; and as the document was not framed with the benefit of deliberation in council, they had not a fair chance to do themselves justice.   They must remember that we have been defending *the recorded action of the House of Bishops* in General Convention assembled, against the informal accident of an hour of haste.   We have appealed from Philip a little excited, to Philip quite sober.   And if our appeal has been triumphantly sustained, it is *so much the more to the honor of Philip sober.* Nobody is hurt ; and there is no harm done ; but it would hardly be worth while for them to try it again just in that way."

Perhaps it is not so strange that one who tore to shreds a serious document like the Declaration of the Twenty-eight Bishops, and made it the sport of his sarcastic humor was not believed to be a very genial and warm-hearted, friendly spirited, and sweet-tempered man.   Plenty of others saw the same flaws, plenty of others ridiculed it, plenty of others made light of it, even though their own Diocesans set it forth as a godly admonition, but no one else treated it in quite so cavalier a fashion.

The Declaration was as ineffectual in staying the advance of Ritualism as a child's dam on the shore would be to keep back a Bay of Fundy tide.*

* In 1868 when it was moved in the House of Bishops that the *Declaration* be adopted as an act of the House, the motion was laid upon the table, although a decided majority of the House then present were among the signers.

But the great successes were not yet wrought, although it is easy enough in these later days to say that the whole ocean was advancing.

Mr. Hopkins defended the whole line of the advance. All t'.e efforts for revived use of Catholic ceremonial, for the establishing of a school of true ecclesiastical music, for the building and arranging of churches in pointed style and Catholic manner, for fulness and exactness of doctrinal expression, for the revival of Sisterhoods and Brotherhoods, and all the rest, found in him a sincere, hearty, and constant advocate. He also defended the lines against the first of the Broad Church attacks upon Christianity. This was notably the case in the excitement over the Colenso affair. With Dr. Morgan Dix and Dr. S. H. Tyng, jr., he worked to secure signatures to an " Address," like the one which was signed by so many English clergymen, against Bishop Colenso.

But, though he was so keen against the Broad Church *attacks*, he saw that they were not always made with the deliberate attempt to poison the springs of the Gospel, but were in many cases the recoil from the Calvinism which so many Low Churchmen had been taught was the true Gospel. Broad Churchmen were few in number in those days in America, and he looked upon the few there were with mild toleration, because he felt they were harmless, and were only taking a roundabout road toward Catholicity.

CHAPTER VIII.

1867–1872.

THE Colenso affair caused the assembling of the first Lambeth Conference in 1867, and Mr. Hopkins accompanied his father, the Bishop of Vermont, then the Presiding Bishop, to the meeting of the Conference. Dr. Hopkins always reckoned the Conference a great feature in the life of the Church. Not many seem to value it as highly as he did, although it is to be regularly assembled at intervals of ten years. He probably had at least as much to do with bringing about the first meeting as any other one man, if not more, and so his feeling in the matter was quite natural. He says : " It was early in the year 1851 that my father, in replying to an invitation from Archbishop Sumner to attend the Jubilee of the S. P. G., made the first suggestion of such a gathering as the Lambeth Conference. That letter was printed in the *Guardian* at the time. . . . About a year later, in 1852, the learned and earnest Bishop Wittingham, of Maryland, then in England, repeated the suggestion in a public speech, which gave rise to some discussion on both sides of the water. Still later, in November, 1854, Bishop Fulford, of Montreal, preached the sermon at the consecration of Dr. Horatio Potter as Bishop of New York. He adverted to the new dogma of the Immaculate Conception of the B. V. M., which was within a few days to be proclaimed at Rome, and in that connection stated the yearning of earnest spirits for the meeting of our whole reformed Church in its corporate capacity. The *Church Journal*, on December 7, 1854, said : ' Let the Archbishop of Canterbury invite all the Bishops of the reformed Church to assemble in Canterbury Cathedral to protest against this new blasphemous fable and to reassert in the face of the whole world the ancient Faith, pure and undefiled.' This article drew forth a very interesting letter from that well-known and influential English layman, Mr. F. H. Dickinson, who mentioned that a friend of his, a member of the Lower House of Convocation of Canterbury 'had been thinking of bringing the subject before the House.' Other articles followed in the same paper, from time to time, keeping the idea before the mind of the Church.

"Now I wrote all those articles in the *Church Journal* myself, being the leading editor of that paper. at the time. I had derived all my strong convictions on the subject from my father. The reunion of Christendom was a favorite subject of longing with him. As long ago as 1835, he devoted the last chapter of his work on the *Primitive Church* to that subject. Toward its close he drew a picture of a great universal council of all who call themselves Christians, meeting to settle their differences by the standard of Holy Scripture and Apostolical Tradition. So glorious was the thought, so entire the rapture of his spirit in dwelling on so bright a consummation, that ere he finished he found the tears running down his face as he wrote. The Pan-Anglican he regarded as only one of the preliminary steps, indispensable to the other—the easiest step to take, and the one to be taken first. So familiar was this idea to me that when the carrier of the *Church Journal* applied to me to write some verses for his New Year's Address at the opening of the year 1854, that was the chief topic to which I devoted my attention, branching out from an allusion to the visit of an English Deputation of 1853 to our General Convention of that year. The description may interest some people as a close approximation to a prophecy of an event *previously unprecedented*, and yet made more than twenty-four years in advance of the fulfilment, with a very fair measure of exactness—even in details."

ANTICIPATION OF THE LAMBETH CONFERENCE.

(Written in 1853 for the first annual address of the Carrier of the *Church Journal* for January 1, 1854.)

" From England's realm the assembled Bishops see,
Gathered once more, for solemn Synod free ;—
State shackles—broken, cast off, once for all—
Shall henceforth never more their powers enthrall.
With them their brethren stand—from mountainous **Wales ;**
From Ireland's soft, green hills and richer vales ;
From Scotland's rugged rocks, 'mid northern seas ;
From wide America's outspread domain,
Stretching from sea to sea ; and north again,
Till Greenland, Labrador, and Newfoundland
Send Bishops, too, to join the lengthening band
That come from tropic isles ; and westward, **on,**
Till golden California, Oregon,

And myriad isles that, in their blindness, be
Like emeralds set within a silver sea,
That wait but morning's sun rising in sight,
To leap at once from darkness into light ;
From twin New Zealand's deep-indented shores ;
From vast Australia's mines of shining ores ;
From Borneo, Burmah, China, and Japan ;
From dusky plains and groves of Indostan ;
From dark Caffraria ; from the deadly coasts
Whence slavery long has shipped her shackled hosts ;
From steep Gibraltar's rock—from all the earth,
Sons gather round the cradle of their birth.
In spotless robes I see them move along,
Passing on either hand—a joyous throng—
Then enter through its western portals ; while
Through Canterbury's huge Cathedral pile
Unnumbered thousands with glad voices raise
The overwhelming burst of choral praise.
Up the long nave they pace ; then, mounting higher
And higher, the line ascends the rising choir ;
Till, rank on rank, their numbers multiplied
Compass the Altar round on every side.
There, let the full Te Deum roll and swell ;
The Catholic Creed its faithful oneness tell ;
Then let the sacred Gifts be offered up—
Break the pure Bread and bless the ruddy Cup.
Then, from full hearts, from greatest unto least,
With breath yet fragrant from the heavenly Feast,
The whole immense assembly lift the strain
That, long ago, on Bethlehem's star-lit plain,
Angels began and Saints shall never cease :
'GLORY TO GOD ON HIGH ; AND ON EARTH PEACE !'
In sacred Council seated soon, I see
The assembled Church prepare its firm decree.

—

" But lo ! the sudden shadows envious rise
    And veil the glorious vision from my eyes."

The service in Canterbury Cathedral, indeed, did not take place in 1867, but it was realized in 1878, at the second meeting of the Conference—the procession of an hundred Bishops entering by the western portal (which is very seldom opened), just as described. The Conference was attended by seventy-six Bishops, among whom were nineteen Bishops from the United States, and all signed the Pastoral Letter. Much the fullest account yet given in print of that meeting is to be found in the " Life of Bishop Hopkins, by one of his Sons ; " but John Henry's journal of the visit he made with his father to England and France gives his own account of some of the incidents connected with it, and some parts of it are here given :

THE JOURNAL OF THE VISIT TO ENGLAND AND FRANCE.

"1867, August 14th, Wednesday.—Sailed at 3.30 P.M. from
New York, in steamer Chicago, Captain James Price, with dear
father, Bishop Odenheimer, with Mrs. and Miss Margaret Odenheimer, fellow-passengers.

"August 24th.—St. Bart's. Gale in evening and night.
Nearly ran on Mizen Head in the dark, at 11 P.M. Narrow
escape.

"August 25th, Sunday.—Bright and beautiful. Exquisite
views of Irish coast from Old Head of Kinsale to Tuskar light.
Said Morning Prayer, Litany, and Epistle. Bishop Odenheimer,
Ante-Communion. Father, Absolution and Benediction. No
sermon. In evening, 8 o'clock, said Evening Prayer and father
preached. A very pleasant service. Holyhead light seen before
retiring.

"August 26th, Monday.—Docked in Sandon Dock, Liverpool,
at 8 A.M. after beautiful views of river and city in the morning
light. Queen's Hotel. To Chester at 11 A.M. To cathedral immediately. Old work almost utterly decayed from destructibility
of stone. Modern work utterly abominable. Evening service
beautifully sung by choir. Tallis precessional. Clergyman opening the service could not intone. We returned thanks for a safe
return from sea. Fine anthem. Boys sang very sweetly and
truly. Some fine windows in north and south chancel aisles, and
in aisle of nave. Yellow wash, white light in nave. Exquisite
carvings in choir; fine old canopies; carved oak eagle; *miserere*
seats. Altar arrangements wretched. Plenty of scaling yellow
wash and decay. Bishop's throne semi-modern botch, much
higher than modern pulpit on opposite side. One transept a
parish church—miserable exceedingly. Fine, but decaying old
cloisters, wine vault, etc. Cathedral built in outside with other
houses. Queer old crooked passages in and out. Bells small,
cracked, *mean.* Could not stay a tenth part as long as I wished.
Returned 5.30 P.M."

This was his first view of a real cathedral, and it is not difficult to fancy him with his eager eyes fastening at once upon
all the details of the structures which his imagination had fed
upon for years, and the keen delight with which he saw them at
last.

" August 27th, Tuesday.—9.10 A.M. train to Tebay junction. Bright day.   Beautiful glimpses of Morecambe Bay at Carneforth. Climbed Westmoreland Fells after lunch at Tebay, and had charming views of soft afternoon shadows among the hills.   Lovely hill and valley views on both sides of the way to Durham, with glimpses of Barnard Castle, and Brancepeth Castle.   Glorious views of Durham Cathedral and Castle (now University) in the evening light, about 7 P.M.   Nothing could be more grand, both for substance and position.   Twilight walk around the cathedral. Examination of north side ; then under the tall trees by path around the west end, with the massive walls and terraces, and glimpses down through the trees to the Wear ; then across the Prebend's bridge, and down to the water's edge beyond, with reflection of the cathedral in the water ; then back over the bridge, with lights from the other bridge shining in the water, and other lights twinkling through the trees near the cathedral ; turned to the right, and, through the great gate, entered the winding little street that runs all round the south and east ends of the cathedral, including an immense accumulation of buildings, entering by a very narrow lane the open spaces at the north side.   On my way, entered the great gate of the quadrangle, and walked down a closed passage to the right (all lit by gas-lights) leading to southeast angle of cloisters, and then under the great oak, and round the hall, Dean's kitchen (hexagonal), and the vast entourage of buildings, but found all gates to the cathedral yard closed. Returned to the Waterloo Hotel (queer, quaint old hostel) at nearly 9 P.M.

" August 28th, Wednesday.—At the cathedral for some time before Morning Service with father.   Went through with him (before and after service) nave, choir, and chancel, Galilee, cloisters, old refectory (with bones of a whale), and down to Prebend's bridge, at the farther end of which father made a sketch, while I went along South Street at the top of the hill toward the lower bridge, getting splendid views of the west front of the cathedral and all the other buildings.   Thence to the hotel by the path just below the west front.   At Andrews' got photographs and saw Mr. Le Keux, the ecclesiastical engraver.   After dinner returned, examined Nine Altars, Bishop Hatfield's tomb, etc.   Afternoon service without organ, and exquisitely done. In the anthem (Gibbons) the boys sang like little angels ; but, as in the morning, procession straggling and broken, dirty surplices, slouchy manners, and irreverence.   Altar arrangements an insult to the memory of Cosin. No candlesticks on the altar. Dean's seat on *north* side and Bishop's on the *south* just like it, both curtained off to keep them from seeing the altar. Bishop's throne enormous, over Bishop Hatfield's tomb, but not used. After Evening Service, with a verger, went up staircase at south-west corner of south transept, through walls, triforium, secret passages, looked down into Nine Altars, south transept, nave, went out on leads of south aisle, out of southwest tower to leads of *both* libraries, and returned by the way we went up. Round the cloisters again, and so farewell. Went over to the castle, and saw old tapestry, chairs, Bishop Neile's grand stair-case, the private chapel, and Bishop Pudsey's beautiful doorway. Candles on the altar in the chapel. At 7.20 P.M. left for York, getting another beautiful parting glance at the station, though more gray and sober than the evening before, and several fine glimpses along the road, the last of which—very fine—was after leaving Loamside. Arrived at York before 10 P.M., and imme-diately went for a starlight and gaslight view of the cathedral, which was an exquisite pleasure in its way. Passed all round it from the south transept (the first part seen) to the whole west end, then back along the south and east and north sides from the street. Stopped at Harker's York Hotel; queer, and com-fortable, but not so queer as Waterloo, Durham.

"August 29th, Thursday.—At the cathedral with father. Attended Matins, sitting in a returned stall on south side. Pro-cession entered orderly, but without music. Service admirably done. Anthem, Farrant. Dr. Beckwith's monument with rec-ord of all his bequests! The Evensong still better than the Matins; a charming anthem, (adapted) from Mozart. The or-gan was finely played after service, and the effect of the trumpet stop, the pipes of which are arranged horizontally, opening down the nave, was wonderfully fine. The *echoes* at every close dur-ing the services, and as the organ stopped, were exquisite.

"August 30th, Friday.—Called on Archdeacon Creyke at 8.30 A.M. for an order to admit me to the triforia; but he was not yet up. Visited Bootham Bar and Monk Bar, ascending the latter, and going all through it, and noting its connection with the path that runs along the inside of the city walls. At a little before ten o'clock tried the Archdeacon again and got the written order I wanted, though rather reluctantly and ungraciously. Mr. Temple, the head-mason, admitted me at once, so that I could ascend to the gallery that runs round the lantern of the central tower, just below the great tower windows, when he locked me in until Matins were over. Looking *down* upon all the ornamental work, the *upper* side of it was seen to be terribly dusty—the undisturbed dust of centuries, though from below it looks clean enough. Could not help thinking that thus God, looking down from Heaven, sees the dusty side of all our good deeds, while we, looking at them only from below, think they are fine enough to be reckoned beautiful in *His* sight. On the floor of the gallery saw a little dead sparrow, which had probably been there for a long time. Modern improvement—spurred on by the two fires of this century, which destroyed the woodwork of the chancel and nave—has provided large tanks in the upper part of the central tower, filled with the rain that falls on its top, and iron pipes lead it down to the gallery where I was, where coiled hose-pipes are ready to convey it in any needed direction. The service began ; and at that immense height of nearly one hundred and fifty feet from the floor, every word of the whole was audible, except that the reader of the Lessons used too much voice by far. The effect of the whole was exquisite, and the delicate echoes from all parts of the building, after each close, were finer than when the service is heard below. The Litany gave greatly multiplied opportunities for hearing this effect. After service went with Mr. Temple all through the triforia, which are lathed and plastered at the back of the triforium pillars, the said plaster being painted *black* to conceal the sham. It is to help the operation of the *stoves* in winter, the stove-pipes being led through the walls, and out behind buttresses above the aisle roofs. Gas lights the choir in a straight line under the triforium, and around the heads of the piers in the nave. The aisles only are vaulted with stone, the rest being a wooden sham put up in the last century. The groins over the aisles are not filled up level as at Durham, but left in hills and hollows above. Ascended the western towers to the bells—the wind playing an æolian harp on the l'œvre boards (slats) of the belfry, and stood in the open pinnacle of the west gable of nave.

" The view of the nave from the base of the great west window inside, is the best. After dinner went with father to the new Roman Catholic St. Wilfrid's Church, nearly under the cathedral. It is apsidal, and a very beautiful specimen of the best of modern art. To Sampson's for photographs. At 4.20 P.M. left for Lincoln ; the railroad ride as smoky and dusty as any in America, stopping thirty-five minutes at Doncaster, where I ran up to see the famous parish church, lately restored, or rather, re-built, after the original design. It is cruciform, with very fine central tower, and is very much in the style of York Minster, though more consistently carried out. Arrived at the White Hart in Lincoln a little after 8 P.M. In the dim light we could see the great beauty of the winding ascent of the hill, and the outlook over the plain below. Before supper father went with me to walk round the cathedral, which was close by, and which we passed on our way to the inn. We went all round the west, south, and east fronts and saw partially the north also, with its singular and beautiful Chapter House. The starlight and gas-light gave us a very peculiar and beautiful effect.

" August 31st, Saturday.—Devoted the day to the cathedral. After Matins went all round with father ; and afterward ascended the central tower, the highest in England, and enjoyed a splen-did view, notwithstanding the smoke and mist. Went all the way through the triforia from east end to west, round both tran-septs. Curious irregularities in various parts. The two sides of the northern transept do not correspond, one having twelve open-ings, the other eleven. The west end of the nave, including the great window, is not in the middle, and the roof ridge takes a turn to match. But the whole abounds in exquisite work, *no-where overdone*, and the stone is in much better preservation than at York. The choral service is very well done, and the pronunciation of the words all through the Psalter is *perfectly distinct*, like the voice of one man. But the touches of harmony in the General Confession at York are far superior to the effect of simple monotone, especially when the note, as at Lincoln, drops a third on coming to the Lord's Prayer. The anthems, modern and highly florid, most artistically done ; one of the boys going up to B♭. In the afternoon notified the Rev. Mr. Venables, the precentor (who is the canon in residence), that we would receive the Holy Communion on the morrow. He very politely promised to call on father, which he did at about eight o'clock, and invited us both to dine with him on Sunday. He insisted, too, on lending me one of the volumes of Murray's " Handbook to the Cathedrals," which was very full of useful information. On the whole, both father and I prefer Lincoln to all the cathedrals we have yet seen.

" September 1st, Sunday (Tenth after Trinity).—Attended Matins, the Dean of Stamford (' peculiar ') preaching a fair, moderate, evangelical sermon. After the Offertory the whole congregation (which was the largest we had yet seen in a cathedral) left the stalls and subsellæ, and occupied the modern benches between them and the altar rail (which is modern, brass, and very good, with vine and grapes running the *whole length*, with text in good raised letters, ' I am the true vine,' etc.).   Not a single note of music from that time to the end of the whole service !   The Dean, Jeremie, consecrated at the north end.   No candlesticks on the altar.   Cold and chilling ! —after the beautiful choral service.   Dined at the precentor's. At 3 P.M. the precentor preached in the nave, father declining his repeated invitation to preach for him.   The pulpit was a miserable modern movable one (the new modern pulpit in the choir is splendidly well done), and several hundreds were present, on open movable benches facing the preacher, whose place was between two piers.   A hymn was sung, and then the ' bidding prayer,' closing with the Lord's Prayer, and then the sermon.   At its close another hymn and the blessing.   The sermon was evangelical, but earnest and good—better than the morning. Nearly the whole congregation then went into the choir for Evensong, the entire space of the chancel from the gate up to the altar rail being fairly crowded ; and the service was delightful.   Took tea at the precentor's, and listened to some very pleasant music from Mrs. Venables (from Mendelssohn's ' St. Paul ') and daughters, from ' Hymns, Ancient and Modern.'   Six lovely daughters, none yet old enough to come out, and all promising to be musical.   Went with the precentor to call on Dean Jeremie, an old bachelor, with whom we spent a very pleasant hour.   He is affable, full of information, and a hard-working member of the Ritual Commission (being Regius Professor of Divinity at Cambridge also).   He told us the late partial report was unanimous, though some expressions in it would be interpreted differently by different members of it, and a few were protested against by some.   The tug of the battle was yet to come. Returning, we took supper at the precentor's, and then to our hotel, after a very pleasant day.

   " September 2d, Monday.—At a little after 8 A.M. started for Peterborough, where we arrived just in time to catch the Creed, Preces, Anthem, and Prayers.   Were shown into a stall by the back way.   The distant voices were very sweet as we entered the nave, and heard them from the remote distance.   Left after a short visit, with great regret, buying my photographs of the verger.   Luncheon with father at the station-hotel, where he

had been waiting for me for some time, having in meantime
been writing a poem on the need of some ritualism to warm up
the devotion *glacé* of the present English cathedral service.   At
3 P.M. started for Ely, where we arrived at a little past four
o'clock, catching an exquisite view of the cathedral and city
from the railway just before stopping.   Drove up to the West
End, and caught part of Evensong, as it sweetly echoed down
the nave.   Quietly we went up together, and took the first we
came to of the open seats in the nave.   The Anthem was admirable, and most charmingly sung, ' O pray for the peace of
Jerusalem.'   Were perfectly delighted with the modern work
under G. G. Scott, which has now been twenty-eight years in
execution.   For the first time in a cathedral, the altar was *not*
the meanest part of the church, but the most gorgeous.   The
altar-cloth was of exquisite needlework ; the reredos of alabaster,
adorned with jewels, colored marble mosaics, and most exquisite
carvings.   Five scenes from our Lord's life are sculptured in high
relief immediately over the altar, in alabaster, partially colored
and gilded ; and exquisite figures scattered all over the reredos
throughout, and as finials.   Much of the old woodwork has been
renewed or restored in excellent taste.   The woodwork of the
choir is all new, and with a wonderful series of carvings in wood,
done in Belgium from English designs, the Old Testament being
on the south side, and the New on the north.   The old rood-
screen is gone, and a new and open one takes its place—to my
regret, in some measure—with the rood in the middle.   It is
very rich and good, in oak ; but has no returned stalls, except
one seat for the Bishop (it is a local peculiarity of Ely that
there is no episcopal throne in the usual place) on the south
side, next the wall, and a similar one for the Dean on the north,
with tabernacles rising far higher than the cross in the centre.   The carvings on the ends of the bookboards in the stalls
and subsellæ, with finials of angels, are beautiful.   The ruins of
the north part of the west end are painfully visible, and other
fragments of ruin appear here and there, but *picturesquely* everywhere.   The Bishop lives in the Close, and quaint and beautiful
paths lead round to the various houses, with many fine trees.
The famous octagonal lantern, which I was prepared to admire
most, pleased me least.   It is evidently a makeshift by those who
had not courage or liberality to rebuild the central tower when
it fell down.   The restoration of the exterior is unsatisfactory in
point of color.   It was hard to tear myself away from this most

magnificent specimen of *modern* work that is good. In the
Choral Service—which is admirably well done—the Confession
is the same as at York ; but they were just then very deficient in
the bass, Durham, York, and Lincoln having voices that went
down to EE, DD, and in one case to CC.

"September 3d, Tuesday.—Raining hard, but went with
father to the cathedral to Matins. Anthem again very beautiful. 'The valleys shall stand so thick with corn that they shall
laugh and sing.' The rain had grown to a thunder-storm, and
while it was so dark that the two standards of gaslights on the
rood screen had to be lit (with beautiful effect upon the woodwork), the lightning flashes illuminated the whole church, and the
peals of accompanying thunder added sublimity to the effect of
the music within. The pattering of the driving rain on the
triforium roofs was very audible, but every word of the *musical*
service was heard through it all without difficulty. After service
saw father home to the Lamb inn, and then returned to study
the stained glass and the ceiling, which I did till my neck ached
almost past endurance. Met in the nave Mr. Taylor, the author
of a number of antiquarian works, and Mr. Charles Minet, of
the Athenæum Club, who kindly offered to give father the en-
trée there during his stay in London. But the talking with
these two, though pleasant, cheated me out of my ascent to the
triforium. At 1.47 P.M. (or rather, half an hour *later*) set out
for Norwich in the rain, where we arrived just as it had cleared,
and in time for Evensong at the cathedral. The shabbiest
service we have yet attended. Not a boy wore a surplice. The
Magnificat and Nunc dimittis were only chanted. The Anthem
needed much more practice, but there was one boy's voice more
delicious in quality of tone than any other we have heard. The
service over, the boys and the rest of the choir went out higgledy
piggledy.

"The woodwork of the choir is in shabby condition. The
restorations now going on are in vile style. The new Dean,
Goulburn, has not had time yet to make himself properly felt.
There is more of ruin, carelessness, chronic and disgusting neglect *here* than in all the other cathedrals we have visited put together. But there are many fine things nevertheless. The
entrance to the cathedral Close, through the Erpingham gate, is
fine. The use of flint with other stone is peculiar and pleasing.
The Norman work is a study in itself; and so is the way in
which the subsequent styles have injured it. The triforium is

larger than ever, and *one* high open arch, without subdivisions,
surmounts each arch of the nave below.   The subsequent *windows* inserted have spoiled it as a *blind* story.   The apse is admirable in effect.   The altar the meanest part of the church, of
course.   The quaint old Norman chapels on the southeast very
'peculiar.   The cloisters are perfect on all four sides.   Nearly
every present residence in the Close has its own pet bit of ruin,
some of them picturesquely covered with ivy.

"September 4th, Wednesday.—Attended the 8.30 A.M. service, which was Choral, with Litany, but without Anthem.
Boys in jackets and trousers as before.   Went round the church
carefully, inside the old Norman chapels, up the triforium and
upper walk above the triforia.   At 11.15 started from the Maid's
Head for London, *via* Ipswich and Colchester; where we arrived,
through rain nearly all the way, at 4.30, and took cab for Westminster Palace Hotel; in reaching which cabby took us twice
across the Thames, giving us fine views.   Walked out with father, and got a look at the Abbey and the Parliament House,
and a new drinking fountain now being erected near by in beautiful style, with marbles, tiles, colors, and gold.   After dinner,
while father was enjoying his pipe, walked out alone, crossed
Westminster Bridge, getting an exquisite view of the Parliament
House with the young moon behind it, and the reflection of both
in the water.   Turned to the left on the other side, and walked
to Lambeth Palace and around the outer wall.   Inquired on my
return past the gate, and learned from the porter that the Archbishop is not in town.   Returned over Lambeth Bridge, and
back to the Parliament House, walking along its northward front.
It is an immense building, and the great tower is superior in
effect, as in size, to any I have ever before seen.   Found the
Abbey exterior more imposing than I had thought at first, both
for size, height, and proportion.   The cleaning process now going on makes it look droll—part cream color or whiter, and
part black as ink.   Returned to the hotel to study the map and
prepare for to-morrow's work.

"September 5th, Thursday.—Attended Matins in the Abbey.
The service not very well done—not equal to Durham, York,
Lincoln, or Ely.   Went partially the rounds, with the guide,
through the chapels.   Was disgusted with the shabbiness of many
things, especially the coronation chair, which is partially decayed or mutilated, and cut over with people's names like an old
schoolboy's desk, looking dirty, mean, and fit only for a rubbish

heap. Restoration is going on, but slowly. Things will be better by and by. The loftiness of the building is great, but too great for its strength. All the aisle arches are bound together with iron rods, *both* ways. (Mr. Foster, clerk of the works, tells me this iron was needlessly inserted by Christopher Wren.) Some of the monuments of Queen Elizabeth's days are the stiffest and ugliest possible. Modern abominations abound. The rabble of modern monuments has indeed taken possession, and they mean to hold it. Henry the Seventh's Chapel is at present in dirty condition. The banners over the knights' stalls have not been changed since 1812, when the last public installation took place, and *all* those whose banners—dusty and dropping to pieces—were then hanging, are now dead. Installations are now by commission from the Privy Council.

" The effects of *light* in the Abbey were glorious this morning, there being a sort of mist, as of incense clouds, through the whole upper part of the building, and the sun's rays made bright beams through the air wherever they shone in. The modern pulpit in the nave is very good. St. Edward's shrine was to me the most interesting monument, though far from showing its original beauty. It is but a mutilated remnant. Walked all the way to our bankers, at Founder's Court, Lothbury, through Whitehall Street, Charing Cross, the Strand, under Temple Bar, through Fleet Street, up Ludgate Hill, past St. Paul's, etc., seeing many famous sites (no pun intended) on my way. Entered St. Paul's on my return, and looked round. The greater part of the exterior is black as ink. Found the interior rather more imposing than I had expected : but as soulless as any Protestant could desire. Lord Nelson's monument, with a big British lion, is *inside the chancel.* Modern monuments, of the patriotic and loyal order, have the whole field to themselves.

" September 6th, Friday.—At the Abbey again, at Matins, and took another walk through the chapels and Poet's Corner. Service rather poor. Returning to the hotel, found the Rev. Thomas W. Perry at the door, and took him up to our room to see father. Had a very pleasant call from him, and much very interesting conversation. It was at the suggestion of Mr. Gladstone and Sir Robert Phillimore (the new ecclesiastical judge) that father's ' Law of Ritualism ' was reprinted here in a cheap edition. Dr. Pusey told him that he had learned from the French bishops things that would greatly surprise the Pope ! The movement among Romanists toward something better is broad and deep.

" Visited St. Alban's, Holborn, but not in service-time. It is approached only through two very narrow and crooked streets swarming with the poorest sort of people, and looks as if it were *used* all the time. It is open every day from 6.30 A.M. till 9 P.M. There is daily communion, and there are *four* celebrations every Sunday; at 7, 8, 9, and 11 o'clock. The church is beautifully fitted up in the interior, the walls being of colored brick, and the chancel richly decorated. The east wall is covered with paintings of scriptural subjects, drawn by L'Estrange, the same who painted the ceiling of Ely. The reredos is richly gilded. There are *five* priests attached to the church, at work all the time, and the work is so severe that they are soon used up. Happened into Lincoln's Inn, was greatly struck by the peculiarities of the place.

" September 7th, Saturday.—Busy all the morning. After dinner, did the Parliament House, finding much more for admiration than I had expected. The Victoria Tower is the finest tower in Europe; and the Clock Tower, with its chiming quarters, is one of the chief pleasures of staying at the Westminster Palace Hotel.

" The wall-paintings are very fine—the two great pictures of Maclise—the Death of Nelson, and the Meeting of Wellington and Blucher after Waterloo—well worth a most patient study. *Apropos* of civil wars, it is instructive to see the leading spirits on *both* sides now represented with equal honor upon the walls of a Parliament House, whose members no longer raise a question either about the loyalty due to the crown, or the liberty which is the legal right of the subject.

" Westminster Hall is a grand old chamber, rich with associations from the most stirring times of England's history; and the crypt is an exquisite specimen of ecclesiastical restoration, though not recognized as a church by the visitors, for the whole crowd kept their hats on in presence of a handsomely vested altar, with candlesticks and candles on (not lighted, of course, there being no service). In the new work now going on in the New Palace Yard to complete the grand entourage, noticed some very fine modern carving, foliage undercut and animals, remarkably well done.

" September 8th, Sunday (eleventh after Trinity).—Rose before 6 A.M., and attended the seven o'clock communion at St. Alban's, Holborn. Some fifty or sixty communicants were present. After getting a cup of coffee and a roll at a cheap eating-house, walked to St. Michael's, Shoreditch, and was present at the latter part of their early celebration there. Only a few present ; but the church is situated very much as St. Alban's is, among the poor and laboring population. There is a long row of tenement-houses on one side of the church ; and at the end of it a modest-looking dwelling of the same kind of brick, with a cross over the door, and an inscription, 'Sisters of the Poor.' The church is in very much the same general style as St. Alban's, Holborn— handsome, roomy, and well appointed in every respect. *Nothing* looks as if it were thought to be 'good enough for the poor.' In both, great cost and ornament, with different colored marbles, have been laid out on the font. Returned to St. Alban's (passing by Smithfield, where the martyrs were burned in the time of Queen Mary, now boarded in for the erection of a market), and, arriving before the end of their nine o'clock celebration, heard *Gloria in Excelsis* sung to old Merbecke's melody, just as I have it in my book. The High Celebration began at 11.15, after Morning Prayer, which was choral, *Gregorian*, and heartily well sung. Not a cathedral in England has yet put as much *life* in the choral service as this free church for the poor ; and in it were four celebrations of the Eucharist, while in Westminster Abbey, with all its splendid endowments, there was *none !*

" Only the two lights were used at Holy Communion ; and the incense, offered at the consecration, was very abundant, and the odor was perceived all through the church. The effect was beautiful and solemnly impressive. The sermon was by Canon Fortescue, of St. Ninian's, Perth, and extemporaneous, earnest, respectably fluent, with only one gesture, and that awkward and constantly repeated ; the subject being the Re-union of Christendom, that day (the Nativity of the Blessed Virgin Mary) being the tenth anniversary of the Association for the Promotion of the Unity of Christendom. After service was over, the Rev. Drs. E. A. Hoffman and E. K. Smith made their appearance, both having been present during the service. Dined with them at the Knights Templars Coffee-house, and went with them in the afternoon to St. Paul's, where we heard Canon Melvill preach. There were over two thousand persons present, filling the whole choir very full and a large part of the rotunda besides. The sermon came in after the Third Collect and the Anthem. Some hundreds went out after the Anthem and before the sermon, and several other hundreds after the sermon and before the concluding prayers. Took tea with Drs. Hoffman and Smith at the

11

Langham Hotel, and attended Evening Service with them at St. Andrew's, Wells Street, where the music was very good Anglican. On our way to the hotel before tea, took a look at the exterior of All Saints, Margaret Street, the finest modern church in London by far ; and after Evening Service at St. Andrew's returned to All Saints (which is within a block) and caught a glimpse of the magnificent and highly decorated interior.

" September 9th, Monday.—Attended Matins at the Abbey, and waited on Canon Wordsworth (in residence that week) for an order to inspect the chapels at my leisure, and the triforium, etc., which he kindly gave me, and I had some very pleasant conversation with him about Church affairs. He looks to the American Bishops to put life in the Council ; and says that the defeat of the Three Bishoprics bill was wholly due to the Bishop of Oxford (Wilberforce), who insists that the Bishops must all have equal chance to be Peers in Parliament !

" Inspected the chapels thoroughly in company with a young artist or architect who was sketching there, but had not time for the triforia. After dinner went to the S. P. G. Rooms to leave father's address, and learned that the Bishops Wilmer (*i.e.*, J. P. B., of Louisiana, and R. H., of Alabama) were at Portland Street Hotel, and called on them at once, but found they had left town for a few days.

" September 10th, Tuesday.—Went by appointment to see Mr. Mackonochie, and had a good talk with him from eleven till one o'clock, which was highly satisfactory in every respect. After lunch in a chop-house went to London Tower, and was shown all through, but had not time to stop and examine one-tenth part of what I wished to see. Among the arms are some revolver guns and pistols of the time of Henry VIII., from which Colt is said to have borrowed his ideas of a revolver. Saw the Crown Jewels and the Beauchamp Tower ; but was most of all pleased with the pure Norman Chapel of St. John. Ascended the Monument, commemorating London's fire in 1666, and had a fine view, though to the west the horizon was not only lost in smoke and mist but it was so thick that the lower parts of the Parliament Houses were invisible, and only the towers appeared above the fog. Walked nearly across London Bridge, and returning, took one of the penny boats up the Thames to Westminster Bridge. A hard shower came up on the way, driving us all down into the stifling cabin, where there was scarcely room to move or breathe. Rain came harder and harder, until I was well wet be-

fore I got to my room.   That evening Bishop Wilmer, of Louisiana, came to call on father, and dined with us, staying till 10.30
P.M.—a most delightful visit to us both.

"September 11th, Wednesday.—Wrote editorial on the proposed arrangements for the Council, as published by the Archbishop of Canterbury, and sent by him to father.   After dinner attended Evensong in the Abbey.   Boys gabbled the Psalms abominably, and organist was more than half the time behind the voices ;
but the Magnificat and Nunc dimittis and the Anthem were beautifully sung.   After Evensong delivered the Archdeacon's order
to Mr. Foster, clerk of the works, who sent a young man with
me all over the triforia.   (In the morning received a very pleasant call from Mr. Thomas Ramsay, with whom all bygones are
bygones.)

"September 12th, Thursday. — The Bishop of Louisiana
joined us at our hotel this morning, having taken the rooms next
to ours—a great addition to our comfort in every respect !
Went with him and father to call on Archdeacon Wordsworth
(this Archdeacon Wordsworth, whose name appears so often in
this journal, was Dr. Christopher Wordsworth, afterward Bishop
of Lincoln) ; but after finding our way to his door through the
curious turnings of the cloisters, etc., found him ' not at home,'
much to our regret.   Then went to the north entrance and entered the Abbey, going round the chapels with father and the
Bishop of Louisiana, examining everything by ourselves.

"September 13th, Friday.—At my room till 4.55 P.M., when
we took the train at Victoria Station for Croydon, where the
Archbishop's carriage met us, and drove us through a beautiful
country to Addington Park.   Fine trees by the way.   The Archbishop received us very kindly, took us out into the garden, and
introduced us to Miss Longley (and afterward to her sister), under
the great cedar (branches spread over more than one hundred
feet diameter).   Flower-beds of bright colors in the green lawn.
Borders each side of the road like rainbows, bands of flowers,
each band being of one tint.   Dined at 8 P.M.   The Bishop of
New Zealand and Mrs. Selwyn arrived before dinner was over.
Spent a delightful evening.   Bright moonlight.

"September 14th, Saturday.—The Archbishop unexpectedly
extending his invitation till Monday morning, I went to London
to get some things we had left behind us, walking all the way (a
delightful walk) to East Croydon, and in the evening back
again.   Overtaken near Shirley Church by the Archbishop's car-

riage, and pressed by Miss Longley to take a vacant seat there, but declined, and finished my walk both ways. Rain began to fall just as I arrived at the palace. Miss Longley sang, and with a remarkable combination of excellencies—unaffected truth, good *timbre*, thorough cultivation, and charming taste and feeling.

"September 15th, Sunday (12th after Trinity).—Saw Miss Rosamond Longley's sketch-book, which has a great deal of merit. Received from her a photograph of the great cedar-tree. Weather clear and cloudy alternately, a perfect English day. The tender half-misty lights on the rolling hills, the walk through lawn and garden, and the road bordered by *eight* parallel tints of leaves and flowers on each side, and the quadruple avenue of old elms, and then another garden, to the churchyard and little parish church of Addington : all in perfect keeping. Grassy and well-kept churchyard, in which Archbishops of Canterbury are buried. The church is of split flints, with freestone dressings : tower, nave of three bays, south aisle, chancel in which are old Elizabethan monuments of a knight and his wife, and two other couples above, kneeling nose to nose on cushions. Three very small round-headed windows over the altar, with tremendously wide splay. Queer old desk with double face, lessons being read toward the Clerk's desk, and the rest, at right angles to the congregation. No organ. All the Canticles (except *Te Deum*, which was read) chanted to the same double chant, morning and afternoon, led by a good baritone voice in the congregation, *all* joining in very heartily, as they did in the responses also. A good sermon from the Bishop of New Zealand, the Vicar taking the rest of the service, the Archbishop holding a service and preaching at Croydon. In the afternoon the Bishop of New Zealand preached again, dear father declining because of his cold, and I declining also, not conceiving it proper for a deacon to preach before an Archbishop and two other Primates. Sate between the Archbishop and dear father in the same pew. After service, was introduced, at the Archbishop's, to Mr. Sharpe, editor of the *Guardian*, and had some pleasant talk with him. Tea under the great cedar on the lawn. Singing from Miss Longley in the evening.

"September 16th, Monday.—Left Addington Park after breakfast, though kindly invited to remain till after lunch. Stopped at the Crystal Palace, Sydenham, where we lunched and remained till past 5 P.M., seeing only an infinitesimal fraction of what there is to be seen there. Antediluvian animals particularly interesting. Returned to London, dear father being very tired.

" September 17th, Tuesday.—Went to Masters' and then to Parker's, for a copy of Keble's Letter on Tract 90, to transcribe for the Archbishop of Canterbury the declaration of Convocation of 1571, about making the Primitive Church the standard. Went with father and the Bishops of Illinois and Louisiana to the preliminary meeting of Bishops at the House of S. P. G., and waited in the upper room until they were done, from 12 M. till 4.15 P.M. Studied maps of colonial sees, and read Parker Society's volume of Grindal's Remains. Returned with father to hotel and lunched. At 7.30 went with father to a very pleasant dinner-party at Mr. J. G. Hubbard's, 24 Prince's Gate, Kensington Road, where we met the Bishops of Cape Town and Ontario, Archdeacon Wordsworth, the Rev. Mr. Perry (who sat beside me), Mr. R. Brett, Mr. Palmer, and others.

" September 18th, Wednesday.—Wrote for the *Church Journal* an account of yesterday's meeting, which made me too late for the Oxford 10 A.M. train. Spent intervening time at Masters', selecting photographs of distinguished men. Took the noon train at Paddington Station, arriving at Oxford (distant glimpse of Windsor Castle by the way, and views of Oxford City—before we reached it—*Newman's views*, see *Apologia*—) at nearly 2 P.M. Walked down Queen Street, and the High, to the Mitre, and dined. Called on Dr. Pusey, but found him engaged, and left father's letter and my card. Attended Evensong at the cathedral, the choral service being very well done, and the Anthem elaborate, though the Minor Canon could not take an interval of a whole tone well. Visited Christ Church, Oriel (seeing the rooms formerly occupied by father, when a guest there), Corpus Christi, Merton, and University Colleges, walking the whole length of the Broad Walk. Then Queen's, St. Peter's in the East, New College and gardens, Wadham, and the New University Museum, which is exquisite, by G. G. Scott. Looked in at the Sheldonian Theatre, the schools, the Radcliffe, Brasenose, and St. Mary's, so to the Mitre. At 8 P.M., again called on Dr. Pusey, and once more found him engaged ; but as he desired me to wait, I waited for half an hour, and then enjoyed a good two hours' talk with him. He was extremely cordial, asked me to stay with him during my visit to Oxford (which I declined), and talked of many Church matters, but especially the

Pan-Anglican, and its proposing to retain the word ' Protestant '
and endorse only four instead of six general councils, besides
setting up our own communion as the model for all the rest of
Christendom.   Promised to call at 9 A.M. next day.

" September 19th, Thursday.—Up at 6 A.M., and resumed my
wanderings around the city by walking down High Street to Magdalen College, which I inspected closely on the outside, the gates
not being open to strangers till eight o'clock.   Walked across
the bridge over the Cherwell.   Wondered at the shallowness and
weediness of the water (worse in the Isis, however, at the end of
the Broad Walk), which must make boating exercise ticklish
business.   Found the small door ajar and went in, going through
several courts and getting into the gardens, when the porter
overtook me and turned me back.   Followed Long Wall Street
to Holywell Church, which is a perfect picture of an English
country church.   Thence up the ' Back Way,' getting a very
fine general view of a large part of the city.   Doubled on my
course and went up Holywell Street and Broad Street to the
Turl, and so to breakfast.   At 9 A.M. called on Dr. Pusey again,
who had been up since 6.30 and had received letters from Bishops present at the Preliminary, which worried him still more.
He said that if the Bishops would only *let things alone* and not
make them any *worse* than they were, the Catholic party could
be kept in hand ; but if they *would* assume the odious term
Protestant (which could only mean protesting against the ' Catholic ' Church), and *would* throw over two General Councils hitherto universally received, he could not be answera-
ble for the consequences.   Went with him at ten o'clock to the
cathedral, and after Matins returned with him to his house and
bade him good-by, declining a warm invitation to return to
lunch.   Resumed my attempts to see the various colleges, etc.
At St. Mary's Church looked in, but found Divine Service going on, and left at once.   Went on to the site of the new Keble
College, nearly opposite the New Museum.   Thence to Parker's
bookstore, where I spent nearly an hour refreshing my memory
as to the Acts of the 5th and 6th General Councils.   Visited the
Martyrs' Memorial, near St. Mary Magdalen Church, Balliol
College, Worcester College and beautiful gardens, with ponds ;
then down a little street to the north, running east and west to
St. John's College and beautiful gardens, then to Jesus College,
and Exeter, where I was specially delighted with the new work ;
the chapel being entirely modern in the highest style, with stone

ceiling beautifully groined.   Looked in at Lincoln College and
the schools, and walked through two stories of the immense
Bodleian Library, seeing several scholars sitting quietly in their
alcoves, and working away as if there were no outside world to
trouble them.   Dr. Pusey does most of his writing here, having
an alcove of his own, and being one of the Curators of the Library.   Peeped in at the Radcliffe, and then went up Market
Street to photographers in Cornmarket, and leaving my marine
glass behind me on the counter.   Lost the four o'clock train in
consequence, but took the five o'clock, which was twenty minutes
late.   Telegraphed to Archdeacon Wordsworth from Reading
that I could not arrive in time for dinner.   Reached our hotel
shortly after father had left for the Archdeacon's, having waited
for me.   Went at ten o'clock for father, and waited for more
than half an hour, walking up and down in the cloisters till he
came out with other Bishops from the Archdeacon's.   Showed
him all my photographs of Oxford before going to bed.

"September 20th, Friday.—Went to the bankers and drew
£50.   In the afternoon went with father to the British Museum, where we met Bishop Talbot (of Indiana).   In the evening
called on Archdeacon Wordsworth, and spent a very pleasant
evening.   The Archdeacon gave me a Black Letter edition of
the English Prayer-Book, 1640, with Sternbold and Hopkins'
Psalms, formerly belonging to the poet Wordsworth.

"September 21st, Saturday.—Started at 9 A.M. for Rochester
(fine views of castle and cathedral before reaching station),
where I visited the cathedral—the meanest I have yet seen in
England, except Chester, and with less of good modern work
than even Chester—and the castle, which is a superb twin.
Bishop Gundolph was a great builder.   After getting photographs, as usual, started at 3 P.M. for Canterbury, where I
arrived at five o'clock, getting fine afternoon views of the cathedral before arriving at the station.   Went immediately from the
Royal Fountain Hotel to the cathedral, which the verger was
just closing for the night.   Persuaded him to show me round—
which he did very completely before going to his tea.   After I
was locked out of the cathedral, spent an hour in roaming all
round the outside, and up and down every walk and archway
and court and gate that was accessible, and all round by the
King's School, and the Norman staircase, etc.   After dark
stopped at the photographer's in the cathedral yard (not the best),
and got the best he had, with two 'Guides.'   After supper,

went to Drury's (the best), and got better photographs and Stanley's book of Canterbury Memorials. Read my Guides and book till midnight.

"September 22d, Sunday (13th after Trinity).—At breakfast the Rev. W. D. Walker, of St. James the Less, New York, came into the coffee-room, to our mutual surprise and satisfaction. Went together all day : at ten o'clock to the cathedral, where we looked about a little before service. Choral service very well done—-choir large and well trained, but surplices rather dirty. Congregation fair for a cathedral. The *Ter Sanctus* was sung for an Introit. The Rev. Mr. Bailey, Warden of St. Augustine's (the first person who has *ever* held office both in the cathedral and in the monastery of St. Augustine, so great was the jealousy and hatred between the two adjoining corporations) preached an excellent sermon on the ninth commandment. After the sermon nearly everybody, choir included, went out, and Holy Communion was celebrated by Archdeacon Harrison without one note of music, and to only one sparse railful of the faithful ! After dinner went to St. Martin's, looking all round it, both before and after service—the visible cradle of the English Church. Saw the font in which (so they say) King Ethelbert was baptized by St. Augustine of Canterbury. (Fine view of the cathedral from the church-yard—Irish crosses.) Walked by St. Augustine's on our return after service, and thence to the rapid little river Stour, and the Abbot's Mill on it, and up the lane to the railway bridge, from which we had a charming view of the cathedral. Thence back by the Stour to the West Gate and out to St. Dunstan's. Returning, looked into an old hospital for three old women, old churches, and various other pieces of antiquity. Thence to the promenade along the inside of the old city walls its whole length, ascending the mound for another fine view of the cathedral. Then round by the new St. Mary Bradin, which we looked into, to our hotel, pretty well tired. After tea we went to St. Augustine's, entered the old wooden gate (so low that one *must* bow going in), were kindly received by the warden and subwarden, attended the 9 P.M. service in the chapel, the great body of the students filling the stalls along both sides of the chapel, being in surplices ; and East Indians, Parsees, and Negroes being well represented. The singing was good, the Psalms were sung to Anglican chants, and the Canticles to Gregorians, *well done*, and refreshing to hear. The chapel is a beautiful one.

"September 23d, Monday.—At 7 A.M. we were up and on our way to the cathedral for the effects of morning light in the interior. Had some difficulty in getting in ; but succeeded, the verger's pretty little daughter opening the outer iron door for us. Spent nearly an hour, especially in watching the effects of the light on the splendid *old* stained glass at the eastern end— the finest *old* glass I have yet seen. Punctually at eight o'clock we were at St. Augustine's again, to breakfast by invitation in the hall. Were seated on the dais with the subwarden and other teachers, at a cross-table ; two longitudinal tables below accommodating the students. The grace and the returning of thanks were both in Latin, with *Gloria Patri* and some verses from the sixty-seventh Psalm—all in Latin. We were thoroughly shown round the place, first by the subwarden and then by the warden—the library and its crypt, Ethelbert's Tower (so-called), the small remains of the grand old Abbey Church, the Students' Cloisters, and all the new buildings. Went with the warden to Archdeacon Harrison's for an order to see the triforia, who gave it to me at once, saying he well remembered father on his visit in 1839. Attended Matins at the cathedral, the service being very well sung. Afterward ascended the triforia tower. Fine views from the lantern of the central tower, and from the triforium of transept. Enormous amount of tree-twigs on the steps brought in by the birds. Took a final look at the crypt, which is the highest, finest, and most extensive in England. Saw the little portion of it which is used by the French Protestants, and has been since the time of Elizabeth. They are very few now—only twenty or thirty. They meet only on Sunday afternoons, and have a sermon only once a month. On leaving the cathedral precincts, tried to find the remains of the old Chequer Inn, but people living on the very site ' did not know ' anything about it. Barely time for lunch and to catch the train. Lovely day of purely English weather and atmosphere, and the rolling country was exquisite in its effects. Fine views of Rochester Castle in passing.

Walked over to Lambeth Palace with Bishop Quintard. Went to Archdeacon Wordsworth's in the evening, to find out what the Colonial Bishops had agreed on, and had much pleasant talk with him and the Bishop of St. Andrews.

"September 24th, Tuesday.—Day of meeting of the Council of Lambeth. Went over with father and left him at the door. Found Dr. Caswall waiting for me at the gate, with the Rev. Dr.

Keene, Mrs. Eames, and a number of other Americans, clergy
and laity : all highly indignant that nobody could get in.   Returned to London Bridge, and took penny-boat on the Thames
to Lambeth, where I walked up and ·down before the inner gateway half an hour until father came down, when we walked to our
hotel over Lambeth Bridge.   Poor day's work to begin with in
the Council.

" September 25th, Wednesday.—Walked to Lambeth with
father across Lambeth Bridge and returned the same way.   Spent
the whole day in my own room, until I went over to meet him
at 5.30.   Better day's work in the Council !   Father made several telling speeches, which gave great satisfaction to the true-
hearted, and helped to raise the tone of the whole assembly.   In
the evening went over to Archdeacon Wordsworth's to borrow
for father a book containing the Act of Elizabeth referring to the
Four General Councils.   Found that he had gone to Fulham to
dine with the Bishop of London ; but the Bishop of St. Andrew's
and Mrs. Wordsworth and her son and daughters kindly helped
me in the search, and I soon came back with the first volume
(there are *five*) of Law's ' Ecclesiastical Statutes at Large '
(Rivington's, 1847), which gave us what we wanted.

" September 26th, Thursday.—Walked over Lambeth Bridge
with father to the Palace.   After returning to my hotel with the
Bishop of Louisiana, went to Archdeacon Wordsworth's for him,
and then over to Lambeth again with a package for him.   Father
has done his duty nobly in the Colenso matter ; but the Archbishop's bargain beforehand with the Bishop of St. David's was
too strong for him.   The General Councils are recognized, and a
Pastoral free from objection is to be issued.   Not a bad day's
work on the whole, but with one bad blot, that ' will not out.'
Spent the evening in our room pleasantly, with the Bishops of
Alabama and Louisiana, and Dean Hines.

" September 27th, Friday.—Accompanied father to Lambeth
Palace over the Lambeth Bridge.   Called for father at 2 P.M.,
and had to wait in the great drawing-room of Lambeth for more
than two hours, chatting with the Rev. Mr. Lingham, incumbent
of Lambeth parish church, and the Rev. Mr. Lloyd, Chaplain of
the Archbishop.   Heard the concluding *Gloria in Excelsis* sung
by the Bishops in Council, at the end.   Was present when they
were all photographed at the door of Lambeth Palace.   Father
and I were walking home to our hotel when, after having crossed
Lambeth Bridge, we were overtaken by cabs sent after the

Bishops by the S. P. G., to catch them for the Conversazione in St. James's Hall, where a great crowd of people had been waiting for over three hours ! Father was placed in one cab and I in another. Was directed to an upper seat behind the Bishops, the Archbishop presiding, and father being the first called on to speak. After the meeting was over, went to our rooms for a few minutes to refit, and then out to Fulham Palace to dine with the Bishop of London (Tait) and a very large company, probably fifty or sixty, among them the Bishop of Oxford (Wilberforce). After the cloth was removed and the ladies had retired, the Bishop of London called father to one side of him and the Bishop of Oxford to the other. Was introduced to the Bishop of Oxford by his request ; and he took me aside to a vacant sofa where we had quite a nice long talk all by ourselves. Evening Prayer in the chapel before we left, the chapel being beautifully decorated in color, with embroidered altar-cloth, and in seemingly ritualistic style : Mrs. Tait (who is cousin to the Bishop of Oxford and a thorough Churchwoman, and has read father's ' Law of Ritualism,' and thanked him for it) playing the organ herself. Reached our rooms very late, and both of us very weary.

" September 28th, Saturday.—Rose at 6 A.M., and wrote for the *Church Journal.*

" At 9 A.M. went with father to breakfast with the Rev. Mr. Lingham, next door to Lambeth Churchyard, where we met again the Bishop of New Zealand and his son. Took seat in the congregation (after seeing father to the Palace drawing-room), and was present at the closing services. Afterward lunched with Canon Hawkins. At 4.55 started for Brighton, where father stopped with the Rt. Hon. Colin Lindsay, President of the E. C. U., who was unfortunately too ill with bronchitis to be visible. I stopped across the street from Sillwood (Mr. Lindsay's place) with the Rev. Mr. Beaulands, incumbent of St. Michael's, etc., taking my meals at Mr. Lindsay's. At 8.30 attended a magnificent service at St. Michael's (the Rev. T. W. Perry being one of the curates). Procession, ' We march, we march to victory,' all down the church and up the middle alley. Gregorian Psalter and Canticles (Helmore), and most elaborate Anthem from Mozart. Lights, flowers, gorgeous vestments, congregation crowded to the utmost. Vigil of St. Michael and All Angels, and the parochial Feast of the Dedication. Vested in white dalmatic, with apparels of red, embroidered beautifully, I sat at father's

right, a deacon similarly vested being on his left. The episcopal throne was on the north side of the chancel, on a step, and
with a canopy over it. A variety of richly embroidered copes
was used, acolytes in red cassocks, etc. Church exquisitely
adorned : the permanent decoration in marbles, paintings, etc.,
being very rich. Sermon by Canon Fortescue, of Perth.

"September 29th, St. Michael and All Angels, Sunday.—Attended early celebration at 8 A.M., *two* previous celebrations having taken place at 6 and 7 A.M. Found very large numbers in
attendance. High celebration at 10.30, preceded by Matins
(Litany omitted till afternoon). Procession, but not all the way
down the church. Exquisite service, Gregorian Canticles and
Psalter. Creed from Gounod, parts of it remarkably fine ; Ter
Sanctus, ditto ; and *Gloria in Excelsis ;* but all very long.
Father preached a very brief sermon, and gave the Absolution and
Benediction. A very large number of communicants—nearly
four hundred during the day. Vestments magnificent, especially
the cloth-of-gold chasuble (Mr. Perry, celebrant) splendidly embroidered and the dalmatic to match. Exquisite jewelled chalice, with niello in the foot, and another with engraving of the
heavenly Jerusalem on the round foot. No incense ; but I saw
the censer and the incense boat and spoon, and know that it is
coming. In the afternoon walked with Mr. Perry and father
down to the pier, and along the sea-shore street, and inspected
St. Paul's, the parent of the seven High Church parishes now in
Brighton, and several more in prospect. Then went to the four
o'clock Litany and catechetical service in St. Michael's. At
7 P.M. another magnificent evening service, crowded to the utmost, with procession all the way down the church. 'Brightly
gleams our banner.' The Anthem of last night repeated : boys
singing up to A and B♭ with truth, clearness, and power truly
wonderful. Sermon by the Rev. Mr. Rivington, one of the curates of All Saints, Margaret Street, who paid a high compliment to
father in the middle of it. All the three sermons were extemporaneous. Mr. Rivington is a son of the London publisher, and
a very earnest and effective preacher.

"September 30th, Monday.—Attended low celebration at
7.30 A.M. The extra services are to last through the octave, all
the offertories going toward the enlargement of the church, which
is greatly needed. Wrote editorial for the *Church Journal.*
Lunched at Mr. Lindsay's, where I had taken all my meals. In
the afternoon left for Newhaven, where I finished my article in

the hotel on the wharf, and we took supper and spent the night.

"October 1st, Tuesday.—After breakfast went on board the Alexandra for Dieppe. Magnificent views of chalky cliffs to the east as we left the harbor, culminating in Beachy Head ; and to the west side also, of similar general appearance. Charming bright, breezy weather. More than fifty vessels in sight at a time. Dieppe was reached at about 3 P.M. French coast almost exactly like the English, chalky cliffs, splendidly perpendicular. Dieppe is in a depression interrupting the chalky line of precipice. The precipices at the left seemed to be pierced with a large number of caves. Entered through masonry piers, and passed into a basin, turning to the right. The castle on the acclivity rising to the west of the city, now used for a prison. Large square tower in the centre of the city, suppose it to be the cathedral. Delayed an hour and a half by custom-house, etc. Started by rail for Rouen at 4.20 P.M. Beautiful scenery, yet not very bold. Multitudes of tall and very slim poplars. Mounds with one or two rows of trees planted on them, separating fields. Roads only wide enough for one cart, with a row of tall trees on each side, planted close together. Brook with both sides made parallel with masonry, so as to look exactly like a canal without a towpath. Village churches mostly poor, cruciform, with tower and low, ugly spire at the intersection. Many factories and tall chimneys.

"Arrived at Rouen at dusk. Went to the Hotel de France. Ran down at once to see the cathedral, and went along the narrow streets at either side, and inside also, the whole length of the nave, to the locked iron doors. Ascertained that there would be service at 7.30 P.M. After tea, went down with father, and attended the service, in the Lady chapel. Father and I took chairs on the left side, furthest back, next the railing. By and by a priest and acolyte came in. The priest entered an ugly low, square desk on the left side of the chapel, about half-way up, and led in what I suppose was a litany to the Saints and to the Blessed Virgin, all whose titles were repeated in full amplification, the people, about one hundred—containing only one man besides us, responding with much apparent devotion. The style was rapid. He then read a brief exhortation in French, and then (the acolyte having entered with the incense) proceeded to the altar, when the Benediction of the Host was given. The people then departed quietly. The effect in the grand old cathedral of immense height (eighty-nine and one-half feet to the ceiling inside), and the bold lights and shadows of the few gaslights, were very fine. After seeing father home, sallied out, and went down to the Grand Promenade by the river side. River glancing with many lights. Trees of the promenade cut away underneath. Bought Murray's and photographs, and took another glance at the cathedral on my way to the hotel.

" October 2d, Wednesday.—Visited St. Ouen, with its beautiful grounds and statue of Rollo ; then the Musée des Antiquités ; then St. Maclou ; then the bridge, and general view. After lunch, started for Paris, where we arrived after four and one-half hours' ride through a charming country, playing hide-and-go-seek with the Seine all along. Took Dr. and Mrs. Evans by surprise, and were received with a most cordial welcome, and any quantity of inquiries about the good folk in Burlington.

" October 3d, Thursday.—Received a pleasant call from the Rev. Mr. Lamson in the morning ; and after lunch he drove out with us in Dr. Evans' carriage (I having before lunch had a very pleasant walk with Mrs. Evans in the Bois de Boulogne) and saw Notre Dame, and La Sainte Chapelle, with its crypt, with glimpses of the Hotel de Ville, Tour de St. Jacques, Tuileries, Louvre, etc. Saw the Palais Royal on our way back. Pleasant little dinner party : the Rev. Mr. Killick, of St. Clement Danes, Strand, Mr. and Mrs. Delano (Twenty-ninth Street, New York), and after dinner the Rev. Mr. Ward (of the Anglo-American Chapel), and Major Hugh Scott, of Gala.

" October 4th, Friday.—Went down town in search of the friends, but could not find them. After lunch drove out with Mrs. Evans and father to the Pantheon, St. Etienne du Mont, the new Trinity Church (unfinished), etc.

" October 5th, Saturday.—Went to the exposition with Mrs. Evans and father, and remained after they had gone home. Lunched there, and in the rain took a cab to photographer's under Grand Hotel du Louvre, where I spent the afternoon. After dinner went with father, Dr. and Mrs. Evans, and the Rev. Mr. Lamson, to the Russian Church to the evening service. Magnificent voices, especially the basses, the deacon intoning on A and B, and another going down to

Was introduced with father to the Abbé Guettée and the Russian Archpriest.

"October 6th, Sunday. Sixteenth after Trinity.—To the Russian Liturgy at eleven o'clock, which was admirably done, but the Entrances were both rather straggling. The vestments magnificent, and the music exquisite. The peculiar architecture of the building, equally effective by day or night. Then went to the American Church, Rue Bayard, and assisted in the ministration of the Cup, father having preached. In the afternoon I preached there from 1 Peter iii. 18, a brief extempore sermon, the Rev. Messrs. Lamson and Duffield taking the service. Went home with Mr. Adams, and dined with him. In the evening (raining) went to the Anglo-American Chapel, Avenue Rapp, near the Exposition, where dear father preached on "I said, I will confess my sins unto the Lord, etc." I said the Creed and prayers on monotone, the Rev. Mr. Root beginning the service, and the Rev. Messrs. Weaver and Wade taking the lessons. Sat up till one o'clock talking with Dr. Evans.

"October 7th, Monday.—At home all morning (raining) laying out route for Rheims, etc. In afternoon went down for photographs of cathedrals and found very few, plodding about from one place to another, without any success. Parisians seem to care nothing for their finest ecclesiastical edifices, such as in England are found everywhere. Rather disgusted with a day's failure. In the evening dined at the Rev. Mr. Lamson's, with father and Dr. and Mrs. Evans; and after dinner, the Abbé Guettée, the Russian Archpriest, Mr. Adams, the Rev. Mr. Gardner, President F. A. P. Barnard, Mrs. Barnard, and others came in. No talk of any theological interest possible. On leaving, took cab (leaving Mr. Adams at the Maison Printemps, by the way) for the Gare de Strasbourg, and the 11.35 train for Rheims. No sleeping conveniences on French trains. Arrived at Epernay at 4 A.M., and remained locked up in the salle d'attente for nearly two hours, to sleep (if possible) sitting on a hard wooden bench, with an alarm-bell (like those of our alarm clocks) ringing all the while in the next room. Arrived at Rheims at 7 A.M. on a misty, cloudy, rainy morning. Walked up the narrow crooked streets (with little or no sidewalks) till I found the cathedral, and went all round it—west, north, east, and south, and even into the archbishop's gardens, and then inside, and carefully examined all the stained glass, which is mostly old and abundant, and *very* good. Having thus spent more than two hours, went to the Lion d'Or, just opposite the west front, and got breakfast. After breakfast, went to the Church of St. Remi, which has much good Norman work, partly outside, but still more inside. Remarkably good proportions, and fine general effect. Went up through the triforia, which are very large and roomy (each bay divided into *two*), paved throughout, and raised in many parts above the line visible from below. Bought full stock of photographs, such as were to be had. But *none* of the north, south, or eastern elevations, the latter of which was as peculiar for its big and quaint animals around the throat of the apse (crowning the parapet in place of pinnacles), as the west front for its hippopotamus, rhinoceros, crocodiles, etc. The new work (under Viollet le Duc) is good, but too fine—too *mincé*. It lacks the vigor at a distance which the old work has. After dinner returned to the study of the magnificent abundance of old stained glass in the cathedral, the west *rosace*, in the afternoon sun, being the most marvellously splendid effect of stained glass I ever saw in my life. It is fully up to one's *ideal*. Ascended the triforia and the southwest tower to the top, the open staircase being in the northeast angle of the tower *inside* the slender open arches. Magnificent view under the arcades of flying buttresses. The open towers at each flank of the transepts floored inside in a valley. Found the triforia *walled-up* at the further side of the passage to give greater strength. Magnificent views of the interior from the galleries at the west end. After supper, stole a final look at the north transept, and saw the moon streaming dimly through one of the stained windows, the great body of the church being buried in gloom, except from the light given by two candles near the door. At 6.40 P.M. left for Laon, where I arrived at about eleven o'clock. This ancient city is situated on the top of a hill several hundred feet high. As it was chilly, and the omnibus long in starting, I left it and went afoot up the hill, the ascent for foot-passengers being straight ahead, up a steep path diversified with two or three hundred stone steps, the widening prospect of streets of lamps below being more and more interesting, and the appearance of the cathedral towers—the cathedral being on the highest part of the hill—growing more and more singular the nearer the approach. At the top of the steps we were not yet at the top of the hill, but met the winding coach-road, and turning to the right followed it till it passed under an arched gateway, and turned to the left winding among narrow crooked streets, to La Hure, a hotel where I spent

the night.   First, however, I explored further along the crooked,
dark, and narrow streets, till I found the cathedral, with the
moonlight resting on its western front, now almost completely
restored.   After examining the western and northern fronts by
the dim light, I returned to La Hure well tired, and gave directions to be called at half-past six in the morning.

   " October 9th, Wednesday.—By seven o'clock I was at the
cathedral, which I examined with fresh interest by day.   It was
interesting in two respects.   First, it was the
only one I had ever seen which contemplated
seven towers, one at the centre of the cross and
two others at the west end, and *two* at the end
of *each* transept.   Of these A, B, C, D, were
built complete, and all nearly alike.   The centre is rudimentary only, and the two eastern
towers of the transepts have only the founda-
tion and the first stage complete.   Magnificent views from above
over a large extent of country, but no water.

   " The west front abounds with animals.   The hippopotamus
and rhinoceros, and two crocodiles appear, with ever so many
smaller animals, sixteen great stone oxen looking out of the open-
ings in the turrets of the towers.   As to internal effect, found it
the *only* French cathedral with a *square* east end, and the only
one where the central tower is used as a lantern, letting in a flood
of light from above.   In all other cases the vaulting there is carried
through similar to the rest of the roof.   Many queer old buildings near it, and the bishop's palace as usual turned into a palais
de justice.   [Laon is not now a bishop's see, having been suppressed by the concordat of 1801, and never restored, as a few
others were during the reign of Louis XVIII.—C. F. S.]   It commanded splendid views from the brow of the hill, looking down
on that staircase.   After breakfast, walked down again to the
station, descending the stairs, having got but very few and unsatisfactory photographs.   Lunched at Tergniers, and arrived at
Amiens at about 3 P.M.   Went at once to the glorious cathedral,
but was disappointed in the western towers, which are but little
higher than the roof-ridge of the nave, and also in the *flèche*,
which is of wood covered with lead.   But the height and majes-
tically powerful structure, with its double guard of flying buttresses, defies description.   Went all round the outside, except
where the bishop's gardens prevent access on the northeast.
Then ascended, with a company, the northwest tower, went out

12

on the galleries of the front, and found the figures of the kings to be over fourteen feet high !—a mistake, because it dwarfs all the rest of the building.   Found that the apex of the wooden roof is about forty feet higher than the stone vault, which last is one hundred and forty feet above the pavement.   Went between the two (looking down a trap-door to the pavement below !) and ascended the *flèche* as high as the steps would take us.   Then down, and on the leads above and below, on south and north sides, then inside to the triforia, which are *windows*, and got splendid views of the interior, with the *three* great *rosaces*, west, north, and south, and. of the whole length of nave and transepts. Descending, studied the effects from below, the *alto relievos* in transepts and around the choir, remarkably fine.   The enormous height, yet majestic strength were a feast.   Bought photographs at the verger's ; but very incomplete.   *Nothing* of east, south, or north elevations ! and *such* a splendid cathedral !   Oh, the barbarians ! and I told them so !   Went to the Gare through the crooked streets at the north side to get a view thence.   Left at 6 P.M. for Creil, where at 9.30 P.M. I got some dinner.   At 11 P.M. arrived at Beauvais, Hotel du Cygne, in the rain—raining all the evening, and so got no sight of the cathedral that night.

"October 10th, Thursday.—At the cathedral before 7 A.M., and a chilly, cloudy, almost rainy morning.   Examined it carefully all round, in the crooked, narrow streets.   The height is wonderful (it is thirteen feet higher than Amiens), but everything else has been sacrificed to that.   There is no nave, or tower, or spire.   The bells are hung *al fresco* over the crossing of the transept, and rung from the pavement of the church by long ropes.   Did not ascend the triforia, because of a High Mass which was sung, and kept the verger otherwise occupied until it was too late.   The celebrant was attended by six boys in cottas over red cassocks.   The chorus was only two men, who sang plainsong in unison with remarkably fine bass voices (not so fine, however, as the Russians).   One old ecclesiastic sat in a stall, and took but little part in the service.   The congregation—besides a school of some thirty or forty girls in charge of some religieuses—not half a dozen persons.   Worse in all respects than daily choral service in the English cathedrals.   The impression of height is wonderful in this cathedral ; but even now *beams* are inserted horizontally between choir-piers and those of the aisles to prevent bulging.   The carvings in oak on the north door are exquisite ; south door later.   Left at 11.05 A.M. without break-

fast, taking a last look at the cathedral from the train.   Got a
few photographs before leaving.   Hasty lunch at Creil.   At
Paris at 2 P.M.   After dinner related my experience and showed
my photographs to Father and Dr. and Mrs. Evans.   Packed up
before going to bed.

"October 11th, Friday.—Breakfasted early, and after a very
warm and affectionate parting from Dr. and Mrs. Evans started
in the 7.45 A.M. train for London, Dr. Evans accompanying us
to the Gare de St. Lazare.   Charming morning: calm, and
bright sunshine, but the morning mists spread a veil over the
whole remoter landscape, heightening beautifully the effects of
the aërial perspective.   Exquisite little views as we played with
the Seine all the way to Rouen, the autumnal tints beginning to
add variety to the foliage.   From Rouen the weather was cloudy,
smoky, and dull.   The passage across the Channel from Dieppe
to Newhaven was still more so, and chilly besides, so as to take
away all pleasure of watching the landscape : but though long
(seven hours) there was very little motion in the boat.   Spent
the time mostly in the cabin, studying Murray's France, and
finding out something concerning the cathedrals of France which
I did *not* visit.   Found it a very interesting study.   Landed at
dark at Newhaven, in the rain.   Took tea there, changed our
French money to English, and started at 7.20 for London.   At
Croydon one of the gentlemen with us in the same carriage
entered into conversation with us, proving to be a Rev. Mr.
Nicholson, formerly a curate of Mr. Denton, and who went with
him and received communion with him in Servia.   He was returning from Paris, where he had gone the whole length of the
city in the rain on Sunday night to hear Father preach, through
admiration of his ' Law of Ritualism.'   He had a friend, a Professor or one of the clergy at St. Sulpice, who was a Gallican of
the Gallicans, and had some years ago done all he could to further
the establishment of Mr. Gurney's chapel in Paris as a representative of the Catholic movement in England, and to help on the
same movement among Romanists in France.   That friend also
told him that, notwithstanding the efforts of the Pope to make
the Roman use supplant the Gallican, the Church of St. Eus-
tache (or St. Eugène, I forget which) was the *only* one in the
Diocese of Paris where the Roman use was thoroughly followed !
Arrived in London at about 9 P.M. and went to the Westminster
Palace Hotel again, rooms 178 and 180.

"October 12th, Saturday.—Took Father to the photographer,

Walker, 64 Margaret Street, Cavendish Square, and had him taken
in his robes, in several positions. Was taken myself also, the
photographer insisting on it. Showed Father All Saints, Margaret Street, where we met Mr. Butterfield, the architect, and the
Rev. Mr. Richards, and were shown over the house kept by the
Sisters. Laid in a stock of London and other photographs. In
the evening showed my new purchases to Father, and then read
to him out of the papers (*Guardian, Church Times*, and *Church
Review*) I had purchased, articles touching the Pan-Anglican,
and the Church Congress at Wolverhampton, till nearly midnight.

" October 13th, Seventeenth Sunday after Trinity.—Attended
early low celebration at Westminster Abbey, 8 A.M. About a
dozen were present. It was the day of St. Edward the Confessor, whose shrine—the only unviolated shrine in England—is in
the abbey, east of the altar. Went to the Temple Church for
Morning Prayer. Full choral service, the Tersanctus for an *Introit*, and choir, music, and nearly the whole large congregation
went out before the Holy Communion, leaving not two dozen
persons to receive. Miserably cold and chilly—cathedral fashion.
The inside of the building, though refitted and polychromed only
a few years ago at great expense, is very dingy and dirty, and full
of smoke. The tombs of the old crusaders—dark effigies lying
full length nearly on the level of the floor—were the most interesting things in the church to me. The stained glass was partly
too dark ; and the rest, to give light, was nearly white glass,
which killed the effect of nearly all the rest. The round part of
the building is very interesting. It is in that that the old crusaders lie. In the afternoon went to St. Barnabas, Pimlico, and
heard some very good Gregorian chanting. The children were
very satisfactorily catechized. The stained glass at the east
and west ends was remarkably good. The rest of the church
was dark and dingy, and full of smoke, but in admirable style,
with a rood screen, and with an earnest, hearty congregation of
the right sort. Clergy houses and schools surround the church
on three sides. Had hard work to find my way to the church,
being misdirected, and the whole day being very foggy and somewhat rainy, like yesterday. At 7 P.M. went to All Saints, Margaret
Street. Found it so crowded ten minutes before the service
began, notwithstanding the rain, that I had to stand all through
the evening, in a place where nothing in the chancel could be seen.
Music delightful : pure Gregorians, sung by a large body of

men's voices, and so unitedly that the words were as distinct as if spoken by only one person. A brilliant anthem was admirably done, with (imitation) harp accompaniment. An earnest and powerful *extempore* sermon was preached by Mr. Rivington, who spoke in the highest and most hopeful terms of the work of the Pan-Anglican, and announced the formation of a new association, under the wardenship of Dr. Pusey, to pray more earnestly for the reunion of Christendom. Saw the Rev. Mr. Richards afterward, who gave me the printed slips concerning the new association. By the way, the Sisters were present at the service in a body. There are *forty* of them in all. They have an orphanage of forty or fifty orphans, a training-school for girls to be put out to service, a dispensary for the poor, an asylum for incurables who come to them to live and be nursed as long as possible, and then to die and be buried; and another hospital for convalescents. For the latter alone they are putting up a building in the country which will cost about $350,000 of our money. And all this is only a *part* of the work done entirely *by one parish*— ritualistic, of course. Their chapel is a perfect little gem; but all the rest of their establishment is as simple and plain as in the cottages of the poor. Walked home to the hotel alone, in the rain.

"October 14th, Monday.—Went with Father to Mason's to be photographed again, in several positions. Then to Masters', who agrees to collect the *Church Journal* bills for five per cent., and then to Hart & Son for chancel furniture for St. Paul's, Burlington. Packed up and left London (after copying Father's letter to Dean Stanley), in the 2.45 train for Liverpool, where we arrived at 8.20 P.M. and went to Queen's Hotel. Dismal English weather—fog, smoke, and rain.

"October 15th, Tuesday.—Wrote communication for the *Guardian*, and a number of letters, to Dr. Pusey, the Right Hon. Colin Lindsay, and others. Copied Father's letter to the Archbishop of Canterbury. At 4 P.M. went down to the wharf to wait for the tender to take us off to the vessel, the Minnesota, which was lying in the stream. She was long coming, but at length we were safe on board, and delighted to find that Captain Price, of the Chicago, had been transferred, with all his officers, to the Minnesota, so that we were among friends and at home at once. Was introduced to Mrs. Price, who was there to see her husband off. Got off at about 8 P.M. Beautiful lines of lights on the Liverpool side of the Mersey, as well as the Birkenhead side.   The lighthouses and floating lights were beautiful also—near and brilliant, with beams of lurid light over the waters; and the moon struggled out through the clouds, giving a combination of varied lights in air and water.

"October 16th, Wednesday.—Spent the day in the cabin, settling the accounts of our whole tour.   Very windy and rough all afternoon, and hardly half a dozen passengers able to come to the dinner-table.   Reached Queenstown after dark, in a gale, and the quiet on entering the harbor was very grateful.   The tender with passengers and mails not coming out in such stormy weather and so late, we stayed all night in the harbor.

"October 17th, Thursday.—Still in Queenstown Harbor. The tender with the Admiral, and a large crowd of steerage passengers, came out to us at about 10 A.M., taking a long time to get everything on board.   By that time the tide was so low, the channel being very narrow, that the big ship could not turn round to get out to sea again.   Beautiful effects of changing sunshine and shadow on the lovely hills around the harbor. About the middle of the afternoon we got off, and encountered a stiff gale outside, in the face of which we made slow progress. Very rough all night.   Dear Father did not sleep at all.   Arranged *cartes de visite.*

[The voyage was a rough one.   But there is nothing in the journal that calls for particular mention.   Two Sundays were spent at sea; on both of which the Church services were read by different clergymen on board—Bishop Hopkins preaching each Sunday, once.]

"October 28th.   SS. Simon and Jude.   Monday.—Begin my forty-eighth year to-day.   .   .   .   Wrote editorials nearly all day.

"October 31st, Thursday.—A bright quiet morning.   Pilot boat No. 19 in sight.   Landed at the Battery at a little after 3 P.M.   In the total of 865 souls on board there were no sicknesses, no births, and no deaths.   The Rev. E. M. Pecke came down on the tender which took us ashore, and gave us letters and other news.   Went up to Mr. Wells' before leaving on the 6 P.M. boat, St. John, for Albany.

"November 1st.   All Saints Day.   Friday.—Breakfasted at the Delavan, then took rail for Whitehall, and on the new steamer Adirondack reached home at 5 P.M., with hearts joyful and thankful to God for all the mercies vouchsafed to us during a voyage of over 7,000 miles!"

Soon after the happy return to Burlington he himself went back to New York and settled down to hard work again.

But early in January a telegram brought him word that his father, to whom he gave first and last the warmest and deepest love of his loving, gentle heart, was dying. The bishop, who had nearly completed his seventy-sixth year, had begun a mid-winter visitation of his diocese. Great fatigue, and exposure to a cold of twenty degrees below zero, after hours in an overheated railway car, had brought on an attack of double pneumonia, to which after a day or two of intense suffering, he succumbed. Henry received the news at an hour too late to reach the earliest train, and, almost frantic with impatience, he bore the delay as best he could, and at last reached his father's bedside, but too late to receive the blessing which the patriarch had longed to give in that supreme moment to his eldest and best-loved son. It was, afterward, a great satisfaction to Henry to know that his brother Theodore, who had ministered to his father in all the hours of pain as a true son by birth and in the priesthood, had received that blessing while the " dear father " was yet alive.

Thus, in the fulness of time, that peculiar family lost the roof-tree. Yet the songs that they had sung to the God they had been trained to love with the completest trust still arose, and their voices did not falter as they sang. To one who was then asked to share for a while the sacred circle of that family, when he expressed his wonder that their trust in God was stronger than their natural grief, it was said, with perfect simplicity and naturalness, " how can we help singing when we know that dear father is gone home ! "

The death of his father changed the current of John Henry's life.

Bishop Hopkins had long before settled it that his biography should be written by his eldest son, and at once he began making arrangements for the sale of his property in the *Church Journal.*

The paper was worth a good deal. It was by all odds the most influential paper in the Church, and during the " hard times " it had not lowered its prices, as some others had done (in vain hope of keeping alive) but had even raised them. Men could not do without it, even if they disliked or mistrusted it. It had made a religious journal as interesting, and quite as entertaining as a secular journal ; and Hopkins was in his prime.

But he sold it for what he could get, and began working on his father's biography. He had given his whole time to the paper, and it would probably have continued to grow under his strong control. But those who took it from him were, although strong enough for good work, unable to give as *much* care to it as he did ; and, after taking a line of policy totally opposed to his, after ten years more it was merged into another, and since 1877 the title of *Church Journal* has not been seen.*

* Until Dr. Hopkins began the Church Journal in 1853, there had been no journalism in the Episcopal Church worthy of the name, after Dr. Samuel Seabury had finished his career as the editor of the Churchman. His work in that paper was more that of a polemic than that of a leader. He liked controversy, and he had a theological mind, and it was the time when the two parties in the Church, the High and the Low, were pitted against each other in a terrible struggle for supremacy. Dr. Hopkins began his career as a journalist at a time when, if party spirit had not been over-come, it was possible to give the High Church party such points of lead and suggestion that it could enter upon a larger life, and much as Dr. Hopkins liked the warfare of controversy, and few men ever had such a relish for the subversion of an antagonist, he soon made the Church Journal the organ of a brighter outlook, a clearer purpose, and a better spirit than had been be-fore manifested in the Episcopal Church in this country. In looking over the files of the Church Journal to-day, you discover that a great part of what is now a precious and priceless possession in the Church was then for the first time introduced by Dr. Hopkins. This was the case in regard to Church polity, the management of dioceses, the greater reverence in con-ducting the service, the improvement of the ritual, and the lifting up of the priestly character as well as the improvement in Church architecture. Every one of these interests received Dr. Hopkins' earnest support, and a great many of them were first suggested by him, and he kept at the work until he had made an impression upon the Church. His paper had a purpose, and it went straight to the mark, and the younger clergy, like myself, found it a source of inspiration in Church life and an excellent educator. It made one feel that the Church had something to say and to do. Then again his writing was always crisp and clear and strong. If at times he seemed to be merciless in his attitude toward his opponents, it was the triumph of princi-ples rather than any feeling of contempt that led him to exult in his victo-ries, and it was an appropriate ending of his work in journalism when he wrote for the magazine entitled The Church and the World, his famous articles on "The Decline and Fall of the Low-Church Party." He was the greatest journalist the Church has ever known. Dr. Hopkins was a genius in jour-nalism, and I have always regretted that he left his work as editor to be-come a parish priest. He abdicated a throne of power in order to take the position where hundreds of men were his equals, but while the editor of the Church Journal he was the most powerful man in the Episcopal Church. He had a mission and a message, and he made himself widely felt. From the beginning of that paper until he left it, he was the most influential fac-tor, outside of the work of Bishop White, that the Episcopal Church in this country has ever known.

REV. JULIUS H. WARD.

Until 1872, that is for full four years, he was at work upon the life of his father. This book, which no one who would be informed as to the course of American Church history can do without, is not only a beautiful example of his devotion to his father's memory, but a work of real literary ability. The way in which he wove together such a fabric from letters, and journals, and Church reports, and newspapers, and made of them one story that reads as if it were the product of his own brain is wonderful. Some critics thought that some of the things therein told ought not to have been allowed to be remembered because they were a disgrace to the Church. To say this, however, is to disregard the warning given by the author in his preface as to his purpose. "My father's life," he says, "was one of almost uninterrupted controversy; and to omit these would be like writing the life of a great general and omitting all the battles. . . ." In regard to the subject of episcopal trials, which touches some of the tenderest points herein alluded to, he says: "I have detailed these things, not for the purpose of reflecting upon individuals, but rather, *as showing some parts of the process by which, as a National Church,* we have obtained our education in this most difficult and disagreeable department of ecclesiastical business; and as some assistance toward other National or Provincial Churches, whose work in this direction is as yet wholly or partially to be done." The book is much more than a life of Bishop Hopkins; it is a compendium of American Church history, and worthy, besides, of ranking high in a purely literary estimate of its value. But his treatment of it was characteristic. He brought out an edition, in costly form, of five hundred copies. He sent copies to all the bishops, as well as to friends, and to very many of those who, in the nature of things would have bought them, and there let his interest in the book, as a merchantable article, cease. During the four years of his work he lived at Rock Point, Burlington; but was a missionary also at Vergennes, Vt., and across Lake Champlain at Essex, N. Y. His missionary work was not limited to the sort of people usually ticketed as "Church people," but reached to everybody, man, woman, or child, who had no one else to care for him. He brought into the Church at Essex, with his whole family, one who, twenty years afterward, during the fourteen months of Dr. Hopkins' last illness, gave him (though three other homes were freely and lovingly opened to him by kinsmen) a home, and tender care, and medical attention as to a father. He was indeed a father to him, having begotten him to God ; but few men realize the greatness of the gift of faith in God, and few men are so strong and faithful, and, at the same time, so sweet and simple and winning as John Henry Hopkins. Dr. E. D. Ferguson and his wife and family, of Troy, must be gratefully remembered by all those who love and reverence the memory of Dr. Hopkins.

He had, for a time, an appointment as missionary at Rouse's Point, which is in the present diocese of Albany ; and in the organization of the new diocese Hopkins, whose work for the division of the old diocese of New York had been finally crowned with success, which was due to him more than any one else, was as prominent as he felt a deacon might be.

He did his best to secure the election of Dr. William Croswell Doane as first bishop, and at once began to work for a further division of the diocese of Albany ! In the first address made to his Convention by Bishop Doane, the need of this subdivision was insisted on, and for years, with every appearance of ultimate success, the movement advanced.

In 1872, being elected rector at Plattsburgh, N. Y., Mr. Hopkins was induced by the bishop to consent to be ordained to the Priesthood, and accordingly he was ordained Priest on the twenty-third of June in that year ; after a service as deacon of twenty-two years ! The same year (or the next) he received from Racine College, then under the care of the lamented De Koven, the degree of Doctor of Sacred Theology.

Dr. Hopkins' work at Plattsburgh was full of his own love and energy. The parish grew much stronger, and he acted, besides, as missionary to all that region. He could adapt himself to any place and to any man, and every one in all the country about who had no one else to care for him was cared for by Dr. Hopkins. His knowledge and love of the Bible, and his power of expressing himself in like simple and direct language (but never falling into the mistake of talking *down* to the level of an uncultivated mind) were so great that he would be taken for one who had no other vocation than to be a missionary. The same thing was true of him afterward at Williamsport, Pa. At that place it was often said that his sermons in the parish church were over the heads of his people ; but when he visited a way-side church, called "the Church of the Good Shepherd," far back among the hills, which he had himself designed many years before he came to live in that region, he spoke with such fulness of scriptural knowledge, such simplicity of style, such deep appreciation of our Lord's own way which made " the common people hear *Him* gladly," that when the news of his death came to those seemingly uncouth Pennsylvania Dutchmen they wept and said that since he who was a very angel to them was now dead, no one would ever love them and tell them God's love as he had done.

In truth his style altered considerably as he advanced in years. It was always marked by a certain compactness, even when it was lightened up by his amazing facility of illustration.   But his habit of extemporaneous preaching reacted upon his written style, and gave it a sort of speech-like quality, so that his ordinary style of writing, always limpid, lost something of its literary grace, and became more like his spoken addresses.   In each he was facile, and each was clear as a sunbeam.   The period of his residence at Plattsburgh was a stormy one in the annals of the American Church.   It marked the culmination and the rapid decline of the warfare against Ritualism, and the setting up of the Reformed Episcopal Church by Bishop Cummins and his associates.

From his own residence of secluded peace, John Henry Hopkins sent out his frequent contributions to various publications. He took his side with great boldness, and advocated in every possible way the lawfulness of ritualism, both in its doctrinal and its ceremonial sides.   He said many things which hurt and wounded.   His openness and complete frankness alarmed even those whom he was defending.   He flaunted his colors jauntily in the very face of his strongest opponents, and exasperated afresh those who might have been pacified if he had been content with a less complete victory.*   This is not the place, nor these the

---

* He wrote a letter to the New York Tribune, November 24, 1877, concerning the meaning of the kindly and fraternal spirit which characterized the General Convention of that year, which had recently ended its session. In this he ran over certain salient points, and summed them all up by saying that " the result of the long war is victory all along the line for Ritualistic advance.   And this victory is so complete that the renewal of hostilities hereafter is hopeless.   That is why we have such delightful peace and brotherly love all round our united household."   He continues : " Nothing would be further from the truth than to suppose that all this means just so much of an advance toward the Church of Rome.   We have insisted that it was the truest loyalty to provide our army with every sort of weapon that is found most effective in the hands of the enemy.   We insist that we are a true branch of the Apostolic Church from the beginning, and that every good thing belonging to that undivided Catholic and Apostolic Church from the

times, for setting forth the history of those days dispassionately.
One thing should be remembered, as to all this, and that is, that
Mr. Hopkins was fighting for others, and not for himself. His
service was simplicity itself in its form to the very end of his
parochial work, and the form of his teaching was modelled
after the style of the typical Anglican divines, except for its lack
of stiffness, and for the entirely unconventional expressions which
he never hesitated to use at any time, when it was better to use
them than not.

Although he was abreast of the most advanced churchmen in
all things, at least in his sympathies, yet he never would have
given offence, even to the most moderate of bishops ; and this,
not from any lack of courage, or because he was double-dealing,
but because of his patience with people, and his understanding of
their needs and of their slowness. Very much that passes for
courage in expression of unusual doctrines is really not courage
at all, for it arouses little opposition, simply because it is not
understood.

True *Church* doctrines in their simplest form are as unpalatable
to those who know and follow the Puritan tradition as the development of the consequences of those fundamentals.

Moreover, John Henry Hopkins was clear-sighted enough to see
that something greater than Ritualism was at stake, and that was the
right of the children of the Church freely to carry out all her teachings. If the movement against Ritualism on the part of the old
conservative High Church party had succeeded the Church would
have been bound down to a cast-iron rigidity of worship and ways
that would have so repressed the spiritual vigor of her life that a
period of more than eighteenth century deadness would have ensued by this time. The Ritualists took the matter into their own
hands, and did with the Prayer-Book, while living up to its system with the utmost fidelity, what never would have been dreamed
of as possible to do with it a few years ago. They acted on this
simple principle that the Prayer-Book itself is our only law of
worship, and that all things in it, not specifically forbidden, may
be done or used. One simple illustration may show this. Ac-

beginning is part of our own birthright, and we mean to have it, whether or
no. We don't intend to have any differences between Rome and ourselves,
except where she is clearly modern and Papal, and therefore wrong, and we
are ancient and Catholic, and therefore clearly right. This is the truest
loyalty to our own branch of the Church, in contesting the claim of a foreign
Church, with a foreign name, to the spiritual allegiance of Americans."

cording to the rubric the Litany is to be said after Morning Service on Sundays, Wednesdays, and Fridays. All schools of
churchmen have interpreted this to mean that it is to be so used,
if there is service on those days. But the rubric does not say it
shall not be said on Tuesday, or any other day; or in the evening, after twelve o'clock, noon. Consequently, it can be said at
any time, and on any day, if the clergyman wishes a service of
penitence. So, too, there is no hour mentioned for the celebration of the Holy Eucharist. The usual Anglican custom has been
to have the celebration after saying Morning Prayer and Litany.

But, since the Prayer-Book does not forbid the offering of the
Sacrifice at an early hour, *before* Morning Prayer, it may be
celebrated thus, if the priest shall find it convenient to do so.
All men see now that the Church has gained immensely in freedom of use of her own formularies. They have become vastly
more effective, and they are used less and less as ends and more
and more as means to an end—the building up of the Kingdom
of Christ. If no more had been effected by those who are called
"Ritualists" in contempt or hatred, they would merit the
gratitude of the Church. Yet what they did, and what they tried
to do, cost the Church many of her dearest sons, some of whom
went into schism because they yielded to the panic which was
shaking the hearts of men who called themselves *par excellence*
churchmen; others were despised and branded as traitors, and
a few gave up their trust in their true Catholic mother and declared her to be no true representative of the Church of God.
The Church suffered deeply in this time of suspicion, and anger,
and controversy.* But for praise or blame in the eyes of the

---

* It is well known that the Ritualistic controversy was really not waged
over the doctrine of the Real Presence and its ceremonial expression. Standard Anglican teachers had never ceased to set forth the doctrine, but usually in so guarded a fashion, and with such evident dread of overstepping the
limits of safety that the natural result had been to make men think it very
dangerous in itself. The revival had simply cleared up these old clouds,
and set forth the doctrine, simply and clearly; the later Ritualists had
simply set forth the truth outwardly as well. Dr. Hopkins' own feeling in
the matter is best shown by the verses entitled "Sparrows in Winter,"
written in the midst of those dreary days of strife. It shows a very different
side from that he usually revealed in his struggles for the Church and her
liberties, and for others.

> Bread on the stones is cast.
> 'Tis winter; and the stones are snowy cold:
> Yet fluttering past
> From leafless trees, the sparrows, young and old,

world, the Church suffered the innovators to remain in her fold.
The ceremonies they brought into the churches were not forbidden ; and in less than a lustrum the movement, begun by a few,
received a great acceleration from the coming into the country of
a society of priests bound by the vows of the religious life, and
acting under the orders of a superior at Oxford. Finally the
growth of Ritualism became so great that one of the founders of
this society, mere acquaintance with whom prevented the consecration of one elected to a diocesan bishopric, was himself
elected to a bishop's see and duly consecrated thereto.

In all this movement from first to last, to say nothing of his

Flock, in their hunger, to be fed ;
And on the cold stones find their daily bread.

　　Love, with a liberal hand,
Throws out its crumbs ; then suddenly withdraws,
　　Hidden to stand
And watch, behind the window curtain's gauze,
Lest human face, too nigh, should scare
The timid birds from this their simple fare.

　　And they are glad, and feed
With eager eye ; and live on daily love,
　　Yet feel none. Greed
And passion stir their little breasts, and move
To bickering wars with wing and bill ;
Yet love looks smiling on, and feeds them still.

　　Hard is this world, and cold ;
And toil, care, woe, and sin, are everywhere.
　　Yet souls untold
Come, from above, to find their sustenance here ;
And, midst the stony drought forlorn,
Find manna waiting for them every morn.

　　God gives that Bread from Heaven ;
And yet His Presence not in glorious blaze
　　Of Fire is given ;
But hidden under veils, lest the bright rays
Of awful light and beauty here
Consume the sinful soul with deadly fear.

　　Men feed and they are glad.
They see not God, the Unseen ; and they turn,
　　With envy mad,
And o'er the very Gifts of Love, they burn.
Yet, fighting, feed, and grow, and will :
And patient God sees, loves, and feeds them still.

—1874.

years of preparation for it in the *Church Journal,* Dr. John
Henry Hopkins was in the fore-front of the battle, the counsellor in difficulties of priests from all parts of the country, the
pest of bishops, whose dearest rights he was defending by taking sides against themselves, the stay for the faint-hearted and
the succorer in distress.   His correspondence was enormous.
Hardly a priest who made any gain in the way of ritual but
wrote to him to tell him of it.   Sooner or later everyone who
became involved in trouble with his diocesan wrote to him about
the course which he might best pursue.   He counselled, he animated, he inspired, all who were in the tumult, and he shared to
the full in all the obloquy which was heaped upon the Ritualists ;
and yet he might have escaped from all if he had been content to
live out his own life and go on in his own ways.   But he was a
churchman, and he was a soldier.   He advised care, patience,
moderation, prudence to those who asked his counsel.   But this
was in private.   When those same men were careless, and im-
prudent, or reckless and foolish, then he did not leave them to
themselves because they had not heeded his words, but he openly
showed himself on their side, and drew the fire of the enemy,
and sometimes rescued them from uncomfortable situations by so
doing, for he was blamed for their having done what he advised
should not be done, as if he had inspired them.   They were excused, as young boys led away by a crack-brained agitator.

Nor was his struggle for liberty in the Church one which sought
for liberty for his own side alone.   Where the Church had not
decreed there was freedom, but not for men of one way of thinking alone.   He recognized to the utmost the full right that Evangelicals and old-fashioned churchmen had to follow out their
ideas so long as they were loyal to the Church.   Nor was he one
who counselled the making of reprisals.   If he was found most
often defending High Churchmen from attack it was because
they were most exposed.   When High Churchmen in turn sought
to hinder the lawful liberty of Low Churchmen he as openly
defended them in their rights.   Dr. Jaggar, an amiable and
excellent Evangelical, was elected first Bishop of the Diocese of
Southern Ohio.   High Churchmen were then in a state of bitter
moroseness over the failures to confirm the elections of Drs. Seymour and DeKoven.   It was hinted that there had been sharp
practice shown in the choosing of the Diocese of Ohio (the northern part of the State), wherein a considerable number of High
Churchmen resided who had furthered the plan of division with

a view of escaping the severity of the long rule of Low Churchism by the Evangelical diocesan (which, of course, he had a perfect right to do under the canon), and it was rumored about that an effort would be made to prevent the consecration of Dr. Jaggar. Mr. Hopkins came out in a letter which condemned the effort in severe terms, and showed the folly of it, and the perfect right of the diocese to choose its own bishop, and how blameworthy it was to put a mark of rejection on a priest for simply being a Low Churchman. Nothing was done. Probably it would have been a failure anyway, but the opportunity of showing how clear was his sense of justice even when the air was ringing with accusation and counter-accusation on all sides, was not lost by him. The very last communication for the public eye that was written by Dr. Hopkins, in June, 1891, two months before his death, was in a similar and more noteworthy cause—the election of Dr. Phillips Brooks to the Episcopate of Massachusetts. However he may have misunderstood the issue, lying, as he then was, very near his mortal hour, and with a weakened system, yet his motive was of the highest, and once more his voice rang out in appeal for justice for one separated by a whole heaven in party position in the Church, he a leader by right in every battle for High Churchmen, asked for fairness and right dealing toward one who misunderstood, and disesteemed the whole High Church position. Both are now in the nearer presence of the Lord they served and loved.

> " There they alike in trembling hope repose,
> The bosom of their Father and their God."

CHAPTER IX.

1874–1891.

Dr. HOPKINS remained at Plattsburgh until the autumn of 1876. He had been, naturally, a conspicuous figure in the new diocese of Albany from its foundation. He had done all that he possibly could do to bring about its early subdivision. He drew up a full scheme for the cathedral statutes, and his draught of the statutes became the basis upon which they were at last adopted. But there had been some trials and some disappointments in his life in that diocese. It had been an object of lawful ambition that he should be sent to General Convention. But in 1874 he was only a supplementary delegate, and had no place on the floor as a member of the House of Clerical and Lay Delegates until, by the departure of one of the regular delegates at the very end of that momentous session, he was called to take his place for a few hours.

He felt that he had not been fairly dealt with, particularly in the matter of the division of the diocese, that he had been treated ungenerously, and that in order to preserve his respect and friendship for his diocesan he must leave the diocese. In the latter part of the autumn of 1876 he was elected to the rectorship of Christ Church, Williamsport, in the diocese of Central Pennsylvania, and this election he accepted, and entered upon his work just before Christmas. The people who came to the early celebration of the Eucharist that Christmas morning were surprised to see that so notorious a Ritualist as Dr. Hopkins had not changed the violet altar-cloth proper for Advent for a white one !

Williamsport is a flourishing and pretty city on the west branch of the Susquehanna. The parish was known as a High Church parish, and it was quite willing for Dr. Hopkins to lead it still further along the ways which were then so much spoken against. But his course was not so much in the way of advancing ceremonial, as in deepening and enriching spiritual agencies. The services increased in number and variety, and soon the weekly and festival Eucharist became the rule in the parish.

13

Even more frequent celebrations came later on, and doubtless, if he had not been so frequently called away from home, he would have established the daily offering of the Holy Sacrifice. But there was no unusual ceremonial at these services. There were no candles on the altar, nor were the Eucharistic vestments used. The bread was "fine usual bread," and the chalice was mixed beforehand in the vestry. Even colored stoles were not used until, after some years, they were given by lay people. The choir was but the old-fashioned mixed choir, and there were no choral services. On Sundays there was an early celebration, and at the usual hour followed the full morning service and sermon. But there was a depth of devotion apparent in these simple services which arose from an entire personal consecration to the service of the blessed Saviour and a full belief in His presence in the Catholic Church. His parochial activities were not fussy, and he was clear of that bane of modern active Church work—the formation of a vast machinery of guilds and chapters for doing useless and useful things with equal efficiency. But he was everybody's pastor in the parish. True as steel himself and faithful to the spirit as well as the form of his vows, he had endless hope for others, never-ending patience with others' foibles or failings, unvarying readiness to listen to every tale of sorrow or of wrong, great gentleness in dealing with those who were trying to learn how to repent, breezy, fresh wit and good humor which blew away selfishness and downheartedness, and overwhelming force for the insincere and the hypocrites.

He had none of that fault of priests—a desire to rule all things, and to keep all things in his own hands. This fault it is which makes so many parsons unmanly and mean. There was none of it in his make-up, for if a man could do a thing that needed to be done, and was willing to do it, he let him do it. And if a man had a right to do a thing, he let him have the right, and he went at least half way to tell him so. He had none of that petty distrust of his vestry which so many priests have. The law of the Church had given the vestry certain powers and duties, and these he gladly let them have without hindrance; and yet he always got his vestry to do about as much as he wanted them to do. He used to say that the best way to get one's rights from others is to give them their own. His work was a great one. It was not confined to the city or to his own missions. He was always at the service of his brother clergy as far as he could be. He visited outlying and distant mission stations; he hunted up the sick ánd the wretched and forlorn; he would travel for miles and miles over mountain roads to comfort a poor woman in distress. He would preach in country school-houses, administer the communion at night to communicants otherwise deprived of that privilege ; at one place he was known as " the Methodist " from the fervor with which he preached. It is hardly a wonder that when he began his agitation for the setting apart of the Convocation of Williamsport as a distinct diocese he was suspected by some (even his own bishop among others) of a wish to be the first bishop of the new see.* For he was active to an astonishing degree in this scheme, which he took up in the very beginning of his life at Williamsport. They did not know him. He was working for the good of the Church, and he would have done the same if it had been his own father who was bishop of a diocese which was ready for subdivision. But his work in this direction all went for nought. It lasted several years, and at one time seemed almost certain to succeed. He raised a good-sized subscription for an Episcopal Fund for the proposed diocese years before it could canonically have been set up—all to no purpose. In one way or another he was thwarted, and at last an assistant bishop was chosen, and the maintenance of two bishops in one diocese has been from the beginning a greater expense to the laity than would have been if the diocese had been divided ; and yet the costliness of division was the great final argument which defeated the movement with the laity.

The following, selected from his frequent letters to his mother, will tell enough of the manner of his life at Williamsport and reveal his activity.

* Before he accepted the call to Williamsport he visited the parish, and, setting forth his determination to attempt the division of the diocese, he made it the condition of his acceptance that the parish should further his efforts, and also that the parish church should be offered to the bishop of the new see, he agreeing in turn *to resign and leave the diocese.* As regards the financial difficulty, the division would require the assessment to be nearly doubled, from fifty cents to *about* a dollar. Yet, in 1882, it was voted to ask for an *assistant* bishop, whose salary was fixed at $4,000, requiring an assessment of one dollar and thirty-five cents ! And the committee which recommended this action had been appointed to consider the best means of relieving the burden of Episcopal duties, after asking certain questions of the parishes. One question was, " How do you think the need of more Episcopal oversight can be supplied?" Only ten per cent. of the parishes replied to this—" By an assistant bishop ! " while eighteen per cent. replied, " By a division of the diocese ! "

The conditions which justify division seem to have existed, but the influence of the bishop prevented it being effected.

Extracts from Letters.

February 28, 1880.—To his Mother : " P.S.—For one funeral lately, in the Hills, I had to drive twelve miles through *awful* mud to the church where the service was held ;· then *five* miles through ditto, to the cemetery ; then ten miles through the worst ditto and *rain* besides, back to Williamsport—twenty-seven miles in all. I left home at 7.30 A.M. and returned at 6.10 P.M., and had service and sermon at seven, same evening ! "

March 23, 1880.—He writes to her : " Last week, on Thursday afternoon, I went up the river twenty-seven miles to Lockhaven, where I was to lecture (on Symbolism) that evening, to help raise funds for the repairing of their church. There was a very good attendance, and they seemed well pleased. I might have returned in a midnight train, but thought it hardly kind to my friends there, and certainly not comfortable for myself. The morning train, leaving before seven o'clock, was also rather uncomfortable. So I concluded to take the 11 A.M. train, which would give me time to pay a couple of visits in the morning. The omnibus was ordered to call for me in time, and I was at my friend's house (a mile and a quarter from the station), with overcoat and arctics on, there being a tremendous snow-storm coming down. But he came not, and so I lost the train, and had to get a conveyance to take me to Williamsport, where one of my lectures on the Sacrifices of the Old Law was to be given in the evening. The roads were shockingly muddy. The snow kept coming nearly all day, the wind being just in my face. I was five hours on the road in a two-horse buggy, but got down in time, chilly, but not hurt in the slightest degree—not even a slight cold ! "

" July 13, 1880.—All last week I was with the Rev. Dr. Charles Breck, brother of Rev. James Breck, founder of Nashotah. He has been preparing a life of his brother, made up mainly from his numerous letters, public and private ; and the mass of material made up over one thousand pages of legal cap paper. He wishes me to put all this in a condition for the printer to go to work on. I read through the whole of it last week, and now have to go all over it, pen in hand, and make any number of corrections on every page ! It is a ' job and a half,' but I suppose I shall get through it some time or other."

" July 30, 1880.—Yesterday our picnic came off—parish and

mission schools united, and adults besides—540 souls! The morning rose bright, but about eight o'clock clouded over, and a few drops fell threateningly: but we concluded to be brave, and started, and the weather was delightful all day long—cool, breezy, and now and then passing clouds to break the force of the sunshine. But we found that there was a 'wreck' on the R.R., half way to 'Hall's Woods.' A cow had sent thirteen freight cars to grief, giving up her own life as a forfeit to her success. We all had to get out, and transfer all the baskets and passengers, and carry five tall tubs, each with twenty-five quarts of ice-cream, and ice too, for some distance around the wreck, and then get into another train, of *freight cars* (all that could be gotten there in time for us). To hoist the ladies up into the freight cars, with no ladders, or platform, or steps, was a part of the fun not down in the programme! But it was *done*, and everything passed off very pleasantly, and *all* got home by six o'clock, safe and sound. *Then I* began to enjoy the day!"

"December 21, 1880.—This afternoon I go to Danville to deliver a brief address on the Organ, at the opening of a new organ in the Mission Chapel there. Last Thursday I was at Renovo (about fifty miles up the river), to see the church there —a little timber affair which they are building from my design. I spent the greater part of the day there, made drawings for the chancel furniture, etc., went to a Church oyster supper in the evening (for the carpets), and got home again by midnight. As soon as I can get the time I am to go to Lockhaven to superintend the putting up of a Memorial Brass, designed by me, in memory of a previous rector, the Rev. Milton C. Lightner. I made the design while at New York at the General Convention. Since my sixtieth birthday I have begun smoking a *little*. I take only one cigar a day, and that at 10 P.M., when everybody else is gone to bed. So far I find it of decided benefit to my voice."

"February 10, 1881.—At a little past midnight last Saturday night I returned from my western trip. The Provincial Synod business was very well done, *as far as it went;* but it did not go *as far* as I wished and hoped. Perhaps it is wiser to move so slowly; but it is very trying to one who sees so clearly what *ought* to be done, and *must* be done sooner or later. Even what was accomplished much more than paid me for the time and trouble of going. The *three* bishops and all the clergy and laity treated me very kindly, and even *more* than kindly. On Thursday and Friday evenings I delivered two lectures to two very fair audi-

ences, and apparently to their great satisfaction. My two sermons, on Sunday morning and evening, seemed to be equally
satisfactory, the only complaint being that they were *too short.*
The following Friday afternoon I started for home again, but
there was detention after detention, so that it was past one o'clock
Sunday morning before I got to bed. But I was up at 6 A.M.,
had my usual early celebration at 7 A.M., with second celebration
at the usual time. In the afternoon I walked out to my Mission,
and had six baptisms after attending to my parish Sunday-school.
Full service in the evening finished my day's work—leaving me
pretty well tired out.

" Bishop Seymour and many others are very anxious to get me
out West; but there is no definite offer of any post, only, they
say, if I come to *any* of the three dioceses in Illinois they will be
sure to send me to General Convention ! "

" March 9, 1881.—Last night I had a very important vestry
meeting. On Sunday I startled the congregation with a thun-
derbolt, as some of them called it, by announcing a call for a
meeting of the Wardens and Vestry on Tuesday evening, to
consider whether the present rector should continue his connection with the parish, or not. Bishop Seymour sent me a very
pressing call to join him in Springfield, to live with him in his
house, at *no* expense for board, lodging, washing, lights, etc.,
and with a $1,000 a year *cash* besides (which would be better
pecuniarily than I am doing here, besides the pleasure of living
and working under a congenial bishop). He promised me, too,
that so far as he *could* promise, if I went there, I should *surely* be
sent to General Convention, as well as to the Provincial Synod.
I then put it to the Vestry, so that if there was the least desire
to have me leave *now* was the time to speak out, when I could
leave them honorably and with no bones broken on either side.
But they did not seem to see it in that light. They unanimously
passed a resolution, earnestly pressing me to stay, and saying that
they believed the desire to be equally unanimous on the part of
the entire parish. Whereupon I told them I would stay—
probably till we get the new diocese. They *know* I expect to
leave them *then.* To-night in the midnight train I go to Baltimore, to preach to-morrow evening in Mount Calvary Church ;
and then return in the night train from there, so as to be here
again by 8 A.M. on Friday morning."

" June 6, 1881.—The past week has given me the most
brilliant triumph of my life, in the adoption by the Diocesan

Convention of Illinois of the Canon of an Appellate Court, drafted by me; and thus completing the organization of our first *Province*, setting a model to all the rest of the Church in America. This comes after *twenty years* of work on *my* part to secure the erection of Provinces, besides all the work that dear father spent in trying to get a Court of Appeals. When I went out to Springfield last January, *I drafted that canon,* but it was of no effect until enacted by the three Diocesan Conventions of Springfield, Quincy, and Illinois. Springfield adopted it unanimously; Quincy with only *one* opposing vote; and now Illinois adopts it *unanimously* on a vote by orders, although the bishop came out *against* it! I am now preparing for a campaign in our Convention for one or more new dioceses.''

"July 5, 1881.—My trip to the West was rather hurried, but otherwise very pleasant. On St. John's Day, June 24th, *Friday,* I went down to Danville first, to attend the laying of the corner-stone of the new and beautiful church to be erected there. There were religious services first, at which the same clergyman preached who preached at the laying of the *first* corner-stone, fifty-three years ago! He was a very old man, and his voice could scarcely be heard. The stone itself was laid by the Free Masons, as was done at the laying of the first corner-stone, fifty-three years before (and as dear father did in Pittsburgh). And the same Grand Master laid the stone who laid the other fifty-three years ago! Certainly a most remarkable coincidence. Before the Masonic ceremonies were over I had to leave to catch the train for the West, which I joined at Sunbury. At Harrisburg I took the main line for Chicago, arriving at Racine on Saturday night, about midnight. On Sunday the Baccalaureate Sermon was preached by the Rev. Dr. Courtney, of Chicago—and it was a remarkably fine discourse, preached entirely without notes. On Monday at the Junior Exhibition I was put on a committee to award prizes for good reading and elocution. On Tuesday evening the Board of Trustees met, and had a stormy session lasting until three o'clock next morning! There was a cold-blooded attempt to put Dr. Parker summarily out of the Wardenship! But it was defeated. The Trustees who did it were so angry at their defeat that they threaten to resign their seats in the Board: and it would be a good thing for the college if they would do so.''

" Wednesday was the Commencement. On Thursday I started for Nashotah, which I had not visited since 1856. Professor

Kemper and Mrs. Adams, his sister, children of Bishop Kemper, showed me quite a number of letters from dear father to their father, written during the Pennsylvania days from 1824 to 1831. They have also diaries of their father's missionary journeys in Pennsylvania from 1812, and would very much like to have me *write his life !* But I am too busy now with other work. The next day, Friday, at eleven o'clock, I started on my return. I had not time to see anybody at Chicago, going or coming. At Erie, on Saturday morning, we received the news of the horrible attempt to assassinate the President. Telegram after telegram, at the successive stopping places, made things worse, until in the evening we were told that he died at 7.15 P.M., and that Mrs. Garfield did not arrive till half an hour after he had breathed his last ! We reached Williamsport at midnight. Next morning I was delighted to learn that the President was yet living, and long may he live ! During all this week I am having the Holy Eucharist daily at 7 A.M., owing to his condition, and the dangers that threaten the country should he die.''

'' September 4, 1881.—Do not feel uneasy about me, dearest mother ; I am somewhat better, though I had only *six* services last Sunday ! ''

'' October 12, 1881.—Last week I travelled only about two thousand miles—to Quincy, Ill., and back, to attend the Provincial Synod of Illinois. Yet I was disappointed. About sixty miles this side of Chicago we found a couple of freight cars off the track, which delayed us (for we could not pass till they were gotten out of the way) for two hours and a half. This made me too late in Chicago. We ought to have reached there by 7.20 P.M. on Tuesday. We did not arrive till nearly ten o'clock, while the Quincy train left at 9.05 P.M. Instead of reaching Quincy, then, Wednesday morning at 8.30, I did not arrive till past eleven o'clock at night, when the synod was all over. . . . I found that the synod had done just right, although not *all* that I could have wished. Next time they may go on and do a little more. The same day at evening I set out on my return, and got home Saturday evening. ''

'' All Saints, 1881.—Last week I was at Providence, R. I., attending the Church Congress, where I had a paper to read on a subject that would not interest *you* at all—it was ' the relation of parishes to the diocese, and of the dioceses to the General Convention, in the matter of jurisdiction and representation.' I also spoke as a volunteer on the subject of liturgical growth, and on theological education. As I am writing to my mother and to please *her*, I will tell her a fact that I would not mention to everyone. At the end of my speech on liturgical growth the little bell sounded its twenty minutes before I was done (as was the case with pretty much everyone else) ; but the audience were so interested that they kept on applauding for several minutes—insisting that I should finish what I had to say. At length I rose and said that I could not ask to violate the law which was laid down for all alike, and then they quieted sufficiently for the next speaker to go on. But though nearly every speaker was caught by the bell in the same way, there was no such *demonstration* made over anybody else. I was specially thanked by the bishop and the committee for my contributions toward making the congress a success. . . . You have doubtless seen the account of the election of a new bishop for Pittsburgh. Immediately after the election I received a letter from a leading layman who told me that ' my letter did it ! ' He had written me, asking me about the Rev. Cortlandt Whitehead ; and I answered him very fully. My letter was read aloud at a meeting of clergy and laity for consultation, and his election was the consequence. A clergyman has since written me the same thing; and also another layman—President Judge of the county in which Meadville is. Also a letter in the *American Literary Churchman* says the same thing so pointedly, that I am afraid it may make some trouble for Dr. Whitehead among the bishops who don't like me. . . . While passing through New York I gave out the contract for the pastoral staff to be made from my design for my bishop here, to be presented to him by his clergy next January on the fiftieth anniversary of his ordination to the diaconate. It will be very pretty, with one hundred and twenty-seven jewels in it, the crook being of ebony, the upper part of the staff of ivory, and the lower part of ebony, and ebony and holly alternately ; with some nice carved work besides. [The greater part of the *cost* of this bishop's crook fell upon him too, though it was presented in the name of all the clergy of the diocese.—C.F.S.] I think he will like *that*, whether he likes the notion of a new diocese or not ! "

" November 25, 1881.—My trip to Fredericksburg, Va., was *very* pleasant. I had three or four days of *almost* complete *rest ;* —more thorough rest than I have had for years. I was received with the utmost friendliness by *all* whom I met. I left here at midnight on Monday the 14th, and reached Washington for a late breakfast at nine o'clock Tuesday morning. I reached Fredericksburg at 2 P.M. On Wednesday I walked out to Marye's Hill (pronounced Ma*ree's*) and saw the site of the terrible battle in 1862 in which Burnside was defeated. I visited also the Federal cemetery on that hill where twenty-two thousand Union dead lie buried. They brought in the bodies from the other battle-fields of the neighborhood, Chancellorsville and the Wilderness. Every grave has a stone at the head, with the number cut on it by which it is recognized in the record book. The whole vast field extends over the top of Marye's Hill (with a magnificent prospect), having a nice wall all around it, and the entire ground is carefully kept in order. There is a neat cottage near the gate, where the care-taker lives. There is no government on earth that has taken such tender care for its fallen soldiers.

" The next day I walked up the river to Falmouth, returning by another way. The third day I crossed the river, and also visited the ferry at which, once upon a time, General Washington flung a stone across the river. On the other side his mother lived for many years. On Friday evening I lectured on the True Relations of Religion and Science, apparently to the satisfaction of my hearers, among whom were the Roman Priest, the Baptist, Methodist, and Presbyterian ministers, and many others of the thinking people of the place. On Sunday I preached three times, twice to the congregation of Trinity Church and in the evening at St. George's. Kinder hospitality I never expect to meet. They are quite ripe for an advance all along the line in Virginia. They say that *all they want is a leader.* I made them some suggestions, but whether they will have *grit* enough to follow them remains to be seen.

" I left on my return Monday morning. At York, Pa., I was left over for a couple of hours and called on the clergyman there, having a nice talk with him about the *new diocese.* That evening I reached Lancaster, where on Tuesday evening I met several of the leading gentlemen for a long talk about the new diocese.''

" December 15, 1881.—Last week at midnight on Monday I started for Washington, where I called on the President for a few brief moments and preached in the evening to a very good congregation at St. Paul's Church, the Rev. Mr. Barker's—a young man who is doing very good and vigorous work. [He was consecrated first Missionary Bishop of Western Colorado in 1893.]

"Next morning I started for Philadelphia, where I arrived at 2 P.M., and stopped at the Rev. Dr. Batterson's, for whom I preached that evening.   He has taken a feeble parish away in the northern suburbs of the city which was almost run out by the Low Church.   He gives them choral service with a surpliced choir, and other 'ritualistic' doings, and the congregation is building up at once !   On Friday evening I preached at St. Clement's, and between times had conversations with some of the leading clergy and laity about organizing the *Province of Pennsylvania,* which is one of the 'big things' I am now trying to work, now that the Province of Illinois is in nice working order.

"I expect to be at the consecration of Dr. Whitehead as Bishop of Pittsburgh, and hope to do something toward the Province of Pennsylvania before I leave the place.''

"Christmas Eve, 1881.—Though the hurry of the holidays is upon us, I took a flying trip to Philadelphia last Monday night, starting in the midnight train and reaching Philadelphia by daylight.   An old gentleman named ——, now living in Germantown, who was formerly a resident of Williamsport and laid out one of the suburbs, gave there to Christ Church a small lot, 100 feet by 50 feet, for our Mission Chapel ; but it was to be used *only* for that purpose, and if we remove to another lot, his gift reverts to his estate.   Now it is in a low mudhole ; is too small for the building we need ; and we shall certainly build elsewhere when the time comes.   But we might as well have the value of that lot to help us ; we might get $200 for it.   Mr. —— is eighty-two years of age—an unbaptized Quaker.   They *say* he is a regular old Turk for temper and obstinacy.   Nobody gave any hope that I should succeed in getting him to give us a quitclaim deed (which was what I wanted).   Even his daughter, a good churchwoman, whom I met in the street on the way to the house, gave me no hope.   I was not personally acquainted with him, and brought no letter of introduction.   His daughter said I should find him walking about the grounds.   The place was very fine—five hundred feet front on the street, with slopes and terraces planted with evergreens and rising twenty or twenty-five feet above the street, with a winding road leading up to the house, which was large, of stone, and with a wide veranda round it, and a fine view therefrom.   Nearly up to the house I met the old gentleman, introduced myself, sailed straight into business, and *inside of an hour* went off with the deed, signed, sealed, and witnessed, in my pocket.

" The rest of the day I spent with Mrs. Vibbert, and she wanted me to sing for her children my song about the Oyster-man, which was *her* delight when she was their age. I took tea at Dr. Batterson's, made three visits, and was off again in the midnight train for Williamsport."

" January 1, 1883.—My first letter of the New Year is to you ! May the New Year bring you all you can desire !

" The last week was an excessively busy one. Four services on Sunday ; four on Monday (Christmas Day). There being *three* celebrations, 7 A.M., 9 A.M. at the Mission Chapel, and at 10.30 A.M. after full service. In the evening we had the Mission Christmas tree—the little building packed to the utmost. On Tuesday service and Holy Communion, and a funeral in the afternoon, going over two miles to the cemetery, and a vestry meeting in the evening. On Wednesday service and Holy Communion ; then a wedding at the church, our parish Christmas tree in the afternoon—with another big crowd ; and in the evening, service and sermon. On Thursday, service and Holy Communion in the morning. On Friday went down and ministered the Holy Communion to a sick tenant at the Hall mansion. On Saturday another private administration to a sick man. Yesterday (Sunday) four services again, and to-day, of course, service and Holy Communion. . . . I mailed you a copy of the Jubilee services at St. Paul's Chapel, in which I suppose, you have already found my sermon. It is the first and only sermon that I have written for more than thirty years ! and the *only* one of mine that has ever yet been *printed*. I do not know whether it will be noticed or not, but if it is, I should not be surprised at plenty of fault-finding."

" February 24, 1883.—On Monday of this week I went to Wellsboro', in Tioga County, to help Rev. Dr. Breck in regard to the alteration of his church. It is an old building of frame, in the country style of fifty years ago, windows half an acre each, all filled with cheap, square transparent glass. He had written me to ask my advice about the size and shape of his altar windows ; but without seeing *all* the rest of the building, what could I say. So I started at 8.30 by train and went to Roaring Branch (about thirty miles). There I took the stage across the mountain to Blossburg, twelve miles, expecting to be the only passenger. But the sleigh was *full ;* and part of the way they crowded three women on one seat. At Blossburg I dined, and hired a two-horse buggy and driver to drive me

twenty miles to Wellsboro'.   It was a bright day, though rather
cold, and I enjoyed the open-air drive of thirty-two miles very
much.   We had daylight enough after my arrival to inspect the
church, and in the evening I made rough sketches, and gave my
advice, and left next morning, returning by the way of Elmira,
where I had to wait nearly six hours for a train !   I reached
home safe and well by six o'clock P.M.

" From Wisconsin the clergy have applied to me to get them up
a pastoral staff to be given to their bishop at the meeting of their
Convention in June, and I shall do it.   It will not be, by any
means, so costly as the one we got up here for Bishop Howe."

" March 6, 1883.—Yesterday I had a very pleasant surprise.
I received a letter from the Rev. Leighton Coleman, D.D., who
is now at Oxford, England, enclosing a note to *him* from Canon
Liddon, the most distinguished living preacher in the Church of
England.   Dr. Coleman had sent him a copy of my Review Article about Dr. Pusey (whose Life Canon Liddon is to write) ;
and the Canon thanks him for it, saying of my Article : ' It is
written with great grasp of the general outline of the subject, and
it occasionally displays an intimate acquaintance with details,
for which I was unprepared.'   Excuse me for transcribing the
words ; but I thought that—coming from so distinguished a man
—they might give some pleasure to my mother.   That article
has brought me more letters of thanks and compliments than any
other I ever wrote."

" April 30, 1883.—Last week I went down to Philadelphia,
starting from here in a dismal snow-storm which continued all
day till it melted into a cold rain, in which I walked about all
the evening in the city.

" Next morning I secured an interview with Bishop Stevens,
who has long disliked me, and who has hitherto bluffed me off,
so that I could not get a word with him.   I got into the house,
however, and would take no suggestion to meet him elsewhere.
I sent back word that I was in no hurry ; had nothing to do in
Philadelphia but to see the bishop ; and would wait as long as
he pleased.   In about twenty minutes the bishop came in, and
greeted me very coolly.   We were together for more than an
hour.   By the time we got through we had come to a mutual
understanding in regard to the Federate Council of Pennsylvania
—he is to introduce the subject in his address to the Convention.
I got him to name a number of gentlemen for me to see on the
subject, who will support the measure in Convention, and be-

fore parting he gave me his blessing. We shall *pull together* on that important point. I afterward saw the gentlemen he spoke of, and one of them, Judge Thayer, has promised to move for a committee on that part of the bishop's address; another —a leading Low Church clergyman—will second the motion, with a speech; all the others will support it, and work for it in advance. So that—unless something occurs to disappoint us—I think the Province of Pennsylvania will be on its legs this year. My resolutions have already passed the Conventions of Pittsburgh and Central Pennsylvania. I came home feeling *very* happy, I assure you, for *nothing* could be done *without* Bishop Stevens and his Convention; and as he is a Low Churchman and did not like me, and as his Convention is Low Church also, and as every effort I had made through others and through letters had been in vain, my final success *personally* is only the more gratifying. Perhaps, however, some other influence may come in and upset it all yet! I shall not feel sure until the Philadelphia Convention is over. Next week I go to New York to the Board of Trustees of the General Theological Seminary, and I expect some tough work there too, of which more when I return."

" May 14, 1883.—Last week was one of the most successful of my life—more so than I could have dreamed of.

" On Monday evening I met, as a member, the Committee of the Board of Trustees of the General Theological Seminary on Amendments to the Constitution—expecting that I *might* be in a minority of *one.* We met in the robing-room of Trinity Chapel. Dr. Dix was in the chair—and there were eight or nine in all, Dr. Heman Dyer (the old head-centre of the Low Church party in New York) among them. The main thing was to try to reduce the board in numbers. It now has nearly five hundred members. Some six years ago they tried to reduce the number to *only* about one hundred and sixty! But they failed somehow even in that. This time, at first, they thought they could not safely venture upon more. But I persuaded them to go farther, and finally they *unanimously* agreed to recommend that the number be only fifty-one besides the bishops (I wanted thirty-one, but yielded so as to secure unanimity). On Wednesday evening we had a tough fight in the Board itself; but finally *carried* our proposal *there* also. If we can get it through General Convention, we shall be all right! I have been working twenty-four years for this! On the next day, in Philadelphia, the Bishop inserted in his Address what I wished him to say about the

Federate Council of all the dioceses in the State of Pennsylvania. A committee was appointed on that part of the bishop's address; a report and resolutions which I had drawn up were presented to the Convention by the Committee, and were *passed*—with only one amendment, which does no harm.   *Each* of the three dioceses has now passed the same resolutions, and each has appointed a committee of seven to meet the others, and the Bishop of Pennsylvania is to call them together, probably some time in September.   This is the greatest triumph of the year, so far!   On Sunday last—Whitsunday—Archdeacon Kirkby was with us in the morning, and gave us a most interesting talk on missions.   In the afternoon our *three* Sunday-schools were all together, for the *first time*.   Trinity Parish split off from our parish some years before I came; setting itself up for a Low Church parish, saying that *we* were too ' High Church; ' many narrow things on both sides have been done to keep up the feeling of *dis*union.   I have steadily pursued a policy of peace and harmony as far as I could; and, as a result of it, the Rector of Trinity, Mr. Foley, will *this* year vote with us on the division of the diocese (which he has never done before), and *proposed* that his Sunday-school should come down to Christ Church in the afternoon, and join ours and our Mission Sunday-school, and all three together be talked to by the archdeacon.   So said, so done.   We had the columns of the church dressed with the Sunday-school banners all round.   We began with our little Sunday-school choral service (words and music both mine); and Mr. Foley made a brief address (he liked our little choral service so well that he is going to introduce it in his own Sunday-school!).   The archdeacon talked to the children in a most charming way.   The four hymns that were sung would have warmed your heart.   The whole three schools had practised them.   We had *five* brass instruments to reinforce the organ; and the volume of sound that went up was such as Williamsport had never known before.   All were delighted.   My organist was so pleased that the tears of joy ran down his face!   A very large share of the success was due to Mr. Dobson, my *good* Deacon. Mr. Foley is going to have a surpliced choir!   Mr. Dobson will do the same in his Mission Chapel.   We *may* do something of the sort also."

" June 16, 1883.—As you doubtless know by this time I was defeated in our Convention in the two things I desired most. The division of the diocese was lost by *one* vote, and my election to General Convention failed by the same. I have taken my defeat with my usual good humor. I am one of the 'supplemental deputies,' however, and may *possibly* get a seat in *that* way, but it is not likely. I suppose I had had successes enough for one season! There were several reasons for our defeat. In the first place, my friends *all* said that, as I had been so promi-nent in the movement all through, *I had better be silent now*—that my speaking would provoke more opposition, etc. So I took their advice, they being *perfectly sure* that they had votes enough to carry it. Nearly all the speeches were made on the other side, and were left unanswered by *our* friends. From what I have been told since by some who voted against us, I am *sure* that if I had torn their flimsy fallacies to rags, as I could have done in a few moments, the result would have been different. Next time I shall take the bit between my teeth and do my own steering. But this beats us for *three years* longer! I may pos-sibly get into General Convention by the time I am sixty-six years old—and probably not then! The bishop has everywhere stirred up the laity against me by calling me an 'agitator,' 'a dangerous man,' 'always extreme,' etc. So they send to General Convention *quiet* men, who will not say a word all the way through, and will probably run home before the session is through!

"I had one *great* success however. Last October I introduced an amendment to our Constitution, so that instead of the clergy *nominating* a man for bishop, and the laity then voting only *yes* or *no* to that man, both Orders shall ballot at the same time, and no one is elected until he has at the same ballot a majority of both Orders. This change was unanimously approved in October, and now has been unanimously adopted, so that it is our law."

"June 26, 1883.—Tell my dear sister that I don't *need* any consolation. I am the most good-natured defeated man that ever was. And it is *easy* to me: for when the *event* shows which way *the Lord* wishes it to be for the present, I am always con-tented, for I do not think myself wiser than He! I know He will bring good out of it in the long run, whether *I* live to see it or not."

Here is as good a place as any for an extract from a letter by Bishop Howe upon this very point: "Just after a defeat in one of these crises, the champion, veiling his disappointment in smiles, made his unobserved way to the Chair, and with a cordial grasp of the hand, said : ' Dear Bishop, I have two characteristics—I never lose my temper, and I never give up ! ' To that decision of the diocese, Dr. Hopkins made no factious opposition.''

To resume his letter to his mother : '' On Monday of last week I went up to Tioga County to help Dr. Breck in remodelling his old frame church. They wanted my advice about *every* thing. The next day, returning, we found a great landslide over the railroad track, which detained us nearly twenty-four hours. I had nothing to eat from breakfast till 9 P.M. The afternoon settled down into a hard rain, dark and dismal. The conductor foraged till he brought in at 9 P.M. a basket with a loaf of bread, some butter in a tin cup, three pieces of cold fried ham, a couple of hard-boiled eggs, and a bit of cheese. I made a good supper ! At a farmhouse, to which we went back, some ladies of the party got beds, but I bunked out on the *seats* of the car with my clothes on, and slept so-so. Next morning we got a good breakfast at the farmhouse, and reached home early in the afternoon. I was to have started that *morning* for Lehigh University to attend their Commencement and see some folks for talk on Church matters. But now the only way I could reach there in time was to take the midnight train and travel all night, and so arrived there just half an hour before the exercises began. So you see I had a rather hard week of it.''

'' Philadelphia, October 18.—Yesterday were carried, by an overwhelming majority, the amendments in the Constitution of the General Theological Seminary for which I have been working for more than twenty-four years ! Instead of between five hundred and six hundred members, that Board will now have only fifty-one besides the bishops. I assure you the result made me very happy.''

'' November 22, 1883.—Last week, on Monday, I took the midnight train for the east, arriving at New Brunswick, N. J., at 10.30 A.M., in time for the choral celebration in Christ Church, in which the surpliced choirs of the diocese took part. There were over sixty in surplices, besides the clergy and the bishop. The service was remarkably well done. At 4 P.M. there was choral evensong, and I preached the sermon, which they all seemed to like very well. The church was crowded to the utmost on both occasions.

'' At 6 P.M. I went on to New York and spent a very pleasant

14

evening with Dr. and Mrs. Dix. Next morning I had a long
talk with Dr. Swope. In the afternoon Dr. Dix took me to
the house of Mr. John Jacob Astor, to show me (by his permission) a magnificent Book of Hours, illuminated on vellum, in
perfect condition, executed about four hundred years ago for
Albert of Brandenburg. The Emperor of Germany (one of his
descendants) was very anxious to get it, but our American million-
aire carried it off under his nose; but it cost him considerably
over ten thousand dollars. The paintings all through the work
were in exquisite miniature style, exceeding anything else of the
sort I ever saw. At 6 P.M. I dined with a very wealthy friend,
Elbridge T. Gerry and his wife, and had much pleasant talk;
and about 9 P.M. went to Dr. Hoffman's (dean of the seminary), and talked with him till nearly midnight. Next day I
went on doing the same, but getting to Philadelphia by 6 P.M.,
where I called on Bishop Stevens (not at home) and others, taking the midnight train again back to Williamsport.

"I was delighted in New York to find a wonderful unity
of feeling in supporting the new assistant bishop (Dr. H. C.
Potter), and that *my personal friends*, Dr. Swope especially,
seem to be nearer to him than anybody else!—a remarkable
fact."

"December 9, 1883.—I leave early to-morrow for Corning,
N. Y., on Church business, about which I will write you more
fully after my return. During the past week I lectured on
Church music, on Tuesday evening, at Bradford, in this State;
on Wednesday preached at Du Bois, where a nice little parish is
growing up out of seed sown by me a year ago; and a little
church is gowing up rapidly, served by a deacon of the diocese
of Pittsburgh. On Thursday morning I administered the Holy
Communion to sixteen persons, and returned home by midnight.
You see, I find plenty to do!"

"December 17, 1883.—During the past week I have again
been 'on the go.' On Monday I went to Corning, N. Y., to
see General Magee, one of the most influential of the rich men
who are interested in the Clearfield Bituminous Coal Company,
who are building the new city of *Peale* in the midst of their
forty thousand acres of coal lands. They have given the Church,
at my request, the finest building site in the new town, and I
want the rich stockholders—especially those who are churchmen—
to give me money enough to build a nice church costing $6,000
or $7,000. They wish me to prepare my plans and get esti-

mates on them, and then they will tell me what they will do.
On my way back I stopped at Elmira to see another influential
stockholder, and at Ralston all night to meet another. All looks
favorable. I reached home Wednesday noon. To-morrow
night I go to New York to attend the consecration of Mr.
Walker as Bishop of Northern Dakota.''

" St. Stephen's Day, 1883.—Last week I took the train Tuesday night, reaching Philadelphia on Wednesday morning—a
dismal snow-stormy day ! I took a cab for three hours, going to
see some friends, and then to Judge Thayer's court-room, where
I had to wait three hours before I could see him. Bishop Stevens
seems disposed to block all my work for the Federate Council of
Pennsylvania by mere inaction. He will not fix either time or
place for the meeting of the Committees of Conference already
appointed from the three dioceses. It remains to be seen whether
I can get him to move on by pressure applied *through others.*
Judge Thayer *will help.*

" In the afternoon train I went to New York, where, next
morning, I attended the consecration of the Rev. Wm. D. Walker
as Bishop of North Dakota. When I was first ordained I was
engaged for ten weeks to hold service for ' St. George the
Martyr,' a parish organization holding twenty-four lots of land
which were to be conveyed to St. Luke's Hospital. These services were held in a private house, away down town, and were
attended by very few. One of the vestrymen who *did* attend was
Bishop Walker's *father,* and he brought the bishop (then a little
boy) with him. I did not know that my connection with him
began so long ago ! I have known him *well* ever since he was
in the General Theological Seminary.

" At the collation in Calvary Church Rectory I had a very
pleasant conversation with Bishop Coxe, with whom I am on
very pleasant terms now. Bishop Littlejohn also had a long
talk with me about the altar plate for his Long Island Cathedral ;
but I persuaded him to employ a regular architect—a friend of
mine. I have not time for it. In the evening I had, by appointment, a *confidential* talk with Bishop Henry C. Potter, which
was on the whole very satisfactory. While there a Mr. Gregory
called to be confirmed by special appointment, and the bishop
asked me to present him, which, of course, I was glad to do.
He (Mr. G.) was surprised and apparently delighted to meet me
on such an occasion. He was engaged to be married to one of my
old flock at Plattsburgh, and she was so anxious that he should

take the Communion with her at Christmas that he came to Bishop Potter to be confirmed specially in time."

"January 22, 1884.—Last week I was off again to the Western part of the State. Bishop Stevens threatens to put in his pocket the three resolutions of Conventions of dioceses in this State, and *not* call together the three Committees which have been appointed to consider and report on the expediency of establishing a Federate Council. As the Diocese of Pittsburgh at my suggestion moved first in this matter, so I wanted them now to *insist* that Bishop Stevens shall do his duty. By arrangement with Bishop Whitehead I went first to Uniontown and attended the Southern Convocation of the Diocese of Pittsburgh. It involved my spending the night (Tuesday) at Altoona, and getting up at four in the morning! I breakfasted at Greensburg, and thought of the time when dear father stopped there to borrow Blackstone from lawyer Foster. We had a very pleasant meeting at Uniontown — the clergy calling me out to speak on every subject that came up. In the evening I made one of the speeches, and reminded them of dear father's work in that western country. Next day I went to Pittsburgh to see Hill Burgwin, a leading layman, who has worked with me for many years, and who agreed to do all that I wanted him to do. I reached home again at 12.20 Saturday *morning.*"

"February 16, 1884.—I have been hard at work trying to get the plans for the mission church at Peale done. You know, too, that I have been trying to get the 'Province of Pennsylvania' established. I succeeded, last spring, in getting the three Conventions of three dioceses in this State all to adopt *identical* resolutions, and three Committees of Conference were appointed to meet and report on the expediency of establishing a Federate Council, the *time* and *place* of meeting to be fixed by the Bishop of Pennsylvania (Stevens). I thought we were *all right*, but when I wrote to Bishop Stevens in December, asking him to let me know when he would call us together, he coolly wrote back to me that as *he* did not see any special reason for our meeting, he was not going to call us together *at all!* The idea of *his* undertaking to *veto* the action of the entire three Conventions (including his own) was a perfect outrage! But I knew it would be useless for me to tackle him *directly*. So I did not reply to his letter. But I made a trip to Philadelphia, and called on Judge Thayer, a prominent layman—the one who, by arrangement with the bishop himself—moved the matter in his own convention, and *carried* it!   The bishop knows that Thayer is not a man to be trifled with.   Thayer was willing to go to the bishop, if some *letter* was written to him by some influential member of the Committee from some other diocese.   So I went to Pittsburgh, and talked it over with my friend Hill Burgwin, one of the best lawyers *there*, and the one who *first* moved our resolutions (at my request) in the Diocese of Pittsburgh.   He entered into my views at once, and wrote to Thayer, who sent his letter (with one from himself) to Bishop Stevens.   And the bishop replies that if Judge Thayer and Mr. Burgwin think it advisable *he will call the Committees together!*   In this change of front, you see, I have kept *myself* out of sight altogether.   The strong laymen are my best helpers.   I expect to hear, before long, that the time is *fixed* and meeting *called.*   The other matter may interest *you* more.   The alumni of the General Theological Seminary have raised an endowment for a professorship in the seminary, and the *first* appointment is soon to be made.   The alumni have the election in their own hands.   Dr. Dix—in a very pleasant note—informs me that he has nominated *me.*   But nomination and *election* are very different things.   To have been nominated so cordially by *him*, however, will I think, be pleasing to *you*, as it certainly was very gratifying to *me.*''

Here is the place to note that Bishop Howe writes, regarding the '' Province of Pennsylvania,'' the various stages of whose growth have been noted in Dr. Hopkins' letters, as follows : '' In one aspect of the provincial system I was happy to find myself in full accord with the earnest and thoroughly informed presbyter.   He was much interested in the adoption and observance of Canon 6 of Title III. of the Digest which provides for a ' Federate Council ' of all the dioceses in any one Commonwealth, for purposes in which they have a common concern, as connected with or dependent upon the civil power.   The organization of such a body in Pennsylvania was largely due to his influence and exertion.   The indifference with which it had been regarded in some quarters, and the fear in some others that the measure might be used as an entering wedge for other and more questionable affiliations, have hitherto prevented that beneficent co-operation in Pennsylvania of the several dioceses from which I had fondly hoped that all would derive advantages, for which we still have to wait.   Dr. Hopkins died in the faith that the benefits of such federation will yet be realized among us,

and in his letter to me expressed that he should ' know and rejoice over it in Paradise,' to which he felt he was hastening.''

" March 12, 1884.—I have just returned from Scranton
where I preached Tuesday evening to a very large congregation
(for a week day evening and *very* rainy at that). I send you a
copy of the *Scranton Republican*, with a preliminary notice of
my coming, which reads as if it were written *specially* to please
my *mother !*

" Annun. B. V. M., 1884.—Last week I was off again, first
on Monday to Watkins, N. Y., to see General Magee, one of
the leading men in the Clearfield Bituminous Coal Company,
to start the getting up of subscriptions among the stockholders
for my new church at Peale, which church I am building for my
other deacon, Mr. Balsley, who began his services there the day
before. General Magee suggested that I write him a letter,
stating just how much I want ($7,500), and that he will show it
to Wm. H. Vanderbilt, and see what he will do.* Mr. Vanderbilt owns more than *two millions* of dollars' worth of stock in
that company ! Next day I went to Elmira first, and saw two
other important men in the Company, finding them kindly
disposed. In the afternoon I went to Tioga, Pa., where I
preached in the evening to a very fair congregation (for a
week day). The clergyman there is doing a remarkably good
work. Next morning, after a celebration at the church, I
started for home, but, at Stokesdale Junction, somehow or other,
I did not hear the conductor announce the place, and I was carried past ! I telegraphed my misfortune to Mr. Dobson, and
went on to Wellsboro,' spending the interval with Dr. Breck,
who was very glad to see me, having lately lost his wife, after
they had buried *all* their children ! He showed me their church,
which had been altered and painted, and in regard to which
they consulted me very often. They are well satisfied with the
result, and it looks better than I ever thought it would, by far !

* This church was built by Dr. Hopkins' sole efforts, after his own designs. With the exception of two or three large subscriptions he paid out
more cash than any other one contributor, and paid every bill for its building when due, borrowing money from the bank to do so, and meeting them,
and paying discounts. If all he did for the church was reckoned at a cash
valuation he would have been the largest single contributor. In short, he
made himself responsible for every cent of its cost. The church was consecrated, and thus put into the bishop's hands. Nor was this the only instance
of his energy and generosity in church building.

" Starting in the four o'clock train, we met detention after detention, landslides owing to the rain, etc., and I did not reach home till nearly midnight.

" It may please you to know that I was specially invited to be present at the consecration of Rev. Dr. Watson, the first bishop of the new diocese of East Carolina, but declined as having neither the time nor the money.   They then invited me the *second* time, offering to pay all *my expenses!*   They could not have done more, if I had been the presiding bishop !   But I am too busy and had to decline again.

" The Province of Pennsylvania looks more favorable now.   I think Bishop Stevens means *fairly*.   Next week I shall take a trip to Philadelphia and find out !

" April 5, 1884.—Monday night I went to Philadelphia, arriving there at eight o'clock.   After breakfast I went to see Bishop Stevens about the meetings of the committees of conference.   I had *succeeded* in *circumnavigating* him !   My two brave laymen did the thing up beautifully for me !   We are now to meet at 8 P.M. on Ascension Day, at the house of Bishop Stevens.   This is their Hundredth Convention since the diocese was organized ; and so they meet on Thursday (Ascension Day) instead of Tuesday *as usual*, and continue their session over Sunday.   I wanted to talk over with him, and *settle on* the exact programmes of what was to be done at the meeting.   But I found him *too sick to talk*.   He had so bad a cold that he was lying covered with wraps, on his library sofa, hardly able to articulate an audible word !   I therefore skipped the long talk, and left—not a little disappointed.   I shall still try to get at the substance of the thing, in another way, however.

" Another thing I had to do was to go to an architect's office in Chestnut Street, and examine his plans for a memorial chapel for Lehigh University.   I did so, and found them such as I could not approve at all !   The architect (under orders, he said, from head-quarters) had tried to combine chapel and commencement hall, two incompatible things.   I have written my condemnation to the president of the University, and *hope* I shall succeed in getting some better plan adopted.   The architect is not a Churchman, and knows *nothing* about Church architecture, except from the teeth *outward*.   It is a shame not to have a *Church* architect to design a *Chapel* for a *Church* University.

" Calling on Dr. Batterson afterward, I learned some very interesting circumstances in connection with Bishop Clarkson.   One was, that the Bishop's last Sunday *East* was spent with Dr. Batterson, morning and evening; and Dr. Batterson gave him as fine ritualistic services as he. could get up—vestments, lights, processions, etc.   After they had returned to the house, and sat down, there was a little pause, and then the Bishop—bringing his fist down with great emphasis—exclaimed—' Batterson !   I would give a thousand dollars if I could have a service like that in my cathedral at Omaha ! '

   " At the great public meeting held to express sorrow at his death, a *Romanist* presided, and a Presbyterian made the leading speech in praise of him !

   " April 16, 1884.—Holy Week and Easter were very busy with us, as a matter of course.   Notwithstanding the criss-cross weather, the attendance was very good.   Easter day was a perfect day, and we had 82 communicants at the early celebration, 68 at nine o'clock at the Mission Chapel, and 70 more at the noon celebration—220 in all, larger by 24 than *any* previous communion in the parish.   The offerings also bring up our fund for tiling the church floor (in place of our ragged carpets) to more than $1,100.   So, we shall put that work through this summer.   The Reredos fund, too, is about complete (except that we shall want $500 more for three fine large *pictures* to complete it).

   " May 8, 1884.—Last Sunday the Bishop was with us.   He arrived at past midnight on Saturday night (or rather, Sunday morning).   I was at the station to meet him, and was up at 6 A.M. for my early celebration, all the same.   In the morning it rained *hard*, but the church was full, and we had 30 confirmed. In the afternoon we had expected to open our new Sunday-school building, but, most provokingly, it was not done.   So I gave the Bishop a rest in the afternoon (which he did not regret), and in the evening \(raining still) we drove him out to our Mission Chapel.   As we knew it would be crowded, we both robed before getting into the carriage.   The little place was crowded *to the utmost*, and many could not get in at all !   The music was *very* hearty and spirited, sustained by a cornet as well as the reed-organ.   During the service the Bishop whispered to me, ' It's very hot here !   Can there not be some ventilation ? '   I answered that he *had* already all the ventilation that was possible. He replied : ' It is worse than the Black Hole of Calcutta ! ' I answered, ' Mr. Dobson has this every Sunday night.'   It *was* hot !   We were streaming from every pore in our bodies. But *sixteen* more were confirmed (making 46 in all), and everything went off in the most gratifying manner—except for the rain and the sweltering within.   I got the Bishop home again, without his catching cold, however, which was rather more than I expected under the circumstances.

"While the Bishop was here I sounded him in regard to the meeting of our Committees of Conference on a Federate Council, and he has consented *at once* to make the motion I wish him to make.   I think that matter will go through *straight.*"

"July 7, 1884.—You may perhaps have noticed that Monsignor Capel, the notorious Romanist lecturer and preacher, has been for some time in this country, and has come out with a pamphlet against our Church.   A consultation among many of the clergy (a bishop being among them) was held at the rooms of the *American Church Review,* and it was *unanimously* agreed that *I* must write the *Review* of it.   So last week, to get *time*— for I am too much interrupted here—I went down to Coleman Hall's, and spent three days, working steadily at my table from breakfast till past 7 P.M., stopping only for dinner.   The article is nearly done, but yet needs a great deal of *finishing.*   It is expected to appear in the August number of the *Review.*"

"*To a priest,* July 29, 1885.—You ought to be ashamed of yourself for getting *any* touch of the Roman fever under *any* circumstances, and if the young lady you write of has helped to cure you, she has done a good work, and give her my love.   If she is the right sort of a woman, you will be all the better for being married *once.*"

"*To the same,* August 4, 1885.—It is a comfort to know that your difficulty was only speculative, and that you are now cured.   Whenever the fit comes over you again, think of the time when *four* out of the five Patriarchs were Arianizing heretics; or of that later time when a paganized *Pope of Rome* could say : ' This Bethlehem *fable* has been a very profitable one for us !' There is a fermentation going on all through the spiritual world, and I believe the dear Lord will bring *good* out of it all.   But I have not time for more—the O. C. R. (Order of Corporate Reunion) is a dishonest humbug !   Last week I held service, on Thursday and Friday evenings, in the Elk Lick and Centennial School-houses in Sullivan County, baptizing —— and administering the Holy Communion to five persons."   [Sullivan County is about forty miles from Williamsport, and occupies an outlying spur of the Allegheny Mountains ; it was not then accessible by rail, and roads could not be worse.]

In 1886 his ambition to be elected to General Convention was gratified, and at the session of that year, which was held in Chicago, he was one of the most prominent figures. He was perfectly familiar with all the work of the Convention, for he had never missed a session from the year 1841, except, possibly, that of 1844.

Very early in the session, Dr. Phillips Brooks offered a resolution of fraternal greeting to the Congregational General Body then in session. Naturally, it was opposed, and on more grounds than one; but Dr. Hopkins came out in support of the resolution, on the ground, chiefly, that since we had begun by making overtures toward a discussion of hindrances to a reunion with all other bodies of Christians, it would be like an affront to refuse a mere courtesy to one of them. He was on his feet a great many times, and his fluency and strength of argument, his sparkling wit, his constant good humor, made him sure of willing listeners. No discussion was dull in which he took part, and with all his sharpness and earnestness he never lost his temper nor self-control. He had no place in any important standing committee, for the President, following the ordinary rule, made him, as a new member, a member of the Committee on the State of the Church. He and Dr. Knight, afterward Bishop of Milwaukee, were colleagues from Central Pennsylvania, and they voted aye on the proposal to change the name of the Church; thus dividing the clerical delegation from that diocese.

The subject of reunion occupied the chief place in his heart, and when the committee having the matter in charge reported the famous " Quadrilateral," he made a minority report which was afterward signed by a considerable number of persons. His own plan, which he had matured in the course of many years, has the merit of clearness and fulness, while it cannot for a moment be misunderstood, or be charged, as the Chicago-Lambeth Declaration of the Bishops has been charged, with shiftiness and doubledealing.

Dr. Hopkins' plan looked two ways. First, premising that no branch of the One, Holy, Catholic and Apostolic Church has ever embodied any formal heresy in the Eucharistic Office, he proposed that to the eighth article of the Constitution be added these words, or their equivalent : " While this Church is responsible only for her own standards, which she has herself set forth, yet she is willing to receive into union any Church using any Liturgy that ever has been used in any branch of the One Holy

Catholic and Apostolic Church in any age.''   In the next place,
not insisting upon any Protestant congregation taking the absurd
name of Protestant Episcopal, or requiring the observance of our
daily choir offices, as if they were of œcumenical obligation, and
asserting, as his own opinion, that our own narrowness is the
chief obstacle in our way of growth, he proposed the following
further addition to the Eighth Article : '' This Church is also
ready to receive into communion any congregation of Christian
persons who will, 1st, accept the definitions of the Faith as set
forth by the undisputed General Councils ; 2d, have a ministry
of Apostolic Succession given either hypothetically or absolutely ;
3d, whose members will accept confirmation at the hands of
a bishop ; and, 4th, who will pledge themselves to use only valid
form and matter in the administration of the two great Sacraments of Baptism and the Holy Eucharist.   This valid form in
the Eucharist to be the recital of our Lord's words of institution
in the course of a prayer of consecration offered to the Father ;
and the matter, bread, leavened or unleavened, and wine produced by the fermentation of grape juice.''   It is to be observed
further, in regard to the proposals relating to union with Protestant congregations, that his plan involved communion with them,
but gave them no legislative authority.   Unity would not be
reached even if such congregations accepted such terms offered ;
but unity would be furthered immensely.   This plan would
establish at once a union of life and restore those persons to
Catholic communion who are now separated from it externally.
But all modes of worship, whether extemporaneous or liturgical,
as well as all control of property would remain for a long time
to come, as they are now.   Moreover it would ensure real co-
operation in Missionary work of all kinds, and thus tend to
produce actual unity.

Dr. Hopkins had made these terms known to the Church at
intervals, for some years, before the Chicago meeting of 1886.
He first set them forth to any large gathering when he preached at
St. Paul's Chapel on the occasion of the semi-centennial celebration of the consecration of the Four Bishops (McIlvaine, Hopkins, Smith, and Doane) in 1832.   He made them known at the
meeting of the '' Congress of Christian Churches,'' especially at
Cleveland, in 1886, when he declared, as a priest of the Episcopal Church before representatives of various denominations, including the Roman Catholic Bishop of Cleveland, his willingness
to give up, for the sake of unity, everything peculiar to the Prot-

estant Episcopal Church.   Thus far his remarks were received
with great enthusiasm, but when he advanced to his true position,
that the Catholic Church was the only centre of unity, and that
her peculiarities were of the Lord's own grace, it was seen that
in his view unity could only be accomplished by union with the
body of the Catholic Church.

The declaration of the House of Bishops, which was adopted
by the House of Clerical and Lay Deputies, and afterward, with
slight modifications, as a basis for negotiation, prevented any discussion of the merits of Dr. Hopkins' plan.   No one has ever
been able to tell how much or how little the Quadrilateral may
mean, and possibly, this plan may be considered, if only as an interpretation of the Bishops' Declaration.

The first election of a clergyman to fill the Alumni lectureship in the General Seminary on Christian Evidences, resulted in
favor of Dr. G. W. Dean, with Dr. Hopkins as the second choice.
Dr. Dean lived but a few years after his election, and upon his
death Dr. Hopkins was elected by a large majority to the vacant
lectureship.   Christ Church had grown so strong during his rectorship that he felt he was not able longer, at the age of sixty-
seven, with the difficulty he had in walking, and his weakened
eyesight, to give the work the attention it needed, and therefore
after his election he resigned his rectorship.   More than eleven
hundred had been baptized, and five hundred and forty-six had
been confirmed during the eleven years of his rectorship.   The
church had been adorned and enriched ; two handsome mission
chapels had been built, besides the new Sunday-school and Guild
Hall, from his designs ; and, besides, he had become personally
responsible for the building of the Church of St. Alban, at Peale,
mentioned in his letters.   The election to the Seminary offered
him work for which he was perfectly qualified, and work which
his decreasing bodily activity would not hinder.

The night before he departed a reception was given him,
which all the parish attended, and many others.   A large sum of
money was given him as a last token of esteem, and so, with
tears he separated from his well-loved people.

To a friend of many years he wrote, October 20, 1887 : " At
last I have a chance to write you some accounts of my experiences since I saw you last, at the close of the $1,000 reception at
the Guild Hall of Christ Church.

" All the rest of that night I sat up working over my disorderly table and its accumulated papers—nearly eleven years of ac-

cumulation. At 6 A.M. I dozed for about half an hour in the big
easy chair you sent me for my bed-room, and then went at it
again. Mr. Woodruff came for his last help and instructions, and
at 9.20 I was off on the train for South Bethlehem (the seat of
Lehigh University).

"At Tamaqua I got a piece of pie and a glass of milk. On
reaching South Bethlehem, I found that my kind host, Bishop
Rulison, had been suddenly called away by the long-expected
death of his mother. Knowing that I was depended upon to
prepare the Letter of Consecration of the Packer Memorial Church
next day, I started at once, without bite or sup, for the University buildings, meeting Dr. Lamberton on the way, who told me
that he would soon return.   I went to work—after long waiting—
about six o'clock, in the drawing-room of the University, with gas
burners too high above me to give me much light; with a very
poor supply of light I managed, however, to finish the work in
time."

The election to the Alumni Lectureship was rejected by the
Trustees; the votes being equally divided.   Thus it was that the
old scores against him were paid off.   In the winter of 1887–88
he visited California, and spent some happy weeks with his
brother Caspar, at Pasadena.   The election was repeated, and once
more it was rejected.   Thus was closed ruthlessly the public
career of this able, brilliant, and self-sacrificing son of the Church
after a suspense of two years, which effectually shut him out from
all occupations.   The Bishops had their revenge for 1871.   *Tan-
tæne animis cælestibus iræ ?*   The action was an outrage in every
sense.   In the first place the fund had been raised by the Seminary
Alumni, and by all rules of custom their nominations should have
been ratified.   But furthermore, according to his powers and opportunities, no one had ever done more for the Seminary than Dr.
Hopkins.   He had defended it again and again from the attack
of some of the very bishops who now voted against him.   It was
an era of good feeling.   The sharp edge of controversy had softened down on all sides.   Men once proscribed and feared had
been advanced to the episcopate with the consent of the whole
Church, and yet, he, who had done no more, and done that openly
and above board, was forbidden to exercise his rare gifts in teaching the candidates for orders.   It is hard to refrain from writing
with severity, and of characterizing these shameful acts as they
deserve.   But *he* forgave, although he was bitterly grieved and
disappointed, and the very sharpest rebuke ever administered by

him to the writer was when he, in the course of a letter to Dr. Hopkins, expressed his feelings in the matter. Yet one thing may be said that may perhaps help the chief actors in the affair to realize how complete their revenge was, when they know that he who resigned a living and a competence in order that physical work beyond his power might be better done by some other, although perfectly competent for the mental work of the case, and whose generosity had ever kept him poor, was in his old age left working all day in the libraries of New York on some contemplated books for the Church, and obliged to barter his books for lodging in the Diocesan House. He writes thus, March 10, 1890 : " The sorting and distributing of my books has been a tedious and wearisome work. About 550 volumes I have given to the General Theological Seminary library, and I received a handsome note of thanks from Dean Hoffman this morning for the gift. My architectural works I have given mainly to my architect nephew, Fred. Camp, who is very glad to get them. Others I shall give to my namesake, John Henry, Theodore's son. The rest I shall give to the library here, in the See House, they in return giving me the use of two rooms as long as I want them. A week or two more, and I shall be at *my own* work once more. Whittaker has agreed to publish in a small volume my two *Review* articles on Mgr. Capel, and my last article on my dear friend Littledale's ' Petrine Claims.' I have at last got through with the proof of Dr. Dean's Lectures on the Evidences."

April 19, 1890. " I think I told you I had been nominated for that Alumni professorship the *third* time, by a majority of *two* to *one*, and had then *withdrawn my name*."

May 29, 1890.—" Yesterday, on starting for the General Theological Seminary, to attend the Commencement, I was knocked down in Broadway by a Broadway railroad car, and bruised somewhat on the lower part of the back. I could not get up without help, which was promptly given me, and I went up to the Seminary and robed for the procession. Coming down the library steps in procession, I thought I had reached the bottom when I had *not*, and as my knees were weak owing to my former accident, they gave way and down I went full length, the second time within an hour ! This time, however, I was not hurt, and went on through all the services without any further catastrophe. At the Alumni breakfast on Tuesday, I was called out for a speech, and received longer and louder applause than any of the other speakers—even the Bishop of New York. At the Commencement dinner I was again called out by the Dean, and the same preponderating applause was given. There is nothing but kindness shown me. Dr. Cady, whom *I* nominated for that Alumni professorship, received from the Alumni one hundred and fifteen votes out of one hundred and fifty-five—some seven still voting for me, notwithstanding my withdrawal. *I* was chairman of the committee to carry the nomination to the Trustees, which I did with not a little satisfaction. I leave for Burlington this afternoon, where on Sunday I am to preach at the ordination of my nephew John Henry, whose course in the Seminary has been *brilliant.* He makes friends everywhere. I shall spend a few days with my doctor on my return.''

Alas! the "few days" were all he had on earth, and they were stretched out to fourteen months of weariness and toil.

June 20, 1890.—"Here I am (Troy, N. Y.), and likely to remain I cannot tell how long. My dear good Dr. Ferguson is ready to keep me as long as I will stay, and does everything for me that he can. But it seems to me that I do not get better, but slowly and steadily worse all the time. That *fall* did me serious injury, I am satisfied. My shortness of breath and physical weakness are both much worse, and so is the swelling of my legs. I brought my historical note-book with me, about Iconoclasm, and have begun to write my book ; but it is desperate hard work ! I cannot work as I used to do ! I am afraid I shall never get my book done ! ''

To Rev. Charles F. Sweet, July 31, 1890.—"My doctor gives me no hope that I shall live long enough to finish my book. I therefore leave it to you—I wish to send you the *Notes* I have made (all in pencil), the manuscript as far as finished, in ink, and leave it to you to work out as best you can.

"Yours, weaker and weaker,

"H.''

To Miss Susan Hall, September 8, 1890.—" I spent a month at Hudson, amid charming scenery and kind friends ; but the larger part of the time sitting all day long in my own room, with my bare feet in a basin, dripping, dripping, dripping—not much to make a letter of ! I get slowly but steadily weaker, and more good-for-nothing, and writing comes harder—I am so sluggish ! But no pain or suffering worth mentioning. I have good appetite for three square meals of victuals and drink, and sleep well o' nights, and it seems ridiculous that I should be so sick ! But when I wish to walk or make any exertion I soon find out how weak I am. How long this is to last I cannot guess ! But I never feel the slightest disposition to be impatient. My only feeling is regret that I shall not be able to accomplish so many things that I have had in my head and heart to do. But they were *all* for the Church. It is the Lord's business, not my own ; and if I cannot do it, doubtless He will find somebody else who will do it better than I should."

To the Rev. E. M. Pecke, October 8, 1890.—"Thanks for your kind note, and *especially* for having remembered me so tenderly at your daily celebration. My physician gives me no hope of recovery ; but my complaint—one of the varieties of Bright's disease—is painless, and I suffer only weakness and weariness. These will increase till the end comes, in a few weeks or months. I am with my dear friend, Dr. Ferguson, who came into the Church under my ministry, with his whole family, more than twenty years ago, and if I were his own father he could not show me more affection."

To his sister, Mrs. T. H. Canfield, November 29, 1890.— " What do you write me such tender, touching letters for ? They are almost more than I can stand. I try to look upon death only as passing from one room into another. I have *no* sense of *parting* from those I leave behind. Probably, where I go, I shall be able to serve them even better than I ever could here. The separation will only be for a few years anyhow—perhaps fewer than we think for, and *then* we shall all be together again, to part no more forever ! "

To the same, December 23, 1890. — " Growing weaker, weaker, day by day, is all I have to say. I wish I *could* drop in on you all on Christmas Day !—But by and by—we shall *all* be together to part no more."

To Miss Hall, February 5, 1891.—" You need not pity me at all. *You* suffer more in one day than I have in all my illness put together. I am quite contented, and more thankful than I can well express that the dear Lord deals so tenderly with me. The only thing that really worries me is, that my good doctor's care is making me a burden to himself and family so much longer than I expected. But, as I tell him, it is all his own doing ! and he laughs, and does it some more ! I have *every* comfort, and can always read, day or night, even when I do not feel strong enough to write. And Dr. Tucker calls to see me two or three times a week, and brings me English Church papers and reviews, and books, to read. There never was a man in my position more comfortably taken care of.''

To a friend, April 7, 1891.—'' As to your question whether it is justice or mercy we are to expect, I would advise you to learn by heart the one hundred and thirty-sixth psalm, where *every verse* ends ' for His mercy endureth forever,' and then hunt the good book through, from cover to cover, and see if you can find it anywhere even once, that ' His justice endureth forever.' Consider also, how we are told that ' mercy *rejoiceth* over judgment,' and see if you can find even *one* place where the rejoicing goes the other way. The bruised reed He will not break, and the smoking flax He will not quench, and you ought to be ashamed of yourself for even suspecting that He would! But all these difficulties are only your *nerves* and not *yourself!*

'' P.S. I have just had a letter from the editor of the *Independent*, clipping a sentence from my *Eclectic* article about the Americanizing of the Church of Rome in this country, and asking me to write more fully about it. So I wrote him an article yesterday. When it will appear I cannot say, probably this week or next.''

The Independent, May 7, 1891.

CHANGES IN THE ROMAN CATHOLIC CHURCH.

BY J. H. HOPKINS, D.D.

'' ' *Semper eadem,*' as we all know, is the claim of the Church of Rome : ' *Always the same,*' although everyone acquainted with Church history knows that it is untrue *in fact.* There is very considerable difference between the Church of Pope Alexander VI. and the Church of Pope Leo XIII., and there is no slight difference between the Roman Church of Leo XIII. and that of Cardinal Gibbons, of Baltimore. The Church of Rome in this country is slowly but steadily being modified by its environment, and the entire results of that change are healthful for the present, and encouraging for the future.

'' This is seen in doctrine, in discipline, and in worship.

'' It is seen in doctrine, because the bulk of the population of this country being Protestant, the Roman preachers have in mind constantly the possibility of some Protestants being among their hearers—especially in their larger and more influential congregations—and they are especially anxious not to offend them too sharply. Often an entire sermon may be heard from a Roman pulpit which might be preached in one of ours without the change of a word. In other cases, there is only a sentence or two out of the way, which might easily be omitted without being missed. Meanwhile, the more odious or corrupt dogmas are seldom touched on, and then but lightly. In this way, though the preachers themselves may be thoroughgoing, yet the multitudes *taught* are gradually being shaped by the modified teaching, whether or no. And it cannot be helped.

" In discipline similar influences are at work. Nationality is seen to be an unmanageable element. When our Roman Catholic population was nearly all Irish, it was comparatively easy to have them politically controlled by the priesthood. But here, Fenianism has been a great and undesigned blessing. The Pope cares a great deal more for the influence of England than for that of Ireland, and to please England is willing to help to put down the national aspirations of the Irish. But whenever a sharp clash has come, politics is on top, and the Pope is on the under side. So, too, when the Roman population of a town is part Canadian and part Irish, it is almost impossible to make them train in the same political party. If the Irish are Democrats, the Canadians will be Republicans. And similar discrepancies will be found where there are masses of Romanists of German, or Hungarian, or Italian, or Polish nationality. The national element is always the stronger of the two. What Papal leadership means was shown not long ago when the Pope came out against the Knights of Labor, and Cardinal Gibbons went to Rome, converted the Pope from the error of his ways, and turned him up on the other side.

" In worship, too, there are healthful changes going on. In the prominence given to the ordinance of preaching, American Romanism is already very different from the ordinary practice of old Roman Catholic countries. And they are learning to give more and more of their service in *English*, so that their people can more intelligently take part. And this tendency will grow stronger and stronger.

" Their laity, too, are learning to come to the front with no little force and point. Great pecuniary scandals, such as that of Archbishop Purcell's brother in Ohio, are gradually opening the

eyes of their laity, and they are slowly but steadily gaining a position in which they can help to manage the vast properties to
which they wholly contribute. In the independent expression
of opinion, too, they are making themselves felt most strikingly,
as was seen at the great celebration with which the Roman University at Washington was inaugurated.

"Another important point must not be overlooked. The
'miracles' like those of Lourdes and La Salette, which are so
prominent a feature in foreign Romanism, do not happen here.
If they are needed for the conversion of unbelievers, there is no
country where they would be more advisable. But whenever
anything of the kind has been started here, it has always been in
some out-of-the-way rural locality, and at once the mandate has
come down from headquarters: 'Stop that! that won't do in
this country!' and the 'miracles' always stop at once.

"Our public school system, too, has been the means of soften-
ing to a very great degree the intense prejudices of thousands of
Romanists, opening their minds and hearts in all their after-life
in a way that they would otherwise never have known.

"Perhaps the most powerful influence of all—though it is
really only the *sum* of all—is in the position which their leading
cardinals, prelates and priests are *compelled* to take, in regard to
the fundamental principles of American liberty. When Cardinal
Gibbons proclaims from the housetops that the Roman Church
has always been 'the zealous promoter of *religious* liberty,' we
should like to see his Eminence study up the History of the In-
quisition! And when he boasts of *Magna Charta* as the work of
his Church, he seems to forget that the Archbishop Langton,
who led in that noble work, was excommunicated by the Pope
for doing it! and that the same Pope declared *Magna Charta* to
be *null and void;* but nobody minded his *brutum fulmen* then,
any more than they do now. To be sure, in order to talk like
American citizens, the Cardinal and all the rest of them are compelled to go dead against the Encyclical and Syllabus, and ever
so much more; but they do it; they do it unanimously; and all
their people go with them most heartily. In all these things,
and many more, they are really approximating the re-union of
Christendom, whether they know it or not. And as the first and
the worst of the evils that brought about the *dis*union of Christendom were of Roman origin, those of us who can *see* these
healthy changes going on may surely thank God and take courage."

To the Rev. C. F. Sweet, April 17, 1891.—"At last I have just recovered possession of the letter from the late learned Bishop Christopher Wordsworth, of Lincoln, in answer to one from me in which I gave him my view of the Iconoclastic Controversy. He calls it, you see, my ' wise and original remarks on the true solution of the Iconoclastic Controversy ; ' and adds that if he should live to write of that period he should ' certainly avail myself of them.' . . . The original scrawl of the learned Bishop you can keep as an autograph, showing how wonderfully great scholars can write !

" My good doctor still keeps me on more vigorously than I could have expected. I am just recovering from rather a severe down turn. I have not left this room since last September. But it seems probable that I may yet last some weeks or months. God's will be done ! "

It was indeed God's will to let him linger some months after that time. Once more he made his voice heard in behalf of Dr. Phillips Brooks, when he was assailed in a spirit, as he deemed it, of unfairness and narrow bigotry.

Dr. Hopkins did not indeed realize from what spirit some of the opposition to that election arose. He considered it to be a skirmish on the lines of the old issue between High Church and Low. In justice to those men it should even here be noted that the issues were deeper and more radical than the former. It was no question of methods, but of first principles. Dr. Brooks was assailed as representative of a party which, while accepting the formularies of the Church in their own private interpretation of them refuses to take them in the sense in which the Church imposes them. Whether Dr. Brooks was justly obnoxious to the charge of disloyalty is another question. It was assumed that he was, and the opposition arose from his known affiliation with the members of the so-called Broad (but really, narrow and illiberal) faction, and because of the constantly made assertion of Unitarians and others who sympathized with them that he was at heart one with them. Besides these, in dealing with the expression of Catholic truths his teaching was so carelessly framed that he had been suspected of holding the received and traditional doctrines of the Church in slight esteem, while even in the words to which he was compelled to give his assent he never set forth their strongest sense. After the election, and while the confirmation was still in question, he was asked in various ways to give some explanation of certain of his words and acts, but this he steadfastly refused to do, leaving his whole past to speak for itself. That there certainly was color for the suspicion against his loyalty to the Faith in the three particulars of belief in the eternal Deity of Jesus Christ, and consequently in the Trinity ; the universal need of redemption, and the impossibility of salvation without a Divine Saviour, and of its application by sacraments ; and lastly in the divine organization of the ministry of the Catholic Church in its triple order of bishops, priests, and deacons, is plain from the fact that his opponents were by no means confined to any one school in the Church, but numbered bishops of all shades of opinion from the High Church in its extreme representatives, to the very limits of the Low Church.

The brave and faithful warning conveyed to him by his own near friend, the Bishop of New York, in the sermon preached at his consecration, is of itself a striking evidence of the doctrinal defects of Dr. Brooks.

Dr. Hopkins, keen as he was, never saw that the lines which divide men in the Church had changed their direction since he was in the thick of the contest. He believed that the High Churchmen had so mastered the field that the battle was to be thenceforth between the old " High and Dry " Churchmen, and the " Catholic " Churchmen.

The Low Churchmen of other days had indeed been scattered, and some of the most earnest of them driven from the Church, unable longer to conceal from themselves the discrepancy between their beliefs and the teaching of the Church. But most of the radical wing remained, and during the era of good feeling which prevailed after 1877 reorganized their broken ranks, and entrenched themselves behind *their interpretation* of the Church Creed, and in a few years prepared to renew the struggle. This time they wasted no strength on sentiment, but attacked from within the very seats of life of the Catholic Church, nay of every Christian sect which believes still in the need of a Saviour for humanity, and thus endeavored to paralyze the Catholic body by the subtle poison of rationalism. These plotters of treason were acting from the same principles which have so many advocates in the various sects of Protestants, where indeed those principles have their native home. To them rallied increasing numbers from all sides in the Church, and not a few are men who at one time or another have been conspicuous figures among the advanced Churchmen. The "tendency to palter with the serious meaning of words which is one of the serious diseases of the times," to use the words of a distinguished Unitarian minister of Boston, has so deeply affected the vitality of even those who are faithful to the Church, that the growth of the dishonest Broad Church party has become sturdy and vigorous. That they must be cast out of the Church which they aim to overturn is evident.

It was his known friendship for members of this revolutionary faction and the unmistakable drift of his teaching which caused the opposition to the election of Dr. Brooks to the episcopate.

Dr. Hopkins never saw the danger, or dreamed that there could be danger. Thus he seized upon some absurd expressions antagonistic to the confirmation of that election, and, rousing himself from his death-bed raised one more clear appeal, this time addressed to his old companions in arms, for justice and fair dealing. All honor is due to him for this last act of magnanimity; though the sole result to him was practical forgetfulness of his own just claims to reverence from some members of the Catholic school, who could not even find a place for his name in the monthly intercessions of a society which prays for the souls of all clergymen who die in the faith : thus intimating their own opinion that he was not one of the "faithful departed." It was high time that some call should be heard that should arouse men from a narrow bigotry like that.

[This incident has been dwelt upon for the sake of history, and as an attempt toward justifying the action of a much contemned member in the Church. Personally the writer cannot believe that Dr. Brooks was in heart disloyal to the faith, notwithstanding his words. If the episcopate was a reward for distinguished service his deep personal merits and singular purity of soul would have entitled him to it. But the episcopate is for the Church, and the evils dreaded have already made their appearance in the increased vigor of liberalism in the Church.]

Dr. Hopkins wrote thus to a friend, who wrote to him in remonstrance :

"June 8, 1891.—My dear Edward : As you know, I am an old soldier, and if there is any one thing I know, it is *how to fight a Church battle.* A fundamental rule is *never* to fight a controversial battle on the personal question of the promotion of an *individual*, especially if he be a man of popularity and power. I am now talking pure politics. Nine men think they understand a *personal* question to every *one* man who understands a doctrinal issue. The Low Church brought down the Onderdonks, and *thought* they had beaten the Oxford movement; but they hadn't. When Seymour and DeKoven were cheated out of their confirmation the stupids were sure they had beaten the advanced movement. But Seymour is a Bishop, and so would DeKoven have been had he lived: and Father Grafton is a Bishop, which none of us would have anticipated in that day. Always show the keenest recognition of the constitutional *rights* of other *parties* in the Church. I did the same thing when some of our stupid friends tried to stop confirmation of Bishop Jaggar on the ground of his having signed a letter of sympathy with Cheney. I came out also in defence of Eccleston when he was attacked: and on the simple ground that so long as there were different parties in our comprehensive Church, *any* diocese had a right to the *kind* of Bishop it wanted. If the opposition to Brooks should succeed, what would be the result? In twelve months the strength of the Broad Church party would be *doubled*. No, no! The fair, square, manly, brotherly handling of all *personal* questions is the best. Fight doctrinal issues by themselves. I am so *sure* I am right in this matter that I would do it over again if I were certain that it would cost me *every friend I have in the world!* And I doubt not that it is partly in answer to your prayers and remembrances that I have been enabled to do my duty."

Two months longer he lingered, slowly growing weaker and weaker. But in all the hours of weariness he never lost his cheery good humor, his loving patience, his trust in God, and his calm assurance of the mercy of the Lord reserved for him in the waiting chamber, and the perfecting of his redemption at the resurrection of the just.

God and His holy will were always set before him, and he had no fear. As a child he had a dream which at the age of twenty-one he wrote down in verse. It had a remarkable influence over his life, and shaped it by its sweetness.

THE DREAM OF A CHILD.

When I was but a little boy,
  In long gone days of yore,
Two old contemporary trees
  Grew close beside our door.

We named the locust " Father," for
 High rose his towering head,
And his far-reaching branches wide
 Their grateful shadow spread.

Close by his side a mulberry-tree,
 We children called it " Mother,"
Seemed with her broad-leaf'd foliage
 Embosomed in the other.

In winter's storm, in summer's shine,
 Still side by side they stood ;
" Father " and " Mother " we loved best
 In all the good green wood.

And under their protecting shade
 We played in sunny weather ;
While over us, like loving arms,
 They twined their boughs together.

One night I laid me down to sleep,
 And in my dreams I saw
A wondrous sight, that thrilled my soul
 With fond religious awe.

Under those loved old trees methought,
 And in their double shade,
I saw a lofty wall run round
 Of solid silver made.

High rose its purfled pinnacles
 Of bright and burnished sheen,
Until they hid their shining heads
 Among the mingled green.

Upon the eastern side, a gate
 Of fretted gold was placed,
And studded thick with precious stones
 That in the sunbeams blazed :

The diamond bright, the sapphire blue,
 The emerald so green,
The ruby red, the onyx stone,
 And topaz there were seen.

And when this sparkling splendor shone
 Before my wondering eyes,
I thought 'twas New Jerusalem
 Descended from the skies

Long time I gazed, then kneeling down
    Upon the grass-grown floor,
As when I said my evening prayer,
    I knocked upon the door.

Straightway it opened ; and I saw
    A Man before me stand,
Who spoke to me with kindly voice,
    And took me by the hand.

His eyes were like my Mother's eyes,
    His voice like Father's seemed ;
'Twas JESUS ! for around His head
    A radiant glory beamed.

He took me in His gracious arms,
    And I sat on His knee ;
Sure even a soul in Paradise
    Never more blest could be.

And there the twelve Apostles were,
    A venerable band :
Four listening stood before their Lord,
    And four on either hand.

He told me that the Saints around
    His FATHER'S throne on high
Once lived upon our earth, and once
    Were children such as I.

And when He blessed me, as I sat
    Upon His sacred knees,
I heard sweet sounds above my head,
    Among the broad green leaves.

'Twas not the little birds, I knew,
    That in the branches sang ;
But golden harps, with angel tongues,
    In joyous concert rang.

And "Alleluia" loud they sung
    As they sang long ago ;
And " Glory be to God on high,
    Good-will to men below ! "

Brothers and sisters all, outside,
    Invited me to play ;
Father and Mother called to me,
    And chid my long delay.

I answered not : for God had touched
    My heart with holy fire ;
How could I leave my JESUS' arms,
    Or that angelic choir ?

And listening to the symphonies
    Of their entrancing theme,
I sank to sleep : and when I woke,
    Behold ! it was a dream.

A dream ! Oh, 'twas a blessed dream
    I never can forget !
And though long years have o'er me rolled
    Its echoes haunt me yet.

When life's sad labors all are o'er,
    And I lie down to rest ;
Oh, let me fall asleep at last,
    Asleep on JESUS' breast !

There let me rest—to JESUS' breast
    By guardian-spirits borne ;
Till loud the angel-trump shall wake
    The Resurrection-morn.

Then I shall join the marriage train,
    With boughs of victor-palm,
A'nd sing the everlasting song
    Of MOSES and the LAMB.

This Dream of a Child (he says in the preface to his " Poems by the Wayside," published in 1883) " was a real dream that came to me at least as early as my ninth year—perhaps earlier. *It left an indelible impression.* The trees mentioned—the locust and the mulberry—grew near the door of my father's house in Allegheny City, near Pittsburgh." During one of those last nights on earth he had such another vision of the peace and calm and rest of Paradise, and in the midst of it was the same JESUS of the child's dream, with " eyes like Mother's eyes, and voice that seemed like Father's voice."

Thus near and sweet were God and all God's ways with him ever.

There was but one more incident which may illustrate that element in his character which was little known to the world, but which

it has been one chief purpose of this work to show : his capacity
for deep personal affection and attachment.   The daughter of his
loving physician (his spiritual son) was to be married.   He had
baptized her, and naturally, from every reason, he was interested
deeply in the affair.   She told him, as time passed on and life
still remained to him, that she had hoped to be married by him.
His pleasure was marred for a time by the fear he might not
live until the appointed time.   But, as months went by, hope
arose, and finally, a few weeks before his death, with the assistance
of Dr. J. I. Tucker, of the Church of the Holy Cross, at Troy,
he was able to perform the ceremony—a ceremony made notable
by his venerable appearance, and his determination to perform it,
though obliged to do so sitting, and marked by his comment
that he had done all the good he could in the world, and he
trusted the Lord would soon take him.   Not many weeks afterward he expressed a wish one night to go to bed somewhat earlier
than was his custom, and, after being helped into his bed, in reply to Dr. Ferguson's question, whether he was comfortably
arranged for the night, he assured him that he was, kissed him a
good-night, and went into a quiet sleep, from which, after about
four hours, without a struggle or change of position, he passed
into that deeper rest that knows no end until the Day break and
the shadows flee away.

Thus it was that he passed away in peace in the early morning
hours of the 14th of August.   His body was carried to Burlington,
and placed where his loved Father's body had been laid before
the burial.   The same vigil of prayer and solemn joy was kept
near it.   On the 18th, the Burial Service was said, the Sacrifice
of our redemption was offered, and then the sacred relics were
borne to the place long before made ready for them near the great
Celtic Cross he had himself designed and erected to mark the
sleeping-place of his Father, and there laid away in expectation of
the mercy of God.

So died one who served the Church with all his power with
unwavering fidelity, complete unselfishness, and unstinted devotion.   Nor was his interest centred in her alone.   No son of the
American Church has had a loftier enthusiasm for humanity or a
humbler love for God.

It was the accident of the time and circumstances that made
his name known chiefly as a keen controversialist, though he had
all the natural gifts that fitted him for the militant Church.   For
he was strong in human sympathy, and felt no enmity toward

the persons with whom he joined issues.   At any time he would
have served at cost of great personal inconvenience one with
whom he may have been in very lively controversy, though no
such merciful measure was meted out to him.   Sometimes, indeed,
he wounded, and wounded deeply, but it was because he seemed
to forget that principles have their embodiment in men.   In his
conflicts he was aiming simply to serve the Church.   In his mind
she was nothing less than a lawful, organic part of the Catholic
Church.   And if he exalted her, it was not that she might glory
in her power as if given for herself, but because he who is in the
possession of power is made capable of higher, wider, fuller
service ; and if this be true of men, much more is it true of God's
Church if she is to be faithful to her trust.   All his plans were
in order to her complete enfranchisement that so she might work
for the good of all men, and, in the words of an Evangelical
clergyman who lived in the same city (of Williamsport), yet " he
was not partisan in the narrow, petty sense of the word.   Though
he might be caustic in exposure of what he deemed our weaknesses, he was never malevolent, and never sectarian in his denial of an equal place for Evangelical and broad Churchman in a
comprehensive body.   He was not underhand, secretive, politic ;
on the contrary, he was frank and straightforward, so unsuspicious
as to be often the cause of his own defeat."   With this last expression of opinion agree the words of Dr. Hugh Miller Thompson, the
present Bishop of Mississippi—that " he had the first characteristic of genius ; he was a boy all the days of his life, fresh, unso-
phisticated, unworldly.   It came to us, in God's guiding of our
lives, to stand opposed in crises of the Church's history.   The
friendship, the affection, were never touched.   I wrote him once,
at such a time, telling him I should in conscience oppose his
views with all my power, but I wanted him to understand that
nothing of that sort could change the deep regard I had for John
Henry Hopkins.   His reply was characteristic.   ' You and I
are too accustomed to square fighting to think less of each other
for a fair blow.'   He always fought with his visor up, a knightly
opponent.   There was no malice, no bitterness.   Indeed, instead,
a cheery boyish enjoyment of the intellectual fray.   Except
Washburn, I never knew a man so incapable of understanding
how an honest attack on his opinion could be construed into
anything personal.   I cannot let his going pass without my
humble tribute to a man dear to me, a friend to whom personally
I owe much of what I have myself thought, or said, that may be

of any worth ; to a gentle soul, much misunderstood, as men of
genius often are ; to a thinker who has left his mark for all time
on the Church of his baptism, and to a Christian knight fallen
with his armor on.''

MONUMENT OF BISHOP HOPKINS, UNDER WHICH LIE THE REMAINS
OF THE BISHOP AND HIS WIFE.

Dr. John Henry Hopkins' grave is at the right, in a line with the two trees
in the foreground.

APPENDIX.

DR. HOPKINS found a way to make his argument for small dioceses *tell* in many questions of Church policy. Before the meeting of General Convention in 1889, the question of proportionate representation was discussed in all the Church newspapers, and in this Dr. Hopkins took a certain share. It was summarily dismissed when brought into *General* Convention. Nevertheless, the principle will probably come up again in *Diocesan* Conventions. He was strongly in favor of the movement, and if his conclusion that "the way to secure proportional representation—or an approximation thereto—is, not by charging the ratio of representation, but by the subdivision of large dioceses," be accepted by the Church, there is this correlative principle that, if State dioceses are subdivided their unity of action in General Convention will, to a great degree, be furthered by their being united in *State Provinces*. As to graduated representation in Diocesan Conventions his words ought to be recorded.

"GRADUATED REPRESENTATION.

" *To the Editor of The Churchman:*
  "It is with no little interest that I have watched the discussion in your columns, and in others of our Church papers, concerning graduated representation. And I have seen, with special satisfaction, that it does not run at all upon party lines. It is an old question with me. In my father's diocese of Vermont, the graduated representation of the laity has been the law for more than fifty years, and has done no harm that I ever heard of. In Central Pennsylvania, on my motion, the same principle was embodied in the constitution of that diocese, and works equally well there. Nor have I seen anything alleged on the other side which even tempts me to change the convictions of years.
  " There are three points to which I would call special attention.
  " The first is, that the title of our General Convention is not 'the bishops and dioceses' of the Church in General Convention assembled; but 'the bishop, clergy, and laity.' And this is further enforced by the rule of order which provides for a vote 'by orders,' when the clergy vote separately, and the laity separately, as distinct orders; the bishops also having their separate vote always, as a House. This mode of voting agrees with the title. If, however, the dioceses are to be represented as such, why should the bishops vote in a separate House? If that theory be correct, then the bishops should sit with

the clerical and lay deputies from their own dioceses, and vote with them.   This is an Episcopal Church, and to take the vote of a diocese when its bishop is shut off in another House, is hardly a church-like way of doing business.

"And in the Upper House the bishops do not vote 'by dioceses;' for if they did, then a diocesan bishop and his assistant would jointly have but one vote, whereas now the assistant, having received 'the Holy Ghost for the office and work of a bishop in the Church of God,' has as full and complete a vote as any diocesan.   Every domestic missionary bishop also has as full a vote as any diocesan bishop, for the same reason; while the missionary jurisdictions in the other House have only a fractional representation, and even so can only speak on questions peculiarly concerning their own jurisdictions.

"If legislation by dioceses is to be the rule, then, to be consistent, not only must our assistant bishops and missionary bishops be deprived of their full and equal vote in the Upper House, but the diocesan bishops must sit and vote with their own clerical and lay deputies, so that 'the diocese' may no longer be considered a 'diocese' while acting without its own head.

"The present mode of voting in the Lower House, 'by dioceses,' is therefore not only inconsistent with the title of the General Convention itself, but is absolutely irreconcilable with the mode of voting in the Upper House.

"The second point on which I would insist is this.   When it comes to the human arrangements for the government of the Church, it is only reason and common sense to take care that, where the Providence of God has put strength, there we should place responsibility.   If, in our arrangements, we place responsibility where the providence of God has placed weakness, what can we expect but weakness as the result?   The proposal to raise in three years a centennial million of dollars for missions, was easily carried through General Convention, with as near an approach to a ' hurrah ' as could be expected in so grave and sedate a body.   But how much of success did the three years produce?   The flabbiness of much of our synodical practical work, both in diocesan and General Conventions, is due to the fact that our laity are not fairly and equally represented, and therefore the vote is no fair expression of the true momentum of the order.   The evil is felt in nearly all our dioceses as well as in General Convention.   When a little missionary parish of a score of communicants has an equal vote, in all things, with a parish of five hundred or one thousand communicants, what does a vote in convention, involving exertion or sacrifice of any sort, amount to?   The majority of those voting have not the power to carry out the resolution which they vote so easily, and everybody knows it.   Those who have the power know that they are not fairly represented in the voting body, and feel little or no obligation to carry its votes into effect.   On our present system, we have organized weakness, instead of organized strength.   And we are coming to feel it more and more, as the unequal growth of dioceses makes the inequalities more and more apparent.

"The third point is this. The Church is not an abstract phrase. The Church is a body of living persons, who have received the grace of God for the work He calls on them to do. The bishop, at his consecration, 'receives the Holy Ghost for the office and work of a bishop in the Church of God.' The priest, at his ordination, 'receives the Holy Ghost for the office and work of a priest in the Church of God.' The layman, at his confirmation, receives the Holy Ghost for the work of a layman—the priesthood of the laity. But who ever heard that a diocese received the Holy Ghost for the work of a diocese? In the 'prayer to be used at the meetings of convention' we find this distinction clearly set forth. It is not a prayer for the diocese. The word diocese does not appear in it once. It is a prayer for 'the council of Thy Church here assembled in Thy name and presence.' And to show that the prayer is not for the corporate entity called a 'diocese,' the prayer goes on, 'Save them from all error, ignorance, pride, and prejudice. . . . direct, sanctify, and govern us in our present work, by the mighty power of the Holy Ghost,' etc. And as all this relates to the persons, how comes it that the priests and laity of a small diocese should have twenty or thirty times as much legislative power as the priests and laity of a large diocese? The thing is manifestly unequal and absurd. In order that representation may be fair and equal, if twenty priests in Arkansas can send four deputies to General Convention, every body of twenty priests anywhere else in the United States should have the right to do the same. If two thousand communicants in West Virginia can send four lay deputies, every other body of two thousand communicants in the United States should have the right to do the same. Of all absurdities, none could be greater than to give to Arkansas or West Virginia twenty times as strong a representation as New York, and then say that all are equally represented!

"I could say much more, but I forbear, only expressing my sincere gratification that the discussion of the question is so entirely free from party feeling of every sort. Another suggestion I would venture to make, and that is, that the inequality of our present system of representation must be corrected in our diocesan conventions, before there will be any chance of carrying a reform in General Convention. And also, our larger dioceses will find it much easier to get something like equal representation in General Convention, by subdividing, than in any other way. In this way the State of New York has already secured five deputations, and could easily double the number. Pennsylvania has three and needs at least as many more. Illinois has three; Wisconsin, New Jersey, Maryland, North Carolina, Ohio, each have two. And the sooner other large dioceses do likewise, the sooner will they approximate to a fair and equal vote in the General Convention of the Church.

"J. H. HOPKINS."

In advocating the principle of proportional representation, there are some points which ought not to be overlooked, though little or nothing has yet been said about them.

16

In the first place, if there is anything in the principle, it ought to be applied wherever it is fairly applicable.   In a diocese there is as much difference between large and small parishes as there is in the National Church between large and small dioceses.   And so long as a diocese grants to its largest and strongest parish, in its own convention, only an equal voice and vote with the smallest and feeblest, with what face can it approach the General Convention and demand a *proportionate* representation *there?*   The answer would be : " If you really believe in the principle of proportionate representation, establish it in your own diocesan convention first, and then it will be time enough to take it up in General Convention."   Until the dioceses, therefore, apply this principle at home, it will be of no use to agitate for it elsewhere.

Dr. Hopkins promoted this reform wherever he could ; the preceding paragraph, indicating that it was for *dioceses* to begin the work of reform in representation of the laity, led to some correspondence with Massachusetts clergymen who were in the mood to advance the work.

" January 19, 1889.—Proportionate representation of the laity has existed for a long time in the diocese of Vermont, and on my motion it has been adopted also in the diocese of Central Pennsylvania.   In the latter case, each incorporated parish is entitled to *one* lay deputy, and one additional lay deputy for each *hundred* communicants as reported to the Convention next preceding : the laity in all cases, like the clergy, voting *as individuals.*   Thus every layman who attends *counts.*   In the other way, any one layman could cast the vote of the parish, and there was no sufficient inducement for the other two to take the trouble to attend.   Moreover, as the lay representation is fixed by the parochial report at the Convention *next preceding,* any large parish which *fails to report* thereby forfeits its additional deputies at the *next* convention, and drops down to the ' one ' of any incorporated parish.

" As to the *basis,* that of communicants is best.   If you make your pecuniary assessments on the same basis, the one will correct the other. If they are tempted sometimes to magnify their numbers for the sake of additional deputies, they will also be tempted to *reduce* their numbers so as to reduce the assessment, and one will fairly offset the other. General Convention will not settle that question.   They will let it alone. As to the general question, the aid of the Holy Spirit is given to the individual, and not to the ' incorporated parish ' or ' diocese.'   This truth followed up settles the whole question."   In a second letter he writes : " Perhaps you will find it serviceable to remind your colleagues that those taking part in our Church councils are not, and never have been at any time, ' bishops, clergy, and *parishes,*' but ' bishops, clergy, and laity.'   And as the bishops are reckoned as persons, and the clergy as persons, the *laity* should also be considered as persons, and not simply as corporations owing their existence as such to the law of the State.   If this does not convince them, nothing will.   How is it possible that State law should give to a civil corporation the right to vote in an ecclesiastical organization, whose powers (so far as the law of the land is concerned) are due solely to the consent of those taking part therein ?

The laity are individuals who have become what they are not simply by any act performed by the civil corporation of a parish, but by the *spiritual* acts of baptism, confirmation, communion, and being under the spiritual jurisdiction of a clergyman of the Church."

Two years later he wrote to the same clergyman, from his physician's house : " March 13, 1891.— . . . Thanks for the copy of your proposed changes as to lay representation.   Nothing short of proportionate representation will cure the flabbiness of our present lay order in Convention.   As I am about quitting this earthly scene soon myself, it is a comfort to me to see others rising to defend the principles for which I have fought so long.   God give you more success than He has given me !   Perhaps *His* time for it had not yet come.

" Yr. obt. servt. in the Church,
" J. H. HOPKINS."

"To the REV. REUBEN KIDNER."

RAIN, LIGHT, HEAT, AND SOIL.

(Wheat No. 6.)

SERMON 29.

"The earth bringeth forth fruit of herself."—*St. Mark* iv. 28.

"No battles about religion have been more fiercely contested than those fought to decide whether a man's believing unto salvation is God's work or his own. The leaders of the quarrel, on the one side, have been jealous for the Lord of Hosts and His Glory. They have been fearful lest pride and self-reliance should take the place of humility and leaning upon God alone for salvation; and lest men should, in the blindness of their conceit, undertake to work out their own salvation as a day-laborer earns his wages. They have, therefore, insisted that man's salvation is all God's work; and in order to be *sure* that they had given God *all* the glory, they have thought it necessary to insist that man has *nothing* to do in it but to be passive under the irresistible influences of the Spirit. They have accounted for the fact that some men believe while others do not, by saying that it was God's decree: that He elected some to salvation and others to the contrary, without the former being any more worthy of the boon than the latter. Anything short of this they have denounced as robbing God of His glory and giving it to man. The other side have been justly fearful lest a doctrine like this should make men grievously careless about exerting themselves in working out their own salvation; and they have therefore enlarged so much upon the necessity of working, and of man's ability to work, and the freedom of his will to go about it, that they have run to the other extreme, and made God's grace as superfluous as their opponents had made man's good works. Thus the battle has raged, waxing from time to time loud and furious, now one party appearing to have the advantage, and now the other; each fighting as if the existence of God's truth depended on his proving his adversary to be a fatalist or a papist, as the case might be. And all the while, the conflict has been as useless as that of the two foolish knights errant in the old fable, who fought long and hard to decide whether a certain shield were white or black; and when they were both dying of their wounds they discovered that the shield was white upon the one side and black upon the other.

". . . An additional cause of mischief has been the disposition of many hard-headed intellects to decide spiritual truths as if they were mathematical problems; or else treat them according to some common

philosophical axiom, rather than according to the Word of God.   They
have not grasped the higher Philosophy of Revelation, by which somewhat of the nature of the ever-blessed and indivisible Trinity is conveyed to those truths which that Trinity has created and revealed.
The Father is God, and the Son is God, and the Holy Ghost is God ;
yet there is but one God.   So the work of our salvation is all Christ's
work, and all the work of the Holy Spirit, and also it is all *man's* work ;
and yet there are not three works, but one only.   This might be illustrated even from the mathematics.   A three-sided figure, for instance,
is *one* figure, yet its being a three-sided figure depends *wholly* upon
each one of the sides, not upon any one of them more than another ;
and the proof of it is, that if you take away one of those three sides it
is no more a three-sided figure ; so that you could not destroy its three-
sidedness any whit more completely by taking away the other two
sides also.

" The beautiful harmony of the plan of salvation finds its best illustration in the works of God, interpreted according to the indications
given us in His own holy Word.   In the parable of the Sower, *the
ground* signifies *man's part* of the work in preparing for the day of
judgment.   And our text, if taken apart from other Scriptures, would
seem to declare that man, of himself, of his own motion, and in his
own strength, relying on his own innate and merely natural powers,
could bring forth fruit to perfection.   It *looks* as if all other agency
were expressly excluded.   ' The earth,' saith our Lord, ' bringeth forth
fruit of herself ; ' not by the aid of any other power : and that not partially, or imperfectly, but completely, and from beginning to end :
' first the blade, then the ear, after that the full corn in the ear.'   What
could declare more fully the sole sufficiency of man, in and by himself,
to bring forth good fruit ?   Where can be the need, according to this
text, of waiting for the grace of God ?

"Yet the reference to the operations of Nature—the very taking of
her most ordinary work for an illustration, implies, by unavoidable
necessity, all that is needed for the correction of this deadly error.
When it is said, ' the earth bringeth forth fruit of herself,' the other
agencies necessary to the result are not *excluded*, but *included*.   And
what these are, we shall proceed to inquire in their order.

" The very parable itself shows that *sowing the seed* is necessary.
For, as the earth does not contain the seeds of all things lying self-pro-
duced in the soil, so the heart of man has no innate knowledge of the
Word and Will of God ; but a Revelation is necessary, and the teaching and preaching of that revelation by the ministry of the Church.
Thus is the seed sown in the ground—that is, brought home to the
heart, so that a man *can*, if he *will*, receive it and cause it to grow and
bring forth fruit.   But the earth is not sufficient to do this merely of
herself.   Suppose a corn of wheat deposited in earth that was perfectly dry, would it ever sprout ?   Most certainly not.   Except to be de-
voured or to decay, there it would remain unchanged even to the
world's end.   And so the heart of man, even when the Word is
preached, if unaided by aught but its own merely mortal and natural

powers, it could never cause the germ of spiritual life to spring; it could never dream of bringing forth fruit unto perfection.

" In the first place, then, the seed sown must have *moisture* from the rain and the dew. And this signifies the operation of the Spirit of God upon the heart, varying, as the moisture varies, in its quantity and in the manner of application. Sometimes it is the invisible vapor in the air, the gentle breathing of a moist breath, the distilling of a silent dew upon the soul, yet without our being able to see or feel it except by its effects. At another time it is like the mist or fog —it is in the shape of doubts that come over the mind, confusing the outlines of all things. But if they only stimulate the doubting soul to a fresh study of the truth, and a renewed trust in God for the discovery of it, they are the sure signs of a clearer sunshine, and will be found to have watered the garden of the soul, like the mist that went up from the earth and watered all the Garden of Eden. Sometimes they are like soft refreshing showers, sometimes like heavy tempests that pour down *almost* resistlessly the torrents of their streams from heaven. How strikingly is this heavenly watering of God's heritage contrasted with the toilsomeness and littleness and meanness of the watering by means of poor *earthly* contrivances, when Moses sets forth the difference between Egypt and the Holy Land. For Egypt is the type of the world; Palestine of the Church. In Egypt it never rained, and the only means of supplying moisture to the soil was by the laborious drawing up of water in machines worked like treadmills, by the feet. These starveling streams were distributed along the fields in narrow channels or canals; and so, with great labor and pains, and at great expense and trouble, a little water was obtained, which was never enough for the parched soil under the continual glare of an African sun. And is it not so with the cravings of the poor souls that wilt and parch in the glare of this world's sunshine—that depend for life and happiness on the artificial streams doled out from its machinery of tantalizing deceits? At what cost and trouble, what pains and patient exertions, are wealth and honors and distinctions obtained? What lavish outlay to secure pleasures that are absorbed in the very using, and leave rather a sting behind! And all these paltry modes of irrigation—after all their costly labor— leave the soul as thirsty as before. But listen to the words of Moses, thus contrasting the world and the Church : ' The land, whither thou goest in to possess it,' said he, ' is not as the land of Egypt, from whence ye came out, where thou sowedst thy seed, and wateredst it with thy foot, as a garden of herbs; but the land whither ye go to possess it is a land of hills and valleys, and *drinketh water of the rain of heaven ;* a land which the Lord thy God careth for : the eyes of the Lord thy God are always upon it, from the beginning of the year even unto the end of the year.' Thus happy is the earth of the Holy Land ; thus favored is the heart that is open to the sweet influences poured out from the treasure-house of God upon His Church. Of that earth are the words of the Psalmist true : ' Thou visitest the earth and waterest it : thou greatly enrichest it with the River of God, which is full of water: . . . thou waterest the ridges thereof abundantly : thou settlest the furrows thereof : thou makest it soft with showers : thou blessest the springing thereof.'

" But is it not enough that the earth be supplied with water, and that from heaven ? What if the seed be buried in the moist earth too deep for the light to reach ? It will then decay without ever sending up its blade to the surface. Or, what if the moist earth, with its seed duly planted, be hid away in some dark cellar or cave, where no light can penetrate ? Will that earth *then* bring forth fruit of herself ? Nay ! the germ may sprout and may shoot forth rapidly to a great size. But the pale, sickly growth will be monstrous in shape, without color or strength, without flower, seed, or fruit, and soon rotting in premature decay. So, without the light of knowledge, without the regular shining of God's Word into the soul day by day, what profits it that some isolated truth should take root and spring up in the dark by itself ? The rank and noisome heresies and errors that have at times sprung up in the Church will tell the tale ! Monstrous in their forms, as rapid as they were unhealthy in their growth, the diseased shoots have brought no good flower nor fruit to perfection, but they crumble and perish in premature decay. *Light* is necessary ! *That* gives color, and tone, and brilliance, and clearness, and strength to bring forth flower and fruit ; and without it, all the rest were vain. And so the knowledge of God's will is needful for the harvest of God's saints. Ignorance—spiritual ignorance—can never be the mother of *true* devotion. But the light that gladdens the soul in Christ's Church is a growing light—the slanting rays of spring rising into the more direct and burning glow of summer, and shining more and more unto the perfect day.

" But if the earth need only moisture and light, why should not the seed sprout in mid-winter ? What matters it that icicles hang from the eaves, and the snow covers the soil ? If that soil be only saturated with moisture, and the frosty air be filled with the glittering sparkle of a bright winter sunshine, why should not the seed *grow*, if water and light are all it wants ? But they are *not* all. The showers of grace may come down abundantly, but only to be frozen by the coldness of the stone-like earth on which they fall. The sun of knowledge may shine with dazzling brilliance ; but it may be only theological knowledge—only a learned head, not an understanding heart. For *this*, a thaw is necessary—something to warm as well as to enlighten. The light of the sun in spring is no brighter than it is in winter : and the truth of God is the same at all times, shining out over all the world with proofs that are ever of dazzling brilliance, and of such strength that no proud mortal can look defiance in their face, except they strike him blind. Yet without the warmth of *Love*, thawing his frozen heart, —they can make nothing grow there, and they will no more profit him in bringing to life the seed of God's Word, than the wheat can grow amid the frosts and snows of winter.

" And these three influences that we have enumerated—the rain, the light, and the heat—are all from heaven. The sun which warms is the same as that which shines. And the rain falls from heaven also ; and although it *seems* not.to be dependent upon the sun, yet we know that it *is* the sun's rays that draw up the vapor from the great deep, and form it into rain-clouds for the earth. Thus the rain also is from the sun, even as the light and the heat, only not so directly ; just as the Holy Spirit, the Comforter, is sent unto us by the Power of God our Saviour—the same who is in His own blessed Person our Light and our Love.

" Now, from what has been said, it will be seen that all these are necessary ; and each one so indispensable that, without it, all the rest were nothing. Without moisture, the light and heat would make a parched drought, when life would die of thirst. Without light, moisture and warmth would only breed unwholesome forms and loathsome abortions rotting in their own slime. Without warmth, moisture and light would be but ice-bound winter instead of balmy spring. And yet, what were all these three without the soil itself to work on ? Place your seed on a stone instead of on the ground, or on a board, or on a smooth rock, and let it *have* rain and sunshine and warmth—but will it grow ? I trow not ! The rain will only wet it, and the light and heat only dry it again ; but they can never make it sprout. It is *in the earth* that it springeth and groweth up, we cannot tell how. It is the earth that bringeth forth fruit *of herself*.

" And this brings us back to our text ; in which, you remember, the whole result is attributed to the earth, although, as we have seen, heaven does three parts for the earth, while the earth does but *one for herself*. Now, will anyone dare to say our Lord has robbed heaven of its rightful glory ? Will anyone say that His lips have denied that rain, and light, and heat, have anything to do with the bringing forth of fruit ? Surely not ! And so we, if we say that man's being saved depends upon his own exertions—that his being lost is all his own fault—if you say that his well-doing or undoing, is in either case his *own* doing : So far from robbing God of His glory, we are only saying what our Lord has here already said : ' The earth bringeth forth fruit of herself.' Without the sowing of the seed by other hands, the earth were nothing. Without the rain, and light, and heat, the sowing of the seed were nothing ; therefore all the glory of all the harvest is due to Heaven above ! But all these, without the earth to perform its part, were also *nothing*—therefore, the whole responsibility rests upon the earth. This is the heavenly arithmetic, where each part carries the whole burden, and yet the burden is but one and the same throughout. That burden is like a weight hanging by a chain of four strong links, where each of the four links bears the whole weight, and yet there are not four weights, but only one. And so here. Our Lord saith : ' The *earth* bringeth forth fruit of herself,' and King David saith : ' Then shall the earth bring forth her increase ' : and yet it is *not* the earth but *God* that giveth the increase. The work of salvation is all God's, and it is all ours too. It is we that work : yet not we, but Christ that worketh in us. The strength is God's ; yet it is ours ; for He giveth it unto us. *We* are more than conquerors : yet it is Christ that giveth us the victory. The glory is all God's, yet it is *ours* too, for we shall shine as the stars forever. And why not? For *all* things are ours, and we are Christ's, and Christ is God's.

" So, then, there is no need of raising a nice and captious question between what is God's work and what is man's work; and there is still less need of our stopping our work until that question be settled. The good ground that is all the while busy making its grain grow and thrive to the utmost of its power, does not, in so doing, despise or set at naught the sunshine and the rain, or rob them of their glory; but it *makes good use* of them in the way that God hath ordained, which is the best glory and highest tribute it can pay them. And that lazy soil, which refuses to exert itself for fear it may be robbing the powers of heaven of their sovereign attributes, will be found in the time of harvest a bare and barren spot, or else, bristling all over with thistles and thorns; and it will be given over to be burned, while the other shall be covered thick with golden sheaves.

" The heavenly influences are not *mentioned* in our text—not because they are forgotten, not because they are of no consequence, not because they are *all*-important—but only because they are the same for all. The sun shines as brightly and as warmly on the roadside, and on the stony field, and on the thorny soil, as on the good ground; and the rain and the dew descend alike on all. Our Father, which is in heaven, maketh His sun to rise on the evil and on the good, and sendeth rain on the just and on the unjust. Therefore, if there be any differences in the results, it is the fault of the *earth*. She bringeth forth fruit *of herself :* and she must be judged by the fruit she brings forth. ' For the earth which *drinketh in* the rain that cometh oft upon it, and bringeth forth herbs *meet for them by whom it is dressed*, receiveth blessing from God; but that which beareth thorns and briers is rejected, and is nigh unto cursing; whose end is to be burned. But, beloved, we are persuaded better things of you.' Ye have received the good seed abundantly; your Heavenly Father hath caused His sun to rise upon you, and hath sent His gracious rain upon you: See then that ye bring forth fruits meet for the service of Him who hath so tenderly cared for you : that ye, also, may at length receive your blessing from the hand of God.

(Signed)   " JNO. H. HOPKINS, JR."

" April 6, 1851 ; two o'clock A.M."
" Preached, first, that afternoon at St. George the Martyr's, New York."

FOR FAMILY PRAYERS.

COLLECTS FOR THE SEVEN DAYS OF THE WEEK.

1869.

"*Sunday.*—O Light of Light, who, in the beginning of the creation of the world, and in Thy Resurrection from the dead, and in Thy sending of the Holy Ghost, didst shine out of the darkness with great glory; shine also in our souls, we beseech Thee, that, walking here as the children of light, we may at length attain unto Thy light eternal; who livest and reignest," etc., etc.

"*Monday.*—O God, who madest a firmament to divide the waters from the waters, and calledst that firmament heaven; grant that Thy Church may daily extend further and further the firmament of heavenly truth, dividing asunder the dark clouds and stormy waves of this troublesome world; through Him who is the Way, the Truth, and the Life, our Lord and Saviour Jesus Christ."

"*Tuesday.*—O God of wisdom, who rejoicest in the habitable part of the earth, making the dry land to appear, and covering it with grass and the green herb, and the fruit-tree yielding fruit after his kind; grant that we may never wander from the green pastures that grow beside the river of life, but may be like trees planted by the water-side, bringing forth fruit in due season unto salvation; through Jesus Christ our Lord."

"*Wednesday.*—O King of Glory, who madest great lights, the sun to rule the day, the moon and stars to govern the night; grant that Thy Church, receiving all her glory from Thee, may beam forth bright as the sun, fair as the moon, and that they who turn many to righteousness may shine as the stars for ever and ever; through Him who is our Sun of Righteousness, Jesus Christ our Lord."

"*Thursday.*—O Holy Ghost, Giver of life, who didst brood upon the face of the barren waters, and they brought forth abundantly the moving creature that hath life and fowl that fly in the open firmament of heaven; brood evermore upon the waters of Thy Holy Baptism, that innumerable souls may be born of Thee therein, and may be so blessed of Thee in this life that at the last day they may be caught up in the clouds to meet the Lord in the air; through Jesus Christ our Saviour."

"*Friday Morning.*—O God of Life, who filledst the earth with living creatures, and madest man in Thine own image, to have dominion over the works of Thine hands; grant that the glory and power given unto him in his innocence may be restored and increased unto us in the Second Adam, by the merit of whose Cross and Passion

Thou hast promised that Thy redeemed shall be made kings and priests unto Thee ; through the same Jesus Christ our Lord."

"*Friday Evening.*—O loving Father, who, in the Garden of Eden, from the side of Adam while he was in a deep sleep, didst make woman to be the mother of all living ; and from the pierced side of Jesus while in the sleep of death upon the cross didst bring forth the water and the blood, and from these madest Thy Church to be His Bride ; grant that we, remaining faithful unto death in the bosom of that Church, may be folded in the everlasting arms of Thy Beloved, stretched forth upon the Altar of the Cross to embrace the world ; through the same blessed Jesus, our Lord and Saviour."

"*Saturday.*—O Blessed Jesus, lover of men, who on Thine own hallowed day of rest didst lie sealed in the stony sepulchre, and in Thy victory over death and hell madest the place of Thy rest to be glorious ; give sweet rest and refreshment to all the faithful who sleep in Thee ; and grant, that when our work on earth is ended, we also may be joined unto Thee in Paradise, and with them may have part in the triumphant resurrection of the just, to be separated thenceforth from them and from Thee, O Lord, no more forever ; who livest and reignest one God, world without end ; Amen."

THE PROVINCIAL SYSTEM.

From "Some Unwritten Books;" *American Church Review*, January, 1891.

AT the Reformation, the theory of the whole movement, so far as the Church of England was concerned, claimed to be a return to the purity of the primitive Church. And at the organization of our American Church that return was made, in some respects, more complete than in England itself. But in other points the restoration is even yet lamentably and undeniably incomplete. Let us consider only the case of our American Church.

The early Church was everywhere divided into provinces of convenient size, and the rule was that the synod of each province should meet at least twice a year, for the hearing of appeals, for the correction of abuses, and for consultations concerning the general welfare. Canons also might then and there be passed, if there were occasion. But it was unheard of that any Diocesan Bishop, with only his own clergy and laity, should ever undertake to pass a canon. "Constitutions" were unknown everywhere.

How does our American system compare with this?

At first when we had only three or four bishops, the Church in this country was organized—to use the proper ecclesiastical term—as one Province. There was not a sufficient number of bishops and dioceses to do anything else. This province, and our National Church, were identical. So in other cases—Scotland for instance—where there was not strength enough for two or more provinces, the province and the National Church were all one. In Ireland there used to be four provinces; though there are now but two. And in England, where there are but two, it would be much better if there were five or six.

But as the nation and the Church have both expanded so wonderfully within our first century, it is plain that a change is required. And the great points are: What should this change be, and how should it be brought about?

First, comparing our American organization with that of the primitive province, what do we find?

Instead of meeting twice every year, our General Convention meets only once in three years!

Instead of being a Court of Appeal, we have no Court of Appeal at all. If a bishop is bad enough to be put on trial, he can be tried and punished; but the court would have no power to rectify the tyrannical abuse of authority for which he may have been condemned.

General Convention can indeed pass canons ; but in subordination to them each separate diocese has its own constitution and canons, and in nearly all the dioceses these can be made and altered without the consent of the bishop himself, for which there is no precedent in the primitive Church anywhere in the whole world. Councils of bishops have made canons without the help of clergy and laity ; but that the clergy and laity should make canons without bishops is a monstrosity unknown to the primitive Church.

Let us go back to the root of the matter. When our risen Lord was about to ascend into heaven, He said to His Apostles : " All power is given unto Me in heaven and in earth. As the Father hath sent Me, even so send I you. Go ye, therefore," etc. He gave no such direct commission of authority to priests or deacons or laity. All that these last, therefore, have at any time enjoyed in the Church, they have enjoyed by gift of communication from the Episcopate, to whom, and to whom alone, the entire power was originally given. But note, that Christ gave the gift to the Apostles as a body—not to St. Peter or to any other as an individual. It is the Episcopate as a body that represents Christ, and received " all power " from Him. Therefore none can make a bishop but the bishops themselves. No election, no appointment, no letters-patent, no popular acclamations, can make a man a bishop. Nothing can make any man a bishop except consecration by those who themselves are bishops already. When the bishops concede to priests, deacons, laity, or the civil government, any share in the government of the Church, or the selection of its officers, that concession is valid, for the bishops originally had " all power." Thus in the original appointment of deacons, the Apostles left it to others to choose the individuals, while reserving to themselves the power of ordination, If the multitude had chosen persons whom the Apostles knew to be unfit, doubtless they would at once have refused to ordain them.

So long as the Apostles were together, and the Church had not yet spread abroad, there was no need of change. " The Apostle and elders and brethren "·could be called together when any tough question was to be decided. But as the Church and the Episcopate extended to far distant countries, the case was changed. The whole body could not be brought together on every question. What, then, was to be done ? Then the episcopate of each province—so soon as it became sufficiently numerous—was organized in a synod. The entire number of bishops represented the original College of the Apostles. All ordinary questions were settled by them. There was an appeal to a larger council only in important controversies of the faith.

Look at the Province of Asia—the example most fully known to us. When St. Paul first carried the full Gospel to the chief city, Ephesus, they had not yet heard of the outpouring of the Holy Ghost. St. Paul laid the foundations, tarrying and laboring there some two years. But within a few years more, look at the change ! St. John is yet alive, and writes the Epistles to the Seven Churches of Asia. Ephesus is the head, for there the good work began. But there are six other Sees clustering around it, and all in the same province, and they evidently form what was soon afterward known as an ecclesiastical province. And so it was, little by little, in all the provinces of the old Roman Empire. Slowly and very sluggishly we are following the example here. The See of New York, which began with one bishop having jurisdiction over the whole State, has grown into five dioceses (there ought to be more than a dozen!), and Pennsylvania has three (there ought to be at least seven, even now). And in Illinois we have the first thoroughly organized province, though with a very imperfect realization, as yet, of provincial powers, and with only three dioceses. But enough has already been done to indicate the general drift of the change required.

And the first principle thus indicated is that the State is to furnish the boundaries of the provinces. There are only three probable exceptions to this—Delaware, Rhode Island, and West Virginia. Delaware and Rhode Island might be permitted to attach themselves for provincial purposes to any conterminous province ; Delaware to Pennsylvania or (better still) to Maryland ; and Rhode Island to either Massachusetts or Connecticut, although, in ancient days, Delaware would be a province by itself with at least three sees, and Rhode Island another province with four or more sees. But perhaps this is too much to expect in these degenerate days. As to western Virginia, the separation of that State was made during our civil war, and in utter violation of the spirit of the constitution, and the boundary line between that and the Old Dominion is the ugliest line on the whole map of the Union. All the other lines are either Nature's graceful lines of coast or river or mountain chain, while all artificial lines are the straight lines of peaceful development. But that ugly West Virginia line is the zigzag scar of the lightning-bolt of civil war, contradicting every other line in the whole map. It would be grateful to all Virginians who love the historic identity of the Old Dominion, to have both the Virginias, according to the old State lines, embraced in the unity of the ecclesiastical province. In every other case, without exception, the diocese now embracing a State or Territory may hope to grow into a province in the course of time.

The shortest and easiest way to accomplish this would be—first, to subdivide each State diocese into at least three sees when the time for subdivision has come. Two might do, as a temporary measure ; but it is unsatisfactory, for the bishops should always have their separate vote as a separate order, and with only two of them they must be unanimous or nothing can be done. Another point is that at first the old Diocesan Convention, with clergy and laity from the whole State, should be continued over unchanged, with its old power of making and altering constitutions and canons, only leaving to each diocese its own elections. In this way, most easily, the power of making and altering constitution and canon can be restored to the *provincial* synod, without any felt loss or surrender on the part of the diocesan conventions. After some years, as the numbers of clergy and laity become inconveniently large, they can be reduced by the diocesan conventions electing deputies in proportion to the numbers of their clergy and laity, rather than have all attending the provincial synod. But this change would leave the legislative power undisturbed where it belongs, with the synod of the province.

Another point that ought to be preserved in our American provinces is that the presidency of the province, or, metropolitanate, should *always* belong to the chief city and original see—to New York, in the province of New York; to Philadelphia, in the province of Pennsylvania, and so on. This chief city is the chief centre of influence in business, in politics, in all other worldly matters; and if it be not made the centre of ecclesiastical influence also, there will always be found there a strong clique of clergy and laity whose influence will too often be opposed to that of the official head of the province or diocese.

Still another point—somewhat new in such organizations—ought to be carefully guarded. Where party spirit runs high, and the metropolitan is of one party, while the other bishops and dioceses may be of the other, it would hardly be fair to give to the metropolitan the sole appointment of committees. The better and fairer rule will be that when a committee is appointed of any specified number from each diocese, then each bishop should appoint the member or members from his own diocese, and if any bishop be absent, then the deputies from his diocese shall freely elect from their own number the member or members called for.

Of course, eventually, the bishops of each province should be the court of appeals for that province. And here two points should be provided for. In the first place, the bishops of the province should, as a body, form the court of appeals, and alone give the final sentence, whatever it may be. And they should give it in writing, each member of the court assigning his reasons, so that—if they are wrong—public opinion may have a fair chance to be heard for the benefit of future cases. In the second place, there should be one clerical and one lay assessor elected by each diocesan convention; besides which, each bishop should have the right, if he please, to name one additional clerical or lay assessor, or both, because he and his convention may not be in thorough harmony, and he has the right to be advised by those in whom he has confidence. These assessors should not be *merely* to give advice. They would probably include those of the clergy who were the best canonists, and laymen who were good lawyers or judges; and all interlocutory questions should be decided by them. It is not possible to insure all bishops as good canonists, and—as our past experience shows—a bishop may be thoroughly conscientious when acting on a court, and yet may have the most extraordinary ideas of *law*. The bishops, therefore, need to be protected against the very real danger of making fearful blunders in matters which they do not understand; and the assessors would relieve them from the decision of all those technical points in which they would be most likely to err. But when these preliminary matters were all settled, then to *the bishops alone* should be reserved the final sentence of the court in the matter at issue. When a State province is established, and with bishops

256 *A Champion of the Cross.*

sufficiently numerous, there are certain other parts of the ancient system which ought to be restored.

In the first place, when a bishop is elected to any diocese within the province, it should be enough to obtain the consent of the majority of all the bishops of the province, instead of asking that of all the bishops in the United States, from Florida to Alaska. The requiring the consent of a majority of the standing committees should be dropped anyhow. There was only a temporary necessity for it at the first organization of our American Church, to make up for the lack of personal knowledge by the English bishops of those clergymen whom they were called upon to consecrate as bishops for these United States. The free voice of clergy and laity is given in the election by the diocese that makes the choice. The consent of the bishops of the province gives the approval of the third and highest order. That was enough in the primitive days. It ought to be enough now. And the metropolitan of the province with others of his comprovincial bishops, should always perform the consecration. If it be the metropolitan see that is to be filled, the consecration should *always* be by the other bishops of that same province ; as in the old days, when a bishop of Rome was chosen he was always consecrated by the Bishop of Ostia and others of the original Province of Rome.

In the second place, when any diocese was to be divided and a new See erected, the consent of the Provincial Synod should be enough, without troubling General Convention. Suppose California wants to be divided, what can Maine be supposed to know on the subject so that it ought to be able to overrule California? No. Each province should settle all such questions for itself. Instead, then, of provinces being a useless, or needless appendage, we should find embodied in them the following important changes :

1. A more vigorous recognition of State lines in our Church work than is furnished by any other religious body in the land, thus giving us a *prima facie* claim to be *the* National Church.

2. A provincial synod making and altering constitution (a constitution is only a more permanent form of canon) and canons, relieving our diocesan conventions of all responsibility in that matter. And eventually it would relieve General Convention of a large part of the legislation—our triennial National Council confining itself mainly to questions of Bible and Prayer-book, and inter-communion, and the restoration of the visible unity of Christendom, leaving all points of ordinary practical administration to the provincial synods.

3. The working of a simple and practical Court of Appeals, before which any and every disputed question might be brought, and settled on the spot.

4. The furnishing of the ancient primary court for the trial of any bishop, with no appeal beyond its decisions except in cases involving doctrine.

5. The simplifying the process of the consecration of bishops in case of vacancy.

6. A similar facility in the erection of new dioceses.

7. One great recommendation of the plan here proposed is that necessarily it must be very gradual in the process of realization. Some parts of our Church (very few) are ready for it now if they only knew it. Others will not be ready for fifty years to come. The full measure of the powers here suggested as proper for provincial synods cannot be conveyed at present. Some of them it may be wiser to withhold until a province shall contain at least (say) seven dioceses. But as one province took its place in line after another—*not all at once*—there would be a much better chance of improvement in a line of advance as yet untried. Mistakes made in one place would be corrected in another; and thus the system would become more vigorous and complete with its gradual adoption.

But one point I would insist on with the utmost obstinacy. The idea of making the meetings of our General Convention not so frequent as once in three years, should be talked down, voted down, knocked on the head, whenever it appears. What! We could meet once in three years just after the Revolutionary War, when there were no steamboats and no railroads, and now, with all the marvellous facilities of modern travel, we are to meet only once in ten, fifteen, or twenty years! The very idea is absurd and intolerable! Why, the Lambeth Conference of bishops from all over the world meets once in every ten years! With our provisions against changes in constitution or prayer-book except when passing in identical verbal form through two consecutive General Conventions, we should crystallize ourselves into future immobility, just when the prospect of the reunion of Christendom demands of us a greater flexibility than ever! And we began the movement too! And what a wickedly absurd position we should be in, if, after inviting a divided Christendom to meet us on the four points, we should adopt a legislative system which should tie ourselves up more closely hand and foot than ever we were tied before! No, no! Even if General Convention reserves to itself only the matters concerning reunion, it will have more than enough to do every three years, and the more the better!

17

THE LAY ELEMENT IN ENGLAND AND IN AMERICA.

(From the *Contemporary Review*, March, 1881.)

FOR more than thirty years I have been a close and steady reader of the leading English Church papers, and most deeply interested in every step of the marvellous Church revival which has been gaining ground year by year during all that time, and is stronger now than ever. The same movement has been making progress on our side of the water, under very different conditions. One peculiar point of observation and thought has been to watch how the life within, on either side of the water, would modify its environment, so as to enable the new spirit to do its full work. For years I have been convinced that the key to the position on your side—the Malakoff whose capture will ensure the surrender of the enemy—is simply to give to the laity in England as nearly as possible the same position which they now enjoy in the Church of America. There has been a steady approximation toward this, beyond question; but its stiffest opponents are precisely those brave men of the advanced school who ought to be its friends, and who have the most to gain from its adoption, because they have the best right.

Nothing would be further from the truth than to suppose that this conviction is a mere piece of our too common American conceit and "bumptiousness." I think I see as many faults, and am as ready to try to correct them, in our American Church as in any other. Nay, it must be frankly confessed that we have no right to pride ourselves on our originality or ingenuity in this matter of the laity. We American churchmen have been guilty of every stupidity and every particle of obstructiveness that was in our power. Wherever it was possible to copy an English blunder we have been sure to do it. Some of our best changes were accomplished, humanly speaking, by accident. Our most real improvements were things into which a kind Providence *drove* us, so that we had no choice left. Yet, after nearly a century of experience of the advantages of our providential position, as proved by a steady gain over even our rapid rate of increase in the population, as also by a still more rapid gain in the tone and strength of churchmanship, we have American stupids (bishops included) who, while abroad among you, talk of the "superior advantages [Heaven save the mark!] of a union of Church and State;" and some of our dignitaries bring back with them strings and rosettes in their hats, and braided coats, aprons, and leggings, and even call one another "My Lord" on the sly, in a semi-jocular manner, when no dangerous ears are within reach. We have a natural genius for making Church blunders over here, and we have not done with it yet. The position taken in regard to the laity, therefore, is perfectly free from any national vanity.

To begin at the beginning. The precise position of the laity, as an organic element in the structure of the Primitive Church, is by no means self-evident. As the entire *depositum* of spiritual knowledge and power was given to the Apostolic College, it must have been the work of time to settle what particular portions of it should be permanently distributed to priests, deacons, and laity. That some such conveyance was contemplated from the first is evident from the fact that the new Apostle, in the place of Judas, was not appointed by Saint Peter (the papal theory), nor by the eleven alone (as some suppose the episcopal theory to be), nor by the eleven and the seventy alone (as some would make the clerical theory to be). The whole "one hundred and twenty" of the "disciples" took part in the election, so that there *must* have been some of the laity voting for the first bishop of the apostolic succession, as well as the eleven and the seventy ; there *must* have been at least *thirty-nine* of these laity, for eleven and seventy (if the seventy were all present) make only eighty-one of the one hundred and twenty. When the order of deacons was created, the "multitude of the disciples" were the electoral body again, though the appointing or ordaining power was reserved by the apostles. In the choice of Church officers, therefore, from bishop or Apostle, which is the highest, to deacon, which is the lowest, the *laity* should have a free voice. At the Council of Jerusalem we find that "all the multitude" were again present, and toward the close they "kept silence," a very significant hint that they had been doing their part of the "much disputing" which preceded. This is a strong indication that the ordinary reading : "The Apostles, and elders, and brethren," means just what we describe as "The bishops, clergy, and laity."

But in the earlier ages, the bishops and clergy being the primary teachers of the new Gospel, would naturally possess so strong a directing power, that the distinct share of the laity in legislation would hardly appear. Indeed, if we look to the power of giving a distinctive *vote*, as an *order*, we find it pretty much confined to the episcopate. A very rigid adherence to the model of the earlier Councils might be found to shut out the priesthood as well as the people, and leave all legislative power to the bishops alone.

As the fresh leadership of early teaching settled down, however, into the well-defined tradition of the second or third generation, the stability of the pyramid was increased by the enlargement of its base. The organic share of priests and people became more highly and firmly crystallized. In the election of bishops it was sometimes manifested with such force as to show the need of further regulation. When one hundred and thirty-seven corpses were carried out of one church after the election of Damasus as Bishop of Rome, it would hardly do to say that the laity had no share in the election of bishops. In the worst of our partisan contested elections, we have never, in America, come anywhere near the liveliness of the Roman laity in the fourth century.

But with the conversion of Constantine a new element had come into play. Slowly in some points, more rapidly in others, the Government absorbed the previous right of the laity, and added other and further usurpations also. This new power was at first exerted as simply " Government *influence*." The forms were left untouched : the *spirit* only was changed. The imperial influence in favor of one candidate was generally sufficient to secure his election. After a time this hardened into a right to nominate, and then at last into a right to appoint and install. So also with regard to Councils. Here, where the position of the laity had been left more indefinite from the first, appropriation by the State, through its powerful *influence*, was more rapid and more complete than in regard to election. All the undisputed General Councils were not only called by the Emperor, but their decisions or decrees received also their κῦρος—their validity as *law*—from *him*. He was the " lay power " entire.

We must now draw a clear distinction between things which have been more or less confused and confounded ever since the union of Church and State began. Everything touching the possession and control of property belongs of right to the civil authority. Our Lord Himself, when on the earth, though He was King of kings and Lord of lords, would not meddle with a case of secular property, even when a man had cheated his own brother out of part of his inheritance. " Man, who made Me a judge or a divider over you ? " was His unanswerable question to one who would engage Him to decide a question of property. Even while the emperors of Rome were Pagans, the Church— as in the case of Paul of Samosata—went into the secular courts for the settlement of the right of property, even church property. Now, for everything concerning the tenure and management of property, the Church is dependent upon the State, *necessarily*, here in America as well as elsewhere. We have no difficulty in getting the State to do for us anything we really need, in this line. In this State of Pennsylvania, for instance, any number of persons may associate themselves together for any religious purpose ; and, having submitted their articles of association to the inspection of the judges of a certain court, and due publicity being secured, when the judge certifies that there is nothing therein " contrary to the Constitution and Laws of the United States or of the Commonwealth of Pennsylvania," the applicants are forthwith recognized and recorded as a corporation at law."

This is *essentially distinct* from the possession or exercise of any power touching questions of doctrine, discipline, or worship, or the election or appointment to office in the Church. But the union of Church and State has so far confused the two that it is not easy to unravel them. And the confusion seems to be inextricable as soon as an Englishman reaches the magic phrase " the Royal Supremacy."

Now, it may startle your readers immensely, but I venture to say that the Royal Supremacy, in its true meaning and intent, exists here, in America, as completely as it does in England. The object of the Statute of Henry VIII. was to put a stop to appeals to Rome in all cases occurring in the ecclesiastical courts in England, those courts having then jurisdiction in "all testamentary and matrimonial causes, and all suits for tithes, oblations, and obventions;" and all these cases were thereafter to be settled *within the realm.* As to America, questions of "tithes, oblations, and obventions" do not occur. "All testamentary and matrimonial causes," so far as civil rights are concerned, are settled by the civil courts, and no Romanist dreams of appealing from them to Rome, any more than do the Quakers.

But we go further than this. The *principle* of the Act of Henry VIII. separates clearly between the civil and ecclesiastical jurisdiction, maintaining that, *in both,* England was sufficient unto herself, without becoming dependent on Rome. The statute says of England, that "the body spiritual" thereof has power "when any cause of the law divine happened to come in question, or of spiritual learning," such cause being "declared, interpreted, and showed by that part of the body politic called the spiritualty, now usually called the English Church (which also hath been reported and also found of that sort, that both for knowledge, integrity, and sufficiency of numbers, it hath been always thought to be, and is also at this hour, sufficient and meet of itself, without the interfering of any exterior person or persons, to declare and determine all such doubts, and to administer all such offices and duties as to the administration of their rooms spiritual doth appertain); and the laws temporal, for trial of property, of lands and goods, and for the conservation of the people of this realm in unity and peace, having been and yet being administered, adjudged, and executed by sundry judges and administers of the said body politic called the temporalty; and seeing that both these authorities and jurisdictions do conjoin together for the due administration of justice, the one to help the other;" etc. Nothing can be more absurd than to argue, that the true meaning of all this is, that secular courts are to judge spiritual cases, or that spiritual courts are to decide secular cases, or that the king, as an autocrat, could overrule either the one or the other. It merely recognizes a fundamental and indelible distinction between civil and ecclesiastical cases, and that *each* of the two kinds of court is to exercise its own powers, without interference from the other within the realm, or from any power whatsoever outside. The same fundamental distinction between the spiritual and the temporal is re-asserted in more than one message sent by Queen Elizabeth to her meddlesome Parliament; and stands permanently embodied in the Royal Declaration prefixed to the Thirty-nine Articles. And the reiterated quotation of all these passages, in all sorts of books, reviews, magazines, newspapers, and other publications, would, so one would suppose, have made the principle itself familiar enough to most Englishmen by this time.

Now this *fundamental distinction* between things and causes properly civil, and things and causes properly spiritual, is American law as well as English law.

Our Civil Courts, where a question of property depends upon the issue, will examine and decide any Church question—so far as that piece of property is concerned. But the decision concerns the Church no farther than that particular amount of dollars and cents, and does not *bind* the Church in *any* spiritual point of view. When an Illinois secular court, after years of incubation, decided that Mr. Cheney was entitled to the possession of his church edifice, *because* he was yet " a Presbyter of the Protestant Episcopal Church in good and regular standing," although at the time of rendering this decision Cheney had not only been for some years deposed from the ministry, but had actually been " consecrated " by Bishop Cummins as a " Bishop " of the new " Reformed Episcopal " sect, what was the consequence? Cheney merely retained possession of a building which was heavily mortgaged, and not very desirable in any point of view; and all the world (Cheneyites included) laughed at the absurdity of the decision.

The very Romanists themselves, in Great Britain, recognize the Royal Supremacy without murmuring. When a Saurin case arises in England, or an O'Keefe case in Ireland, of the very sort that, before the Reformation, would have been evoked to Rome, what do your Romish ecclesiastics do about it? Do they evoke it to Rome? No more than if they were so many Protestants. Cardinals, bishops, and priests, monks and nuns, obey the *subpœnas* and other processes of the civil courts, and accept their decisions, whether they like them or not, as quietly as if there was no such city as Rome, and no such person there as the Pope.

And it seems to be an entire mistake to suppose that the power now exercised by the Crown in regard to the *congé d'élire*, and convocation, and various other matters, has anything to do with the Royal Supremacy. The Royal Supremacy is an incident of the Crown, *necessarily co-extensive with its jurisdiction*. Will anyone say that the Royal Supremacy has been *abolished* in the Dominion of Canada, or in any other of the constitutional colonies? Is it abolished in Ireland, or in Scotland? Nay, is it abolished in England itself in regard to all persons *except* those who belong to the Established Church? The very asking of the question is enough. It is abolished nowhere. It would be just as correct to say that none but members of the Established Church are " subjects " of the British Crown.

This is clear enough as to the Civil Courts. As to the Spiritual Courts it is not so clear. But the positive and direct declaration of the Statute of Henry VIII. is, that spiritual questions shall be decided by *Spiritual Courts* only, without appeal to any power outside the realm. When the State, in process of time, recognized the existence of two or more religious organizations, with legal rights, within the realm, the *principle* of the Act was not thereby destroyed, but only rendered more active. The organs for the settlement of spiritual questions merely became more numerous, so as to decide those questions according to the communion in which they may arise. If it be a spiritual question among Presbyterians, the Presbyterian Spiritual Courts will settle it. If among the Baptists, then the Baptist Court. If among the Methodists, then the Methodist Court. If among the Romanists, then a Romanist Court; each and every of them managing their own

Courts to suit themselves. In any case, if property interests be involved, the Civil Court may review the decision so far as civil rights may be involved; but its sentence will bind no further than that.

All the particulars, therefore, in which the Crown now has more or other powers touching the Established Church than touching any other religious body in the empire, are simply *outside* the true meaning and intent of "*the Royal Supremacy*," and may be entirely altered and removed by law, without touching the Royal Supremacy in any degree.

In all these other matters, however, the Crown now absorbs and uses powers that originally and properly belonged to the *laity* as an order within the Church itself, and which *ought* to belong to the laity *now*, if only the laity were so organized for that purpose as to be able to use them.

With us, they are so organized. And let us compare the general features of the two systems. No man has an *ex officio* place as a lay deputy or officer of any sort in the Church of America. He must be *elected*. And the only ostensible ground on which he *can* be elected, is because he is a Churchman, and is sufficiently interested in the Church to serve without pay. *Your* laity, in the only organization you have (your Parliament), even in its best days, when admitting only Church communicants, was composed of men chosen for *secular* objects; by methods of *secular* agitation, whose parties rose and fell on *secular* questions; and to which spiritual questions or interests could scarcely at any time be more than incidental. This contrast, alone, ought to be enough to settle the whole question. But when, besides this, your only legal organization of the laity of the English Church first ceased to be communicants, then admitted a nation of Presbyterians, then another nation chiefly of Romanists, then Jews, and now Atheists, and yet still clings to the spiritual power of the lay order in the Church of England herself, while keeping the order of the clergy all the while tied up in a double-bow knot, how *can* reasonable men suppose that to be a plan preferable to ours?

Let us now compare a few details. And in so doing, the secular lay power—the government for the day—will be contrasted with the Church laity among us.

As to legislation: Without a writ from the secular lay power your Convocation cannot come together at all. Our Church laity have no such control over us. Our Conventions all meet at fixed constitutional times, as a matter of course. Special meetings are called by the bishop, or by standing committees, which generally consist of both clergy and laity.

When your Convocation has come together, you cannot even discuss any matter of legislation without a Letter of Business from your secular lay power. Our Church laity have no such gag in our mouths. When we are assembled in Convention, *any* member may introduce any matter of proposed legislation he pleases, and the House can discuss it as long as they like, and come to what conclusion seems good to them.

When your Convocation has come to a conclusion, it is of no force unless your secular lay power sees fit to approve it. Here there is some nearer comparison ; for with us a *vote by orders* may at any time be called for (and on some subjects the vote must be taken that way), and without the consent of a majority of the lay order present nothing is done. But practically there is a vast difference between this and your way of doing (or rather *not* doing) things. For, first, our laity are Church laity, chosen and coming there because of their interest as Churchmen, and they are therefore eminently fit to be trusted. They are also present during the whole discussion, they are compelled to hear what the clergy have to say, and to answer it face to face if they can ; and they are protected from the pressure of secular interests, or secular entanglements, in coming to their spiritual conclusion. In all Church matters they are thus *being continually educated* by their membership in such a body. They there learn things concerning the working system of the Church which they might never learn in books, and which they would never hear in sermons or in private conversations. And nothing is more interesting than to watch some clear-headed layman, from General Convention to General Convention, growing continually in strength of judgment, clearness of insight, and boldness of advocacy, until he is numbered among those on whom the clergy rely as their constant and conscientious helpers in every Church contest, and towers of strength for the maintenance of every Church principle. On the contrary, your secular lay power is inaccessible to Church teaching or Church argument ; the clergy cannot make it listen, has no control over its adjournment or consideration, and is therefore completely at the mercy of its ignorance, its caprice, or its secular interests.

Whenever your discussions are at all displeasing to your secular lay power, it can prorogue your Convocation on the spot, and send you all home, willy-nilly ; or your Archbishop—generally the mouthpiece of the secular lay power rather than of the Church—can do it of his own motion. There is no such sword suspended by a thread over the head of any of our Conventions. Assembling at the stated constitutional time, so long as a quorum is present, *nothing* can prorogue or adjourn the session, except the free vote of the body itself. In the case of the General Convention it requires a joint vote by both Houses. Neither can terminate the session by its own sole act.

But some among you lift up your hands in holy horror at the idea that we give to our laity an equal vote with the bishops and clergy in all questions of *doctrine*. So we do. But let us look a little more closely, and not jump too suddenly to a conclusion.

Nobody among us pretends that the Lord gave His commission to *teach* to any but the bishops and clergy—to the bishops alone *absolutely :* to the other clergy only derivatively, but yet substantially and authoritatively. That commission was not given to the laity. Wherever the bishops and clergy went, in primitive times, they preached and taught, and the laity received the faith from them with meekness and docility. But how is it now ? Have the clergy received the revelation of any *new* doctrine, heretofore unheard of by the laity, and which the laity would, therefore, be likely to reject ? Certainly not.

Among Romanists or Dissenters there may be room for new doctrines, or new denials of old doctrines, but not among us. The only question of doctrine that can arise, is as to the clearer statement of some things which have fallen partly out of sight in the popular apprehension. And as to these, why should we fear the laity? What are they, anyhow doctrinally, to the clergy but as the armature of soft iron to the magnet? Who has taught them what they *now* hold, except the bishops and clergy? If that teaching has been faithfully given, why can we not trust the laity to echo it correctly? If that teaching has *not* been faithfully given, let the bishops and clergy correct *themselves* first, and then, within a generation or less, they will find the laity ready to go with them. It would be *most unwise* to legislate afresh on doctrine, until *the picked men of the laity*—those chosen for their intelligent interest in Church matters, and those alone—are sufficiently educated by the bishops and clergy to see the propriety of it. To legislate in advance of this degree of co-operation would be *to ensure schism.*

We say thus much as to *new* legislation on doctrine. But there is no great cause for alarm in this direction. What we are all most concerned about is, to see that we *lose* no part of the doctrinal treasures which we still retain. Now, on our American plan, *no* doctrinal change can be made without the identical action of two consecutive General Conventions, each voting by its three orders; and the want of concurrence on the part of any *one* order (even by a tie vote), at either of those two General Conventions, is enough to defeat the change. That is to say, suppose the whole three orders were unanimous in favor of the change in 1880, and in 1883 the clergy and the laity were equally unanimous for it, while the House of Bishops should be equally divided, it would *fail.* If the order of bishops can be trusted, neither clergy nor laity can do any harm. If the order of clergy can be trusted, then neither the bishops nor the laity, though unanimous, can do any harm. And there may be cases when the simple slowness of the laity may save the Church from weakness or rashness on the part of both bishops and clergy. All readers of Church history will remember those terrible Arian times when " the ears of the people were more orthodox than the tongues of the priests."

There is another consideration which I commend most earnestly to the notice of thoughtful men. The laity, with us, have their say on the election of every bishop, and on the candidacy and ordination of every priest and deacon, and on the parochial call of every rector of a parish. But it is also true that the clergy have their measure of influence on every part of the operations of the lay order, on the selection of vestrymen in their parish, on the appointment of lay delegates to their Diocesan Convention, and on the choice of lay deputies to General Convention. These last are usually chosen by concurrent vote. No man can go as lay-deputy unless a *majority of the clergy* vote for him, as well as a majority of the laity. Neither can anyone be chosen a clerical deputy unless he receive a majority of the lay votes, as well as a majority of the clerical votes. This looks perfectly equal, and in theory *is* so, so that no layman can take any exception to it. But *in practice*, except on very rare and extraordinary occasions, the clerical vote is the real determining power, and the lay vote, sooner or later, coincides. If a clergyman is a person of any real weight of character, his vestry is very soon just what he chooses to make it—the lay deputies to Convention are those whom he wishes to be sent; and, when there, they vote as he does. Nor is this any unfair interference with their right. They have a right to act with their clergyman if they like; especially when they have called him themselves, and love him, and take pleasure in agreeing with him and helping him and his influence in every way. Thus, too, in all our Church Conventions, the clergy take part as in their life-work, which they thoroughly understand, and in which they have the effectiveness of soldiers of the regular army. The laity, however, take their part generally with far less of ready confidence and effectiveness. In other words, they are rather like the militia. And unless some singular want of judgment, or some unusually mischievous element makes itself felt, the preponderance of the clergy in all that is said and done is natural and continued. Sooner or later, on our plan, the laity *must*, and *will*, take the tone which bishops and clergy give them.

Whenever there is a temporary discrepancy between the two orders, it is almost invariably due to one of three causes : 1st. It may be owing to temporary panic, seizing upon the comparative ignorance of the laity, and exciting them to resistance before there is an opportunity to enlighten them as to the true facts of the case. All that is necessary is to keep cool, have patience, let the tempest in a teapot die away, and then the whole may be easily explained, and the laity will accept the explanation. 2d. It may be due to ignorance merely, without the panic, in which case it is even more manageable than in the other. An absence of the worry and hurry, and a little time and patience, are all that is required. 3d. There may be something in the constitutional organization which has a *natural tendency* to make the laity feel that they are unfairly used ; and if this be so, it is sometimes very easy to get up a very mischievous excitement.

For instance : There are two modes of electing diocesan bishops among us. The Pennsylvania and Virginia method gives to the order of the clergy the right to nominate a man to the laity, and the latter can only say *yes* or *no* to the nominee of the clergy. This is giving, apparently, a very important prerogative to the clergy; and, very curiously, it prevails mainly in dioceses which were Low Church at the time when they adopted it. The other is the New York plan, by which both orders ballot simultaneously on a perfect constitutional equality, and there is no election until some one candidate has a majority of *both* orders at the same ballot. This is the High Church plan, and is far preferable for the *reality* of clerical influence. The other plan is like the silly dog in the fable, who lost the meat in order to grasp at the shadow. And this will be clearly seen on a little closer examination. If both clergy and laity really have their minds set upon one and the same individual, either mode would work the same result. But suppose the clergy desire a man who at first sight is not so acceptable to the laity—how then? The *feeling* that this is so would be very perceptible before the Convention came together. Some among the lay opponents would be sure to say that " the laity don't come here merely to register the edicts of the clergy." The laity may, by a strong majority, prefer some other name than the one sent down by the clergy. But they have no way by which they can manifest that preference, except by defeating every name sent down by the clergy, until the clergy shall send down the name desired. What chance is there then for the first choice of the clergy? *Simply none at all.* The first time it is sent down it is negatived. What shall the clergy do? Send down the same name a second time? What is likely to be the effect of that? It is an implied rebuke to the laity—an implied suggestion that their first action was hasty, or from want of due consideration, or was prejudiced or unjust. Is this likely to put the laity in a better humor? They are more likely to say *no* the second time than the first; and it will get worse every time until the laity become perfectly unmanageable. The first choice of the clergy (perhaps their second or third choice as well) will be defeated, and the election will probably fall upon one whom nobody desired and nobody even thought of before the contest began. But on the other plan, the clergy having apparently no organic advantage over the laity, the two orders come together without that artificial predisposition for a disagreement. Each order votes for the man it prefers, and can *show* its preference, and continue to show it, ballot after ballot, as long as it pleases, without any offence being implied to the other order. If the clergy are divided into cliques, the laity will probably carry in their man. But if the clergy understand one another (a majority of them) and stand shoulder to shoulder, the laity will soon feel satisfied with the open compliment they have paid to their candidate, and will, vote by vote, come round to the clergy's candidate, until at length he is elected.

The same general principle applies to any *constitutional inequality* between the two orders, which is not absolutely required by essential principle. To give the laity a separate vote on doctrine cannot possibly do any harm. But it may do great good, by promoting that *solidarity of feeling and interest* which is of inestimable value.

While on the subject of elections, I cannot resist the temptation to make two practical suggestions, though they are aside from the main subject before us. The first is, that the *sooner* an election is held the *better*. " The King is dead : Long live the King!" is the best model. Ten days were not suffered to elapse after the Ascension before St. Matthias was in the place vacated by Judas Iscariot. And when the subject was brought up, the Apostles did not leave it open for several days to give an opportunity for electioneering and canvassing and slandering, but they went into the choice *at once*. In all elections of bishops, the primary instinctive action is best—based, as it must then be, on the *already publicly known* standing of men for ability and character. The most common use made of days or weeks intervening, is to give the second- and third-rate men a chance to blackball the first-rate men, who otherwise would be the spontaneous choice. So strong is my feeling about this, that, if it were in my power, the law should be that the clergy and laity should attend the funeral of the dead bishop in the morning, and, on returning from the grave, go *at once* into the election of his successor, without stopping for either meat or drink ; and that any number of the clergy and laity thus continuing in session without any adjournment or recess for any purpose whatsoever until an election was made, should be a sufficient quorum for a valid choice. The second suggestion is, that nothing *more* than a simple majority of both orders present should be required in order to elect. To require, for instance, a majority of *two-thirds* merely means that a little clique of about *one-sixth* of the body shall have power to *defeat the majority ;* the consequence is, the defeat of the strong man and the election of some one who is weak enough to have no enemies. It is our favorite American way of killing off (politically speaking) the natural leaders of parties, and promoting men in their places who can be more easily used. Both these suggestions would tend greatly toward *minimizing* the evils naturally incident to a popular election. In decisions about doctrine, *moral unanimity* should be required. In the election of individuals to office, a *simple majority* is the wisest and most efficient rule.

To pass now to another matter, though one of great importance—the forming of corporations for the holding and managing of Church property. They are with us almost invariably composed largely, if not of a majority, of laymen. Sometimes, as in Pennsylvania, the State law requires this. The consequence of such an arrangement would naturally be to put an end to all projects of spoliation. " Hawks will not pike out hawks' een." The idea of plundering the clergy is very attractive to some minds ; but the plundering of *corporations of laymen* is a very different matter. It is then always remembered that "the rights of property are sacred." The management of Church business might, in some respects, be thus rendered more clumsy and tedious, sometimes even sluggish ; but, in the long run, the property would be safer. Look at the fate of Church property held solely in clerical hands all over the continent of Europe, and in other countries also. Clerical management secures rapid acquisition, and often to vast amounts, but is *invariably* followed, after a certain lapse of time, by wholesale confiscation. And this is not the effect of doctrinal differences ; but it is the *laity as an order* taking to themselves that *control of property* of which the clergy, by superior finesse, had for too long a time deprived them. This lesson is taught us as clearly by Spain and Italy in the nineteenth century as by France in the eighteenth, or by England and Scotland in the sixteenth. And if the laity thus act, organized as the civil government of the day, it must be remembered that this is the *only* organization of the laity which the Church, for ages previous, had encouraged or known anything about.

We have, indeed, a protection which is unknown among you. We have a written Constitution, and a Supreme Court of the United States. Our Church property has been declared to be, in so far that of private corporations (as distinguished from public corporations), that no State Legislature can, by any act of confiscation, take it away from us. And if any such Act should at any time be passed, the Supreme Court would declare it to be " null and void," because " unconstitutional." The very *possibility*, therefore, of such a thing as disendowment—that is, wholesale robbery by act of the Civil Government—is inconceivable in our American system. The existence of this danger among you only makes more necessary that *organic solidarity of interests* between clergy and laity which would speedily take all dreams of disendowment out of the range of " practical politics."

And now let us look at the tough subject of patronage, beginning with the lower sphere of the parish clergy, and afterward proceeding to bishops.

No part of our American system has called forth more constant complaints from among ourselves, or more severe criticism from elsewhere, than the giving to our parochial vestries the power of calling a rector, and too often, the practical power of starving him out or of driving him off when he has worn out his welcome. " The hideous vestry system," and the terrible disease of " *vestryitis*," have echoed and re-echoed through our newspapers, and in episcopal addresses and platform speeches, until one would think it was the worst plan of solving the patronage problem that ever was invented. Yet, instead of being the worst, it is actually *the best* known at the present day in any branch of the apostolic Church. At any rate, it is incomparably better than yours in England.

Our system, indeed, is yet in its infancy, and has many evils to contend with, which are properly its own. In the first place, the English churchmen who come over as immigrants to this country, too often bring with them the idea that beyond baptisms, marriages, and funerals, they do not need to trouble the Church at all ; or that, as there is no Church established here *by law*, there is none which it is at all their duty to attend. If they do attend, they are so accustomed to a clergy supported by existing endowments, that they cannot be made to feel that there is any need for them to contribute toward current expenses. Any farther interest they may show is probably in the way of fault finding or bullying, because things are not exactly as they were in the parish they came from " at home." So the English element—where any such element is to be found—is not much of a help. And too often a large part of the American element is but lately drawn in from the much more numerous and powerful sects around us ; and persons attracted to the Church only in their maturer years, are too apt to bring with them the mental habits which were those of their previous lives. Their sectarian idea always was, that the pews were the source of power ; and that it is the first duty of the pulpit to please and fill the pews ; and that, if the preacher don't do that, he ought to quit. Hardly anywhere are there any " endowments " of any sort, for the current expenses of clergy and parish. These *must*, somehow or other, be paid by the congregation, or by some missionary organization ; or the clergyman must starve, or live by his own private means, or leave. Now, the problem is, to *compel* people to support a clergyman by their *voluntary* offerings, when they *do not choose* to do it. It is possible, indeed, to put a legal remedy in the hands of a clergyman, but when he has come to the point of suing his people and levying on their property to get his salary, what good is his subsequent preaching of the Gospel likely to do, either to himself or to them ? With ancient endowments, the income of which would support him, independently of the good-will of the parish, the case would be different. In parishes among us that have sufficient endowments, the tenure of the rectorship is as steady and as sure as in England. These are, indeed, as yet, very few, and for the most part they are not desirable. Suppose that a clergyman—no matter for what cause—has lost his acceptableness, so that a large part of his people will no longer attend his ministrations, and that the longer he stays the worse it gets. What is the result on *your* principle ? The clergyman gets his living all the same, with less and less work to do. The people neglect religion altogether ; or, after a few years, seeing no hope of any speedy change in the Church, they begin to go to the Wesleyan chapel or the Independent meeting, and after ten, fifteen, twenty, or thirty years of such a " permanent rectorship," the bulk of the population are permanently alienated from the Church. On our plan, the rector would have been starved out or driven away (I purposely use the strongest words) in a year or two at the furthest, and the coming of a new man would have given a chance, at least, of better satisfaction and growth for the future. It is not often, on our plan, that dissenting congregations are built up out of the ruins of our parishes. The clergy, indeed, sometimes have a hard time of it ; but the clergy exist for the sake of the people, not the people for the sake of giving a support to the clergy ; and whenever the preference *must* be given, the interest of the flock should prevail, and the clergy, like their Master, be content to suffer in the service—and move on. So far as my experience goes, when there is dissatisfaction in a parish, it is quite as likely to be the parson's fault as that of the people. The being in Holy Orders is no sufficient excuse for any man to dispense with prudence, tact, knowledge of mankind, acceptable manners, or any other good gift. And a clergyman is at least as much bound to show due consideration for the feelings and convictions of his people as they are for his. A neglect of these considerations *will* work according to the laws of human nature, as surely as a priest's hand, if he thrust it into the fire, will get burned. It is not best *for the clergy themselves* that their income should be *entirely* independent of their devotion to duty. We are all human. And that we should find, when we do our duty diligently, a little more encouragement than when we neglect it altogether, will do none of us any great harm. Of course this is written, not for exceptional cases, but for the general run.

Now, as it is clear that our plan, on the whole, works less harm than yours, where the priest is personally unsatisfactory, let us next look at the other side. Suppose a priest builds up his parish to an extraordinary degree of health and strength ; and his being made a bishop, or his accepting a call to another post of labor, or his death, should cause a vacancy, how shall it best be filled ? On our American plan,

the vestry—generally some seven, nine, or twelve of the leading laymen
of the parish, elected annually in Easter week—can call any priest of
the Church in good standing, in any diocese, and no bishop has a
canonical right to refuse him if he comes with clean papers. These
Easter elections of vestrymen are generally mere forms. When the
parish is at peace, scarce half a dozen voters ever attend, and a little
judicious influence, exercised kindly by a wise rector, will in a few
years give him a vestry thoroughly in harmony with himself. In case
of his death, they will surely get a successor as perfectly in harmony
with his tone and spirit as they can, and *nobody can hinder them.* If
their beloved rector has gone to another field, his influence will regulate
the succession almost as a matter of course. Those astonishing calamities which startle us so often, as happening among you—where a united,
harmonious, zealous parish is scattered to the winds, or blighted in a
day, by the arbitrary appointment of a new incumbent utterly out of
harmony with his predecessor—are *simply impossible* on our American
plan.

With us, therefore, the *evil* that a priest may do in a parish is more
transient, and the *good* that he may do is more surely *permanent,* than
with you. Our plan—with all its drawbacks—is better than yours in
both directions.

Its excellence will be equally apparent if we try it by another test.
What should we put in place of it? The favorite plan *here,* with
those who are dissatisfied, is to give the nomination to all vacant parishes to the bishop of the diocese for the time being. This might do
very well in ancient days, when the bishop was the channel of the
direct apostolic tradition. But in our days, when we are trying to
work a true spiritual reform in the Church from within, it is a totally
different question. Tradition, as we all know, is of the essence of the
episcopate. The instinct of bishops is almost invariably to hand down
the working system of the Church just as they received it. As they
are mostly elderly men by the time they are consecrated, their effort is
to perpetuate the tone of the past generation, rather than to encourage
that which is advancing in the present. *Every reform from within,
therefore, must count upon the bishops for its enemies for at least a
whole generation ;* and it will be a fortunate thing if the opposition
does not continue for two or three generations. And this is well, for
otherwise changes would be too easy, and all stability would be destroyed. If the new movement be of God, it will not die out, but will
only be deepened and steadied and strengthened by opposition. The
long struggle will teach humility to the human instruments through
whom it is carried to success. The first generation will be kept humble
by opposition, denunciation, and defeats, and possibly defections and
blunders. The second generation will be kept humble by knowing
that, though they may reap the fruit, they did not sow the seed, or bear
the burden and heat of the day. And the final triumph will be far
more permanent than if it had been more easily gained. Look at the
episcopate of England to-day, with the Primate of all England (Abp.
Tait) at the head of it. They are *now* ready unanimously to commend

the wonderful Church revival that began with the Oxford movement of more than forty years ago. But the episcopate of England was *equally unanimous in condemning it forty years ago.* And even now, though unanimously approving it, they are almost as unanimous in condemning the Ritualistic movement of to-day, which is as inseparably connected with the other as the butterfly is with the caterpillar. If the nomination to vacant parishes, therefore, be given to the bishops, every possible reform of the Church from within will be smothered in embryo. To urge other considerations, from the danger of family jobs for sons or sons-in-law, or cousins, or partisan friends, or the like, is needless. You all know much more about those things in England than we do here; not that our bishops here are any better than yours by nature; but here a kind Providence gives them no chance to do any thing of that sort—thanks to our vestry system.

Another plan of providing for the patronage is to give it to a *central board*, whether clergy or laity, or both, or to them jointly with the bishop. The inevitable working of this plan is, to give the preference to the *mean average*, and to taboo all " extreme men " of every school. The tendency of this is to increasing *narrowness*, generation after generation. Extreme men are of the greatest value, because they keep the arms of a true comprehensiveness wide open. A bishop might *possibly*, now and then, be brought to regard extreme men with some favor; but a central board, never! The guaranty of our comprehensiveness is, therefore, the freedom of vestries in making their own calls, just as, with you, it is an incidental benefit resulting from the present anomalous condition of Church patronage among you. But our form of it is the safer, and with less danger of abuse. We have no Dean Stanley. We have no Stopford Brooke.

If the power is to be lodged neither with the bishop nor with a central board, so a combination of the two would be worse than either alone, for it would ensure all the faults of both, and give no chance for the good points which might possibly be found now and then in either the one or the other. Of course, if a bishop be of the right sort, one who knows how to win and keep the confidence of his people, he will be consulted in many, if not in all, cases of vacancies in his diocese, and his advice will be practically equivalent to a nomination. But if a bishop be of the right sort, he will have this influence anyhow, and no canon could take it away from him. If he be *not* of the right sort, no canon ought to give it to him, for he could never be trusted to make the right use of it.

In a country like ours, the idea that the right of nomination to vacant parishes should be bought and sold in open market, or run with the possession of a certain estate, is of course out of the question.

Now, if the right is not to be given to the bishop, nor to a central board, nor to one private individual, to whom *can* it be entrusted but to a *local* board, the leading persons of the congregation concerned—in other words, the vestry? They are *personally* the most deeply interested. *They* are to receive their spiritual ministrations from the priest appointed. *They* are to benefit by, or suffer from, his personal peculiarities. *They* are to furnish his income by voluntary contributions out of their own pockets. *They* are more directly interested, therefore, than bishop, central board, and all other parties put together. To intrust the selection of the priest to them, therefore, must necessarily be the safest and the least liable to objection of all modes thinkable.

Nor is it correct to say that this really involves the absurdity of the taught choosing their own teacher, the sheep ruling their own shepherd. It does no such thing. No person is eligible, by any vestry, until he has been duly examined by the canonical authorities and solemnly ordained to the priesthood by a bishop, that ordination being, on the lowest view, the certificate of the episcopal order that that priest is canonically qualified and fit to take charge of any cure of souls to which he may be called ; and so long as that priest is " in good and regular standing," that position " is a standing guarantee to the same effect." When any vestry calls any priest, then, they simply *take the bishops at their word*, that the priest is a proper man to be called. As to all the infinite variety of points touching personal appearance, voice, manner, character, tone of theology, grade of ritual, and what not—all of which are within the canonical comprehensiveness of the Church— the parish is a better judge of what it really wants than anybody else ; and to trust it to make its own selection, by its own vestry, is less likely to be seriously abused, than to trust the power of selection to any other party or parties less directly interested in making a *good* choice. (The idea of a popular election by all the communicants of a parish, is open to objections of another kind, and has no friends on this side of the water in our Church.)

But the toughest and most important part of the patronage problem is, the selection of the persons to be consecrated bishops. Now, in theory, the bishops are the rightful, original, perpetual, indefeasible chief rulers of the Church—the one channel through which alone our historic succession from the Apostles can be demonstrated—the one channel through which alone a valid ordination can be obtained by any priest or deacon. *Ecclesia est in episcopo.* If any true representatives of the Church can be found anywhere, they should—in theory— be the bishops. And the bishops themselves are never weary of reasserting this, their traditional position, and claiming the fulness of their traditional power. But when there is a conflict of true interests between the Church and the civil government, where—since the revolution of 1688—have your bishops always been found ? Suppose that the relations between England and France were such, that all nominations for promotion in the British army were to be made only by the king or emperor or president of France, and a war should break out between the two countries, how many victories would be won by the British armies ? In *every* such contest, except only the immortal seven in the reign of James II., your bishops have, as a body, *invariably sold you out to the enemy.* And nothing is more natural. The priestly power which they received from the Church, they shared equally with twenty thousand other priests. The honor of being selected to be a bishop, they owe, not to the Church, but to the Prime Minister of the

18

day; and, like human beings, they are grateful to the power that made them. It is not only that they always take Cæsar's side; but it is the calm and serene unconsciousness that there ever can be any difference between Cæsar's interests and those of God, that is amazing to the churchly mind. Look, for the crowning instance, at the way in which the *judicial* and *disciplinary* powers, inherent in the episcopal office from the beginning, and maintained more or less clearly through all the ages down to the year 1879, were then coolly, nay eagerly, *made a present of* to Parliament and a purely Parliamentary judge! And now the whole episcopate is howling with indignation and rage at the faithful priests who are willing to go to jail in the hope of recovering, to these treacherous prelates, that precious jewel of their order, which they had themselves so shamefully, nay, shamelessly, thrown away!

No measure for Church Reform is worth thinking of which does not include—if indeed it does not begin at—the restoring to the Church the selection of her own bishops. And yet this seems to be a matter in which the waters have yet hardly begun to stir. Years ago, when the new sees were first spoken about, with an endowment to be provided by private individuals entirely, it seemed as if the time were surely at hand for a change. If the Government funds had provided the endowment, it would have been natural enough for the Government to nominate the new bishop as usual. But that Government should give *not one penny*, but should *require* an endowment to be raised of from £20,000 to £80,000; that *all* this should be paid in out of the pockets of private individuals, and that Government should then impudently pocket the patronage created by private liberality—in advance—seemed to be *impossible*. And yet it took place as easily as if it were "all right." To me, it was simply amazing.

But what remedy is possible? It clearly will not do to restore an absolute right of choice to the cathedral chapters, reduced as they are, and appointed in such a way as to make them no better representatives of the Church than the bishops themselves. It will not do to abolish the *congé d'élire*—the last faint reminiscence of the former rights of the Church, thus kept alive as a hope for the future. It will not do to have bishops made merely by letters patent, and thus abandon the Church's ancient right altogether. To attempt to alter the law may at present be unwise, as it would probably be unsuccessful. But a sensible Prime Minister, who feels the delicate and difficult responsibility of the nomination of bishops, might easily find a way to cut the Gordian knot. When a see was vacant, or a new see erected, he might say, officially, that the one name presented to him before such a day by a majority of the clergy and laity of the diocese concerned, voting by orders and by ballot, should be the name inserted in the letter missive that accompanied the *congé d'élire*. This mode of settling *his own choice of the individual* would be so popular in the Church at large, that no successor would dare to depart from the precedent thus set. And the old forms, with a new soul in them, might go on until the reorganization of the Church could make the process a little more direct.

But take care not to be deluded by any proposal that the Church shall send in *two* or *three* names, of which the Prime Minister shall select *one*. So long as the selection of a name is to be left to him *in any measure or degree*, he is sure to choose the one that the *State* can rely on, rather than the Church ; and the Church will continue to be cheated in the result. Let there then be *one* name ; and as the Church has done *all* the *choosing*, she will have a fair chance to secure fidelity in the one chosen. Remember how the Pope manages to amuse his priests with allowing them to send him three names for a vacant episcopate, and then he chooses *one* of them—or some one else whom he likes better. The actual determining as to the particular individual, ensures the *inner allegiance*.

This asking for a nominee on the part of clergy and laity *presupposes* some organization of the laity by the *voluntary act of the Church*. This is the best way for it to originate, rather than to wait for an Act of Parliament to constitute the lay body, as in the case of the Church of Ireland. If the Church begins it, she can easily insist, from the first, that none shall be eligible except regular communicants. In this point we made one of our many blunders, not corrected yet, in all our Diocesan Conventions, but amended years ago in regard to our General Convention, which alone deals with doctrine. When the body of laity is thus constituted by the Church, and in working order, no act of disestablishment would venture to set it aside or constitute another and a different lay body.

The proposal of the Convocation of Canterbury for the establishment of a " Provincial House of Laymen " is very good as far as it goes, but it would not be found so effective, if meeting and debating separately from the clergy, and only on certain points. *Co-ordinate powers and position*, meeting and debating in *one body*, but with the *vote by orders* as the protection to each order, is the true thing to aim for. The provincial idea, also, does not go far enough. One great cause of the deadlock of Church machinery in England is the existence of only two provinces, one of which is so numerous that it is constantly tempted to feel as if it were the whole ; while the other is so small, that it is tempted to pursue an obstructive course, if for no other reason than to prevent its being overslaughed altogether. If the Welsh dioceses were reconstituted into a province, with an Archbishop of St. David's at their head, it certainly would not hinder the revival of Church growth, now so happily begun within that Principality. And if two or three other provinces were erected within the present overgrown province of Canterbury, there would then be less obstruction from mutual jealousies, and every one would then feel the *necessity* of having one national synod in which the entire English Church should act as a unit— bishops, clergy, and laity. To this alone should the delicate work of *legislation* be intrusted. On our American plan, where each petty Diocesan Convention makes its own " constitutions " and body of " canons " (subject, of course, to those of the General Convention), the work of so-called " legislation " is run into the ground.

There is one most important point to be touched on, which I have never so much as seen any allusion to, in all your discussions on the subject. There has been plenty said, indeed, about the danger of an *imperium in imperio*. Some years ago I read the report of a speech by a leading Non-conformist, who declared himself entirely opposed to the disestablishment of the Church of England. He acknowledged that it would be greatly to the benefit of the spiritual life and vigor of the Church to be set free from the State : " But," he asked, " what in that case would become of the liberties of the *State ?* " The Church would embrace more than a majority of the people in one organization ; and religious zeal being a stronger motive generally than any ordinary political object, no Parliament of England would ever be able to resist the Church. " To preserve the independence of the *State*," he said, " he must continue to oppose the idea of restoring freedom to the Church." I have never seen any attempt to answer the objection. Yet there is an answer.

The history of the Church shows a general, and seemingly irresistible tendency, on the part of purely clerical synods, to get into conflicts with the civil power for supremacy. During the whole mediæval period (and the Papacy is merely a prolongation of that, in its worst features) the feudal system culminated instinctively in one visible head. If two men will ride on one horse, one must ride behind. Both the Pope and the Emperor were determined to ride *first ;* and neither was willing to ride behind the other. The modern theory is truer and better in every way. It is to separate the spheres, so that each shall be supreme *in his own sphere ;* and that there should be wise and careful and kindly co-operation where the spheres overlap. The development of modern civilization shows, more and more, that if there is to be *one* master, it will not be the Pope, much less any other cleric. His ancient domineering over kings and kaisers has so far changed, that there is not now an emperor, king, or president anywhere in the whole world to lift a musket for him, or to care for all the anathemas or interdicts he may be foolish enough to utter. *No purely clerical legislative body* will now be tolerated anywhere in the civilized world.

Now, the true operation of the laity, when admitted into fully co-ordinate position in all Church synods with the clergy, will be to *destroy all probability of dangerous collisions beweeen the Church and the State.* And the reason will be clear, on a little reflection. In all free countries Government necessarily assumes the form of government by party. In every National Church, the lay members, as well as the clerical, will be attached more or less to *both* political parties. But in the case of the clergy, the religious interests are so entirely predominant, that it would not be difficult, on grounds of conscience (or what seems to be such in times of excitement), to produce a corporate resistance to some legitimate exertion of power on the part of the State. The case as to the laity, however, is very different. In a body of such vast importance as the National Synod of England, it would only be natural and proper, and indeed inevitable, that Churchmen of great national eminence should, from both parties in national politics, be sent as lay deputies to the synod. Now, the life-calling of the laymen, in cases like these, is *practical politics.* They are professional *experts* in this direction, just as the clergy are professional experts in the direction of doctrine, discipline, worship, and Catholic tradition generally. In case any measure were proposed that would have an undue political bearing, if it were one that the Conservatives could make something of, some Liberal laymen would be found to object instantly : and if it be one that would help the Liberals, some Conservative laymen would be equally on the watch. When the laymen were all united, it would be clear that the Government *ought* to, and *would* respect the conscientious convictions of so large a body of the people, of *both* parties. The operation of this has often been most beneficially manifested in our General Conventions, where Judges of the Supreme Court of the United States, Senators of the United States, Governors of States, Members of Congress, or those who have once filled such offices, often come as simple lay-deputies from the dioceses in which they reside, and give to the Church the benefit of their experience of a lifetime. The wholesome effect of it always is to teach prudence and propriety, and to keep the Church from meddling, though with the best of motives, in that which is really none of her business. Thus, with the laity in their proper co-ordinate position, the anticipated difficulties of an *imperium in imperio* would never occur. The laity would be a perpetual *flux,* by which the constitutional antagonisms of the clergy and the State would be reduced, melted, moulded, moderated, compromised, or entirely removed. *The importance of this consideration cannot be exaggerated.* The large proportion of laymen with national reputations that would be brought together in any meeting of a synod representing the entire Church of England, would at once *command* the perfect confidence of all Englishmen, that no such body would ever run amuck against the legitimate powers of the British Parliament.

Such a position, given to such laymen, would likewise render disendowment—except perhaps a few cheese-parings of sinecures and such like—morally impossible. Neither party would venture to advocate it, for fear of bringing down upon them a greater *loss* of political power than they could possibly make up by gains in any other quarter through a policy of spoliation. With the laity in Synod, the whole nation could easily be made to see that disendowment meant really that one part of the laity should rob another part of the laity by act of Parliament. And when that was seen, it would not be done, it *could* not be done.

And now for a few general considerations in closing.

Ever since the time of Constantine, wherever there has been no form of Church organization to secure to the Church laity their proper influence, the lay power, organized as the civil government, has domineered over the Church from the outside, and every now and then plundered her by wholesale, besides insisting on the right to control the promotion to all her chief offices. The natural leaders and constitutional rulers of the Church, in all these ages, have been under first mortgage to her most formidable enemy. The struggle to regain *something*, has led the Church to submit to the Papacy on the continent ;

and the degradation of religion on all sides has led to continental infidelity and communism.

In England, after the papal difficulty had been gotten rid of, the other was intensified, until the results—though not so deep-seated, acrid, and inveterate as on the continent—are nevertheless so vast as to stagger the power of apprehension. If she had *merely retained* the ground she held at the opening of the Reformation, with its natural increase, making no fresh conquests, only think what the British Church would now be! But the terrible loss of spiritual flexibility and power involved in her " established " relations with the State, has cost her nearly the whole of Scotland, four-fifths of Ireland, nearly the entire mass of the great Protestant sects that dominate this country, and nearly one-half of the home population in England besides! What further proof of the " great advantages of our *establishment* " do sensible men require?

On the other hand, the poor little Church of Scotland, almost exterminated by her connection with the State, is reviving to a wonderful degree, a majority of her sees having either built or begun cathedrals within the present generation.

The Church of Ireland (*fit experimentum in corpore vili*), brought to an almost intolerable degree of degradation by her State connection, has been mending ever since it ceased. Remember the bear-garden at the beginning of her synodical sessions, with Lord James Butler as high-cockalorum of the Protestants on the rampage, and the terrible threatenings of what " the laity " were going to do with the " remnants of Popery " in the Prayer-book! But being compelled to meet the clergy face to face, in equal discussion, year after year (though the clergy were nothing to boast of as a whole), the Irish laity have been *learning*, year by year, what nobody could make them learn before. And slowly, but steadily, the tone of the whole body has been rising, until, when the " revision " was completed, those were *least* satisfied with the result who themselves had set the ball in motion. And if the bishops and clergy had only been a little more firm in the use of their vote by orders, the result might have been somewhat better still. But if the experiment has worked well, even in Ireland, it cannot possibly work otherwise than well in any other part of the Church.

In this country, notwithstanding our long colonial asphyxiation, when the Church was deliberately smothered by the State for State purposes; notwithstanding the fact that she was well-nigh extinct at the close of the Revolutionary War, loaded with political as well as religious obloquy, and that it was a whole generation before even the gift of the episcopate brought back to her the signs of returning life; notwithstanding the fact that we have faithfully copied as many of your blunders as we could, besides making others of our own; notwithstanding our " hideous vestry system," our non-communicant membership of vestries and conventions, and faulty tenure of Church property; notwithstanding our imperfect judicial system; our failure, thus far, to establish provinces, our feebleness of plan in having the senior bishop by consecration as the presiding bishop of our national Church, and other drawbacks too numerous to mention—we have, nevertheless, during nearly a century since our full organization, been *gaining steadily* on our growth of population, even although that growth is the most rapid that the world has ever seen, and although it is so largely made up of foreign elements which are, for a generation or two, almost wholly beyond our reach. Nay, more than this: our influence has perceptibly modified every other leading variety of religion in this country, so that the general movement, which is more or less perceptible, is steadily and predominantly a movement toward us. We are the evident centre of gravity of all the varieties of Christianity now known in the land.

Your own colonial Churches all tell the same story, each in its own proportion and degree. Not one of them has failed to give the laity an organic place and co-ordinate position. Not one of them has lost in strength, zeal, power, or tone of Churchmanship. All have gained.

And let me appeal specially to the experience of advanced men at home. What would the whole movement of the great Catholic revival have been without the laity? Where would have been the enormous gifts for churches, church schools, and all manner of good works, that have made the Anglican Church during the past forty years the marvel of Christendom, without the laity? Where would have been your two "fighting" societies—the English Church Union and the Church of England Working Men's Association—without the laity? They have proved themselves, in *every* way, fit to be trusted. *Then trust them.*

And how can you hesitate? Your secular lay power now monopolizes—practically in entire independence of the bishops and clergy—the absolute control of Church legislation, Church discipline, and the appointment to high office in the Church; and even impudently claims the power of legislation on doctrine without consulting the Convocation; besides constantly threatening you with that wholesale confiscation of which they have given you more than one specimen in former days. Your alternative is to grant to the 'Church laity, organized as such, an *undivided third part* of that power which is now tyrannically usurped in its entirety by the secular lay power—an undivided third part, to be exercised at every point, under the supervising influence, and modified by the indispensable co-operation of, the two orders of bishops and clergy : and yet you hesitate !

Anyhow, whether you advocate it or not, the change is coming. It will soon be on you, whether or no. Resistance is useless. By resistance you may force it into some very undesirable position. By boldly and fearlessly going *for* it, you can ensure its being realized in its best shape, and reap the earlier benefit from its triumph. It should be the first point, the chief point, in your " plan of campaign," instead of being omitted altogether, or left to drift along at the mercy of a " fortuitous concourse of atoms." In short, with the laity properly organized by the voluntary action of the Church, and that position subsequently recognized, directly or indirectly, by the State, the benefits of disestablishment would be substantially gained already, and disendowment would be made well-nigh impossible.

It is with the utmost diffidence that I submit these thoughts to the brave brethren who are dearest to me in England. The venture would not be made but for the reflection that one who lives close under the base of a lofty mountain seldom sees its shape, because the nearer, though lower, foot-hills shut out the sight. Only one who views it from a certain distance can truly delineate its outline of grandeur and beauty. If this thought will not plead my excuse, I would then urge that I have resisted for many years the desire to write on this subject, and only at last have reluctantly executed my task. If even this will not bring me pardon for taking the liberty to write as I have done, I shall be content to accept the rebukes of my English brethren in loving silence, and trouble them with no further intrusion hereafter.

JOHN HENRY HOPKINS.

WILLIAMSPORT, PA.,
January 20, 1881.

LETTERS OF DR. R. F. LITTLEDALE.

Dr. Hopkins was sometimes called " the American Littledale," and, in some points, there was a certain likeness between them. Yet the comparison is unjust to them both. The two carried on a regular and very frequent correspondence. Very many of Littledale's notes were written in Latin on postal cards, and signed *Parva Vallis ; i.e.*, Little Dale. Some of these were astonishing in the audacity of combinations and rhymes.

The first of the letters here given relates to Dr. Hopkins' article, "Three Points," in the beginning. The latter part of it has a reference appropriate to Hopkins' article on " The Laity in England and America." There was no possibility of reconciling the views of the two priests upon this point. Dr. Hopkins stood almost alone among high Churchmen in justifying the present relations of the laity toward the legislation of the Church.

" 50ᵐᵃ Sunday, 1888.

"MY DEAR DR. HOPKINS : Yes, I had worked out all three of your points, the wilfulness of the Reformed breach with Episcopacy, the mainly political character of Elizabeth's penal code, and the comparative slightness of Anglican failures. I particularly noted that as to the last point, the respectability of Quakerism and Methodism, the two sects to which the Anglican Church has given birth, when compared with those which have sprung out of the Church of Rome—a strong point in our favor.

" I can give you Roman Catholic testimony in favor of No. 2, should you wish to deal more fully with the matter on some future occasion.

" I hope your move to Burlington will give you strength as well as leisure for Church work of a literary kind. The Erastianism of the American Church, far more subtle, searching, and dangerous than our

English Erastianism—I mean, of course, the lay synodical vote—the 'call' system, and the power of the vestries, is *the* rampant evil which now most needs to be extirpated. The plea that the laity cannot carry a vote against the bishops and presbyters breaks down when stated conversely that the bishops and clergy cannot carry a vote against the laity, though the matter might be the attempted condemnation of some heresy—say spiritualism—that chanced to be widely popular amongst lay folks, and to which the Church would be virtually committed by the failure to condemn. That is the ultimate difficulty that no plausible defence of the lay vote can get round ; it places the powers of teaching, binding, and loosing in the wrong hands; wrong as uncommissioned by Xt., wrong as incompetent for lack of necessary knowledge. Upset this, and your name will rank with Seabury's as a benefactor to the American Church. I am in bad health, rather more so than usual, but I hope I may say 'Faint, yet pursuing.'"

" Rogation Monday, 1889.

"MY DEAR DR. HOPKINS : I am very glad to know that you will review my ' Petrine Claims,' because you will know where the salient points really are, and will make the public know them too. Kindly emphasize what I say in my Preface of the legal nature of the argument, and the relative subordination of theology throughout, as deliberate, and not resulting from oversight.

. . . " I am much interested just now in a revision of the Scottish Liturgy which is on foot. I have sent in many suggestions, but I have no guess how they will be received. The draft is more tentative and timid than I quite like, but I admit the difficulties in the way of the heroic method of treatment, especially as the English bishops have to be conciliated on issues where the English rite needs pulling up. Thanks for sending me Dr. Richey's *Parables*."

> " Ecce nova forma chartæ
> Orientali ex parte
> Factæ Britannorum arte,
> Tam Mercurio quam Marte,
> Rhythmis, quos hic vides, fortæ
> Denarii pretio et quartæ
> (Viles census etiam spartia)
> Missa ab Hetrasco, Larte,
> Tibi, Joanni Henrico,
> Cui millies salvere dico,
> Mirandulâ doctiori Pico,
> Meo tamen et amico,
> Maneas ut semper talis
> Hic precatur parva Vallis.
> Dab. Kal. Julii., mdccclxxv."

DR. HOPKINS TO DR. LITTLEDALE.

" Felix es, O Parva Vallis !
Tuta semper sis a malis !
Sint tutamen tibi montes,
Tibi fluant vivi fontes,
Tui rores, tui flores,
Tui redolent odores,
Tamenetsi tuæ rosæ—
Manibus in Puritanis,
Infidelibus, profanis,—
Aliquantulam spinosæ :
Kal. Sep., mdccclxxv.—Plattsburg, N. Y."

"THREE POINTS."

An Essay read before the Associate Alumni of the General Theological Seminary, in the Seminary Chapel, New York, May 31, 1887.

FOR many years three points have presented themselves to my mind with great force, in considering the relations of different parts of Christendom to one another, and yet I do not remember having ever seen that attention paid to them which they seem to me to deserve. Nor shall I be able to do them justice now. The full consideration of them would require far more of time and of books than a country parson can command, and far more of opportunity to listen than our brief annual meeting could afford. All I can do, therefore, is to set before you a few sketch-like hints, which, perhaps, some one having more leisure and learning may work up hereafter in a manner not now possible to me.

I. The first of these three points is in regard to the loss of Apostolic order in the Reformation movement on the continent—the chief point of organic difference between the Anglican Reformation and the others. It is commonly said that this loss was a matter of necessity— that they had to do without bishops on the continent because none of the bishops would take part with the Reformers.

The point I would make is that, historically, *this is not true.* There were bishops enough to have preserved the Apostolic succession for them, if they had cared to do it; and the neglect was, therefore, due to other causes.

The full proof of this can hardly be given without a minute search of the more diffuse records of the times; for our general historians would hardly stop to notice facts which are not in the front rank of importance from their point of view. The facts which I shall lay before you are gathered mainly from Reverend Henry M. Baird's " History of the Rise of the Huguenots of France "—a work in two octavo volumes, covering the history of only sixty-two years in all, and thus affording unusual room for minuteness of detail, although Mr. Baird is not a Churchman, and does not dream of making out the point of which he so unconsciously furnishes the evidence.

The two who are named first among the French Reformers are the learned Lefèvre, of Etaples, and the ardent Farel. The third, he says, was Guillaume Briçonnet, Bishop of Meaux. His father had been a cardinal, as well as Abbot of St. Germain-des-Prés, and Archbishop of Rheims, and had anointed Louis XII. at his coronation. As cardinal he had headed the French party in the Conclave, and in the service of his king had faced the dangers of an open quarrel with the Pope.

The cardinal was now dead, having left to Guillaume—born before his father had taken Holy Orders—a good measure f that royal favor which he had himself enjoyed. He was made Archdeacon of Rheims and of Avignon, Abbot of St. Germain-des-Prés, and lastly, Bishop of Lodève and of Meaux. He showed early his reforming tendencies by his efforts to make the luxurious inmates of St. Germain observe better discipline. Briçonnet was appointed Bishop of Meaux in March, 1516, and about the same time was sent by Francis I. as special envoy to treat with the Pope. He had been at Rome on similar business in the time of Louis XII. The knowledge thus gained of the way in which things were done at Rome, convinced him of the urgent need of reform ; and he resolved to begin the work in his own diocese.

He invited both Lefèvre and Farel to make their home at Meaux ; and they came, followed soon by Michel d'Arande, Gérard Roussel, and others of the same sort. " A new era," says Baird, " now dawned upon the neglected diocese of Meaux. Bishop Briçonnet was fully possessed by his new-born zeal. The king's mother and his only sister had honored him with a visit not long after Lefèvre's arrival, and had left him, confident of their powerful support in his intended reforms. " I assure you," wrote Margaret of Angoulême wrote him, not a month later, "that the King and Madame are entirely decided to let it be understood that the truth of God is not heresy." And a few weeks later, the same princely correspondent wrote that her mother and brother were " more intent than ever upon the reformation of the Church." The effect of the new preaching at Meaux was great. The wool-carders, weavers, and fullers accepted it with delight ; the day-laborers flocked from the neighborhood at harvest-time, and carried back the new enthusiasm to their secluded homes. Bishop Briçonnet himself was active in promoting the evangelical work, preaching against the most flagrant abuses, and commending the other preachers whom he had invited. He actually said to his flock : " Even if I, your bishop, should change my speech and teaching, beware that you change not with me ! "

Under Briçonnet's protection Lefèvre made and published (in 1523) a translation of the New Testament, and then of the whole Bible, into French, which was earlier than a similar work was done in England. The bishop freely supplied copies to those who were too poor to buy. He introduced the French Scriptures into the churches of Meaux, where the innovation of reading the lessons in a tongue that they could understand astounded the common people. The delighted Lefèvre wrote to a distant friend : " You can scarcely imagine with what ardour God is moving the minds of the simple in some places to embrace His Word, since the books of the New Testament have been published in French. . . . At present, throughout our entire diocese, on feast-days, and especially on Sundays, both the Epistle and Gospel are read to the people in the vernacular tongue, and the parish priest adds a word of exhortation to the Epistle or Gospel, or both, at his discretion." All this was far stronger encouragement than the great Catholic revival of our own day ever received from any bishop in its earlier days. True, stern and formidable opposition soon arose. Briçonnet was cited be-

fore the Parliament of Paris to answer, in secret session, before a commission. He was dealt with in such wise as to break his courage, and
stop the public instruction of his people in the Holy Scriptures. He
was acquitted of the charge of heresy, indeed, though they made him
pay two hundred livres as the expense of bringing to trial the heretics
whom he had helped to make. A man converted in that way is very
likely to be " of the same opinion still."

But Briçonnet was not the only bishop who sympathized with reform. He was a noble as well as a bishop; but the same side was
taken by one nobler than he, and higher both in Church and State.
This was Odet de Coligny, the elder brother of Admiral de Coligny,
and of D'Andelot, of the blood royal, who was created Cardinal of
Châtillon at the early age of thirteen, and afterward Archbishop of
Toulouse, and Bishop and Count of Beauvais. As early as 1551 he
was pretty well known to be in sympathy with the Lutherans. In
Easter week, 1561, there were outbreaks of violence against the Protestants in many parts of France, one of the most noted of which was
at Beauvais, Châtillon's own cathedral. He had openly fostered the
preachers of reform in his diocese. " But," says Baird, " even the personal popularity of the brother of Coligny and D'Andelot could not, in
the present instance, secure immunity for the preachers who proclaimed
the gospel under his auspices. The occasion was a rumor spread
abroad that the cardinal, instead of attending the public celebration of
the Mass in his cathedral church, had, with his domestics, participated
in a private communion in his own palace, and that every communicant
had, at the hands of the Abbé Boutillier, received *both* elements ' after
the fashion of Geneva.' Hereupon the mob, gathering in great force,
assailed a private house in which there lived a priest accused of teaching the children the doctrines of religion from the reformed catechisms.
The unhappy Adrien Fourré—such was the schoolmaster's name—was
killed; and the rabble, rendered more savage through their first taste
of blood, dragged his corpse to the public square, where it was burned
by the city hangman. Châtillon himself incurred no little risk of meeting a similar fate. But the strength of the episcopal palace, and the
sight of their bishop clothed in his cardinal's costume, appeased the
mob for the time; and before the morrow came a goodly number of
the neighboring nobles had rallied to his defence." Surely, one of the
most striking incidents of those strange days was to see a Roman cardinal receiving the Huguenot communion, and afterward masquerad-
ing in his cardinal's vestments to prevent his being torn in pieces by
the rabble of his own people for the act! Again, in the preparations
for the famous Colloquy of Poissy, in the same year, 1561, when the
assembled bishops were about to join in the Holy Eucharist, we read
that " Cardinal Châtillon and *two other bishops* insisted upon commu-
nicating under both forms; and when their demand was refused, they
went to another church and celebrated the Divine Ordinance with
many of the nobility, all partaking both of the bread and of the wine,
thus earning for themselves the nickname of Protestants."

Two years later, 1563, Pius IV. issued a bull, calling for summary

proceedings against sundry French bishops, Cardinal Châtillon being
at the head of the list, followed by seven others; but as he was rash
enough to insert the name of the Queen of Navarre also, the French
court made such a vigorous response that the bull was either recalled
or dropped, and the proceedings against the bishops were indefinitely
suspended.

In the year 1565, the Pope's new Nuncio demanded that the red cap
should be taken from the Cardinal of Châtillon. But the latter, who
chanced to be at court, replied that " what he enjoyed, he enjoyed as
the gift of the Crown of France, with which the Pope had nothing to
do." And his uncle, the old Constable, was even more emphatic.
" The Pope," said he, " has often troubled the quiet of this realm, but
I trust he shall not be able to trouble it at this time. I am myself a
Papist, but if the Pope and his ministers go about again to disturb the
kingdom, *my sword* shall be *Huguenot.* My nephew shall give up
neither cap nor dignity which he has for the Pope, seeing the King's
edict gives him liberty to keep them."

Three years later, in 1568, it seems that Cardinal Châtillon had been
excommunicated by the Pope, condemned of schism, and was dead in
the eyes of the law, and Catherine de Medici had promised to surrender
him into the Pope's hands. Châtillon had come to court, under the
King's safe-conduct, to treat for peace after the second civil war.
Cardinal Santa Croce, the Nuncio, entering the council-chamber, boldly
demanded the performance of Catherine's promise then and there.
Catherine did not deny the promise, but said that this was an unsuit-
able time for its fulfilment, owing to the King's safe-conduct. To this
the Nuncio replied that no respect ought to be had toward Châtillon,
for he was an excommunicated person, condemned of schism, and dead
in the eyes of the law. At this point the Duc de Montmorency broke
out : " Madame, is it possible that the Cardinal Châtillon's delivery
should come in question, being warranted by the King and your
Majesty to the contrary, and I myself being made a mean therein?
Wherefore this matter is odious to be talked of, and against the law of
arms and of all good civil policy; and I must needs repute them my
enemies who go about to make me falsify my promise once made."
After these plain words Santa Croce departed, without attaining his
most cruel and dishonorable request.

Later in the same year, 1568, it was in contemplation to seize Châtillon in his episcopal palace at Beauvais. The third civil war was then
raging. But he received timely warning, and escaped through Normandy to England, where Queen Elizabeth received him at court with
marks of distinguished favor. He succeeded in getting Elizabeth to
send substantial help to his distressed friends in France.

In 1570, about two months after the declaration of peace, Cardinal
Châtillon, who had been deprived by the Pope of his seat in the Roman
conclave, had also been declared by the Parliament of Paris, on motion
of the Cardinal Bourbon, to have lost his bishopric of Beauvais on
account of his rebellion and his adoption of Protestant sentiments.
All such judicial proceedings had indeed been declared null and void

by the terms of the royal pacification; but the parliaments were very reluctant to yield obedience to the royal edict. The King sent orders to the first president of the Parliament to wait upon him with the records. And when, after a second summons, they were brought, the King, with his own hands, tore out and destroyed every page that contained any action against the Cardinal Châtillon.

But we must be brief in other cases; for these were not all. We find mention made of Michel d'Arande, who was Bishop of Saint-Paul-Trois-Châteaux, in Dauphiny, and yet sympathized entirely with the Reformers, and was in confidential intercourse with them; also of Gérard Roussel, who was appointed by the Queen of Navarre to be her preacher and confessor, and rose to be Abbot of Clairac and Bishop of Oléron; yet he remained to his death a sincere friend of the Reformation. In his own diocese he set the example of a faithful pastor. Even so bitter an enemy of Protestantism as Florimond de Raemond, contrasting Roussel's piety with the wordliness of the sporting French bishops of the period, is forced to admit that " his pack of hounds was the crowd of poor men and women whom he daily fed; his horses and attendants a host of children whom he caused to be instructed in letters."

Another prelate is mentioned, the Bishop of Senlis, as being so much in favor with the Queen of Navarre that he translated for her into French the Book of Hours, omitting all that most directly countenanced superstition. We read also of Cardinal Sadolet, Bishop of Carpentras, who readily certified to the falsity of the charges made against the Waldenses, exerted his influence with the vice-legate to induce him to abandon an attack on one of their villages, and assured the inhabitants that he firmly intended, in a coming visit to Rome, to secure the reformation of some incontestable abuses.

Another prelate we read of, Chatellain, Bishop of Macon, who was at one time favorable to the Reformation, though his courage was not equal to his convictions.

Much better known, however, was Montluc, Bishop of Valence, who, in 1560, when the Huguenots petitioned for liberty of worship, was their warmest and most uncompromising advocate. . . . This bold and eloquent harangue of the Bishop of Valence was followed, in the same discussion, by one still more cogent from the aged and virtuous Marillac, Archbishop of Vienne. He urged that " it was vain to expect a General Council, since between the Pope, the Emperor, the Kings, and the Lutherans, the right time and place and method of holding it could never be agreed upon by all; and France was like a man desperately ill, whose fever admitted of no such delay as that a physician be called in from a distance. Hence the usual resort to a National Council, in spite of the Pope's discontent, was imperative. *France could not afford to die in order to please his Holiness.* Meanwhile, the prelates must be obliged to reside in their dioceses, nor must the Italians— those leeches that absorbed one-third of all the benefices and an infinite number of pensions—be exempted from the operation of the general rule. Simony must be abolished at once, as a token of sincerity in the desire to reform the Church," etc., etc.

Besides all these, we find Du Val, Bishop of Séez, in Normandy, mentioned in the same group with Bishop Montluc, and that Abbé Boutillier who administered the Holy Communion in Genevan fashion to Cardinal Châtillon.

A very high authority gives us some other names. It is the bull of Pius IV., already mentioned, in which, after Cardinal Châtillon, he adds Romain, Archbishop of Aix; Montluc, Bishop of Valence; Gelais, Bishop of Uzès; Roussel, Bishop of Oléron; D'Albret, Bishop of Lescure; Giullart, Bishop of Chartres; and Caraccioli, Bishop of Troyes, who had resigned his bishopric, and had been ordained a Protestant pastor—*eight* prelates in all.

Besides all these, Jervis, in his " History of the Gallican Church," gives us the names of Jacques Spifame, Bishop of Nevers; Pelissier, Bishop of Maguelonne; Etienne Poncher, Bishop of Paris, and afterwards Archbishop of Sens, as sympathizing with the Reform, in the early period of the agitation, and Barbançon, Bishop of Pamiers, in the later.

We have now enumerated no less than nineteen prelates, among whom are three archbishops and two cardinals, who are shown to have sympathized with the Reformation; and of these, no less than *eight* are certified to us by the Pope himself, as Protestant enough to be excommunicated. The Reform party, therefore, had bishops enough to have kept up the apostolic succession, had they chosen so to do. The plea of necessity, therefore, is utterly idle. They had them, but they would not use them. All consciousness of the importance of the question of valid orders seems to have been so utterly lost in the fierce controversies of the time that it never comes to the surface. Nay, so completely was it ignored, that we find one of the above bishops, an Italian, Caraccioli, accepting a new ordination as a Protestant pastor.

[This action of Caraccioli, and of other French bishops not named by Dr. Hopkins, was in exact agreement with the Calvinistic and Independent theory as to "gathered Churches." The first founders of *English* Independents refused the title of ministers of Christ to nonconformist clergy, as well as to the conforming prelatical clergy, because they lived in the Church of England, and did not leave it, as Separatists. Robinson said to the non-conforming clergy, " You have the same office as the mass priests, because you have been ordained by bishops." He also said to Bishop Hall, of Exeter, " Episcopal ordination *prevents* its receiver from being a minister of Christ, and it is to be renounced as a part of that sham clergy derived from Rome." Of himself, he said, that though ordained by a bishop, " I cast away my *popish priesthood*," which, be it remembered, he had received from a bishop of the post-Reformation Church of England.

These incidents will set forth the very basis of modern congregationalism, and show also how utterly unhistorical is the " good-natured " admission by Congregationalists that Episcopalians are good Evangelical Christians. If such had been the theory of the founders of their bodies, no separation from the Church of England would have been caused by them. They also show the crass ignorance of history of those among us who seek to meet them on their own ground. Such liberalism is an insult to the true liberality of the mother Church, and treason against Christ.

The French bishops did not continue their orders, because they renounced their episcopal ministry in accordance with the Calvinistic belief. C. F. S.]

II. The second of the Three Points I am to touch upon is this : In England the Reforming party, as such, never drew the sword to defend themselves from persecution. They bore the persecution patiently, so long as it pleased God it should last. All the rebellions that were made in England during the Reformation period proper—except the personal movement for Lady Jane Grey—were made by the opponents of Reform. As a reward for this patience and endurance, so it would seem, the good Providence of God accomplished the needed reform without disturbing a single foundation-stone of the old Church. But in France and in Germany, and in Scotland and elsewhere, impatience and persecution provoked civil war, and that of the most obstinate and hurtful kind. This caused *two* great evils. First, the religious question was tangled up and lost in the political question. The other great evil is, that the going to war utterly lost all the *spiritual* fruit that otherwise would have borne by persecution patiently endured. The early Church went through her ten persecutions without once resorting to armed defence against the most outrageous and cruel oppression. And this patient endurance—by the blessing of God—conquered the mighty Roman empire. So, in England, the burning of nearly two hundred of the Reformed party during the reign of Philip and Mary, patiently endured, turned the hearts of the nation so strongly, that after the accession of Elizabeth there was no serious obstacle to all the Reformation that was needed. In France the glorious martyrdoms, so bravely endured by Leclerc, Pauvan, De Berquin, Du Bourg, and innumerable others in the early part of the movement, produced a wonderful popular effect, which was spreading with astonishing rapidity. Even Catherine de Medici herself declared her intention to hear the Bishop of Valence preach before the young king and the court in the saloon of the castle. In that same year, 1561, three weeks before the arrival of Beza to take part in the colloquy of Poissy, she wrote to the Pope of the " impossibility of restoring to unity (the number of those who had forsaken the Roman Church) by coercion, and declared it a mark of Divine favor that there were among the dissidents neither Anabaptists nor Libertines, for all held the creed as explained by the early councils of the Church. It was consequently the conviction of many that by the concession of some points of practice the present divisions might be healed. But more frequent and peaceful conferences must be held ; the ministers of religion must preach concord and charity to their flocks ; and the scruples of those who remain in the Church must be removed by the abolition of all unnecessary and objectionable practices. Images, forbidden by God and disapproved of by the Fathers, ought at once to be banished from public worship ; baptism ought to be stripped of its exorcisms ; communion in both kinds

19

to be restored ; the vernacular tongue to be employed in the services of the Church, and private masses to be discountenanced."

Surely a wonderful letter to be written by such a person as Catherine de Medici, and to such a person as the Pope ! From it we may easily estimate the force of the current by which she was surrounded. Again and again the Court seemed on the very point of taking sides with the Reformation ; but every time the mixing up of rebellion with Protestantism spoiled the prospect. A little more of patient endurance would have won the victory, and in such a way as to retain the ancient foundations of the national Church undisturbed. A few hundred might have been added to the number of martyrs in the meantime ; but what was that compared to the tens of thousands that perished in the civil wars and massacres? Baird defends the Huguenots in their taking up arms. Yet they had endured persecution for only about one generation, while the early Church bore it for nearly three hundred years. Even Baird, however, is compelled to admit that what he considers justifiable was actually destructive. He goes on to state the full consequences of this terrible blunder of his friends, which, nevertheless, he attempts to justify. He says :

" The first civil war prevented France from becoming a Huguenot country. This was the deliberate conclusion of a Venetian ambassador who enjoyed remarkable opportunities for observing the history of his times. The practice of the Christian virtues of patience and submission under suffering and insult had made the Reformers an incredible number of friends. The waging of war, even in self-defence, and the reported acts of wanton destruction, of cruelty and sacrilege, turned the indifference of the masses into positive aversion."

The same evil consequences, only to a far greater extent, followed the terrible Thirty Years' War in Germany—probably the most horrible civil war that has ever cursed any Christian country. And the same cause produced the same effects. It was not because the Reformed had no friends among the bishops, but because they were too impatient of persecution to be willing to wait until the Lord's work should be done in the Lord's way. And the same impatience led them to overthrow the ancient authority of bishops in the Church of God and originate a new ministry of their own.

Now, we have seen, in our own day, though after a much milder fashion, the operation of the same general principles. The great Catholic revival of the past half-century is one of the most wonderful that the Church has seen in any age or in any land. One great object of it was to revive the true doctrine that bishops are in the Church by *Divine* right, and that the powers given to them by Christ and the Holy Ghost cannot be taken from them by merely human authority. Yet at the beginning, the entire Anglican Episcopate—with much fewer exceptions than we have found in France—was *opposed* to the Revival. Many were discouraged at this, lost heart, and left us. But a little reflection ought to have satisfied them. The primary instinct of the Episcopal Order is, and rightly, to hand things down to their successors exactly as they themselves received them. When, therefore, after the lapse of ages, the Church has gradually accumulated errors in various directions, and the spirit of Reform is sent forth by the Holy Ghost, that Reform must always *expect* to find the Episcopate as a body *opposed* to it.

The bishops, as a body, are rather more elderly men than the average of the rest of the clergy. They represent the age that is just ending, rather than that which is just beginning. And with their primary instinct of keeping things unchanged, they oppose every improvement as an innovation. The feeling of the bishops was almost unbroken for a quarter of a century after our Catholic Revival began; and even now, when it is more than half a century old, a faithful and devoted priest in Liverpool—Rev. J. Bell-Cox—has lately been sent to prison by a bishop—a Low Church bishop, his *own* bishop—for that fidelity to that great Revival; he being the *fifth* priest who has cheerfully gone to jail in the same great cause. In all these fifty years and more, all the persecution that could be brought to bear has been borne cheerfully, with *no* attempt to retaliate, or secede, or form a sect, or usurp the canonical authority of the bishops. Yet all the while, preaching and teaching, and writing, and ritual, and organization for work among the poor, and the revival of the religious orders, and much more, have gone on with unflinching energy and courage, until at length we have finally conquered the decided majority of the Anglican Episcopate itself.

And that episcopate is now about as unanimous in commending the great Catholic Revival as they were forty years ago in condemning it. When one has mastered the *theory* that the bishops will certainly, at least for a generation or two, oppose any and every attempt at Reformation from within and from below, he will be less likely to lose heart and courage when he finds that the theory is borne out by the facts. And it is well that it is so. If changes could be brought about too easily, we should lose all stability—there would be nothing but change; whereas now, when a change for the better has been slowly and painfully accomplished, it is a satisfaction to know that it will last. Moreover, when a movement is really begun by God the Holy Ghost, and is carried on with equal courage *and patience*, there is no danger that any opposition by the bishops of the day will ever be able to put it down, no matter how hard they may try. In a generation or two, the Reform will be represented and maintained by the bishops themselves. Let patience, therefore, have her perfect work. With heavenly patience the new life is like leaven, that spreads its influence from soul to soul, until the whole Church is leavened. With impatience and civil war, that new life becomes rather like the destructive forces of Nature, by which the solid mountain is rent into two opposing cliffs, which frown defiance on each other forever, and unite no more.

III. I have left myself but little time for the *Third Point*, which is not so closely connected with the other two, but which, I hope, may be helpful to some minds. When a steel bar, freely suspended, is rubbed so as to develop positive electricity at one end, it is always found that the same action has at the same time spontaneously developed an equal amount of negative electricity at the other end. The amount of electricity produced may thus be tested, with equal correctness, from the negative end as well as from the positive.

Now, this third point is simply to compare the great communions of Christendom *by their failures.* We are all familiar with the positive comparisons—so familiar that sometimes the very familiarity makes us suspect that there must be some undiscovered fallacy about them. Let us, then, try the negative for once.

But, you may say, what do you mean by the negative? I will explain. Let us look at the three great communions of Christendom —the Roman, the Oriental, and the Anglican. So long as we are divided no one of us has any authority from God to claim that we are *entirely* right in all points of difference, and that the others are *entirely* wrong. We *must* be, all of us, right in some things, and wrong in other things. And in so far as we are wrong, we shall have our *failures*, as well as our successes. Now, I propose to compare our failures. And—as one ought to do—let us begin with ourselves.

Our failures, then, may briefly be described as the English-speaking Protestant denominations, so far as they have sprung out of the English Church. As for those which have sprung directly from the various Reformed bodies on the Continent of Europe, of course the Church of England is not responsible for them. All these denominations are without the historic episcopate; and this points to a great fault in the English Church, largely owing—as are most of her faults—to her union with the State. At the time of the Reformation, Cranmer earnestly desired to increase the number of episcopal sees in England from twenty-three to forty; and King Henry VIII. gave him reason to hope that it should be done with endowments from the Church property seized by the crown. But, instead of that, only six new sees were erected—one of which soon ceased to exist, and there the increase stuck for three hundred years. If that proposed enlargement had been made, it is highly probable that dissent from the Church of England would never have amounted to much. But when—with the steadily growing population—there was no growth in the episcopate; when the time and attention of bishops were largely absorbed by their duties in Parliament; when their spiritual duties were more and more neglected, visitations being made only once in from three to seven years, and in some cases not at all; what could be expected but that a type of earnest piety should largely prevail from which bishops were entirely left out?

Then again, in her catechism, the Church of England has taught nothing about Confirmation or Holy Orders, or of the organization of the Catholic Church, *not one word!* What wonder then that some of her people should easily come to think that Confirmation is of no great use, and that one kind of minister of the Gospel is as good as another, and that any and every kind of sect is a Church? Other faults might be mentioned also, especially the suspension of the synodical action of the Church for nearly one hundred and fifty years. But no matter

how great the evils of these divisions and losses, with all their controversies and jealousies, thus much must be allowed : On the whole,
and with few exceptions, these denominations all accept the Bible, and
use it in the version given them by the Church ; they all profess to
accept the Apostles' and the Nicene creeds ; they all claim to keep up
the ministration of the two great Sacraments ; their baptism is almost
universally a valid baptism ; they are earnest and zealous in a great
variety of good works, and not infrequently in liberality and zeal they
set us an example which we should do well to follow.   They are, on
the whole, a very respectable set of failures.   And the separation from
us is not so wide or so deep as in any other of the cases which we shall
mention ; while the general confession of the evil of disunion is more
outspoken and sincere, and the prospect of reunion far more promising
than we shall find anywhere else in Christendom.

Let us look next at the Oriental Church.   Her great failure is Mohammedanism—a far worse and more destructive failure than ours ;
for Mohammedanism is rather a heresy arising out of Christianity than
an original and separate religion.   It includes a recognition of both
the Old and New Testaments—of Abraham and Moses and Christ.
The faults that provoked this terrible reaction were rather the faults of
the decaying and slavish absolutism of the old pagan Roman empire,
which Christianity could not save ; together with picture worship and
saint worship which grew naturally out of the other, aggravated by the
irrepressible dialectics of the Greek mind in defining and over-defining
the nature and relations of the Persons of the Blessed Trinity.   Mo-
hammed threw off Christian baptism, and retained the old circumcision.
He made one clean sweep of the Trinity and of the Incarnation.   He
made God to be a simple unit, and himself to be God's greatest and
final prophet, and the sword to be the chief propagator of his religion.
The later organization of the Janissaries is a horrible travesty, worthy
of the Devil himself.   The Turks levied a tribute on Christians of
children—baptized Christian childr en—who were violently taken from
their parents before they were old enough to understand the truths of
Christianity, and were then carefully trained up as Moslems, and were
sworn to fight—as their life-work-—that very religion into which they
had been baptized in infancy.   No wonder that such a weapon became
ultimately intolerable even to the Sultan who wielded it !   There can
be no question that Mohammedanism—the great failure of the Oriental
Church—is incomparably worse than ours.

But the Church of Rome affords a failure far beyond either of us.
As she has carried her practical corruptions, her additions to the Faith,
and her passion for *absolutism*, both in Church and State, to such tremendous lengths, so in the intensity of atheistical continental communism she has developed a failure incomparably worse than even
Mohammedanism, and beside which our Evangelical Protestant denominations appear like positive blessings !   The horrors of the first
French revolution were bad enough.   The Commune of Paris has
shown that it would improve on the old horrors, with greater ones of
modern invention, the moment it should have a chance.   The intense

hatred of anything like Christianity, or even of a belief in God, is startling. Only think what the condition of a man's mind must be who deliberately shoots dead a priest who was standing at the altar and reciting the Apostles' Creed—his only motive being *hatred* of the Creed
which the priest was reciting! Roman repression has been manufact-
uring the concentrated oil of vitriol which threatens to destroy everything that it can get a chance to *touch*.

The comparison of our failures, then, while it ought to teach an Anglican modesty, and deep sense of our own shortcomings, has in it also
an element of comfort and encouragement. We have not been so long
on the wrong course, and have not driven our errors so deep, and have
not brought forth such desperate results as the others ; and therefore,
as to what we still have to do, we may well " thank God and take courage."

DECLINE AND FALL OF THE LOW-CHURCH PARTY.

(From " The Church and the World " for April and July, 1872.)

To one who looks at the present state of parties among us, and compares it with that which existed from thirty to fifty years ago, the change is wonderfully striking, and that in a twofold point of view. The personal alienation and bitterness are now incomparably less than they were then; while, nevertheless, the points now at issue are so much further advanced, and of so much more importance in themselves, that one would naturally expect greater heat and violence, rather than less. And this singular decrease in real bitterness has taken place in spite of the efforts of the losing party to work themselves up into hostile zeal by using the most extravagant phraseology. To read their writings one would think that something terrible is going to happen; so terrible, indeed, as utterly to frighten them out of the proprieties of speech; but when one meets them personally, one finds that these truculent writers are as pleasant and amiable a set of gentlemen as one could well meet upon a summer's day. The formidable phrases, used by them so freely in type, would seem really to be " all sound and fury, signifying—nothing." Yet they do not signify nothing.

There is no need that we should be unjust toward the Low-Church or " Evangelical " party. The true Catholic, above all other men, knows that every great aberration from truth and right within the Church contains a lesson which needs to be learned by heart, if similar evils are to be avoided in time to come; and still more, if those which exist are ever to be removed. But as there is an unbroken continuity in the history of the Church, each period bringing to maturity the seeds that were sown in the period preceding, so it is very hard to give a satisfactory review of the present condition of Church parties, from the difficulty of knowing where to begin.

The heart of Christianity as a power in the world—we do not mean the head work, which may be called theology; or the bony framework, which may be called the Apostolic hierarchy; or the flesh, which may be looked on as the general body of the laity brought in contact with the world; or " the blood thereof which is the life thereof," which is, of course, the grace of God; or the locomotive power, which is the missionary system; but we mean simply the heart, that impulse of *will* which is felt consciously or unconsciously by every fibre of the whole wondrous structure : and this heart of Christianity, as a power in the world, has always been its *Asceticism*. The kingdom of God has not moved onward in this world by means of those whose grosser natures are satisfied with just so much of religion as may be enough to save their own individual souls, and who care for nothing beyond this, which they regard as the prime and sole necessity; for these selfish creatures can give no impulse to anything, except such as can be gained, by accomplished tacticians, from the skilful manipulation of mere dead weight. Christianity has grown by means of those who were capable of rising above what is the minimum for personal salvation; who kindle with the love of Christ, until they yearn to show their love to Him in the utmost of labor and self-sacrifice of which poor human nature is capable. And this is what we here call Asceticism. A deep, all-penetrating sense of personal religion as a peculiar relationship existing immediately between Christ and the redeemed and loving soul, and stimulating that soul, as its chief joy, to do " all for Christ," is the root-principle of Asceticism. One such soul can give more of power to Christianity than countless swarms of those who are content with merely saving their own souls, and beyond that make no further change in their previous relations to the world, the flesh, or the devil.

During the early ages of persecution, the whole body of the Church might well have been regarded as Ascetics; for even to profess as much faith in Christ as was necessary for the saving of one's own soul, was then worth a man's life, to say nothing of the chances of torture besides. As might be expected, the irresistible impulse of onward growth was great in proportion to this universal Asceticism; and during the first three hundred years the Cross conquered the empire of the Cæsars, and vast regions beyond its bounds. After the conversion of Constantine, when the world invaded the Church, Asceticism took refuge in the deserts, and soon—under the changed circumstances of the contest—the Monastic system embodied and organized the Ascetic principle, and was the life-essence of that tremendous struggle for the Faith, whose formal victories were registered, for all time, in the decrees of the General Councils. The monasteries, too, bore the chief brunt of the fight in conquering and civilizing the swarms of Northern barbarians, whose fresh forces, thus early Christianized, alone rendered it possible that the rottenness of Roman civilization should be changed into the actualities of modern Europe. They alone preserved the treasures of learning through ages of darkness. They alone contended with the kings and princes of the earth, and by their indomitable courage and pertinacity during ages of union between Church and State, prevented that union from rendering the Church the mere tool of secular statesmen, or the pasture-ground for the hungry cattle that are the curse of kings' courts. In their splendid success lay their greatest snare. Order after order rose by heroic self-sacrifice, and made itself a power in Christendom, soon to become rich in worldly wealth, and to find its early zeal smothered in the abundance of the good things of earth which that zeal had drawn forth as a spontaneous harvest from the hearts of the men of the world. The salt had at length lost its savor, and was cast out, and trodden under foot of men.

Another sort of Asceticism then broke forth, which undertook to enforce the three vows of Poverty, Chastity, and Obedience after a new fashion. The Poverty was made to apply to the service of God, which was stripped down to the utmost possible bareness. The Chastity was interpreted to mean that it was the duty of all men, especially the clergy of the three Sacred Orders, to marry as many wives in succession as they had the chance. And the Obedience meant, that all men must be compelled to obey the saints; these new-fashioned Ascetics being the saints, the true Israel, unto whom—and unto whom alone—the Scripture promises were made; while all other kinds of Christians were regarded as Moabites, Amalekites, Babylonians, or some other variety of Biblical heathen. The full triumph of this kind of Asceticism during the Great Rebellion proved it to be more intolerable than ever the old sort was, and the demonstration was made in fewer years than the other took centuries; so that, on the restoration of the Stuarts, the people were glad to get free from it by throwing off almost all semblance of seriousness in religion. Asceticism of every kind being dispensed with, worldliness in living and latitudinarianism in belief became more and more general. The heart of the Christianity of the land was being eaten out, until the eighteenth century made it doubtful whether religion were not about to disappear of the dry rot. And from this fearfully low tone the Roman Communion, and the Oriental also, from various causes, suffered quite as extensively as the Anglican, and in some respects more so.

With the appearance of Methodism things began to mend in England; and the essence of the improvement was in the reappearance of a real Asceticism, such as the origin of Methodism indisputably was. A deep, all-mastering sense of personal religion lay at the root of it, and a burning love for Christ, which could not be satisfied with merely getting religion enough to save one's own soul, but which overflowed with irresistible yearning to do something for Christ in gratitude for His great gift to us, and found the noblest field of action in carrying the glorious gift of the saving Gospel to others. The previous deadness, while the population was still increasing, had left a steadily accumulating mass of ignorance, carelessness, and vice, which was rapidly gaining upon a Church whose vitality was failing because her Asceticism was gone. The Reformation destroyed many churches, and built none. It wonderfully diminished the numbers of the clergy. The Great Rebellion carried the work of destruction still further. Those were the years during which, as Dr. South said, one might as soon have expected stones to be made into bread, as into churches. Methodism believed in poverty, in so far, at least, that its chief field of labor was among the poor and neglected, and its manner of living was such as characterized the lower classes. In the qualifications of its ministers or preachers, in the style of its humble chapels and class-rooms, in its open-air services and camp-meetings, its desire to accommodate and benefit the poor was made palpable to a Church which had neglected the poor; and the original intention was, that it should be a religious order within the Church. As to Obedience, Methodism exacted a compliance with rules of enforced confession, of attendance on class-meetings and frequent services, of plainness of apparel, and of abstinence from dancing, theatre-going, and other social enjoyments, all of which savored strongly of the sternness of self-sacrifice under the old monastic system. Touching Chastity, however, Methodism had nothing to say beyond the current principle and practice of all true Protestantism—to wit, that it is every man's and every woman's right, if not duty, to be as much and as often married as the civil law will allow.

The crying need of the Methodist movement, the portion of Asceticism which gave it the real power which it possessed, and the unfortunate infirmities of temper and blindness which produced the gradual alienation of Methodists from a worldly and latitudinarian Church, resulted at length in the formation of a somewhat similar party within her pale, the Evangelical party, as it delights to call itself. In essential principle it was the same as the Methodist movement, though in intensity, organization, and power it was far weaker. Being a portion of the National Church, it had only the loose organization of a party, not the close and powerful organization of a religious order. Obedience, therefore, which meant something real among the Methodists, meant little or nothing among the Evangelicals in the Church. As to Poverty, the chief field of the Evangelicals was among the upper and middle classes of society, and very little among the really poor. They did not enforce confession as boldly as the Methodists did in their class-meetings, and thus were, in one source of moral and spiritual strength, inferior. Plainness of apparel, and abstinence from social pleasures, were enforced much more feebly than among the Methodists, partly because of the presence of a large aristocratic and cultivated element among the Church Evangelicals, and partly because the practical vigor of Methodist discipline was wanting. But the fundamental idea of personal self-consecration was there; of personal love to the Lord Jesus, nourished by more frequent services than once a week, overflowing in constant acts of love, and deriving reality from more or less of honest self-sacrifice and laborious self-denial, to say nothing of rich gifts to the treasury of the Lord. It was the first stage of revival, within the Church, from the deadness of the eighteenth century, and as such, did a noble and good work.

But in proportion to the earnestness and depth of conviction with which the Evangelicals were animated, was their hatred of all who opposed them. This was intensified by their narrowness. They were narrow theologically; for, while grasping strongly the essentials of personal religion and personal devotion to Christ, they ignored to a great degree the Church and the sacraments. Wesley tried hard to preserve the reverence due to both; but he failed; and the Evangelicals sympathized heartily in the failure. They were narrow intellectually; for no branch of culture was regarded with sympathy outside of their own range of revival reading. The architecture of an old-fashioned Methodist Bethel, and the music of a camp-meeting tune, fairly represented the degree to which the Wesleyans had made the arts the handmaids of religion : and the Church Evangelicals had even less originality than that. They were narrow socially; for, in the Church of England, the Evangelicals were a close clique, with just enough of tantalizing affiliation with the aristocratic classes to prevent any extensive work among the poor. All this narrowness, combined with their thorough-going earnestness and intensity, made them bitter and denunciatory to a remarkable degree. All who did not pronounce their shibboleth with precisely their strength of aspiration, were unhesitatingly declared to be "destitute of vital piety," by which they evidently meant, were sure of eternal damnation; for they were positively certain that nobody could be saved unless his piety was "vital," as *they* understood it.

They did, as we have said, a noble and good work notwithstanding. Religion was, with them, the one overmastering consideration, in comparison of which all else was as nothing. Their warm love for Christ led to vigorous action, in certain directions (whether it was always wise, is another matter). The rapid and steady growth of the Bible Society was largely due to their anxiety to diffuse the knowledge of the Word of God. The Church Missionary Society testified to their zeal for Foreign Missions. Their Sunday-schools were a means of great good at home. Their desire to affiliate—on the platform at least—with Evangelical Dissenters was, in reality, a groping for some sort of Catholicity, a confession that the entire and voluntary isolation of any small section of the believers in Christ is a self-condemnation in the sight of Him who prayed so earnestly that all His disciples might be One. They revived the idea of Asceticism in several important respects, though hating the word itself as being pure "Popery." Their week-day devotional meetings were a half-way house toward the restoration of daily prayer. Their hymns were one of the best parts of their service to the Church. Glowing with real fervor, these hymns were the first that had popular strength enough to break the frozen uniformity of Tate and Brady. The Evangelicals fought for, and maintained triumphantly, the liberty to sing hymns, without first waiting for the approval of either Church or State; and, outside of the regular services appointed in the Prayer-book, they similarly demonstrated, in their prayer-meetings, the existence of a liberty which has since been put to good use by the Catholics. Certainly in these two points —hymns and extra services—the Evangelicals have earned a right to our grateful remembrance, which we shall always be prompt to acknowledge. We assure them that the liberty which they thus proved to exist, they *now* can never take away, no matter how much they may desire it.

Let us next turn our attention to the Church in the United States.

At the time of our first organization after the Revolutionary War, we had inherited mainly the lowest type of eighteenth century Church-and-State religion, which was found in nearly every part of the country where the Church was known at all, outside of New England. In Connecticut, having from the first been free from the curse of governmental protection, and born and nourished in the wholesome air of persecution, her distinctive principles were forced sharply to the front, and were sufficiently well believed in to be valiantly fought for against all assailants. It was to this part of our Church that we owe, possibly, the procuring an Episcopate at all ; certainly the changes in the Eucharistic office of our Church which make it so vastly superior to that of the Church of England. But everywhere else there was barely enough of Churchmanship to say that life was left. What shall be said of the " Catholicity " of the Churchmen of South Carolina, who only consented to come into union with the General Convention on the express understanding that no bishop should ever be sent into that State ? What shall we say of that in Virginia, where even the bishop, for many years after the Episcopate was obtained, despaired of the revival of the Church, and where the number of our clergy even *now* is hardly as great as it was before the Revolutionary War broke out ? On that soil where the State Legislature had, by law, fixed the salaries of the clergy at so many pounds of tobacco *per annum*, and made the amount collectable by the sheriff out of each planter's crop, one may safely say that the Divine Source of the spiritual power of the Church was very likely to be lost sight of. Especially was this the case when for an hundred and fifty years there had been the constant effort to erect an established Church in these several Colonies, which should be an Episcopal Church ; yet in all that time no bishop had ever been seen or appointed, no confirmation, ordination, or consecration had ever been actually witnessed anywhere in the land, and no discipline could be executed anywhere according to any practical system of canonical law. That the Church, thus deprived of the presence of her vital Order, and of all the organic offices of her hierarchy, loaded with the obloquy of scandals which she was not allowed power to correct, burdened with all the odium of legal connection with a civil government which was becoming constantly more odious to the people, and finally identified, during the Revolutionary struggle, with Toryism and allegiance to King George, and a supposed longing for the restoration of monarchical government ; that a Church with all this to contend against, and well plundered of most of her glebe lands and churches besides, with her clergy almost annihilated, and her people—never well grounded in Church principles at all—scattered away like chaff before the wind ; that a Church like this, popularly supposed to be only an " Act-of-Parliament Church " anyhow, should even be able *to live*, in the midst of the thriving and popular sects that rejoiced in the perfect triumph of religious liberty, was wonder enough. Nothing short of the power of God could have made it take root and grow as it has done.

And it was, for a while, a bare continuance of life—nothing more. The Apostolic Order—without which there can be no Church in the sense of the Catholic Creed—was happily secured to our Church of America, but it was at a time when, if left to herself, her theological tone was so low that she would have thrown the Catholic Creed itself overboard without a struggle or a regret. It was, however, the latitudinarianism of profound indifference, not of actual heresy ; and when it was found that the Nicene Creed must be restored, or the Episcopate could not be had, it was restored promptly, without objection and without qualification, emasculation, or amendment, just as it stood in the

Prayer-book of the Church of England. At first there was in this country a general consent that bishops might be tried, sentenced, and punished by their own clergy and laity in Convention assembled, and should not have any separate voice in the legislation of the Church. The infusion of high sacramental doctrine from the pressure of Bishop Seabury and the Connecticut Churchmen, would certainly have been defeated but for a degree of doctrinal deadness which prevented the possibility of a correct estimate by the majority of its importance; and this was aided by a practical indifference to the Communion office, which was then used only three or four times a year at most. Before there was a thorough awaking from this lethargy, the Institution office had happily been also secured—another treasure, due, like the former, to the Churchmanship of Connecticut.

It was mainly through that portion of the Church which had been strongly tinged with Toryism, that Church life and spirit were preserved in such wise as to render a revival possible, and this was, for a time, an obstacle difficult to overcome. Bishop Provoost was a Whig, and a latitudinarian, who hated the Tory Bishop Seabury very cordially. Bishop White, though not a latitudinarian, was yet, on some points, what used to be called a Low Churchman in England fifty years before; and never could see that the principles of his famous pamphlet " The Case of the Episcopal Churches Considered "—in which he proposed to resort to ordination by presbyters in case bishops could not be had—were untenable and intolerable. Bishop Madison was President of William and Mary College, and, as nearly as possible, nothing else.* All these were gentlemen of the old school, and as free as possible from any tinge of Methodism, or enthusiastic fervor, or " Evangelicalism," in the party sense of the word. They regarded it with hearty opposition. The venerable Bishop White—who was the least remote from it, and who was commonly so modest and careful and gentle in the expression of his opinions—never minced matters when on that subject; and even when he was an octogenarian, on hearing a speaker in his Diocesan Convention claim that " their bishop was a Low Churchman," he repudiated it with unwonted energy. " As the word is understood among us now in this country," said the old man, " you might as well call me a Turk or a Jew!" On the other hand, Bishop Seabury, who had been a Tory, was the chief means of preserving our Catholicity. Bishop Moore, who had been a Tory, laid the foundation of that Churchliness in New York on which Bishop Hobart was afterward to build so splendidly. And in the pamphlet warfare which accompanied the revival of true Church principles among us, the political or Tory phase of the question was from the first thrust strongly into the foreground by its opponents.

For some years after the completion of our organization under the " Constitution " there was no marked manifestation of party, as we understand the term now. Things were as yet too nearly dead to permit

---

* For seven years, from 1805 to 1812, no Convention was held in Virginia; and in 1813 the Rev. Mr. Meade thought it would be the last attempt of the sort, and that the Church in Virginia was " Lost, lost, lost ! "

anything so much instinct with life as a sharp party warfare. And as the progress from half-death to life is slow, so the development of party spirit was gradual. At first the only symptoms of the birth of an " Evangelical " spirit were to be seen in an occasional parson who was warm with Methodism, either from sympathy or previous personal connection ; and who manifested his fondness in a way not specially suggestive of a familiarity with Church principles or the Canons. They had personal fervor, however, a thing which it was almost impossible to discover in the public services of their brethren as then generally conducted. With no singing of the Canticles, no responses except by the clerk, no hymns except for a few festivals and special occasions, no psalmody but Tate and Brady, no baptisms except in private, and no Holy Communion except three or four times in the year, there was really a great work for the Evangelical party to do. And under its vigor the Church of America soon began to wake up. But the weakness of the party at the first may be gathered from the words spoken by Bishop McIlvaine at an annual meeting of the Evangelical Knowledge Society, that " he recalled the General Convention held when he was a candidate for orders. Key was the only one who was allowed to stand up in defence of Evangelical truth. Three clergymen, with the chairman, constituted the whole Evangelical force in the Lower House."

It was not long after this, however, that their strength was greatly increased. In Virginia, the fervor, moral courage, self-sacrifice, and high social position of the Rev. Mr. Meade were the chief means of bringing to the Church in that State a sort of resurrection from the dead. Wherever he went, his preaching drew crowds ; and his depth of earnestness, his graceful gesture, and his voice of winning sweetness, gave him everywhere a remarkable success in attracting ardent souls to the fold of Christ. In Pennsylvania, under Boyd, Bedell, and Bull, the Evangelical party rushed up into rapid life and strength ; and, in the important matter of electing an assistant and successor to their venerable bishop, they came within one vote of snatching the victory from the friends of Bishop White, and making Mr. Meade eventually the Bishop of Pennsylvania. The *Recorder* had been previously started by them, and became an important means of extending their affiliations all over the country. The establishment of the Alexandria Seminary gave them a theological training-school entirely under their own control, and insured them a certain advantage all over the South. The wonderful success of Bishop Philander Chase, and the unfortunate complications which embroiled him with Bishop Hobart, threw all the prestige of his work into the hands of the Evangelicals, and seemed to promise them entire possession of the West. The mild influence of Bishop Griswold, with full opportunity to mould the infancy of five dioceses, rendered it apparently certain that Evangelicalism would rule all New England outside of Connecticut. Maryland was half theirs already, as was Pennsylvania. In all the horizon there was nothing clearly outside of their speedy grasp except New York, Connecticut, New Jersey, and North Carolina.

We have alluded to the element of fervid Asceticism which was the one essential of true religious life in the Evangelical party. Its narrowness, its sad lack of theology, of Catholicity, and of knowledge of human nature, its utter ignorance both of its own true place and work, and of the relation in which they stood to the world, caused it to excel, in bitterness of feeling and expression, every party yet known among us. Every strong development of religious love must indeed have, commonly speaking, its special development of antipathy. " Do not I hate them, O Lord, that hate Thee? " is ever prominent in its feelings. Now, the Evangelical party was so situated as to be endowed with a double portion of this antipathy. The eighteenth century coldness was regarded by it as a condition, not of diminished or suspended animation, but of absolute death. It was a very dull and quiet kind of Christianity, indeed; very undemonstrative, and not at all aggressive; but the Evangelicals were sure that it was " deadly," that it was " not vital piety," that it was totally destitute of " the life and power of the Gospel." It was a " preaching of mere morality," without any of the savor of " the doctrines of grace." It was hated cordially, therefore, as being mere latitudinarianism, Pelagianism, naturalism, and therefore " another gospel," deserving all the anathemas that S. Paul could utter. This was the phase of hatred that resulted naturally from the dull era, against which their revival was originally directed.

But side by side with their movement against dulness and deadness, there was, as we have seen, a revival of true Catholicity beginning to make itself felt. The Churchliness which was first manifested from Connecticut, and soon after began to flourish in New York, was quite as genuine a revival as the other, and—to say the least—quite as much needed. Its love, for a time, may not have been quite so fervid; but its culture was broader and deeper. It had some theology. It had a firm grasp of fundamental Church principles, and would by no means let them go. This drew upon it the other part of the Evangelicals' double capacity for hating. Every Church principle which·the Evangelicals themselves ignored, was by them dubbed " Popery; " or, if the Popery of it could not be made manifest to any reasonable understanding, then it was more conveniently, and even more unanswerably, labelled " Popery in disguise." That nobody besides themselves could see it, was only an additional proof of the jesuitical art with which it was " disguised."

And perhaps here is as convenient a place as any to point out some of the essential weaknesses which, from the first, rendered the decay of the Evangelical party in the Church of America only a question of time. Their fundamental points of opinion were all either unchurchly or positively anti-Church. In England, where the union of Church and State exists, and the higher Church preferments are in the gift of the State, it is of the highest convenience to statesmen to encourage the existence, within the Church, of that party which does not really believe in the Church to which it professes to belong; for by nominating such men to high office in the Church itself, they render it morally certain that, in case of a contest between Church and State, the natural leaders of the Church will be mortgaged in advance to support the supremacy of the State, or the " Royal Supremacy," as they call it there. Nominees to office in the Church who have no serious religious differences with Dissenters, will always be more popular with the nation at large when nearly, if not quite, one-half of the people call themselves Dissenters—a condition of things which no wise statesman or shrewd politician can afford to ignore in making his appointments to high office in the National Church. It is precisely this which led to the appointment of Dr. Tait as Archbishop of Canterbury, by a government which *professed* to be the peculiar champion of the rights of the Church. Hence the necessity for such a class of Churchmen ; and hence, too, the certainty that a considerable portion of them will receive high promotion so long as the union between Church and State continues, no matter how small their numerical following may be among the clergy and laity.

The common ground between Erastianism and Dissent is this : The Erastian does not believe in the distinctive principles of the Church— does not believe that she has any spiritual powers which man can neither give nor take away ; for if so, it would be possible that the Church might be right in a contest with the State, which contradicts the fundamental principle of Erastianism. The Erastian believes it his bounden duty to obey the command, " Render to Cæsar the things that are Cæsar's, and to God the things that are God's." But he understands it in a peculiar fashion. As Cæsar is mentioned first in the above formula, Cæsar of course is entitled to the precedence in every case of conflicting claims. And if this will not do, then it is remembered that " the whole heavens are the Lord's ; the earth hath he given to the children of men "—that is, to Cæsar. Therefore, so long as we are on the " earth," the will of Cæsar must be supreme : and in England the will of the people comes sooner or later to be the will of Cæsar. The Dissenter also holds that there is nothing in the distinctive principles of the Church which is obligatory, provided the will of the people happens to be the other way. Only he does not wait for the formal parliamentary expression of the will of the people as a nation ; any respectable portion of the people satisfies him, in regard to matters which, as he agrees with the Erastian, do not exist by a spiritual authority which is divine. Hence, in England, there has always been a strong religious affinity between the Low Churchmen in the Establishment and the Dissenters outside ; and this sympathy is one main element of the *political* advantages of promoting Erastians in the Church. But when the high places of the Church are thus filled—when the chief rulers of the Church are promoted because they do *not* hold her principles, but sympathize with those whose proper place is outside of the fold—we can understand what was the condition of the people of God when Herod, *the Edomite*, was king at Jerusalem. It was while Herod was king that Christ was born at Bethlehem. It may be that a similar triumph of the Church's enemies within the Church herself may mark the nearness of the time of His second coming.

In this country, however, the elements of the problem are very different. Here there is no union between Church and State. Except some coquetting of politicians with the Church of Rome, there is nothing to be gained politically by affiliation with any body of Christians, much less with any one communion in preference to others. The State, as such, has no voice whatever in electing the rulers of the Church. No laymen even have any voice therein, unless they belong to some parish of the Church, and have made themselves sufficiently prominent in Church work to secure their election as delegates in the Diocesan Convention, or as diocesan deputies to the General Convention. The chief circumstance, therefore, which makes Erastianism powerful in the Church of England renders it impossible in the Church of America. The principle of Erastianism—which is the entire supremacy, in everything, of the lay power in its organized form of civil government—cannot, indeed, exist among us, except in so dwarfed and mutilated a form as deprives it of all real power for harm. As having any direct reference among us to the civil government, it has simply disappeared entirely. In its lower and weaker form—that of an appealing to the laity, or looking to the laity as a power to overrule the bishops and the clergy—it is incapable of much mischief, even in the most excited times. For, though no change in Church laws can be made without the consent of the laity, the laity can make no change without the separate consent of both bishops and clergy. That the laity can withhold the support of the bishops and clergy, in order to compel their compliance, is but partially possible in the abstract; and it is so generally impracticable in the concrete, that it may be safely disregarded. The threat has never yet been made on any scale worth notice; and it will be made many times before Churchmen will conquer their repugnance to the baseness of carrying it into execution. On the other hand, no lay delegation can be sent to the Diocesan Convention without good chance of clerical influence in making the election, and constant conference and co-operation with the clergy during the sessions, both orders debating in one body. As the clergy must generally be far more familiar than the laity with the subjects under discussion, the representation of the laity in our Church councils is chiefly valuable as giving an excellent opportunity for the clergy to educate the leaders of the laity in many important matters not properly embraced in sermons or homilies, and also as preventing the possibility of any serious jealousy ever arising between the clergy and laity as distinct orders, *both* having given free assent to all the laws of the Church, and to all changes made therein.

But it will be seen at once that the motives which lead to the election of our lay delegates are totally different from those which lead to making a man prime minister in Great Britain. The lay delegate serves at his own expense. He has no earthly object to gain in serving at all, and nothing to lose by staying away. Indifference to Church principles will rather make a man prefer not to be elected, or will induce him, if elected, to find it personally inconvenient to attend. So also with the clergy. Where the Church is free, and on a perfect legal

20

equality with all the sects in the land, many of which are more numerous and wealthy than she is, why should any man wish to be a clergyman bearing her commission, unless he really believes in her principles? And even if a few disloyal men should obtain orders, from personal or local or temporary causes, how can they ever rationally expect that the very fact of their ostentatious disloyalty should lead to their promotion by the free voices of those who *do* believe in what they profess?

The natural force of these plain conditions would seem to lead to the simple conclusion that a low-church party—where there is no union of Church and State—is an impossibility. And if all men were perfectly logical, it would be so. In a free country like this, there is no sufficient reason for any man's belonging to any Church the principles of which he does not believe in. But there are many circumstances which have combined to produce and to continue that unchurchly party among us, and which will insure its partial existence for a long while to come; but a full consideration of them will show the reasons why that party is disappearing more and more from the councils of the Church, and why it is certain to grow weaker and weaker so long as it continues to exist.

The originally low and latitudinarian tone of nearly the whole of our Church that was left after the Revolution was so deplorable that, as we have said, even partisan Evangelical life were a clear gain in many respects ; and latitudinarianism had no strength to resist the new impulse, unless by partaking of that other and better life—the revival of Church principles in their proper fulness and strength. Hence, the rapid rise and spread of the Evangelical party. But as the life of the Evangelicals was really a reflex within the Church from the greater glow without, it was impossible in the nature of things that it should be made dominant or permanent in the Church itself, all of whose distinctive principles it expressly and ostentatiously ignored. This consideration alone would have been enough. But there was another which also was sure to be fatal of itself, and that was, that the whole Evangelical movement rested, both in theory and in fact, on mere individualism. There was no coherence, except such as should be made and kept up by an organization within the Church resting on voluntary action, and working outside of all her canonical machinery; whereas the other and better revival—recognizing the Church as a visible body, and looking upon her canonical machinery as resting on and embodying in action her own distinctive principles, which were heartily believed in —had the immense advantage of needing no party organization other than the canonical machinery of the Church herself. The Church party, therefore, labored for general and united action in all things. When unable to carry its measures, it did not withdraw and set up an opposition affair which it could control by itself, but it waited patiently and struggled bravely until better days should come, compromising from time to time, until strong enough to do better. The *prestige* of united action in general institutions, which its superior intelligence enabled it to establish before it could be prevented, has, therefore, been steadily and increasingly gained by the Church party.

To pursue this policy was, indeed, logically impossible for the Evangelicals. Individualism is their root-principle; and even when they have a majority, they are not willing to trust themselves to that majority, lest at some day it should fail them, and the *individual* should find himself bound in some way he should not like. They were theresore compelled to make their sphere of action fractional. They struggled only for a part; while the Church party struggled for the whole. As a natural consequence of this, the practical influence of the one has been growing wider, and that of the other narrower, all the while. When the Church party succeeded in establishing the General Theological Seminary under the organic control of the whole Church, the Evangelicals established the Alexandria Seminary, which is *not* under any such organic control; and the Gambier Seminary is equally free from it. When the Church party organized the Church Book Society on as general a basis as was in their power, the Evangelicals for a long while patronized the American Tract Society's publications, preferring those which were totally destitute of all Churchliness of tone, until it was found that this was too barefaced an ignoring of their own Church to be entirely popular even with their own people. They then organized the Evangelical Knowledge Society, in which they could still profess allegiance to the " Church of their affections," while ignoring or opposing her distinctive principles. Yet, even so, the field of its literary exercise has been shrinking to such an extent that a large portion of its business has come to be the publishing of cheap editions of that very Prayer-Book, which pamphlets published from the same counter declare to be full of the germs of popery. When the Church party succeeded in organizing the work of Missions, the Evangelicals—contrary to their primary and natural instincts—consented to come in and take part. At that time they felt but little interest in the Domestic field. It lacked the brilliant glow of romance which lent a glory to the Foreign field.. The latter, too, was more wholly dependent on that individualism which lay at the root of Evangelicalism, and thus enlisted all its sympathies: while the Domestic work, entirely free from all that was exciting or impulsive, depended more for its success upon the quiet and careful use of ordinary means, and thus was the first care of the Church party. Whether there was at the time any express understanding to that effect, or not, it is certain, as a matter of fact, that, from that day to this, the Domestic Committee has consisted of a majority of the Church party, while the control of the Foreign Committee has been wholly in the hands of the Evangelicals, where it still remains. The natural consequences of this may easily be imagined. As new dioceses have been formed in the Missionary regions of the Church, they have almost uniformly come in as staunch members of the Church party: while the Foreign field brought no accession of strength to the Evangelicals in the General Convention until the late admission of foreign missionary bishops to seats in the Upper House. These two votes, however, came too late to be of any service, and the presence of bishops from China and Africa is too uncertain anyhow to be depended on.

It was not very long before some of the wiser heads among the

Evangelicals began to see that they had made a mistake somewhere, and that the West, which had once promised to be theirs in a lump, was now looking in another direction. Gambier was managed so ill, and Nashotah—which had brilliantly outflanked Gambier with regard to the Great West—was doing so well that they saw mischief was ahead. The missionary bishop system, too, was beginning to show its fruits, as diocese after diocese dropped in. But what was to be done? While their own friends were in control of one committee of the Board, and fairly represented on the other, how could they honorably set up an opposition organization in any part of the field? But a true Evangelical never yet allowed his honor to interfere with either his piety or his party; and the Philadelphia Association of Evangelicals was formed to do work which already properly belonged to the Domestic Committee. It was not that the Domestic Committee used its position for High-Church party purposes; but it so happened that the major number of bishops who needed missionaries were of the Church party, and the large majority of clergymen available for that work were of the same sort. If a majority of the Committee had been Low-Church, the result would have been just the same, had they honestly worked under the rules laid down by the General Convention for the guidance of the Board. No question of party was ever made by that Committee in appointing a missionary. The Evangelicals, however, were never willing to do Church work after this fashion. A part of their narrowness was in their conscience; and that conscience—so they often said—would not allow them to give money where any part of it might possibly be used to support men who were not preaching "the gospel" as they understood it. They were content to take part in nothing which they could not control. In the foreign work, as a general rule, they have sent out only those who were of their own way of thinking. If any foreign missionary was found to be clearly of the other school of theology, he was made to feel so uncomfortable that at length he had to give it up and come home. The Philadelphia Association concentrated the feeble forces of Evangelicalism in the domestic field so as to make them tell; and thus, by sharp management, they at length contrived to secure two new Western dioceses on their first organization—Iowa and Kansas; and they may probably have another in Nevada. But "what are these among so many?"

The animus of the two parties was never more plainly shown than in regard to that same Philadelphia Association. The Evangelicals were determined to occupy a ground so restricted that a number even of their own friends could not unite with them. The Church party, on the other hand, though keenly sensible of the unhandsome way in which they were treated (and some things were said which had better been left unsaid), on the whole, stretched their charity; and, saving their principles under a bare formula, made their practical system so elastic that the money contributed by Evangelicals could be used for Evangelical party work, under the direction of the Philadelphia Association, while passing nominally through the hands of the Domestic Committee, a majority of whom were of the Church party.

[It would be well if the members of the advanced wing of the High Church party now would heed this warning, for there have been deplorable instances of exactly such refusals to work through the constituted organs of the Church on the part of members of *this* party.]

But even this was found to be too close a connection with the Church party to be as effective as the Evangelicals desired ; and the American Church Missionary Society, and still later the Evangelical Education Society, have yet further carried out the programme of the entire isolation of the Evangelical element from the other operations of the Church. For themselves it is a mistake. It is a confession of helpless, hopeless weakness. It is a proclamation to all the world that they cannot hold their own on an equal chance ; but must as far as possible prevent all practical contact, in order to keep their party from being gradually absorbed by that which constitutes the great majority of the bishops, clergy, and laity of the Church in America. They still retain their old control of the Foreign Committee, though one of their leaders made an effort, at the meeting of the Board in 1868, to get rid of that also, as the last link that binds them to any general organization for practical work. Even in the Evangelical parishes the interest in the foreign field had fallen off greatly, as Dr. Cotton Smith then avowed, owing to their dislike of being connected in *any* way with a board whose domestic work is not controlled by Evangelicals. That is to say, those Evangelicals whose zeal for Christ and the salvation of souls started the Africa and the China Missions, and had been so lavish of money to sustain them, and had gloried in the self-sacrifice of the missionaries who belonged to their own party—those Evangelicals who had kindled the zeal of many thousands by the example of their laying down their lives so cheerfully in their Master's service, and for the good of the poor benighted heathen—those same Evangelicals, had run behindhand in their contributions more than $32,000, and were probably willing to starve out their own great work in foreign lands, if by so doing they could only insure one more point of total practical alienation from their brethren of the Church party at home ! The debate proved, however, that all Evangelical men were not yet ready to take this melancholy and suicidal position. The attempt at separation has never been renewed in the board ; and so the Foreign Committee goes on as before.

Our sketch has shown how the conscious inferiority of strength on the part of the Evangelicals has gradually led them to abandon the whole sphere of Church work, except where they can exercise entire control ; and that is now almost nowhere, except in such voluntary associations as they have started, and the basis of which they have made narrow enough to insure the exclusion of all others. Indeed, they would have worked themselves out to this result much sooner than they did, had it not been for several incidents of notable importance, which, for a time, gave them an apparent strength much greater than they really possessed. And here we must return once more to the most unpleasant part of our duty—the remarking upon the double share of bitterness which has characterized the controversial warfare of

the Evangelicals. As they were sure that their own Evangelical platform was essential to vital piety, and that the piety of all who did not
stand on it was dead, worthless, and destitute of saving grace ; and as
the root of all their movement was individualism, so their opponents
were in like manner individualized. As, on the Evangelical hypothesis,
all their opponents were devoid of true religion, so the Evangelicals
had every reason to believe in the truth of every scandalous story that
was told or made up against any individual opposed to them. Whatever blackened their opponents only proved that those opponents were
in reality what, if the Evangelical platform were true, they *ought* to be :
and, of course, the Evangelical platform was true. This element of
personal bitterness would have been quite enough of itself ; but it was
intensified by that combination to which we have previously alluded.
The contemporaneous revival of a truer Church feeling was regarded
by the Evangelicals as essentially Popish ; and, since, like all true Protestants, they hated the Pope even worse than the devil, so this part of
their antipathy was hotter, more bitter, and more unscrupulous than the
other. Every inch of advance in Church doctrine, discipline, worship,
or usage, has been fought against with the utmost pertinacity ; and no
pains have ever been spared to create the popular impression that every
such thing was Popery, even though the perfect model of it could be
found in the second or third century. In 1814 the chanting of the
Canticles in morning and evening prayer (they had always been *read*,
in this country, down to that time), was denounced as Popery ; just as
the same nickname has been given, with the same propriety, to the revival of the glorious old Gregorian tones in our own day. Gothic
architecture, recessed chancels, preaching in the surplice, altar-cloths,
the daily service, were all Popery, and " taught transubstantiation," and
what not. The ceaseless iteration of this stupid cry produced really
deep and bitter mischief in the earlier part of the movement, because
then it was believed in ; but now it is beginning to be laughed at. Our
Evangelical friends have been crying " wolf " so long and so loudly,
that the sensibility of the longest ears is wearing out.

But when the war against " Tractarianism " first broke forth, the
terror was fierce and deep. Tract No. 90 set many people fairly wild.
In this frame of mind the Carey Ordination produced a genuine *furor*,
a fervid upboiling of public feeling, in comparison with which all that
has been said and done about Ritualism is a mere bagatelle. The
scandals growing out of the cases of the suspension of the bishops of
Pennsylvania and New York—two great pillars of the Church party—
gratified both the elements of " good hating " combined in the Evangelical breast ; and since many who did not belong to the Evangelical
party acted with them on the issues involved in those cases, it gave them,
for the time being, the appearance of a great preponderance of power.
The secession of Dr. Newman and so many other " Puseyites " to the
Church of Rome was a never-ceasing arsenal of weapons for Evangelical warfare. It was not taken into consideration that the violence of
Evangelical abuse and the intolerance of Evangelical persecution were
really the causes which *drove* many of these men out of the Church of

England : and when they went they were attacked afresh for going.
The Gorham Judgment was regarded as a great doctrinal triumph for
the Evangelicals ; but, on careful examination, it was not very comfort-
ing after all, for it only showed that Gorham might be tolerated, and
not by any means that his doctrine was the true doctrine of the Church
of England. However, it produced another batch of secessions to
Rome, which were fresh elements of strength for the Evangelicals in
irritating and keeping up popular prejudices and misunderstandings as
to the real points at issue.

Meanwhile, the extraordinary unanimity of the outcry against Tract
No. 90 was working out a new result. The essence of that famous tract
consisted in the statement that, in interpreting the Thirty-nine Articles, " we have no duties toward their framers." This was thought
to interpret those Articles in a " non-natural " sense ; to be " evading,
not explaining, the Articles ; " and the hubbub raised about " dishonesty," " jesuitism," and what not, was enough to deafen all other voices,
and almost to prevent the power of rational thought. But the idea that
the private views of the Reformers as individuals should rule the interpretation of formularies which had passed through several revisions
subsequently (the last being by the Churchly divines of 1662), stirred
up the spirit of investigation into the *real* history of the Reformation ;
and it was found that the popular Protestant traditions of the eighteenth
century were one thing, and the real opinions of the Reformers in many
respects a very different thing. The researches among old archives
and State papers every day brought to light fresh facts in favor of the
Church party, and damaging to their opponents. Especially in regard
to the doctrine of the Holy Eucharist was this evidence conclusive.
The suspension of Dr. Pusey for two years from the University pulpit,
for preaching the ancient doctrine on this subject, was a challenge
promptly and victoriously answered ; and, as a natural consequence of
this victory, the disposition to set forth visibly the substance of sound
Eucharistic doctrine placed the capstone on the ecclesiological revival,
which, in the midst of the most vociferous and unscrupulous opposition,
had steadily gained ground : the altar-cloths and other adornments began to be common. The Westerton and Liddell cases—Protestant
mobs having failed of their object—settled a fact, to the great astonish-
ment of the Evangelicals, that, as a question of *law*, the Church party
stood on such strong ground that they could not be touched by coercive
process without fresh legislation ; and this established the basis on
which the present so-called Ritualistic movement has grown up. Its
advocates have claimed, from the first, to be within the plain letter of
the law ; and in the disgraceful series of prosecutions gotten up and
pushed through by the Evangelicals against them, the decisions of the
Judicial Committee are such manifest perversions of law and justice,
merely in order to gratify Protestant prejudice, that each legal victory
for them has proved to be a popular defeat. When 5,000 priests
protest against a decision, the back of the court, as a moral or spiritual
power, is fairly broken. The Evangelicals have procured a decision
which makes against the Ritualists in some points ; but it compels the

Low-Church deans to wear copes in their own cathedrals, and by irresistible implication pronounces that preaching in a black gown is illegal ; a result which has all the popular effect of a broad joke at their expense, purchased with a heavy outlay of their own money. The party there is dwindling, as it is here, but the causes are in many respects so different that we must drop that branch of the history altogether, or our work will spread beyond our limits.*

To resume our outline of the decline of the Low-Church party in this country : We must remember that the essential principle underlying their whole organization was, that individually they sympathized more with the vital piety outside of the Church than with those inside who hold to her distinctive principles ; and therefore, on every occurrence of a popular agitation among those denominations, there has been a fresh blunder made by the Evangelicals within the Church. When revivals were the rage, the Evangelicals sympathized ; and because they were partakers of a movement which interested great numbers of people, they felt that they must be adding to their own strength : but before long the fervor went down, and then our Evangelicals were surprised to find that they were actually weaker than before. When the temperance excitement arose, they very generally went into that likewise, on the same instinctive principle, and with the same general result. When anti-slavery began to ring from the pulpits of the sects, the Evangelicals were the only ones who even felt inclined to give the same sort of gospel among us ; but before the breaking out of the civil war, this tendency was kept under restraint by the fact that Virginia, a slave State, was the stronghold of Evangelicalism, and several other Southern dioceses had similar ecclesiastical sympathies. With the uprising of the North, after the attack on Fort Sumter, all this was changed ; and the Evangelicals once more yielded to the primary instinct of their religious life, which is, to go with the crowd of the Orthodox Evangelical denominations in every popular movement. And this, as in all previous cases, turned to their injury, only more completely than ever, because it bit deeper. The idea that successive temporary excitements, having no connection with Church principle or Church life, *could* really build up a solid strength within the Church, was, of course, preposterous : but our Evangelicals, who never reason correctly, took it for true wisdom, and perpetrated the same blunder over and over again with an amusing pertinacity. They may have heard that " the Church is an anvil that hath worn out many a hammer ; " and yet they always sympathized with the hammer, and never with the anvil. During the war,

---

* We omit all adequate mention of the marvellous Church revival of our age, which began with the Oxford movement, and which, in less than forty years, has built ten times as many churches as were erected in the previous three hundred years, to say nothing of the extension of the Anglican episcopate almost over the world ; while in schools, literature, the arts, and everything affiliated, however remotely, with the Church, the progress has been equally great. Nor can we say anything of the noble, pure, and full Asceticism, which is the heart of it all. Our subject is, not the growth of the Church party, but the Decline and Fall of the other.

therefore, they thought they had " a sure thing ; " and after the General Convention of 1862 their triumph seemed to be complete.

But there were others who saw deeper than they did. If the country were to be permanently divided, then the Evangelical policy was the best ; but if the country were to be reunited, and the Church also, then the war policy, for the Church, would be fatal. Sound Churchmen, therefore, who held that as Churchmen they had no concern whatever with politics; and those also who firmly believed that the unity of the country would be restored, and that then the greatest triumph of the Church would be to give a glorious example of the spontaneous re-union of separated brethren ; all these united fought their way through the war, enduring any amount of personal abuse for " disloyalty," "sympathy with traitors," and other such bitter and crazy nonsense, until the return of peace, when their patient courage was abundantly rewarded. Those who thought they had triumphed gloriously in 1862 were left a sorry remnant in 1865, too feeble even to secure the inser-tion of a protest on the Minutes : and of all the Southern dioceses there is *not one* that can now be relied on as staunch to the Evangelical party. Even Virginia has lost the heartiness of her ancient devotion, and is keeping up an earnest thinking as to what all this means. Thus the most brilliant triumph of our Evangelicals was also the briefest, and the most fatal to themselves.

Another piece of short-sighted unwisdom has all along characterized the Evangelical policy ; but as it is a logical necessity in their position, it is certain that they will continue it zealously to the end of the chap-ter. Their own particular party creed being very short and simple, so far as its positive teachings are concerned, and being precisely the same that constitutes the popular religion of the day, and therefore is well known to everybody ; it is simply impossible to render the col-umns of their periodicals or the pages of their books interesting at all, unless by means of the double antipathies which are so dear to them. As the larger part of their labors is thus devoted to a propagation of the gospel of hatred, which they have made peculiarly their own, they may be safely depended upon to rake up and publish, and keep pub-lishing, every extreme or unwise thing done by their opponents. Their charity, too, is so great that, as a general rule, they either assert or in-sinuate that the whole Church party is responsible for every extrava-ganza of doctrine or practice that can be discovered in any Ritualist. They delight in printing, at full length, with all the strange-looking technical words (which pass for something horrible because they do not know what they mean), the most elaborate accounts of Ritualistic services. The sympathy which exists between them and the denomi-nations, ensures the copying of these accounts in the numberless issues of the sectarian press ; and the secular press sympathizes, of course, sufficiently to add still further to the publicity of every piquant detail. Take S. Alban's, Holborn, and S. Alban's, New York, as samples ; and compare the brief and infrequent mention of them in the Church press, with the interminable columns that have been devoted to them by the Low Church, sectarian, and secular papers. The disproportion is ab-

solutely laughable. The opponents of Ritualism seem judicially blind
to the fact that they are thus constantly giving it the benefit of an
enormous amount of gratuitous advertising—an amount of advertising
that hundreds of thousands of dollars could not have bought, but
which they are thus making a present of to those whom they hate
most. It is no wonder that the Ritualists are in very good humor with
such a way of carrying on the war. They may laugh who win. The
constant crowds present at Ritualistic churches are largely due to this
handsome system of hostile advertising. Among the many who come
expecting to be horrified, the larger part find that it is not so horrible
after all. A second and a third visit render it still less obnoxious ; and
finally, in many cases, the enemy is turned into a friend. And, as we
have said before, there is no danger that the Evangelicals will cease this
mode of building up their opponents and undermining themselves ; for
if they once stop their tirades against Ritualists and Ritualism, what
can they fill their columns with that anybody will find it interesting to
read ?   And as for the Church party, it *must* continue to grow, so long
as its bitterest enemies kindly persist in thus advertising it so enor-
mously—for nothing.

Another disadvantage of the Evangelical party, as a party, is, that
its own inconsistencies have gone far to destroy its credit with precisely
those plain common-sense people to whom it delights to appeal. When,
after reading Evangelical editorials for years against the Popery of
crosses and flowers in churches, and lights burning by day, they at
length find Dr. Tyng himself crowning the spires of S. George's Church,
Stuyvesant Square, with two great crosses, and adorning the interior
with other crosses that cannot easily be numbered for multitude ; when
they find flowers enough crowded into the chancel of the same S.
George's Church to deck for a high festival half-a-dozen Ritualistic
altars ; and when they find the gas-burners in full blaze all round the
interior of the same S. George's Church, while the sun is brightly shining out of doors ; what are they likely to think ? Moreover, after reading, for years, hot denunciations against the " meretriciousness " of
adorning churches with colors and gold, when they at length see more
than twenty-five thousand dollars spent on the inside of the walls of
that same S. George's Church merely for colors and gold, what is the
result as touching the godly sincerity of the Evangelical party in its
fierce and wholesale denunciations ? Plain, common-sense people
don't see any difference in principle between having crosses on spire,
font, pulpit, roof, gallery, and pavement, and having a cross upon the
altar—especially as they have so long been taught that the altar is not
a whit more sacred than any other part of the church. They don't
see how flowers can be all right on the first Sunday after Easter in the
afternoon, and all wrong on Easter-day in the morning. They don't
see how fifty lights in the nave should be good Protestantism, and two
lights on the altar be flat Popery. They don't see how colors and gold
can be consistent with vital piety on walls, beams, stonework and
woodwork, upholstery and altar-cloths, and yet be fundamental and
deadly doctrinal error in a vestment of the minister. And the conse-

quence is, that the louder and the more furiously these Evangelicals rave
and ramp about the Popery of such things when done by the Ritualists, the more easily plain, common-sense people smile and shrug their
shoulders, and see no occasion to be alarmed in the slightest.

It is not to be supposed that the Evangelicals have been unconscious
of their own decay. Even before the breaking out of the war, one of
their prominent men gave privately to one of the Church party the real
reason why they had organized separate Evangelical societies within the
Church. It was, he said, a matter of necessity to do so, in order, if
possible, to prevent their whole party from gradually coming over to
ours. They had discovered the strong tendency in that direction, and
knew that the only way to stop it was to prevent, as much as they
could, all actual contact of the two parties in the practical work of the
Church: an actual contact which the Church party has always sought,
and by which it is sure to grow; while the other party shuns it instinctively, because it has found it destructive. All that the iron pot
asks is a chance for a fair bump; while that is naturally the sort of fairness which the earthen pot is most anxious to avoid. The only desire
of the Evangelicals, on the contrary, is to stand far enough off to render
misapprehensions easy, and correction impossible. But if they were
aware of this before the war, much more palpably was it forced upon
their consciousness after the war was over, and when they had discovered the destructive consequences of their mistaken policy. The famous
breakfast party at Delmonico's was intended as a formal rehabilitation
of the Evangelical party in its previous position; but the damage done
is such as breakfasts cannot repair. On reckoning the diminishing numbers of the Evangelical array in the General Convention—the only test
of proportionate strength in the general legislation of the Church—the
truth was visible to the most unwilling eyes. "My leanness, my leanness!" was the cry of the knowing ones of the party. And in one of
their most thoroughgoing organs, within less than two years after the
war was over, there were open utterances of the most gloomy forebod-
ings. Our limits will not permit us to give extracts; but we state the
evident drift of the remarkable articles to which we allude.

They began with a melancholy retrospect of Evangelical mistakes,
laying chief stress upon their folly in assenting to the division of the
Mission work which was effected on the reorganization of the board in
1835, they taking the Foreign Committee while the Church party controlled the Domestic. They might have known—it was said—if they
had thought a moment, that as the fruits of the Domestic work were
speedily admitted to General Convention, while those of the Foreign
field were not, such a division of their forces would soon make the
Church party so strong in General Convention and in the Board, that
they could take the Foreign Committee too, whenever they were so
minded; and that had already come to be the case. [All this was true;
but how could the Evangelicals have prevented it? In 1835 they were
yet in a minority, and therefore could not dictate terms to the majority,
much less insist on controlling both committees. And if they had begun
thus early their now favorite plan of isolated work, it would only have

injured them, by this time, much more than it actually has ; for it would have been in operation just so much longer.] However, the Evangelical editorials to which we are referring went on to show the immense growth of the Church party ; that almost every new diocese organized in the mission field now came in as a High - Church diocese ; that, as fast as Evangelical Bishops died, their dioceses were almost certain to elect High-Churchmen in their places ; and that the older and larger dioceses were being put through a course of subdivision which would probably in every case add still further to the High-Church strength ; so that what with their own losses and the gains on the other side, there was every human probability that, in ten years or thereabouts, the Evangelicals would not have a single vote left, either in the Upper or the Lower House of General Convention ! Next came the consideration as to what could be done to cure or even modify the evil. And it was not obscurely shown that the best, and indeed the only, thing that could be done, was, *to get up a Schism*, while they were yet strong enough to make one ; for that in a few years, at the present rates of change, they would be too weak to be able to make a schism, no matter how ardently they might then desire it.

It took some time for the brillant idea embodied in those Evangelical editorials to work its way to the acceptance of the more radical leaders of the party. There were two grounds on which it was thought the needed preparation for a schism could be made. One was, to sound so loud an alarm about the fearfulness of Ritualism as to frighten some people into a readiness to seek refuge from the monster in a schism ; and the other was, to provoke, if possible, some exercise of discipline against Evangelical irregularities, upon which the cry of " tyranny " and " persecution " could be raised, so as to command further sympathy. These were not very ·promising attempts, either of them ; but the case was getting to be desperate, and what else could be thought of.

It has often been a cause of devout thanksgiving on our part, that a kind Providence has, for many years past, sent us opponents in the Church who have very little common sense, and no tactics at all. When their own party is already a minority, and is growing smaller day by day, they seem to think that the surest way to make it grow larger is to start some more extreme policy, which will split the few that are left, and drive the better part of them into our embraces. Then again, our position being defensive, and their programme requiring them to begin the attack, only look and see how wisely they have managed it. When an enemy is entrenched in a stronghold, with many successive lines of defence, and each approach guarded by many outworks, a true and wise strategy will reduce the outworks one by one, and bring on the decisive contest as near the citadel as possible. This being the wise course, the Evangelicals instinctively took the opposite, and risked the whole campaign on the first and feeblest outpost they came to. If defeated there, the Church party had fort after fort, rampart after rampart, to which they could retire in succession, and continue the fight ; but if the assailants were repulsed at that first outpost, good-by to them ! The outpost chosen by the Evangelicals was the canon forbidding any

clergyman of the Church to officiate within the territorial limits of
another clergyman's parish without his express consent; and the famous
young Tyng case arose, and roared its way through all the newspapers
in the land.

The consequence was a total defeat for the Evangelical party. They
had secured the "tyrannical" verdict out of which they hoped to make
party capital enough to serve as the foundation of a schism; but the
foundation seemed to be laid in a quicksand, and immediately disappeared. When, in advance, there was an attempt to dragoon the
whole party into an agreement upon the radical platform, the conservative section of it rallied, and put an extinguisher over the blaze at its
first kindling; and in consequence the language of the Philadelphia
Declaration was more mild than exciting. It was thought triumphant
strategy for Dr. Tyng to declare himself entirely satisfied with "*the
Prayer-Book as it is.*" Even the Bishop of Ohio, in publicly fraterniz-
ing with the Presbyterians was careful to avoid any phrase which expressed a conviction of the validity of Presbyterian "Orders." There
was evident motion in the water; and yet the watched pot would not
actually boil. And when, after the protracted and intense excitement of
the trial, and when every art of the demagogue had been exhausted in
order to enlist the public press, and bully the court, and kindle the popular
passion to a readiness for an outbreak, all this formidable preparation
broke into nothing, like a puff-ball, when the sentence was only an "admonition." It was impossible, with a straight face, to make "tyranny"
and "persecution" out of *that.* At the meeting of indignant partisans
held immediately after, and while their blood was at the hottest, there
was an attempt to declare for a schism on that basis; but it failed ignominiously, even then and there. It appeared, even at such a moment,
that if some of the clergy went into a schism, they could not depend
upon their own laity to go with them; that many of their own people
did not approve of the flat disobedience of a canon which had provoked
the trouble; and that the great preponderance of voices, even among
themselves, was *not* for a schism, unless the next General Convention
should refuse to relax that canon. It was therefore agreed to "*agitate,*
AGITATE, AGITATE," for the repeal or modification of that canon.
If that were refused, terrible things would happen! Some wished to
insist on alternative forms being added to the Prayer-Book in certain
places; but they were regarded as rather radical, and the party would
not commit itself to so extreme a position.

The only other point upon which there was anything like a general
rally was upon the right to "exchange pulpits" with non-Episcopal
preachers outside the Church; in vindication of which some clergymen,
who ought to have known better, broke the canon deliberately, in the
hope of thereby proving that it could not mean what it says. A noble
Pastoral by the Bishop of New York led to a pamphlet war, in which,
as the clear result, the Pastoral was left in possession of the field.
This line of business, however, culminated in the Hubbard case, in
Rhode Island, of which more hereafter.

The days and weeks rolled onward slowly toward the meeting of the General Convention; but the determination to "agitate, agitate, agitate," amounted to comparatively little. Memorials were numerously signed indeed; but the signatures had to be drummed for, and when they were laid before General Convention they had not the weight of a feather. The agitation grew cooler and cooler, instead of hotter and hotter: until—not long before the 1st of October—the very Evangelical papers which had made it their specialty to get up the excitement openly groaned over the total failure of their agitation, and confessed the entire indifference of the bulk of their own party in regard to it. This, of course, was fatal to any attempt to secure a relaxation of the Tyng and Hubbard canons.

But our wise Evangelicals are not content to fail like other people. They must needs go about to make the assurance of failure doubly sure. And they succeeded gloriously!

It will be remembered that it was the influence of the Moderate Evangelicals which overruled the attempt of the Radicals to clamor for "an alteration of the Prayer-Book, or schism!" The Moderates insisted that nothing more must be attempted than merely the relaxation of those two canons: and they claimed triumphantly that *they* were content with "*the Prayer-Book as it is.*" The Prayer-Book, they said, had always been Evangelical in its real meaning, for was it not the work of the glorious Protestant Reformers? The Evangelical interpretation was therefore the natural, the true, the only honest interpretation. But when the agitation for an amendment of those two canons was found to cool as rapidly as mutton gravy in a cold dish, then the Radical Evangelicals broke out, on their own responsibility, in the most brilliant and successful manner. An anonymous pamphlet, in a pink cover, appeared (written by an Evangelical priest since deceased), and bearing the sensational title, "*Are there Romanizing Germs in the Prayer-Book?*" This pamphlet is of such importance at this point of our subject, that, notwithstanding the fearful calamity in which its writer lost his life not long after, we cannot pass it by. We shall review it, not as representing its writer so much as the school of which he was the representative; and as a blunder of that school, it is so significantly rich, that we hardly know how to refrain from quoting nearly the whole of it. It defines Romanizing germs to be "seeds of spiritual death to every organization in which they are allowed to root and grow. They choke, in due time, the most precious and fundamental truths of our faith. They change the sinner's sure and steadfast hope into a rope of sand." This is fearfully emphatic language, especially when applied to "the Prayer-Book as it is," with which Dr. Tyng is so entirely satisfied. Moreover, this pamphlet does not profess unlimited faith in the Reformers; and here we gather the fruits of the fresh study of the Reformation which was made necessary by the challenge given in Tract No. 90. This pamphlet corroborates Tract No. 90 on both sides of its work. As a matter of principle, it recognizes no duty to the Reformers, but to amend their work, and reject their ideas when erroneous; and as a matter of fact, it acknowledges that the views of the Reformers, and of the final revisers of the Prayer-Book, were what is now called " Romanizing," and were by no means identical with the popular Evangelical Protestantism of the present day. But let us go to details.

The pamphlet recognizes the fact that Elizabeth retained *eleven* of Bloody Mary's Romish councillors, and added only *eight* Protestant ones of her own selection; while for years the Papists "repaired to their parish churches without doubt or scruple," and priests officiated at the parochial altars. " The Liturgy," it says, "was published early in Elizabeth's reign, when there was hope of compromise with Rome, and hence is *Romish.*" Alluding to the changes since made, it candidly confesses : " We cannot fairly assert that the Prayer-Book which we now use is the one left us by the Edwardian Reformers;" and adds, very properly : " When interpreting the amended portions, we cannot, of course, refer to those worthies, any more than we can properly appeal to Hamilton and Jefferson to explain the amendments recently made to the Federal Constitution." And it says further : " It was a strange admission made by Dr. Bayford, Gorham's own counsel, that ' Roman Catholics might conform to the Church of England without violating their consciences.'" This is Tract No. 90 in full, only " a little more so," so far as general principles are concerned.

As to the Rule of Faith, which Protestantism makes to be "the Bible as each man's private judgment understands it for himself," the pamphlet finds that this is by no means the doctrine of the Prayer-Book. For Article VI. (the Articles, it seems, are erroneous as well as the Prayer-Book) declares the Apocrypha to be read by the Church " for example of life and instruction of manners;" and the Homilies are recognized in the Articles also; and " Ancient Authors" are appealed to in the same category with " Holy Scripture;" and "the Ancient Canons" are recognized as having power to "command" us, and are " linked with the Holy Scripture to regulate our *discipline ;*" so that "morality, doctrine, polity, and discipline," are all affected by these "traditions of men." As to the Homilies, our pamphleteer is particularly emphatic. In them, he says, " the Apocryphal books are described as 'the infallible and undeceivable word of God.' Baptism and justification are used as synonymous terms. Baptism is spoken of as the 'fountain of regeneration.' We are said to be 'washed in our baptism from the filthiness of sin.' Matrimony is denominated a sacrament. The Fathers are appealed to as authorities. The primitive Church is recommended to be followed as most incorrupt and pure." And all these passages in the Homilies, he insists, "form an integral part thereof,* and are to be read diligently and distinctly, that

* These passages, we suppose, are omitted in the "abridged edition" of the Homilies published by the Evangelical Knowledge Society. The pamphleteer seems to reflect upon the American Church Missionary Society (a purely Low-Church organization) for including "Articles, Liturgy, and Homilies " as standards of "principles and doctrines." "Accordance with them," he says, is thus "made an article of our faith." He condemns his own partisan societies for really professing to believe all that is held by the Church party !

they may be understanded of the people." And he thus states the logical consequences of such teaching : " The ' Homilies ' of Cranmer and his associates are excellent, but are not the Homilies of Chrysostom and the saints of his time as weighty ? The ' Ancient Authors ' testify to the fact of Episcopacy, why should they not of its prerogatives ? The ' Ancient Canons ' command on one point of discipline, why not on another ? " Precisely so ; and hence he thinks that Prayer-Book doctrine leads straight to such as this, which he quotes from Dr. Dix :

" Divine, or, as it is called, Catholic, faith is a gift of God and a light of the soul, illuminated by which a man assents fully and unreservedly to all which Almighty God has revealed and which He proposes to us by His Church to be believed, whether written or unwritten."

And he adds : " This point having been reached, it follows as a necessary sequence that the sacramental and sacerdotal ideas with which all patristic writings are surcharged, will be accepted and proclaimed." Just as if the same Convocation of 1562 which adopted the Thirty-nine Articles had not expressly " accepted and proclaimed " that very thing, when they enjoined that all preachers should " in the first place be careful never to teach anything from the pulpit, to be religiously held and believed by the people, but what is agreeable to the doctrine of the Old and New Testament, and collected out of that very doctrine by the Catholic Fathers and ancient Bishops." The object of the very men who set forth the Articles is thus proved to be the special horror of the Evangelical pamphleteer ! It is amusing, too, to see the fanatical opposition of such men to the mention of the " unwritten " word of God. Why, their great Protestant tradition, that the Holy Scriptures " contain all things necessary to salvation "—a tradition embodied in our Constitution, and which is so far made an article of faith that no man can be admitted to Holy Orders without subscribing it—cannot itself be found in Holy Scripture at all ; and cannot be proved but by the aid of those same " patristic writings " which are so " surcharged with sacramental and sacerdotal ideas." The Evangelical Protestant who denies *all* " unwritten " tradition, cuts the throat of his own hobby.

The three great treasures confided to the Church being the Ministry, the Word, and the Sacraments, and our Prayer-Book being thus shown to be " Romanizing " in regard to " the Word," it is next found to be no better off as to the Ministry.

The Prayer-Book has the word " priest ;" and the pamphlet says that " for the real significance of ' priest ' in this rubric [before the Absolution in Daily Prayer], we must consult the reactionary spirit of 1662." And again : " Our *Declaration* is simply abreast of the first twelve centuries, which cover the formative period of the Romish system." And so he goes on to prove that our priests are clothed with proper priestly powers, and perform properly priestly acts, in " consecration " and " oblation " in the Holy Eucharist, in benediction, and in the forgiving and retaining of sins. He states that in our American Church, the " form most com-

monly used " in ordaining priests is that which begins : " Receive the
Holy Ghost for the Office and Work of a Priest in the Church of
God ;" and that these words "are avowedly used because they are
Christ's words." He admits that " all this is the most blasphemous
frivolity, if it be not the deepest truth," though evidently convinced
that it *is* " most blasphemous frivolity." He admits that the Prayer-
Book teaches the Apostolic Succession ; and that it means thereby " a
tactual succession whereby grace is communicated from one to another
for the exercise of ' sacerdotal functions ' in a ' sacerdotal connection ';"
that, in accordance with this view, " *exclusiveness* is the prevailing practice of our Church. All *ministers* are reordained. *Priests who are of
the Succession*, though they be Roman or Greek, are not reordained."
The " functions " of the priest are acknowledged to be " supernatural "
and "the dogma of *transmitted grace* " to be " distinctly stated." Mas-
kell is declared to have made only " logical deductions from the Prayer-
Book doctrine " when he said :

" The members of the Church of England, by God's blessing, well
know that none but a priest can stand in their stead before the Holy
Table, and offer in their behalf the solemn prayers and praises of the
Office of the Lord ; that none but a priest can consecrate the elements, . . . A denial of the Christian sacrifice leads easily to the
denial of the priesthood."

And the following form of Absolution, from the Church of England
Prayer-Book, is put in the same category :

" Our Lord Jesus Christ, who hath left power to His Church to
absolve all sinners who truly repent and believe in Him, of His great
mercy, forgive thee thine offences, and by His authority, committed to
me, I absolve thee from all thy sins in the name of the Father, and of
the Son, and of the Holy Ghost. Amen."

And he quotes Goode's admission concerning the Ordination formula, that " the existence of such language in the Prayer-Book leaves
it open here (unfortunately, I think) to adopt a papistical interpretation ; " and yet Goode, he tells us, was " ever slow to acknowledge that
anything in the Prayer-Book is not ultra-Protestant."
On the subject of the Ministry, therefore, the Prayer-Book is no more
to be trusted by an Evangelical than on the Word ; but its Romish
errors on the subject of the Sacraments are the worst of all !
Thus he begins with Baptism : " The Romish dogma is expressed
with sufficient explicitness by the current phrase BAPTISMAL REGEN-
ERATION." In regard to the Baptismal Office in the Prayer-Book, he
says, " its doctrinal statements are so integral a .part of the service, that
every baptized person, however illiterate, must become a party thereto." Moreover, " the service is positive in its declarations, logical in
its sequent steps, and remarkably contrived to declare with great distinctness the doctrine involved. Objection to it belongs to its *structure*

21

as much as to any of its expressions. It is an ecclesiastical monograph on the doctrine of Baptism." Again :

" The word ' regenerate ' conveys the central idea of these offices. We cannot agree that this word has lost its ancient, or rather its original, meaning. We have failed to obtain from those who hold this view any satisfactory historic proof of such changes. It is, indeed, no longer used by all synonymously with ' baptize,' because all the Christian world does not now believe, as it once did, that the ' baptized ' are ' regenerated.' . . . Moreover, the Prayer-Book does not seem to leave much room for doubt upon this point. In Article XXVII., regeneration is used synonymously with new birth, and is a translation of the Latin *renati*."

After full quotations from the Offices, the writer says : " If, after this recital of these explanatory clauses, it is still asserted that regeneration or new birth means only some ecclesiastical change, we are constrained to inquire, What ideas of ' the state of salvation ' are prevailing among us ? " He then goes on, at length, to prove that the Office declares the vital importance of regeneration ; that it is to be sought in Baptism ; that this object is declared to be gained ; and that God is solemnly thanked for it. This, he says, implies the *opus operatum*. The protest of 1553 against this Romish error, he tells us, " was withdrawn in 1571 (Queen Elizabeth's reign), and has not since been restored ; in which respect we have ceased to be Protestant." He concedes freely that Ambrose, Tertullian, and the whole primitive Church, taught the doctrine he condemns ; and gives up the whole body of the Reformers, too, with equal candor :

" When Dean Goode wrote to Mr. Spurgeon that the baptismal service involved questions of ' what might be called historic theology,' he seemed to us to yield everything. For baptismal regeneration was the prevailing belief among all classes of theologians for years after the Reformation. Nearly all, if not all, of the catechisms framed at that time are tainted with it."

After quoting some of them, he concludes that " the Edwardian reformers, as a body, believed in baptismal regeneration." The attempt to evade the force of this by showing that they were Calvinists (Dean Goode's view) " would not help us out of our present difficulty." And the men of 1662, equally with those of 1552, " believed that ' baptism is our spiritual regeneration.' " He sets forth in order *five* different modes that have been employed by Evangelical men to get over, or under, or around the language of the Prayer-Book ; but dismisses them all in disgust (Mr. Gorham's included), as being totally destitute of Scriptural authority : " Here are no less than *five* different explanations, all or any one of which destroys the unity of the baptismal service, and violates its plain letter." And he adds : " The laity, for the most part, are ignorant of or unwilling to accept them."

As to the Holy Eucharist, the pamphlet tells us that in 1662 " a new spirit was breathed into our Communion Service "; and the antipathy to the use of the words of our Lord—a strange antipathy for a Bible Christian—reappears : " We regard as unfortunate the use of the Scriptural language, ' Eat My Flesh and drink My Blood,' as it is used in some parts of the service." The opening words of the formula of reception are " constantly used to sanction high views of this Sacrament." It goes on to " object to the *Consecration* and *Oblation of the Elements*, and to the *Invocation*," calling special attention to the additions in our American Book, which make it, in the view of the pamphleteer, so much worse than the English. He objects to the doctrinal phrase, " but also to be our spiritual food and sustenance in that holy Sacrament "; and affirms that by the language of " the black rubric," concerning kneeling at the reception of the Holy Communion, " room was made for the entrance of the consubstantiation idea which now so extensively prevails among us." The grievances on this sacrament are summed up as follows :

" In the use of Scriptural language in a wrong connection, in the consecration and oblation of the elements, in the invocation, in the reverent handling and eating of what remaineth, in the doctrinal phrase alluded to, in the want of explanation of the reasons for kneeling, and for the participation by the clergy before the people, we have seeds which, under certain circumstances, will germinate into Romish error."

And as a specimen of such logical error, a quotation is given from Bishop Overall, who, on the words " we, and all Thy whole Church, may obtain remission of our sins," etc., remarks : " This is a plain oblation of Christ's death once offered, and a representative sacrifice of it for the sins and for the benefit of the whole world, of the whole Church."

So the poor Prayer-Book cannot be trusted as to either the Ministry, or the Word, or the Sacraments !

But the Catechism is a special grievance besides ! " We regard it," says our pamphlet, " as a fruitful source of Romanizing doctrine, and as the instrument most useful in instilling in the minds of the young the germinal ideas of the sacerdotal and sacramentarian theories." Left to this, the poor child " would know but little of the finished salvation which is in Christ, and of the precious grace which flows from Him to every believing soul." Only think of it ! That miserable Catechism actually teaches " that there are duties to be done, rather than riches of grace to be enjoyed." And he concludes thus :

" The large number of catechisms issued by the Evangelical Knowledge Society, and by other publishing houses, as well as by individuals, show how great is the want which they are designed to meet. The different character of the teaching they set forth is a standing protest against that which every clergyman is commanded to teach his children at least once a month. Doubtless, if the Catechism were less frequently taught, our people would less easily be led into Romanizing error."

After thus abandoning the whole Prayer-Book field to the Church party, our pamphlet is quite consistent in much that it says of that party:

" The sacerdotal party are neither small in numbers nor aliens in our ecclesiastical commonwealth. Nor yet is their influence on the decline. They have been an integral part of our Church from its beginning. They have ever been numerous and influential enough *to mould its prevailing sentiments*, and, as we have seen, *to establish their own doctrinal status by material changes in the Book of Common Prayer.* Their growth, and the acceptance of their peculiar doctrines, have been at least coequal with the extension of the Church. Indeed, to the eyes of many they seem like a flowing tide gathering force, and sweeping away clergy and laity, churches, institutions, and dioceses. The Evangelical party, the true representatives of the Protestant Edwardian Reformation, with all their societies and earnestness, have been as impotent to stay this tide as Canute on Britain's sands. They have, on the other hand, felt the power of this overshadowing influence, and have become in some degree infected with semi-sacerdotalism and semi-sacramentarianism, which has dashed their courage, weakened the force of their convictions, and unjointed their armor of aggressiveness."

And the Prayer-Book is the cause of it all!

" A ' Prayer-Book Churchman ' is a current phrase, expressive of this fact. Dr. Pusey and his friends have ever declared in all sincerity that they have ' made their way ' by the Prayer-Book. It seems like folly to assert that a large body of our people, intelligent as they are, have been led to adopt a doctrinal system the very opposite of that which they believe is taught by the Prayer-Book, their much-loved formulary. The present position and influence of the sacerdotal party can, in our opinion, be accounted for in only one satisfactory way: they are built upon, and are the outgrowth of, the Romanizing germs in the Prayer-Book. So long as these remain, disciples thereof will multiply."

While candidly saying, " We cheerfully accord to the sacerdotal party entire conscientiousness of conviction. Their doctrinal views doubtless seem to them *in entire accordance with the Bible and the Book of Common Prayer,*" this pamphlet declares, of its own friends, " We are firmly convinced that clear views of Bible truth have led to the *non-natural* interpretation of the Offices. Yet how often have the Gospel teachings of the pulpit been neutralized by the instructions of the Prayer-Book ! " And again we read :

" It is a noteworthy fact, that during three hundred years, a large and influential sacerdotal party have existed within our Church, and come down to our time in uninterrupted succession. Their rallying cry has been these very doctrines. They have vindicated them by appealing to the natural interpretation of the Occasional Offices, our popular theological formulas."

And again :

" The constant repetition of the declaration of baptismal regeneration has forced many to believe, at last, *what has been so often spoken in unbelief.* Defections from Evangelical truth among us are to be traced to the insidious influence of the Offices. The testimony of the Articles has been but little felt, because they have been a sort of clerical dessert (some decline dessert), while the Offices have been daily food. . . . Humiliating as it is to confess all this, we feel that nothing is to be gained, and much may be lost, by attempting to conceal what is patent to the world. . . . One marvels to see how busy are some Sacerdotalists in plucking the blossom of Ritualism from the plant of High Churchism, as if it were of abnormal growth, and not the natural efflorescence. One grows sad while observing the many Evangelicals who try to stay the tide of High Churchmanship by quoting the Prayer-Book. In view of these facts, we are forced to regard the Prayer-Book as the fountain whence flows that stream of Romanizing influences which is rapidly growing into a mighty river, and, with its many branches, penetrating our whole Church."

But while thus conclusively recognizing the honesty of the position of the Church party, and the fact that the standards of the Church clearly teach their principles, the picture drawn by the pamphlet of the position of the party it represents is pitiable in the extreme. As to the Baptismal Offices, he says there is one question which it will not do to pass by :

" It is this : *How can Evangelical men use these Offices and yet remain faithful to the truth as it is in Jesus?* We would answer, in their behalf, that few of them administer heartily : some under protest ; some refuse ; the majority of them apologize for their action, by putting a *non*-natural sense upon the Offices. When asked to explain them they explain them away. . . . *Every Evangelical minister*, then, *speaks to his congregation with a mental reservation*, and heartily thanks God for doing what he does not believe, in all cases, is done ! Is it possible that the servants of God, who, above all others, are to provide things honest before all men, are compelled to resort to such equivocation, and that public Offices can be framed only on such a principle ? If we suppose that this hypothesis is good when applied to the minister, what has charity to do with the child's own declaration, ' Wherein I was made,' etc. *Are we to teach our children to lie?* "

Then again, in a passage to which we have already referred, after considering the five Low-Church explanations of the Baptismal Offices, he says :

" Here are no less than five different explanations, all or any one of which destroys the unity of the Baptismal Service, and violates its plain letter. They are so constantly obtruded as to suggest great sensitiveness of conscience behind them. They have been unceasingly offered, but without relieving many of a sore burden which the service imposes. Some have outgrown the scruples of their consciences, but every new generation is obliged to pass through the same struggles as those who have gone before. The world is slow to believe that popular devotional formularies are so recondite in their meaning that a vast amount of historical lore is necessary for their right interpretation, and has been quick to style these various explanations ' traditional, evasive expedients,' bad in principle, and unsatisfactory in result."

Again :

" An increasing number of the clergy are struggling under stress of conscience, tortured with doubts as to their duty. . . . They do not wish to get rid of their scruples by outgrowing them. Yet they cannot, without deep pain, use parts of some of the Occasional Offices. They shrink from the continued repetition of unsatisfactory explanations. They regard with alarm the influence of the Prayer-Book upon many of the souls committed to their charge. This stress of conscience dulls their enthusiasm and abates their influence. . . . We cannot use or give a Prayer-Book without, in some sense, becoming a party to its errors."

And the prospects ahead seem to be as little inviting, or rather, still less so :

" Still further it may be asked, Would not a revision to-day be less Protestant than it would have been twenty years ago ? Will it not be still less Protestant if it takes place twenty years hence, supposing the policy of the future to be, as in the past, Micawber-like ? * Have we power to hinder such revision if the dominant party resolve to make it ? What, then, is our hope of diffusing Evangelical truth throughout our communion, of relieving distressed consciences, of preventing a Romanizing revision, but in such agitation in reference to the Romanizing germs in the Prayer-Book as will call attention to the doctrines which they naturally develop, and will prepare the way for their extirpation ? "

And the opening part of the pamphlet speaks of " the thickening calamities in our body politic," admitting that the very work which is

---

* The revision completed in 1892 has completely verified this doleful prediction of the Low Churchmen of 1867. Such relaxation of rubrics as was granted was made in accordance with the customs of " Ritualists," and the doctrinal statements were made stronger, while the enrichments were precisely such as were asked for by High Churchmen.

proposed " must increase the sad embarrassments and the weighty re-
sponsibilities of the times in which we live." Poor Evangelicals ! We
do not wonder that they feel blue !

This remarkable pamphlet at first was offered for gratuitous distribution, being widely mailed to clergy and laity all over the country.
Sound Churchmen were so delighted with it, that within a few days
applications from several of them were made for some five thousand
copies in the aggregate, to be used as "campaign documents" for
Churchmen. A dim consciousness that a mistake had been made then
dawned upon some of the Evangelical leaders, and applicants were told
that there were "none on hand." The second edition was marked on
the title-page : " PRICE TEN CENTS, POST-PAID."

If this pamphlet had been the only thing of the sort, and if—being
anonymous—it had not been issued from a responsible office, it
might have passed for a High-Church hoax. But very soon after appeared another pamphlet, in a blue cover, evidently by a different hand,
and with differences of treatment, but marvellously agreeing in the
chief points we have noted. It is entitled, " *Revidenda ;* or, A brief
Statement of those things in the Liturgy which should be revised and
altered," etc. It acknowledges that since the time of Edward VI.
changes have been made " with the view of conciliating High Churchmen and Romanists ; " and that " the *real* presence of Christ in or with
the elements is not ignored." It admits that " The Baptismal Service
being at the foundation of the ritual and Liturgy of our Church, we
find all other parts of the ecclesiastical system built upon it, and in more
or less harmony of design ; " yet he would destroy it root and branch.
The author of it declares that the use of the word *priest* " in any sense
other than that in which any disciple may claim it, is unscriptural and
sinful." As to Ordination, we are glad to learn from him that the
alternative form in the ordination of priests, " Take thou authority,"
etc., " is now seldom used ; " and he adds :

" So here we see the minister at his second ordination is invested
with rights and privileges not granted to the deacon. He argues, If
those priestly words are used, surely I have the right to interpret them
in accordance with the well-known and straightforward meaning of
them. The burden of proof that the words do not teach that I am to
forgive sins, lies with those who deny the literal interpretation. So it
does, etc."

Touching the Declaration of Absolution in the Daily Prayer, he
says :

" We cannot expect members of other Churches to be posted and familiar with the exceptions, explanations, rebutting evidence, and lines
of argument, by which Evangelical men keep a good conscience [?] in
the use of the absolution service [*sic*]. Give it the ' priestly ' interpretation, and it is blasphemy, and many of us would never use it again if
that is fairly proved. Allow that it is *probably* the sense, and the most

fair and reasonable view of it, then the conscience is entangled, the use of the form is attended with misgiving, weight, and regret."

Among other familiar places, the Institution Office is faulted heavily : " It is a fungus ; but like all plants of that kind, the ideas in the Institution Office have rapidly increased, and have spread the false and corrupting sacerdotal theory until it has nearly covered the whole denomination." Of course, the writer wishes all these things to be entirely removed ; but the most noticeable things he says are in corroboration of the confessions of the other pamphlet as to the intolerably dishonest position of the Evangelicals at present :

" The real grievance is, that we do not like *to read aloud* passages and words, from *one* point of view, under cover of some sort of mental reservation, or according to a rather far-fetched interpretation, which are generally understood by our congregations in *another* sense, and— as is claimed by those who are entirely satisfied with the Offices—in their plain, primary, and literal sense. . . . It is not always possible to avoid being compromised and placed in a false position, when, in connection with others, the services are used, and an interpretation by emphasis or gesture is given by the officiator. . . . The use of the expressions under consideration, and the avowed or implied position that they are taken and understood in a different sense, becomes *a training in equivocation.*"

After showing the evils of dishonest subscriptions to the Articles, he continues :

" The same course in reference to the Liturgy has ended in a similar result. The danger, that the habit of mind, and the practice of interpretation and double sense, will extend to the words of Scripture themselves, and thus the same equivocation, glossing, and practical reversal of their divine statements will be apparent, is not one merely to be apprehended. The evil has been most sadly and widely exemplified, and threatens to affect all religious teaching."

This confession that the Broad-Church school, and the skeptical tendency, are the direct outgrowth of Low-Churchism, is very striking, and perfectly true. But the evil, our author says, will not stop with the things of religion :

" The practice will be adopted in secular matters, and engender and encourage prevarication and equivocation, the result of mental reserve, in all the relations and business of life. There will be an entire want of reliance on the plainest and most earnest and solemn declarations, and the query will be changed from ' What is truth ? ' to ' Where is truth ? ' Thus it will be seen that the evil principle once introduced, or allowed, spreads its contagion, and taints all the good with which it comes in contact. The double or less obvious sense becomes a cancer on the face of truth. In the name, therefore, of plain, honest speaking, in the name of public morality, in the name of true religion, let us preclude the need or the possibility of anything like equivocation."

And yet once more, in his concluding summary of " plain reasons " why the Prayer-Book should be revised, he thus words one of them :

"Because various formularies of the Church cannot now be read without apparent mental reservation ; and it is most undesirable that Christian ministers should even appear to understand and interpret words otherwise than in their plain and strict meaning."

General Convention, therefore, is implored to give relief to the " consciences " that are so sorely aggrieved.

The Moderates among the Evangelicals are left, by this dashing movement of the Radicals, in a very uncomfortable position. They try to " explain away " the plain language of the Church, and claim that it does not mean what it plainly says. But the world is beginning to smile at so small a minority attempting to affix new meanings to the English language. All Romanists, all Dissenters, all of the Church party (comprising five-sixths of all Churchmen), and now all the Radicals, who are the only really aggressive portion of the Evangelical party itself, are agreed that the Standards of our Church teach what the Church party holds ; and even the most pious impudence in the world will soon be shamed out of the attempt to assert the contrary. *The Episcopalian* is particularly severe upon the " explainers " among its own friends. It says (January 13, 1869) :

" Some say, ' Pooh, pooh, we find no difficulty in the use of the book. We mean so and so by the words. We have wisdom—we know that an idol is nothing in the world ;' we can sit in the idol's temple and eat things offered in sacrifice to that false god, yet it gives us no trouble ; we eat to satisfy hunger, and do not regard appearances. Others explain and explain, and try to reconcile the objectionable expressions, and when a comfortable position helps them to invent, they get along pretty well. Others use the services, and suffer in mind and conscience, crying, ' Oh, Lord ! how long ? Lord, what wilt Thou have us to do ? Is it Thy voice, " Come ye out from among them, and be separate, and touch no unclean thing"?' Others decline their parishes, refuse to use the obnoxious services and expressions, and are censured for using the defective modes. They deny the teachings which they regard favorable to the false theory, refuse to be responsible for their pernicious influence, and conscientiously suffer and wait for the day of deliverance. With these we sympathize ; with these serious and anxious thinkers, feeling after God, and inquiring His will, we affiliate ; in their interest we exert ourselves. Their fortunes are ours ; their lot is our chosen inheritance. Where they go we will go, and there we hope to remain. Their God shall be our God, and their people our people."

So the moderate Evangelicals are confessed to be not only dishonest, but mercenary also ! " When *a comfortable position helps them to invent*, they get along pretty well." Is not this rather severe upon certain Low-Church Bishops, to say nothing of many others whom we could name ? Well may they exclaim, on reading such articles, " Save us from our friends ! " But their chagrin cannot prevent the effect of the blow. These pamphleteers will be found to have done to their own party as fatal a service as General Hood rendered to " the Lost Cause " when he turned his face northward, and undertook to " cut off General Sherman's communications."

Careful readers of the pink pamphlet will have noted its clear threat of schism, if the demand for relief of " consciences " by means of revision were not complied with :

" The Romanizing germs in the Prayer-Book are an offence to their consciences. They feel that they have a right to claim such relief as, not being unreasonable in itself, may be granted without yielding any essential of the faith, or destroying the unity of the Church. If they are denied this relief, it will be necessary for them to seek it wherever they can find it. Their stress of conscience will not allow them to rest content in their present status. . . . On S. Bartholomew's day, 1662, two thousand clergymen, including such men as Baxter, Owen, Alleine, Howell, Flavel, Poole, went out from the Church of England, because relief to their conscientious convictions was denied."

This threat of a schism, as we mentioned at first, was openly made in a leading Evangelical paper, on the express ground that a schism was the only means of preventing the entire absorption of the Low-Church party.* It has been repeated again and again, in various forms, by others of their organs, especially *The Protestant Churchman* and *The Episcopalian*. It was openly talked of, and generally agreed to, at the indignation meeting which followed the sentence upon young Mr. Tyng ; and then and there the chief point at issue was, the *time* at which the schism should be made, some being clamorous for making it at once, and others declaring that it would be better to wait until they should see whether the next General Convention would grant them the " relief " which they demanded ; and if it would *not*, then they would go for a schism unanimously. Various suggestions for independent action, amounting, in fact, to schism, have been repeatedly

---

* [This threat of making a schism was at last carried out, and in 1873 and 1874 the " Reformed Episcopal Church " was organized. Bishop Cummin, then Assistant Bishop of Kentucky, was the only prelate who joined the new sect. It was a great loss to the Church that *any* high-minded and pious clergymen and laymen should feel impelled to leave the Church ; yet they could not accept the Prayer-Book as it is, and honorably followed their consciences. Their places are illy filled by the Broad Church clergymen, who openly deny that they are bound to believe the doctrines of the Church, and even deny the Deity of Jesus Christ, the Inspiration of the whole Bible, and the need of a Redeemer from sin.—C. F. S.]

made. For instance, *The Protestant Churchman* of April 2, 1868, in
a leading editorial on " The Liberal Branch of the Protestant Episcopal
Church," said :

" There are only three ways in which the relations between these
parties can be adjusted. One is by the elimination from the Church of
the sacerdotal party; another is by the elimination of the party of the
Reformation ; and the third is by some arrangement by which both
can remain in the Church, each divesting itself as far as possible of
every responsibility in regard to the other. The third method is the
one we would now consider.

" We take it for granted, on this supposition, that the sacerdotal system is to remain in the Church in such a form that it will be impossible
to compromise with it. The first effect of this will be that the legislation of the General and Diocesan Conventions must be restricted to a
very narrow sphere. It would be impossible to legislate beyond the
narrowest limits without interference with conscientious convictions,
and without provoking resistance on the one side or the other. There
will, from the necessities of the case, come to be virtually two ecclesiastical bodies, organically connected together, each ordering for itself
most of those matters which have heretofore been provided for by the
General Convention.

" The Liberal and Evangelical party has long since adopted the
policy—which it is now too late to reverse, even if it were desirable—
of leaving the organic Church institutions in the hands of the opposing
party. What it needs now in order to secure for itself the prestige
which the control of Church organizations gives to its opponents, is
to assume itself a quasi-ecclesiastical character, and assert and maintain
for itself a position of virtual independence in the Church. . . .

" This much is certain, that the divergence of parties in our Church
is now so great that they have not common ground to stand upon. It
is impossible that both should agree in any legislation except of the
most general character. It would be intolerable that one should legislate for the other. If, then, they are to remain together, each must be
permitted to order its own affairs in its own way."

We give this extract, not because of any specific importance in it, but
merely as a sample of the wild schemes that are passing through the
brains of the few thinking men who yet cling to a dwindling and dying
party. What can be more absurd, in a free country which has just triumphed in the greatest civil war the world ever saw, waged in order to
compel the minority to submit to the majority when acting within constitutional forms of law—what can be more preposterously absurd, in
such a country, than to assert a permanent right on the part of the
minority to disobey all legislation, *because* it is so small a minority as to
be unable to secure any appreciable weight in the legislative body that
governs the whole? On the same ground, when the Republicans control more than two-thirds of both Houses of Congress, the Democrats
are freed from any obligation to obey the laws enacted by such a Con-

gress! " It would be intolerable that one party should legislate for the other ; " therefore the minority must " assert and maintain for itself a position of virtual independence in the country !" This is secession doctrine with a vengeance ! The old theory used to be, that a Sovereign State had the right to secede. This new theory is, that any number of Sovereign individuals have the right to secede, though they be not numerous enough to carry a single State in the Union ; and the *fewer* they are, the better is their right, and the clearer their duty, to secede ! When a great party has run down into such drivel as this, it is about time to order its coffin and write its epitaph.

But in order to measure the utter fatuity of this scheme of a schism, we must go back once more, and notice the great event which has really crushed out all possibility of vigorous life for a Low-Church party hereafter in the Anglican communion. We refer to the Council of Lambeth ; the full greatness and importance of which has not as yet begun to dawn upon the minds of more than a few. An absolute majority of all the bishops of our Communion were there present, and *all* signed its Synodical letter, and agreed to its resolutions. So large a number of the absentees have since sent in their entire adhesion, that a heavy majority of each separately organized portion of our Communion is now committed, irrevocably, to the maintenance of what was there done. Now the chief reliance of the Low-Church party is upon the Thirty-nine Articles (which they misunderstand) ; and the Council of Lambeth utterly ignored the Thirty-nine Articles. The Low-Church party glories in the being " Protestant ; " and the Council of Lambeth utterly ignored Protestantism. The Evangelicals hold themselves up as the models of all true religion, and repudiate all idea of the reunion of Christendom except upon their own party platform ; and the Council of Lambeth did *not* set up our Communion as the model for all Christendom, but candidly confessed our own short-comings, coldness, and need of great improvements. The Evangelicals abhor the idea of recognizing the Primitive Church as a standard, since they regard the Sovereign Individual (provided he be an Evangelical) as superior to all the rest of Christendom ; whereas the Council of Lambeth recognized " the undisputed General Councils " as the unquestionable standard of the faith of the whole Anglican Communion. There is not a plank— not even a splinter—of the Evangelical platform left standing, by the action of that Council. Low-Churchism, word and thing, is utterly thrown overboard and done for. And there were enough Low-Church bishops there present to commit their whole party, and really to sign away, for all future time, its very right to existence.

But besides this positive action, there was something else. Colenso is a Protestant—a pure Protestant. He believes in private judgment, and in the Sovereign Individual. He declares himself a " Liberal " Christian—thus claiming the same distinctive word which Unitarians delight in, and which *The Protestant Churchman* has proposed to take as equally appropriate to its wing of nominal " Episcopalians," whenever the schism is complete. Perhaps, if they were to send for him, Colenso would consent to come over, from Natal, where he has only two or three clergy and parishes to own him, and be the "Liberal" Bishop of the new "Liberal Church." They might agree happily in altering the Prayer-Book, for Colenso would heartily indorse the idea of the author of *Revidenda* that revision should proceed on "the principle of *omission* rather than of *addition*." "It is proposed *to diminish*," he says, "rather than increase, the dogmatic assertions of our standards." Now before the meeting of the Council of Lambeth it was confidently stated that, in case of a schism, there would not be wanted among our American Evangelicals a sufficient number of bishops to keep up the Succession. But when they met at Lambeth, they found that Colenso was not invited, and did not dare to come. They found that although, from technical reasons growing out of the relations between Church and State in England, the Council was prevented from acting *formally* on the subject, yet that, on every ground except the Queen's letters patent and royal mandate, Colenso was utterly cast out, and no member of the Council would have anything to do with him. And American Evangelical Bishops could easily reflect that, in *their* case, there would be no "royal mandate" or "letters-patent" to impair or impede the universality and promptness of *their* rejection, in case *they* should go into a "Liberal" schism in these United States. Since that Council, therefore, we have seen no more public statements confidently claiming "at least three bishops" as ready to head the schism; but privately we have heard of very edifying confessions that their Evangelical Bishops "came back from Lambeth with their mouths stuffed with cotton." It is certain that not the slightest semblance of encouragement has been given by any Evangelical Bishop to the notion of getting up a schism, Moreover, there is not a single diocese which would go, even if its bishop went; and it does not appear that more than just one parish could be found to go with its minister, should *he* choose to become a schismatic.

And now comes Mr. Cracraft, with his famous letter to Bishop McIlvaine renouncing the ministry of the Church; for, logically, here is the best place to mention it, and historically it brings us back from our Lambeth digression to a resumption of our sketch of the "agitation" which was to affect the General Convention of 1868. This letter appeared just after those two notable pamphlets—the *Romanizing Germs* and *Revidenda*. And it corresponds wonderfully with them in all their strong points, besides the additional interest of announcing an action in logical consistency therewith.

Mr. Cracraft—who had been a priest in the Church for a quarter of a century or thereabouts, and a large part of the time in the Diocese of Ohio—writes to his "dear friend" the Bishop of Ohio, "asking to dissolve his connection with the Protestant Episcopal Church," for sundry reasons. First, because "the plain, literal, and historical teaching of the Offices of the Prayer-Book" would make him to be "a PRIEST, in the *sacerdotal* sense." "With me," he adds, "the conviction is irresistible that the minister in our Church is considered a *priest* in this anti-Protestant sense." And he goes on to prove it. He next asserts that "the proper accompaniment of the character here defined is, I con-

sider, obviously furnished—an ALTAR ; " and he proves *that*—which is a
bitter irony on the Bishop of Ohio himself, whose most strenuous exertions of Episcopal prerogative have been directed to the denial that we
have any Altar, and who has always refused to consecrate any church
which had not, in place of an Altar, a wooden table, with legs. But
regardless of the bishop's feelings, the cruel Cracraft goes on next to
prove that the priest and altar are not without their proper Sacrifice.
A portion of the Consecration Prayer, he says, " is expressly called the
' *Oblation.*' "   And he pointedly continues :

" All, I suppose, clearly understand oblation to mean an offering—
a sacrifice. Taken in its *natural* and *historical* sense, this oblation
prayer can only be understood to teach that the Lord's Supper is not
only a memorial, but a *Sacrifice*. In glancing back over this, we shall
find, I think, fully presented, first, a *priest*, in the sacerdotal sense ;
second, an *altar*, on which the sacrifice is to be offered ; and finally, an
offering, to be presented to God in the sense of a sacrifice."

Next he asserts that the priest has the " priestly *power of absolution* " ; which he proves with equal clearness.   Then, as to Sacramental
efficacy, he proves clearly that the Church teaches Baptismal Regeneration : " The sacramental theory—the outward sign and the inward
grace *essentially coherent*—is here fully sustained."   As to the Sacrament of the Altar, he finds that in the Prayer-Book it " is authoritatively
defined that the grace of this sacrament is *the real presence of Christ
Himself in* the outward elements."   And as to both sacraments, he
says, " It is difficult to conceive how any language can more forcibly
express a sacramental theory than that with which we are here presented."

Having thus come to clear views of the doctrinal teaching of the
Prayer-Book, Mr. Cracraft honestly asks :

" Can I longer perform *Offices* that I believe pronounce and teach the
sacramental theory that I have so long thought I was opposing ? . . .
I am convinced that the honesty and simplicity of the Gospel, in which
I should be clothed, forbids it ; nor can I soothe my conscience on the
subject. . . . I must do violence to my convictions if I go forward
and give my co-operation in the propagation and upholding of errors
so vital and so dangerous to the souls of men."

He considers first, indeed, whether it may not be his " duty to stay
and combat error in the Church where it exists."   For some time he
thought it was ; but he had " only to consider the past to obtain a con-
vincing answer."   And he goes on remorselessly to say :

" The unsatisfactory results thus far, I think, leave no hope for the
future.   The sacerdotal and sacramental theories have not paled before
their combatants, nor become less potent in the Church from the
assaults made upon them from the standpoint of the simplicity of the

Gospel, or the doctrine of salvation only by faith. The influences in the ministry and episcopacy of the Church are now, more than ever, thrown ponderously into the scale on the side of these errors. This I believe to be true of the Diocese which God has so long intrusted to your care. Who that contemplates your position, as one of the foremost champions for the truth in this conflict, can fail to see that while the weapons of your warfare have been bright and glorious in this great struggle, you are yet girded about and hedged in by the influences which you have so long opposed? And though not literally left alone in the conflict, yet so inadequate are the forces that act with you, in the episcopate and out of it, that your and their final subjugation is manifestly only a matter of time."

When reading Mr. Cracraft's glowing phrase about the " bright and glorious" weapons of Evangelical warfare, one cannot help wondering whether the same thing is referred to which we have found our other Evangelical writers describing as " mental reservation," " compromising honor and morality," using words in a " non-natural" sense, " teaching our children to lie," " a cancer on the face of truth," etc.

The alternatives so loudly clamored for by those who devoted themselves to the business of " agitation," namely, " Revision of the Prayer-Book, or Schism!" were not unnoticed by Mr. Cracraft. " Some," he says, think that " a change can be safely anticipated in the Prayer-Book. Some even believe that a *reconstruction* of our Formularies can be expected at our next General Convention, and comfort themselves with these hopes." But he quietly and conclusively adds :

" The more discerning, I think, entertain no such expectations. The best informed are more than convinced, while hoping it may be otherwise, that the action of that body will but strengthen the hands of the Ritualists and Sacramentarians."

And as to a Schism, he says : " I would say *Amen!* to this with all my heart, but I cannot regard it as a well-grounded source of comfort. Others may." And he goes on, with cold-blooded and exhaustive logic, to show, that such a schism must be either *with* the Apostolic Succession, or *without it.* If without it, " few would organize for a higher and purer form of evangelization." And again : " Few would contemplate separation, unless Episcopacy, as of Divine appointment, and the consequent doctrine of Apostolical Succession, should be carried with it." The schism, therefore, without Bishops, " could have no numerical strength." But how would it be if the Schismatics *have* Bishops and the Succession?

" *With these*, in the workings of the great future, the same results, now giving all this unrest, would certainly be reproduced. These *high claims* lie at the foundation of all anti-Protestant exclusiveness, all Churchly pretensions, all Ritualistic and Sacramentarian arrogance, and would render it, in the end, as much in the way of the march of mind, as much opposed to liberal institutions, religious unity, and Christian fellowship, as the present structure now is, that they would try to improve."

We never saw, from an enemy, a clearer recognition of the great truth, *Ecclesia est in Episcopo.* Wherever there are Bishops of the Succession, there the whole circle of Church doctrine, discipline, worship, and usages, *will* return sooner or later. Even a Low-Church schism, going out with only Low-Church Bishops, would eventually come to raising the same fruit on the same old tree. So perish the notion of getting up a schism! Without Bishops, it would be impracticable; with Bishops, it would be of no use. But the melancholy part of our last quotation is the confession that in breaking away from " the Church of the living God, the pillar and ground of the truth," the leadership which a schismatical Evangelical wishes to follow is (not the Bible, which is vulgarly supposed to be their object, but), first of all, " the march of mind," and next, " liberal institutions; " in which Colenso, and all Unitarians and Neologians would precisely agree with him. But what can be a more complete sentence of death upon the Evangelical party, than his thus showing that all except " a few," *even of that party itself,* are so bewitched with the doctrine of the Apostolic Succession that they will not surrender it; and that this doctrine which they thus hold, really implies all that the Church party claim!

With this stab under the fifth rib, given " most affectionately " to the Evangelical party by a conscientious Evangelical in a letter to his own " dear Bishop," the General Convention of 1868 met; and it is not difficult to perceive in its action how much effect all the " agitation " of the previous year had produced.

The demands of the agitators were fourfold.

First, a relaxation of the Canon on Intrusion, or what may be called the Tyng Canon.

Secondly, a relaxation of the Canon against the ministrations of any but Episcopal Clergy in our Churches, which may be called the Hubbard Canon.

Thirdly, a Revision of the Prayer-Book, so as to take out the *Germs of Romanism,* or allow the Evangelicals to use alternative forms whenever they did not like what is now required to be said.

Fourthly, that something should be done to put down Ritualism.

And they were totally defeated on all four.

First, as to the Tyng Canon, which cost many more words than it was worth. Mr. Tyng himself was present, and remarkably active—every seat in the Convention being furnished gratuitously with a copy of the thick pamphlet containing the account of his trial. By a curious coincidence, the Church in which the debate and decision took place was the same in which he was " admonished " by his Bishop, in pursuance of the verdict and sentence of the court. The greater part of the pertinacity shown in attempting to amend that Canon, had nothing at all to do with the Tyng case; and of all the speakers on the floor during that long and repeated debate, young Mr. Tyng's course of action was upheld, excused, or defended, by not one—absolutely *not one*. Instead of showing any disposition to nullify the law, even Ohio declared that in no Diocese was there a more honest determination to obey the Canons than in Ohio; and yet where is there an " Evangelical" Diocese, if it be not Ohio? The climax, however, came from Old Virginia, which used to be regarded as an Evangelical pillar as strong as Ohio. It was a clerical deputy from Virginia who showed the intolerable mischiefs which were sure to flow from practices like Mr. Tyng's, even when indulged in from the purest motives; and by way of giving an inimitable touch to the satire of facts, he quoted at large a case that happened among the Presbyterians, where " preaching the Gospel " after that free-and-easy fashion had produced a local feud of seventeen years' duration, and had compelled the enactment of a rule among them which was the precise equivalent of our Canon, and is in force among Presbyterians to this day ! Mephistopheles himself could not have thought of anything more cutting than that. As might have been expected, the General Convention obstinately refused to amend the Canon at all, even when the advocates of some change had succeeded in gaining the reluctant consent of the Committee on Canons ; and the whole subject was " indefinitely postponed."

Secondly, as to the Hubbard Canon. The feeling in regard to Mr. Hubbard was very different from that in regard to Mr. Tyng. There was about the former a simple-hearted earnestness, an amiable and enthusiastic wrong-headedness, to which Mr. Tyng could lay no claim ; and the exciting scenes of the Revival going on about him at the time of his action, were very different from the croquet-playing on Saturday evening which preceded Mr. Tyng's Sunday display before the Methodists of New Brunswick. Moreover, Mr Hubbard had saved all possible trouble by agreeing to a statement of the facts ; and he had not yet been found guilty. The court did not announce its decision until long after the General Convention had adjourned. But the pleas urged in his behalf were well understood ; and, far from relaxing the terms of the Canon, the General Convention screwed it up a little tighter, and blocked with special care all the verbal rat-holes through which the Jesuitical interpretations of Mr. Hubbard's friends had attempted to enter and eat out the heart of the Canon itself. This being done, it was of no consequence what the court should do with Mr. Hubbard; and their letting him off because the framing of his presentment was a botch is of no importance to any one but himself. The hair-splitting technicalities by which alone he was acquitted will be of small comfort to a conscientious man, especially when viewed in the light afforded by the action of the General Convention. In this protracted and repeated discussion, too, the time and attention of the House were chiefly consumed by other amendments than those connected with the Hubbard case ; and among all the speakers, there was found to approve of Mr. Hubbard's course, *not one*.

Thirdly, as to Prayer-Book revision, to afford relief to the Low-Churchmen. There was only one attempt to do this, during the whole Convention. A layman from Kansas moved to strike out, from the

22

form in the Ordination of Priests beginning, " Receive the Holy Ghost,"
the words : "Whose sins thou dost forgive, they are forgiven ; and whose
sins thou dost retain, they are retained." No sooner was the motion
stated, than it was moved and seconded to lay it on the table ; which
motion was instantly carried—apparently not a little to the surprise and
indignation of the layman from Kansas. And so strong was the feeling
against any such action, that, a few days after, that same layman, having
the floor on another subject, took the occasion to explain that " it was
not *his* wish that the Prayer-Book should be altered in any sense ;" and
to cap the climax, it was a lay deputy from *Virginia* who moved " that,
in the judgment of this convention it is inexpedient to alter the Book
of Common Prayer." The only proposals for alteration that could even
obtain a hearing, were from the other side ! On this subject, therefore,
—the one on which the pamphlets had made their greatest efforts—
their friends in the House were not strong enough even to make a fight.
And how could they ? The pamphlets had expressed that, for two or
three hundred years, Evangelicals, while claiming to possess the only
pure and vital religion in the Church, had been constantly practising
prevarication and equivocation, mental reservation, the using of words
in a non-natural sense, compromising honor and morality, "teaching"
their children " to lie " whenever they taught them the Church Catechism
and so forth ; and that after doing all this most piously and pertina-
ciously for two hundred years or more, their consciences were now so
tender that they must have immediate relief, or they would surely
plunge into schism. What a wonderful kind of piety it is, to be sure !
During all this time, by its own account, it has prevaricated, equivocated,
compromised honor and morality, and what not, rather than commit
schism ; but now it has changed its mind, and—its conscience being
at present very tender—it will commit schism rather than equivocate
and compromise honor and morality any longer ! It is hard that such
true piety should be put to any such alternative as that. And it is no
wonder that piety of so peculiar a description should not have been
thought, by General Convention, worthy of special exceptional legislation.

Fourthly, as to the putting down of Ritualism, the battle was longer
and stronger, because the Evangelicals had many allies who by no
means belong to their party. But even the combined strength was of
none effect. The minority report, which condemned certain specified
things by name, could not pass ; so those specified things are not condemned. The majority report, which condemned certain general principles, without going into details, and thus could be made to mean
anything or nothing, could not pass ; and thus no general principle of
Ritualism was condemned. In the resolution adopted, not a particle
of additional power was given to the Bishops beyond what they had
before ; so that it amounted to just nothing at all. And in the Pastoral
Letter, though a general phrase bore against Ritualistic excesses, yet
when all the facts are weighed, its true worth will not be mistaken.
The original draft of a Pastoral Letter, which spoke out against the
Ritualists in a style that would have suited the " agitators," was *thrown*

out bodily. The attempt to pass the famous " Declaration " of the twenty-eight Bishops, as an act of the House of Bishops, *failed.** The condemnation of erroneous views supposed to be taught by Ritualists, was so ingeniously framed as really to condemn errors that are held by nobody that we ever heard of. Viewed in this light the phrase condemning Ritualistic *excesses* amounted to nothing at all. So on this point the defeat of the Evangelicals was as total as on any other.

Nay, the course of events had all the effect of a practical joke turning universal laughter upon the opponents of Ritualism. For whereas it was supposed that some members voted to remove the sessions from Trinity Chapel (where it was very difficult to hear), chiefly to get rid of the mild Ritualism of a surpliced choir ; they found themselves, when moved, not only in the Church where Mr. Tyng was sentenced, but also before a beautiful white marble Altar, and a large Altar-cross between two candlesticks with candles. And, on the very day when the decisive vote was taken, the feast of SS. Simon and Jude, there had been an early celebration at that Altar, with candles burning, and a goodly company of communicants present, some of whom were devoted Evangelicals a few years ago, but now rejoice that they have found a more excellent way. There were few present who did not perceive and enjoy the exquisite irony of the position. And the beauty of it was, that it was entirely unintentional. The committee which selected the Church of the Transfiguration solely for its acoustic properties, had no Ritualistic leaning. On the contrary, when it was resolved to use that Church, one of them sounded the rector as to whether those articles could not be removed. His answer was very manly and proper. He said that if he had offered his Church to the General Convention, he should feel it his duty to make it acceptable to them ; but since they had come to ask him for the use of it, they must take it as they found it, and nothing should be removed. And so it was. And —except one passing allusion—the " Ritualism " which they had before their eyes was not unfavorably commented on during the whole of the discussion on the subject.

As the Evangelicals were totally defeated in the General Convention 'of 1868 on all the four points they made, it was to be expected that— if they were consistent—a schism should startle the Church forthwith. The Moderates had persuaded the Radicals to postpone the attempt, in hope of some favorable action by the General Convention. That expectation was utterly, ignominiously, disappointed. The Radicals now had the argument all their own way. But the schism did not come. The House of Bishops, with a tender and politic regard for the feelings of the disappointed ones, on the last day of the session suddenly made them a present of a Low-Church Missionary Bishop, whose election was carried in the Lower House. Instead of an outburst,

---

* It is most gratifying to know that the debate in the House of Bishops on this subject was on both sides worthy of that House, and that the harmony which in the end prevailed was in no small degree due to the wise churchmanlike counsels and touching appeals of the Presiding Bishop.

therefore, there was an entire calm ; and that, too, although *five* new
Dioceses were either admitted or consented to at that Convention, of
which the Evangelicals got *not one.*

At the first anniversary of the Evangelical Knowledge Society thereafter the Moderates felt so strong that an attempt was made to wipe
out the damaging effects of the Radical pamphlets by a Resolution
" that the work of the Society in largely publishing and circulating the
Prayer-Book meets with the approval of the Society ; " and recom-
mending also " the circulation of a compendium of its history, to show
its source and its evangelical character." But if the Moderates were
found to prevail in the General Councils of the Church, the Radicals
had the mastery in their partisan gatherings ; and the resolution was
so strongly objected to as reflecting on the author of the tract on
" Romanizing Germs," that it was finally *withdrawn.* This was tan-
tamount to an indorsement of that pink pamphlet by the party.

It was not long before another pamphlet of the same kidney was
issued from the office of *The Episcopalian* in Philadelphia, *Prayer-
Book versus Prayer-Book,* in which it was stoutly denied that the discovery of Romanizing Germs was a sudden or a new thing. It said :

" This discovery has not been sudden, nor is it of to-day. There are
a great many in the Evangelical ranks who have been aware all along
that there are certain words, expressions, and usages in the Offices,
that, if taken in their *natural and grammatical sense,* would inculcate
error. Impressed with this fact, they have never taken them in this
sense. They have always explained them away. They were *taught
so to do at their Low-Church Seminaries.* . . . Every Evangelical Clergyman remembers how his Theological Professor labored at
expositions, *e.g.,* of the Baptismal Service for Infants ; and to-day
there is not one of them who will take up that service, and use certain
expressions in their literal and grammatical sense."

This reiterated charge of wholesale, deliberate, chronic, and conscious dishonesty in the use of our standard formularies, has never been
disproved by the Moderates, and never can be ; and in this one fact is
involved, really, the sentence of death on the whole Evangelical Party.
The new Papal Dogma has " conquered History " only because the
Pope excommunicates all who refuse to swallow it. The Moderates
have no such power. If their true position were demonstrated only by
their opponents, the proof might be resisted on the ground that it was
due to party hostility ; but when the confession is made over and over
again by their own friends, and the proof is published by their own
presses, and sold over their own counters, and maintained triumphantly
in their own partisan societies, and there is not even an attempt to
gainsay it, the total extinction of that party among honest men is only
a question of time. The Moderates will die strangled by the bowstring
put round their necks by their Radical friends ; and the Radicals—
honest and outspoken as they are—will cease to exist, because by their
open confession it is clear that they hold certain notions which were

never held by any branch of the Church in any age or country, and are irreconcilably opposed to Holy Scripture as interpreted by the Primitive and Undivided Church—nay, they clearly refuse to accept certain parts of the Catholic Creed of Christendom itself. We have given the more space to those pamphlets for this very reason. From the time of their appearance and acceptance by the leading organs of the party, that party has been like a little fish left at high-water mark on a sand-bank by the receding tide; not yet dead, but sure to die. Its subsequent acts are but like the spasmodic yet vain endeavors of the little fish to jerk itself back again into the water, but which only exhaust it the sooner by wearing out its small remainder of life among the drying sands.

The Radicals, knowing the logical strength of their position in their own party, now determined to force the fighting, and called the Chicago meeting for the following June (1869)—their object being to commit the whole party to the policy of "Revision or Schism." Not one of the Low-Church Bishops, however, belonged to the Radical party. Lambeth had cured them, if there were any who really needed the cure; and before that meeting, the Bishop of Ohio issued a letter (to which we shall refer again), candidly acknowledging that the "soul-destroying heresy of Baptismal Regeneration" (meaning thereby that persons baptized in infancy were sure of salvation without ever experiencing either repentance or faith in their later years), was not, and never had been, held by High-Churchmen at all. He earnestly opposed the Revision policy. Nearly all the Evangelical Bishops took the same course; so that while *The Episcopalian* was exhorting its friends to observe the 15th of June as a day of extemporaneous prayers for the Chicago meeting, "that its deliberations may result in setting us free from whatever taint of Popery or error may lie in our Prayer-Book," that same paper admitted that all who went to that meeting would go "without the approval of their Bishops."

After all the noise made in advance, the Chicago meeting was a ridiculous failure, there being only some thirty members present, clerical and lay, and not a Bishop among them. The President was a layman; and even in this small squad, the President on taking his seat utterly denounced the idea of a schism, with only the causes which then seemed to lead to it. "This," he said, "was not a meeting for such a purpose. He could never have been one to attend a meeting for such a purpose." A clerical speaker declared that "Secession was no remedy for the evils they deplored. Enlightened Christianity already groaned under the weight of secessions and separations." It was evident that their alternative of "Revision or Schism" had already lost its latter half, and the true alternative was, Revision or—nothing at all.

But the Radicals—short of a resolution to secede—had everything their own way. One Clergyman declared that "for twenty-four years he had never used the Baptismal Service without a certain qualm of conscience in regard to its phraseology; and men older than himself stood in the same position, and were within hearing of his voice." Dr. Newton said, that "if a Clergyman were to be deposed because his

conscience would not allow him to use the word 'regenerate' in the
Baptismal Service, they would not long have to wait for an opening out
of their difficulties." Dr. C. W. Andrews confessed that " the great
blunder of the English Reformation " was the construction of the Baptismal Service with this " regeneration " in it (and, if we remember
aright, he showed on another occasion that Low-Churchmen had invented no less than seven different modes of explaining it away, but
none of them was entirely satisfactory). A layman's remark, that they
did not contemplate secession, but that they did contemplate " being
driven out," was received " with cheers." On the contrary, resolutions
pledging loyalty in all matters of " faith, doctrine, worship, long-estab-
lished rites, ceremonies, and usages of the P. E. Church, as our bright
and uncompromising Protestant Apostolic inheritance," were not only
declared to be out of order—the offerer being interrupted divers times
while speaking—but the Rev. Mr. Cheney went so far as to " hope that
those resolutions would not be suffered to go before the public." Mr.
Cheney's remarks, in view of his subsequent course (his presentment
was formally made four days after), are well worthy of note :

" When the young men now demanded revision, they but followed
out logically what the Bishops had taught them in other days. He saw
the students of Alexandria and Gambier, and they were almost unanimous for revision. The men who had been taught by Bishops Mc-
Ilvaine and Johns were unanimous for revision. As Bishop McIlvaine's
Letter [against revision] and character had much influence in the com-
munity, it seemed proper that they who demanded revision should put
themselves right. . . . As for himself, he was not going out of the
Episcopal Church. No man could put him out. He would fight out
the battle in the Church ; and if they all left him, he would climb to
the mountain-top of communion with his God, and claim that *he* was
the Episcopal Church ! "

The meeting ended in passing four resolutions, 1st, in favor of Revision (it appeared that the Offices of Baptism, Confirmation, Holy
Communion, Ordination, and Institution were all to be altered) ; 2d, to
agitate, agitate, agitate ; 3d, that their Evangelical " *American Church
Missionary Society* should extend its work to Foreign Missions, or
another new Society should be started for that purpose ; " and 4th, in
favor of uniting with outsiders in the Bible Society and other " great
national institutions."

The advocates of " schism " were naturally somewhat disgusted ; and
one of them pointed the moral of the Chicago failure by renouncing
the ministry of the Church. The letter was written close upon the
adjournment of the Chicago meeting ; and the difficulty in his mind as
to Baptismal Regeneration was thus expressed : " I cannot consent to
address God in my prayers in terms which would be falsehood if I
used them in my preaching." Bishop McIlvaine answered it, displac-
ing him according to Canon, but adding : " I cannot but have a sincere and affectionate sympathy with you in your circumstances, nor

will I withhold the expression of my regret that in the chief cause of
your action the laws are what they are.   I am decidedly in favor of
some change in the Prayer-Book, so that by some change of words, or
some provision of other optional words, the difficulty in your mind
may be avoided."

A change came o'er the spirit of the dream of other Evangelical
Bishops also, about this time.   Among the Radicals whom they had
so successfully embarrassed or baffled at Chicago—for even the secular
press laughed at the smallness of the meeting, and the inability of the
little company of thirty to agree entirely among themselves—among
this small number, we say, or those who sympathized with them, were
men of great importance.   And when Mr. ——'s private chaplain " se-
ceded," and Mr. ——'s private chapel no longer was reckoned as part
of the Diocese of Ohio, and it was found that wealthy laymen were
likely to sympathize with Mr. ——, the Evangelical Bishops, with the
wisdom of the serpent, began to take a somewhat different view of the
situation.   Bishop ——, in his second letter to Bishop McIlvaine on
the subject, says : " *We cannot afford to lose* those from our ranks who
are decidedly and conscientiously in favor of certain liturgical changes
and modifications ; " and he is therefore willing to advocate some revision of the Prayer-Book in order to keep them—to make, indeed, large
suggestions of revision ; but not that *he* felt the need of any change
himself.   By October, significant intimations from Ohio were published,
showing that Bishop McIlvaine and Bishop Bedell — and probably
other Bishops—had come to the conclusion that " the principle of *omission* or *alternate phrases*" might be extended to the Baptismal Service.   At least, it " was seriously contemplated, even by those highest
in authority and influence."   It was plain that the Radicals could not
be ignored.   They were too strong and too important for that.   They
were evidently bent on a general rally, too, at the first occasion ; and
they must be met on their own ground, for a trial of strength.

In November, therefore, at the annual meetings in Philadelphia, there
was a pitched battle between the Moderates headed by Dr. Alexander
H. Vinton and the Radicals under the leadership of Dr. Cotton Smith
—the Bishops carefully keeping themselves out of the fray.   Dr. Vinton
was the Chairman of a Committee of Observation, which had been appointed " to discover the duties of the hour, and the means of discharging them."   As Chairman, he made a brief verbal report, in which he
stated that the Committee had unanimously agreed to report that " they
had nothing to suggest, and nothing to say on the subject assigned to
their consideration "—which was not only cool, but rather contempt-
uous.   As one of the Radical organs described the effect of it, " This
announcement startled the large number of Clergy and Laity present,
and excited a great deal of feeling.   It was hard to determine whether
disappointment, amazement, or disgust predominated."   Notwithstanding the assertion of unanimity, Dr. Cotton Smith, one of the Committee, presented a minority report, proposing the organization of an
Evangelical Brotherhood, the details of which were read by the Rev.
Dr. Muhlenberg.   Discussion became lively.   It was proposed to re-

commit the subject to the same Committee, that they might sit again, and think better of it. But that was speedily rendered impossible, for one member after another rose and resigned his place on that Committee.

The debates were very sharp and protracted, the Moderates doing the larger part of the talking, and the disagreements were as marked as possible. No more stunning contrarieties have ever been developed in any discussion between High and Low Church, than were here uttered among Low-Church themselves. Mr. Cheney denounced the two Canons (the Young Tyng Canon and the Hubbard Canon) in strong language, declaring that a failure to recognize non-episcopal ordination as " a divine ordination," or a failure to accord to it " true validity " was " a sin against the HOLY GHOST ! " Dr. Vinton, on the contrary, said that Evangelical men could not be united in the effort to repeal those two Canons. He added that " some Evangelical men prefer the Prayer-Book as it is, and have a way satisfactory to themselves of explaining away its language. Their consciences do not trouble them. They will never join in any effort to revise a word or line of the Liturgy. . . . much less will they ever fight for a new Prayer-Book." But while the discussion on Revision was going on vigorously, it leaked out, and began to be whispered round, that the Evangelical Bishops had made up their minds, at a private meeting just holden in New York, to change front on the subject of Revision. At length the statement was openly made on the one side, and flatly contradicted on the other ; and as the dates of the differing informations given to the two sides were as near together as to day and yesterday, one may easily understand how sharp the skirmishing was.

But the Radicals were right. The Evangelical Bishops knew perfectly well that their best milch kine were on the Radical side of the house, and they must do something to encourage them to let down their milk ; for if these magnates should desert to the Presbyterians, what would become of the exchequer ? " Justification by faith only " could not be expected to risk a loss of three or four truly pious millionaires at one fell swoop. The Circular of the Nine Evangelical Bishops was already in type at the very time the Moderates were confidently denying the possibility of such a thing. When the meeting came to a vote, the Radicals carried their resolutions in favor of " a full and thorough revision of the Book of Common Prayer," by the handsome majority of 74 to 46. Moreover, rejoicing in their strength, they passed another Resolution calling on the Nine Bishops to " consider whether there be grounds for presenting for trial any Bishop or Bishops who may be alleged to hold, and to have taught. . . . doctrines contrary to those held by the P. E. C., with the view of having the real doctrines of our Church affirmed and settled by the authority of its highest judicature." This was more than the Nine had bargained for. After this resolution had been footballed through the newspapers for some months without doing anybody any harm, one of the Nine, endorsed by another of the Nine, published a letter showing the utter absurdity of the idea, and especially, that the calling

on the whole Nine to engage in the business rendered it practically an
impossibility. Indeed, the impotence of this trial‑shot was only
laughed at from the first ; and the Bishop of —— must have had some
difficulty in keeping his face straight long enough to write a serious
answer to the proposal. *The Episcopalian* newspaper, however, could
not see the joke ; but fairly boiled over with " bitter disappointment
and provocation," and gave the Bishops some " plain talk, some strong
and blunt Saxon "—hoping that its proposed new " Reformation will
not stop till complete Revolution is made in the Constitution of the
Church—until every vestige of Prelacy is swept away ! " which is very
likely, seeing that no change can be made in that Constitution without
twice receiving the vote of the House of Bishops itself !

But to return : soon after the November meeting the Circular of the
Nine Bishops was in everybody's hands. In it, they kindly provided
both for the Moderates and the Radicals. As Moderates themselves,
they say : " We have always been fully persuaded that our formularies
of faith and worship, in their just interpretation, embody the truth of
Christ, are warranted by the teaching of Holy Scripture, and are a
faithful following of the doctrines professed and defended by our
Anglican Reformers "—which is very fair, old-fashioned, High-Church
doctrine. But they find " very serious indications of a state of mind
among many of the Clergy and Laity. . . . contemplating action
most earnestly to be deprecated " [*i.e., schism*]. And it had become
" painfully evident that many in our Church are so burdened and distressed in the use of certain expressions in our formularies " that something ought to be done " in brotherly kindness and charity for their relief." The result was, that " *if alternate phrases* or *some equivalent
modification* in the Office for the Ministration of *Baptism of Infants*
were allowed, the pressing necessity would be met, and a measure of
relief would be afforded, of great importance to the peace and unity of
the Church." The Circular concluded by hoping that " the next General Convention " would have such " large-heartedness," etc., as to
" consent to the relief already indicated."

It was not many days, however, before the Bishop of New York sent
out his noble *Pastoral* in reply to the Nine. Its note rang out like a
trumpet, giving no uncertain signal for battle : and every sensible man
knew from that moment, if he had not known before, that the giving of
any *such* " measure of relief " was about as likely as to see the sun rise
in the west. With a perseverance akin to despair, however, the Radicals in their organs, pamphlets, agents, etc., went on " agitating " and
getting memorials signed, to be sent in to General Convention, and
comforted themselves with the dream that something would surely be
done this time. Thus the little fish, after a desperate twitch of its own
tail, gets, from the height of six inches above the sand, a momentary
glimpse of the retreating sea, and believes that in just a few minutes it
will escape the dry death, and bathe once more in the waters of life all
over !

Meanwhile, a very different part of the same great battle was being
fought out in a very different way. At every turn of the contest, the

Evangelicals brought up the Ritualists as their great grievance, after all. They could not see why, if Ritualists who believed the standards of the Church in their plain literal sense were tolerated, the Radicals could not be tolerated also in denying them. It was a queer parallel to run, to be sure ; but then those brethren have a queer way of putting things, now and then. Their parallel lines generally cross one another at right angles. And there were many among the Moderates and among the old-fashioned High-Churchmen who thought that, by a combination among themselves and the Radicals, the Ritualists could be put down once for all, and then all the rest would be " a happy family "—as it was well known they had always been before. Accordingly, in a very quiet way, preparation was made, in the General Convention of 1868, for a campaign in that direction. The list of offences for which a clergyman may be put on trial was—with very little remark—altered, by inserting " any act which involves a breach of his Ordination vows "—just for symmetry, as it was urged, because this was already one of the things for which a bishop could be tried, and therefore it ought to apply also to priests and deacons. It was put through under old-fashioned High-Church leadership, but—as it seemed to us at the time—by a sort of tacit mutual understanding with brethren on the other side, who, if they had thought the edge of the new enactment was to be turned against themselves, would have made the air vocal with the most sonorous remonstrances and protestations. But if it was meant only for the Ritualists, they had no objection.

Hardly two months after the adjournment of the General Convention, and actually before its Journal was published, the Bishop of Ohio began to put it in operation against one of his clergy, who was guilty of the enormity of having a surpliced choir and processional hymns : which things the bishop assured him were " against the laws and usages of our Church ; " informed him that this was his bishop's " godly judgment " to which he had vowed obedience ; called his attention to the new legislation of General Convention making him liable for trial if he disobeyed ; and summoning him, in fine, to instant surrender. Not a little noise was made when people began to see the operation of this innocent-looking, " symmetrical " change in the Canon ; and when able counsel from other dioceses came on to help the faithful Ohio brother to fight the battle, old-fashioned High-Churchmen from New York came out with a pamphlet to sustain the intolerable tyranny attempted in Ohio, thus strengthening the impression that a mutual understanding had existed from the first in regard to the whole campaign. We shall do nothing more than merely allude to this subject here. It is, by itself, more than enough for a whole article. But nothing is more intolerably preposterous than the assumption that any and everything a bishop chooses to say to one of his clergy is " a godly judgment " or a " godly admonition," which is to be implicitly obeyed at once on pain of punishment. Bishops are not all wise men. All bishops are not equally wise at all times. It is a conceivable case that the command given by a bishop should be, in point of fact, not " a godly judgment," but an ungodly want of judgment ; and what becomes of the vow of

Canonical obedience then ? If it is not a supposable case that a bishop should show an ungodly want of judgment, how can we possibly justify our opposition to the Bishop of Rome? Or how can we prove that the Bishop of Rome is not quite as likely to be infallible as the Bishop of Ohio?

But to continue our sketch of facts. The first court organized to try the Rev. Mr. Tate broke down of its own accord, on the first day, because a clergyman had been appointed as one of the court who was not eligible according to the Canons of the diocese. The Diocesan Convention then greatly altered the Canon, restricting the number from whom the court should be drawn, and giving the bishop the power to appoint the president of the court. A new court was thereupon assembled, and after four days' debate about its own existence, declared itself dissolved, owing to irregularities in its own formation, and prominent among those alleged was the fact that the bishop had wrongly excluded one name from the drawing, so that the selection was from twenty-three names instead of from twenty-four, as the Canon required. The laugh at this double break-down was getting to be rather severe upon Ohio; but it was mingled with indignation when letters written for the public by the president of the court (appointed by the bishop), revealed the fact—with apparently an utter unconsciousness of its turpitude—that the majority of the court had made up their minds to condemn Mr. Tate before hearing a word of evidence in the case, and had likewise settled that his sentence should be "suspension from the ministry!" If this is a specimen of the "godly judgment" of Ohio, what a wonder it is that we do not all render implicit obedience at the first word of command! "Obedience can never be wrong," may be the voice of Ohio; it is also the voice of the Jesuits calling upon all "Catholics" to submit at once to the Infallibility decrees of the Council of the Vatican. Both doctrine and practice are pure Ultramontane Popery.

Mr. Tate finally, of his own accord—as he had professed himself willing to do from the first—yielded to the bishop the two points of ritual objected to by him, but under protest as to the bishop's views of law, couched in these words: "Claiming for myself, that, while using them I conscientiously believed, and still firmly believe, that I have violated no law of the Church or vow of my Ordination: "—a protest by no means satisfactory to the bishop. And the hornet's nest of troubles likely to grow out of the attempt to crowd down the throats of the clergy by main force these new views of "Canonical obedience" and "godly judgments," has been found sufficient to prevent any similar attempt in any other diocese. In the only other where there was a probability of it, the bishop very wisely stopped short of attempting an Ecclesiastical trial; and the ill-feeling found vent in that meanest and most sneaking method of manifesting ill-will—the refusing to admit into Convention the laity of a parish whose clergyman is unpopular, but whom they cannot put upon his trial for any Canonical offence.

The attempt to put down Ritualism in that way has thus proved to be a ridiculous abortion.

But ecclesiastical trials are a two-edged weapon, and one edge may cut deep while the other is too dull to cut at all. The Cheney case was the poetical response to the Tate case. The latter began early in January, 1869; the Cheney case was not begun until some months afterward; so that if there was any cry of " persecution." it was an effective reply to ask : " *Who began it?*" While the Radicals were holding their ridiculous little meeting in Chicago, of thirty persons, the preparations were being completed; and four days after it adjourned, the presentment was made. And there was no break-down on the part of the court. After every possible resource of tactics was exhausted, including injunctions from the civil courts, carried up to the highest court in the State, the result came at last; and he who had defiantly courted discipline from the first, was formally and canonically deposed from the ministry of the Church of God.

It was a fatal blunder on the part of the Radicals. It will be remembered that at their little Chicago meeting, the idea of their being " *driven out of the Church* " was received " with cheers." Mr. Cheney's resistance and defiance of the clear and unquestionable law of the Church, was *intended* to bring down upon him a punishment which, it was calculated, would be sufficient to " fire the heart " of the Evangelical clergy and laity, and thus rush them into a secession. The attempt was made ; but it failed. A few clergymen went to Chicago to officiate for Mr. Cheney during his preliminary suspension. Circulars of " moral support "—so-called—were signed and circulated (about sixty clerical names, we believe, formed the longest list ; but there were several millionaires among the laity). As an agitation of any magnitude, however, the thing fell dead. It is one thing to suffer as a martyr : another thing to suffer as a mere wilful breaker of the law. Mr. Cheney played for the former stake, but won only the latter. The general verdict, even among his own party, is, " Served him right."

We must now go back once more to take up another dropped stitch. At the little Chicago meeting in 1869 it appears that there was a Committee on Revision formed (or already existing), of which the Rev. Geo. E. Thrall was the chairman, there being ten members in all. This committee were to go to work in good earnest to revise the Prayer-Book, which was accordingly subdivided among them in sections, and they wrote to their friends in all quarters asking to be informed " what were the alterations which they desired." This looked like business, and saddles the party with a heavy share of responsibility for the ultimate result. One of the speakers, however, was blunt enough to say, that " however this revised Prayer-Book might please themselves, it was questionable whether it would gratify the General Convention. He wanted to know whether, if such a book was prepared, they were ready to stand or fall by it. *He* thought that Evangelical Christians would rally to their support." This was the beginning of the movement which resulted in the new *Union Prayer-Book* which made its appearance last summer—about that period of the season when dogs do most generally run mad. There never was a clearer illustration of the old adage, *Quem Deus vult perdere, prius dementat.*

That book is the best ever sent forth by the Evangelicals, because it is the most honest. It goes further, and does better, than even the Radical pamphlets from which we have quoted so largely. Its beauties are too numerous to be exhausted, should we give a whole volume to their contemplation. But we shall specify only two points, as the best of all.

So long as the Evangelicals accepted the standards of the Church, and claimed to hold them in their true historical sense, it was a work of no little difficulty to convince them clearly of vital error. Their views might be mixed, or muddy, or ill-balanced, or defective, or a variety of other things : but it was rather hard to call them heretical. And so long as they were not clearly heretical, it would have been a violation of charity to call them so, no matter how firmly we might have been persuaded of the fact ourselves.

Now nothing is more unanimously agreed on among all branches of the Catholic Church, than that it is *heresy* to deny any part of the Catholic Creed—that Creed which has been accepted everywhere, always, and by all. If the Union Prayer-Book, therefore, wished to keep any character for orthodoxy, it would have left the Creed untouched. But its compilers were happily too honest for that. They have omitted from that Creed two things, which show where the root of the whole difficulty has been from the beginning. Their opposition to Baptismal Regeneration is found, not only in their baptismal office, where we should have expected to see it of course : but they have omitted *entirely* from the Creed the words, " I ACKNOWLEDGE ONE BAPTISM FOR THE REMISSION OF SINS." This is an open confession that their baptismal difficulty is due to their being *heretics* in denying an article of the Catholic Creed; and that *they know it*. In like manner, their other great point, of the validity of non-episcopal orders, is really due to the fact that there is one of the Four Notes of the Church as contained in the Catholic Creed, which *they* do not believe in. Accordingly the honest and intelligent compilers of the Union Prayer-Book have utterly omitted the work APOSTOLIC as a descriptive title of THE CHURCH : which is flat heresy again, openly and unblushingly proclaimed before the whole world.

On publishing this precious book, two clergymen, with consistent honesty, renounced the Ministry of the Church, and then, on the first Sunday of September, set up a meeting-house of their own, with their new book : and awaited the great sensation that should result, when all the Evangelical Denominations of Protestants should flock to their standard. Alas for the vanity of human expectations ! A few articles in the papers, and these bold heretical heroes were forgotten ! The Protestant denominations went on quietly as before, just as if nothing had happened : and within a few months, an unpaid mortgage turned one of them out of his new brick meeting-house into some Hall, and the other slipped into some agency or other in order to eke out a living.

But this was a beautiful preparation in September for the General Convention that met in October. Such an unanswerable manifestation of the real nature of the evil that had been painfully festering in the Church for so long, and had at length come to *such* a head as the heretical Union Prayer-Book, was death to all hopes of "Revision," or "omission," or "alternate phrases." Some still kept a stiff upper lip, and whistled loud to keep their courage up, and memorials were to be forwarded in numbers nobody ever knew how great. But the Nine Bishops who had committed themselves to the idea that General Convention would grant "this measure of relief" were in a very awkward predicament, knowing their game to be hopeless, and not seeing how they could escape an ignominious failure.

All these circumstances must be taken into consideration, in order to be able to estimate truly the meaning and weight of the *Declaration on Baptismal Regeneration* which has so wonderfully puzzled our newspaper commentators.

The Nine knew perfectly well that it was utterly idle to attempt Revision, or alternate phrases, or to touch the Prayer-Book in any way likely to please their friends. Nothing that came within ten miles of that sort of thing would be looked at for an instant in the Lower House, to say nothing of the Upper. The Bishops "went into council" on the matter, therefore—shut out their own secretaries, banished their door-keepers below stairs, shut their windows, stuffed the key-hole, barred the bottom of the stair-case—and then began to talk over the situation. The Nine begged piteously that something — however slight—should be done, to get them out of their predicament. If they went home without anything, they would lose their hold over their fractious people, who had been making this long disturbance about their consciences, and nobody knew how much mischief would happen. The Nine were evidently in a very tight place, and in danger of a heavy fall : and their brethren, after long debates and much persuasion, concluded to try and agree on something which would "let them down easily," as the phrase is, and break no bones. Several forms of Declaration were discussed, but were open to the serious objection that they might be supposed to mean something definite. At last, this danger being avoided as wholly as is possible in human language, they sent forth the following, in a shape which binds nobody :

"We, the subscribers, Bishops of the Protestant Episcopal Church in the United States, being asked, in order to the quieting of the consciences of sundry members of the said Church, to declare our conviction as to the meaning of the word 'regenerate' in the Offices for the Ministration of Baptism of Infants, do declare that, in our opinion, the word 'regenerate' is not there so used as to determine that a moral change in the subject of baptism is wrought in the Sacrament."

And the Pastoral Letter, after quoting it, goes on to say that "This declaration was made in the loving hope and confidence that many consciences might thus forever be freed from false impressions, which have been prevalent, concerning the teachings of the Church as respects spiritual religion and personal piety. . . . Baptism does not supersede

the necessity of repentance, of justifying faith in Christ, growth in
grace, and in that ' holiness without which no man shall see the Lord.' "

Now, after reading this over very carefully, let us go back to the
letter on the subject published by Bishop McIlvaine more than two
years before, to see what new comfort—if any—has been gained by
the Evangelicals in this " Declaration " of the House of Bishops. In
that letter, addressed privately to a Clergyman at the East, who was
disturbed by the cry for " Revision or Schism," and published in reply
to the urgent request of many, Bishop McIlvaine says, first of all, that
the fault found with the Prayer-Book might as well be found with the
Bible itself :

" Is not the need of explanation in some parts of the Prayer-Book, to
prevent erroneous impressions, the result of the closeness with which
they copy the very words of Scripture, without explanatory comment?
For instance, the words in the ordination of a Presbyter, to which so
much objection is made—are they not almost the very words of John,
xx. 22, 23 ? and do they not need as much explanation as they stand in
his pages, as they do in the Prayer-Book ? "

This is clear and satisfactory, and unanswerable as against the " Revision or alternate phrases " which he and the rest of the Nine subsequently asked for. But next, as to the terrible error which the Evangelicals have all along professed to be so horribly afraid of, but which
nobody that we know of has ever held or taught, the Bishop of Ohio is as
clear and strong as possible—far *more* so indeed than the *Declaration*
of the House of Bishops. Speaking of regeneration as a *moral* change
—the being " transformed by the renewing of the mind "—the Bishop
says that it " is *not* found inseparably connected with Baptism, either
adult or infant, *by any, even the most advanced teachers of what is
currently called Baptismal Regeneration.* . . . Others, as *Romanists* and *Tractarians*, while applying to Baptismal Regeneration the
most exalted language, reduce it to the being *sacramentally* united to
the Church as the incarnation of Christ and depository of His grace,
and so made partaker of Him. To bring forth the fruits of the Spirit
is no necessary evidence of that regeneration. *I know of no class of
writers in the Anglican Church* who find the regeneration of all infants in Baptism in the sense of *an implantation of actual goodness*—
that is, a goodness which, as the child grows in age, will produce the
fruits of righteousness : " and he then quotes Bishop Bethell, and Moz-
ley at some length, showing that what Evangelicals so commonly and
obstinately insist that their opponents teach on this subject, is a " tremendous contradiction of experience," rendering Baptism " an un-
meaning, absurd, and incredible abortion."

Now compare this clear, vigorous, sweeping, outspoken language of
Bishop McIlvaine in 1869, with the cautiously guarded " Declaration "
of 1871 : and it will be found that the *only* semblance of an idea contained in the latter is precisely the same that was boldly and fully set
forth in the former. *What, then, have the Evangelicals gained?*

They have simply gained the privilege of the Japanese aristocracy—the honor of dying by their own hand.   It is said—we know not how correctly—that the form of opinion signed by the Bishops as their " Declaration " was in reality drawn up by the Rev. Dr. Andrews—the same who at Chicago declared that the putting of the word " regeneration " into the Baptismal Office was " the great blunder of the English Reformation ; "—the same who declared in the autumn of 1870 that " Baptismal Regeneration is the cancer of the Church," and that " there can be no peace until it is revised " out of the Prayer-book ; the same who published a pamphlet showing *seven* different ways of interpreting Baptismal Regeneration as meaning *no* Baptismal Regeneration, and declaring that none of them all was satisfactory : this same Dr. Andrews, it seems, is the one to draw up the mild, watered-down " Declaration " of 1871, which is a confession, on the part of the Evangelicals themselves, that all the hard things they have said on this subject, for generations past, against High-Churchmen, Tractarians, and even Romanists, are slanders ; that all the fault they have found with the Prayer-Book itself on this subject is groundless ; and that nobody has been to blame for all the trouble but their own narrow, blind, intolerant, obstinate selves.   All the Evangelical Bishops united in asking for this precious paper.   They begged hard for it.   They promised faithfully that, if their brethren would only give them this precious " Declaration," they would go back to their dioceses, and tell their friends who had the tender consciences that this was all they ought to ask, all they could expect, and that they must be contented with it, and be good quiet boys for the future.   And when it was all but unanimously signed—every Evangelical Bishop setting his name to it—their friends everywhere smiled and sang and shouted as if they had gotten a victory !   Bishop McIlvaine himself was so delighted that he writes of it, " We could hardly believe our senses."

But what has been the practical effect of it ?   Has it put new life into the Evangelical party ?   Were there any evidences of such a result thereafter, in either House ?   Not at all.   Not a lisp was heard in either House—not even a motion was made in any way whatever embodying any of the old Evangelical watchwords.   The Low-Church partisan gatherings ceased.   A calm as of death settled on the whole Evangelical business.   The party was as quiet as a Japanese gentleman is after he has accomplished " the happy despatch "—called in their language *hari-kari.*   The previous condition of the clamorous little party was like that of a loud-winged insect, transfixed on the pin of a naturalist and fastened tight to a board, whence for hours the air is filled with the noise of his restless but useless buzz : until at length a drop of sweet oil, judiciously applied to its head, changes its mind so suddenly that it " can hardly believe its senses," but is thenceforth content to buzz no more.

In plain words, the Evangelical party, as a tactical element in our Church politics, is henceforth dead ; and it is the " Declaration " that gave it the *coup de grace.*   From the moment of its appearance, that party disappeared, and was absorbed bodily into the old High-and-Dry party, the object of union being war upon the Ritualists. A letter of Bishop Cummins furnishes their motto : " *Toleration of Ritualists is treason towards God ; it is ruin to the Church.*" So far was this disposition for entire unity carried on the spot, that some of them threw out most tempting intimations that the separate partisan Societies, which are the darling jewels of the Evangelicals, would be given up—amalgamated with the general Institutions of the Church—if only some legislation against the Ritualists could be carried. So far indeed are their hearts weaned from delighting in the solitariness of those partisan " voluntary Societies,"—which have heretofore been their special joy, their pride and their boast, their banner of defiance and their citadel of strength—that their change of manner was so striking as to be now and then amusing. The Bishop of Lichfield was addressing the Board of Missions one evening, and the salient point of his speech was a glowing commendation of the American Church for *avoiding* " voluntary Societies," and committing her whole mission work, and all her other branches of practical operations, to *organic* instrumentalities, under the high sanction of the legislative power of the Church. His commendation was in reality a *censure* upon the whole theory and practice of the Low-Church party for twenty or thirty years past ; and all that time the Bishop of Ohio had been one of the leaders of that entire policy. Yet during that admirable speech, the venerable Bishop · of Ohio sat within two feet of the speaker, listening with a calm placidity of countenance truly beautiful : and when the speech was ended, the Bishop of Ohio—the senior Bishop present—rose, and moved " the thanks of the Board to the Lord Bishop of Lichfield for his admirable and instructive address "; and the vote was, of course, unanimous, nor were any complaints made by anybody. It was a worthy companion picture for the Altar-scene in the Church of the Transfiguration in 1868.

In what we have said, we would not be supposed to omit disingenuously a reference to Bishop McIlvaine's letter, printed in the London *Record*, giving his account of the way in which that " Declaration " business was transacted, and what the document really means. We do not wish to criticise a venerable Bishop needlessly : and therefore we take it for granted that, while writing parts of that *Record* letter, the good Bishop totally forgot the other letter he had written on the Baptismal question (quoted above) in 1869. On no other hypothesis is some of the language of the *Record* letter capable of any explanation whatever.

It so happened that we were in Baltimore on the day when that " Declaration " was sent down to astonish the Lower House and everybody else. We met one of the Bishops who signed it and asked him what it meant ? He said it meant just about nothing at all. We asked him then, Why were not the Bishops content to say just nothing at all ? He replied, that the Nine were in a very tight place, and pleaded so earnestly for *something*, no matter how little, with which they might pacify " tender consciences," that they had not the heart to refuse them. We then asked, Why they did not send the Nine to the

23

Catechism, where they would have seen that the " *Repentance* whereby they forsake sin, and *Faith* whereby they steadfastly believe the promises of God made to them in that Sacrament " are things that infants " cannot perform " by reason of their tender age : but that they are things which, " when they come to age, themselves are bound to perform ? " He laughed and said that that was, of course, all that the " Declaration " meant ; but that if the Evangelicals were content with a Declaration that manifestly meant nothing more than was in the Catechism already, it was " their own lookout." We replied, that we thought the House of Bishops ought to have had *more respect for itself* than to put forth a solemn Declaration which was either a truism, or would seem to mean something that was never intended. He admitted it ; expressed strong dislike of the whole thing ; said that he had been unable to sleep the night after signing it, owing to the uncomfortableness of his reflections ; but that it was purposely put in a form that could bind nobody ; that it was the shortest way out of a difficulty that troubled some of the brethren ; and he was confident that as it meant nothing, and was worth nothing, it would soon die and be forgotten. He was not the only Bishop whose signature of that document cost him a sleepless night and uncomfortable thoughts of his head upon his bed. But the account he gave of the business was about correct : and it is not worth while for either friend or foe to value that negative " opinion " at more than it is worth.

The Low-Church party, as a tactical element in Church politics, has now, as we have said, ceased to exist. There are only two parties left in the field : the High and Dry or Old Fogy High-Churchmen and the Advanced or Catholic party on the other. So rapid is the movement among us, that those who, a quarter of a century ago, were thought to be dominant in both Houses of General Convention, are now—nowhere : while the Catholic party—then not strong enough to be known or felt—are now, in the very first General Convention where the lines have been drawn in the new place, strong enough to defeat the fresh and formidable combination against them in a pitched battle, and will, before many years, command a full working majority in both Houses.

But though dead as a tactical element in our Church politics, it must not for a moment be supposed that the Evangelicals as individuals, as a school, as a clique, have disappeared. By no means. They have able men, strong parishes, societies, seminaries, newspapers, wealth in abundance, and a certain amount of liberality and zeal : but they have no future to look forward to, except that of further decay. They may build up Institutions, and endow them : but, in a few years, those Institutions will be ours, endowments and all. They may organize new parishes : but before long those parishes will be found to have sound Church rectors, or may need to call in even a Ritualist to prevent a death of inanition. They may educate and bring into the Ministry under Evangelical auspices many young men : but the irritating and insulting pledges as to " opinions " required of such men before they can draw their pittance—a narrow policy growing narrower by judicial blindness—is the best possible preparation for a change of ecclesiasti-

cal position as soon as they are in self-supporting parishes of their own.
Such changes are taking place from day to day : and the Evangelical
leaders know it.

We have alluded more than once to the extraordinary bitterness and
violence of language used by our leading Low-Churchmen concerning
their brethren in the same household of faith. Dr. ——'s well-known
speech will not be forgotten : that he would " as soon put his feet
within the pale of hell, as in a ritualistic menagerie," and that the
Church party are " frogs and lice," and the " children of the devil,"
while the Evangelicals are "the children of God." The author of
" Romanizing Germs " says of the doctrines of the Church : " They
result in an ecclesiastical organism, in an exclusive priesthood, in sacramental efficacy, in patristic authority ; which are to our eye the sure
signs of spiritual death, the marks of a candlestick whose light has gone
out, of a Church that has a name to live but is dead. . . . Romanism, like a subtle poison, is coursing through our body ecclesiastic.
Racking pains, partial paralysis, intestinal ulceration, general debility,
testify of the poison's hold and power." The author of *Revidenda*
calls it " muffled Popery," and *The Protestant Churchman* describes it
as being " a development of the sacerdotal system, until it is essentially
that of the Church of Rome." But no matter how strongly they may
declare the Church to be " dead " with this Romanism, it is clear that
they do not mean it ; for they do not disguise their anxiety to continue
in organic unity with all this false and " deadly " doctrine, yea, even
with the extremes of Ritualism itself. The author of the " Romanizing Germs " says, after claiming full liberty for his own friends : " if
it be urged that the Ritualists would make the same demand, we say
heartily in reply, Let their demand be granted. If we are to have indeed a comprehensive Church, let all shades of thought be free to
develop themselves." All they claim is, a little more liberty for themselves within her bosom, and there they are content to remain. They
profess to desire no breach of that Church Unity which now so sweetly
binds together the living and the dead. But when a living man really
is bound to a corpse, he is not of such a contented spirit. He does not
declare that he will remain bound, and that nobody shall loose him.
He does not quietly limit his aspirations to one additional thickness of
paper betwixt himself and the corpse. It is evident, therefore, that the
Evangelicals are once more using language in a non-natural sense.
They may now and then be coarse and violent, or even vulgar in their
mode of expressing themselves ; but it is only " pretty Fanny's way."
They are not really so truculent as their language seems to indicate.

They are, indeed, our Ecclesiastical Bourbons—they learn nothing,
and they forget nothing. They go on repeating like parrots the same
phrases which were their favorites from thirty to fifty years ago, utterly
unconscious of the vast change of circumstances, which has affected them
quite as much as any others. They have adopted, one after another, a
great number of things which at first they vehemently denounced as
" Romish," and which—in others—they vehemently denounce still, unconscious of the laughter of their contemporaries. Was there ever a

more complete change of place on the part of two bodies of combatants, than there has been since the publication of Tract No. 90? Then
there was a universal Protestant chorus against the Tract, as dishonest,
evasive, Jesuitical, as involving mental reservation and the use of
words in a non-natural sense ; and our Evangelicals vaunted themselves as the only honest men in the Church, who alone held our
standards in their *true* sense—the very sense of the Reformers who
made them.   Now, however, the tables are completely turned.   With
a matchless genius for blundering, the same columns of the same
pamphlets still boast of being the sole representatives left among us of
the true views of the Reformers, while side by side they record the confession, which the controversies and researches of the past few years
have wrung out of them, that " the Reformation, as taken up and forwarded under Elizabeth's auspices, could not have been radically
Protestant, nor the Liturgy, its written expression, altogether free from
Romish taint ; " that it was the express object of that arrangement to
retain the Papists in the communion of the Church of England ; and
that for a time it was successful in accomplishing this object, for
" Papists ' repaired to their parish churches without doubt or scruple,'
and priests officiated at the parochial altars ; " that since the adoption
of the Articles in 1571 " we have ceased to be Protestant " touching
the *opus operatum* in Baptism, and that " baptismal regeneration was
the prevailing belief among all classes of theologians for years after the
Reformation ; " while, moreover, " the Baptismal service being at the
foundation of the Ritual and Liturgy of our Church, we find all other
parts of the ecclesiastical system built upon it, and in more or less harmony of design."   And having made these discoveries, it is further
cheerfully confessed by the Evangelicals that they must " accord to the
sacerdotal party entire conscientiousness of conviction.   Their doctrinal views doubtless seem to them in entire accordance with the Bible
and the Book of Common Prayer : " while, in the same breath, these
Evangelicals, these former paragons of honesty and straightforward-
ness, these haters of mental reservation and equivocation, these abhor-
rers of the iniquity of using words in a *non-natural* sense, shriek out in
the torture of a wounded conscience the confession that *they* are in the
constant habit of perpetrating all these abominations, while their opponents, against whom they have been launching false and furious accusa-
tions for thirty years past, have all the while been honest men, who
understand Holy Scripture in the same sense as did the Primitive
Church, and who interpret the standards which have come down to us
from the Reformation, in the very same sense that was meant by the
Reformers !

Yet these changes of party warfare have a meaning much deeper and
larger than their relations to local struggles.   The present state of
things is one result of the great tidal wave which has for more than
half a century being steadily sweeping upward from the depths of
eighteenth century latitudinarianism and degradation, and still bids fair
to keep on, until the Reunion of Christendom shall bless the now divided hosts of the Church Militant, and this whole world shall be con-

verted unto God. In its frantic violence of language, and its wilful blindness to the facts that are going on about us, the dwindling and helpless remnant of the Evangelical party is like a man, who, within closed shutters and by the light of a farthing dip, is loudly and passionately demonstrating to the uneasy handful about him, that the house they are in is immovably anchored on the rock, and is therefore safe amid the darkness of night and the raging of the storm : while, if he would but open his shutters and look out, he would see that the mighty freshet had long ago lifted his little shell of a house, and that he has already floated down many miles on his course toward the great Sea, which is One : while the outgush of a glorious Dawn would render his farthing dip useless for the purpose of giving light, and he would hardly like to keep it burning as a " symbol " of the brilliance of the errors which have so long deluded him !

If logic, or reason, or consistency, or historical knowledge—if the convincings of opponents or the confessions of friends—had any real mastery over the Evangelical mind, it might safely be set down from henceforth as done for. But the little that is left of it may well rely upon its proved ability to set all these at defiance. It will, indeed, disappear from its former prominence in the Councils of the Church. The party which once had all New England, except Connecticut, now has not a single diocese there that it can call its own. In the Middle States it has only Pennsylvania, and by no very strong majority. The new Diocese of Central Pennsylvania was secured by the Moderates, by the turn of a feather, the new Bishop receiving the votes of several High-Churchmen : and in two or three years the control of that diocese will be in other hands. In the South, outside of Virginia, they have nothing. And in the West, the vote in the Cheney case tells us that even Ohio is not secure ; while Iowa and Kansas are not to be permanently depended on ; and Nevada has not yet been admitted. This is positively all ; and there is no prospect of *any* further gain for them in the future. As an element in Church legislation, therefore, they have, as we have said, become extinct already. Ichabod, Ichabod !

But, as individuals, as parishes, as cliques, they will last for some time to come. The doctrine of justification by faith only, without works, is always welcome to a certain proportion of the rich and fashionable congregations in our large cities. Wherever a popular preacher can announce " a pure Gospel " of that sort to sinners in their rented pews, when the united annual incomes of those sitting in the middle alley alone would amount to from five to twenty millions of dollars, it will be antecedently probable that that congregation will be Evangelical.

Moreover, it must never be forgotten that the Church is steadily absorbing large numbers from the denominations around ; and that, too, from the force of many concurrent causes which have nothing to do with careful reading or conscientious conviction. Causes social and political, causes intellectual and æsthetical, and many others, are constantly bringing to us numbers who—for a time at least—have no reason for the faith that is in them, except that the Drift has landed them among us. Such persons will for a long time be ruled by the popular Protestant prejudices of the country : and so long as they neither read nor think, neither feel nor care, they will naturally perpetuate what has heretofore been called " the Evangelical party." There must be a lowest form in every school : and the Church is a school. There must always be an " awkward squad " at every recruiting station : and the Church Militant is an army, which cannot hope to recruit its ranks with those only who are able to serve like trained veterans from the outset. But, as a great party struggling hopefully for the mastery within the Church, the old Evangelical party is dead, dead, dead. It came to its end at the General Convention of 1871. Were strict justice to be done, the coroner would sit, and the verdict would be *felo de se*, without any suspicion of " temporary insanity." But this would be rather hard on so religious a party, and would, by the rubric, deprive it of Christian burial, which would be a pity. We, for our part, shall therefore make no objection to the milder return of " Died a natural death," or " by the visitation of God "—whichever the surviving friends may prefer. And, notwithstanding its morbid antipathy, while living, to the idea of prayers for the departed—we love it well enough, after all, to inscribe affectionately upon its tombstone—*May it rest in peace!*

THE CATHEDRAL SYSTEM IN THE CITY.*

(The regular quarterly paper, read at the meeting of the New York
Ecclesiological Society in January, 1855. By the Rev. John H.
Hopkins, Jr., M.A.)

WHEN one who is thoroughly imbued with the fundamental principles
of the working of the One, Holy, Catholic, and Apostolic Church from
the beginning, examines the *theory* of our present Church constitution,
he finds the main features of the structure all in their right places. No
general canon can be made without the consent of the Bishops. Each
Bishop is *ex-officio* President of his own Convention. No Priest or
Deacon can be made except by him, nor received ordinarily from one
diocese to another, nor transferred from one parish to another, without
his sanction. No parish can be organized, and no Church consecrated,
but by him ; nor can any permanent parochial connection be formed but
by his authority. Generally, too, where there is any organization for
Diocesan Missions, he has substantially, if not formally, the appointment of the stations and the nomination of the missionaries; and the
same is the rule under our general Missionary Board. Thus the glorious
old Church axiom, *Ecclesia est in Episcopo*, and the resulting rule,
Οὐδὲν χωρὶς Ἐπισκόπου—*nothing without the Bishop*—seem to be
theoretically the life and soul of our whole ecclesiastical system. But
when we look at the practical position of the Church we discover that
much of this theory is only theory, and is to be found nowhere except
on paper. We do not find that the Bishop is the centre of all the *visible*
fabric of the Church. We do not see how he well *can* be the soul of
the Church's practical life and action. We see nothing whatever that
can insinuate even a suspicion that the Bishop is the essential embodiment of Divine Power in the Church. This may seem strong language ;
but let us look at *facts*, and see whether they do not justify it.

What constitutes a diocese, as the word is popularly understood
now ? A number of *parishes*, with *priests* and *people*. The parish
churches are prominent fabrics. They speak for themselves. The

* This article is very much condensed from the original. There is also,
in the journal of the Ecclesiological Society, a companion article on the
cathedral system in rural dioceses. Dr. Hopkins wrote many articles on
the cathedral system (especially as to New York City, in the early years of
the Church Journal), and he used to say that not less than twenty millions
should be expended on the cathedral, and its endowments for all purposes.
He believed that the ideal place for it in New York was on the high ground
between the Harlem and East Rivers.

parish priest is always to be heard of by inquiring for him at or near his Church. If there be a Bishop, what difference does it make in the appearance of the diocese? None at all. The Bishop has no church of his own, except he be also a parish priest; and then he serves at the call of a vestry, and is more or less under their control, like any other priest. Here, in New York, many miles off we can already see the spires of the parish churches, and their splendid fabrics stand proudly forth on our chief thoroughfares; but where is the Bishop's Church? He has *none.* When not actually engaged in his canonical visitation, he appears to have no business in any Church, except by invitation or permission of its Rector. Every man in the ministry seems to have a local habitation and a name, except himself. We beg pardon; he *may* have a *local habitation.* By diligent inquiry, or by searching the directory, the stranger finds his way down some obscure side street, and in the midst of a row of houses he may find one which bears the Bishop's simple surname on the door-plate. It is near no Church, and is just across the way from a Presbyterian meeting-house. It has little or no convenience for the special hospitality enjoined upon every Bishop at his consecration, being only a residence, like that of any private gentleman. There is, in fact, no *external* circumstance whatever to distinguish the position of our Bishops from the so-called itinerant bishops of the Methodists, except that, in public official ministrations, our Bishops wear expensive robes of black satin, and lawn sleeves with ruffles round the wrists; while the Methodist Bishops officiate in citizen's costume. Of all the great body of the Church in its manifold connections, there seems to be no one person or thing either dependent upon the Bishop, or set in motion by him. And those stated duties to which he is specially pledged—hospitality and constant preaching of the Gospel—appear to be made by his peculiar circumstances specially impossible. Even when he ordains, it must be in somebody else's Church, and by permission of its Rector, for he has, as we have already said, no church of his own. The same ostensible anarchy reigns throughout all the practical working of the Churches. One Society has its headquarters here, another there. For Diocesan Missions you go down to Water Street. For General Missions you go up to the Bible House. For Bibles and Prayer-Books you go over to Thirteenth Street. For other Church books you must repair to Broadway. There is no visible connection with the Bishop in anything, nor with each other in any operation. It would seem as if the object were to scatter the strength of the Church as much as possible; to *avoid,* by all means, the setting the candle in a candlestick; to *shrink* from placing the city on a hill *for fear* people should see its strength, and unity, and beauty; but rather to sink its several fragments among the waves of the world's life; to smother it away in holes and corners, that it may be kept " out of sight, out of mind," as much as possible.

Now, how is it that a theory which is instinct with such central strength, unity, and beauty, on paper, has slidden into such slovenliness, indifference, and disjointedness — such miserable weakness, awkwardness, and inefficiency, in practice? It is, in fact, one of the many ill results of the Popish corruption and Erastian malpractice, that have so largely tainted the channel through which our historical Church has descended to us from the Apostles of our Lord. Both of these disturbing causes have so far marred the magnificent vigor of the Church's own primitive plan, that it could now hardly be recognized any more were it not that features which have long been changed in every outward seeming, have still been retained, faithfully traced upon our paper system, if nowhere else.

The corruptions of Popery during the Middle Ages laid the foundation for all the mischief that has since followed. Bishops then became entirely too worldly in their character. They were Barons more than Bishops, and chief Princes rather than chief Pastors. Non-residence was the prevailing vice among mediæval Bishops. Whether on political affairs at the capital of the country; or engaged at Rome in ecclesiastical intrigues for translations and pluralities, or promotions of one sort or another; or in some part of the multifarious proceedings which were always attracting men and money to the papal court; a Bishop's own diocese was often, of all Europe, the part which was least likely to see anything of his Lordship. And when he was in residence for a brief space, it was ten to one that the secular business of his Barony, or getting in his revenues, occupied nearly all his time. Besides which, in very many cases, Bishoprics were conferred upon those who, from youth or incapacity, could perform none of the functions of a Bishop, except taking and spending the income of the See ; or upon those whose high office at the court of either king or pope would not permit a residence in the diocese. The See, in such cases, was conferred only as the most convenient mode of making a present, to a prosperous courtier, of a handsome income, with little or no duty attached.

As the inevitable consequences from all this things went sadly to waste in nearly every diocese. The priests and the people learned to do with Bishops as they do in France with things which it is impossible to procure. They *did without*. And when the head was thus unhappily out of the way, of course, confusion and disorder reigned among the members. It was easy for one wealthy monastery after another to gain from the Pope an exemption from its Bishop's visitation and control : for the monks were always willing to pay a very handsome price to the Pope for such a piece of parchment ; and the Bishops generally cared too little, or knew too little, about their own dioceses to oppose it. Nay, this practice increased to such an extent, that at last, it invaded even the ancient citadel and stronghold of a Bishop's personal and unquestioned power—his Cathedral. Here, in primitive times, he used to reign supreme, with his priests and deacons and deaconesses and minor officials about him, like the general of a great army—a true captain in the Church militant— surrounded by his staff, and by all the means for the readiest and most efficient action with the rank and file. Yet even here, constant absence and obstinate neglect on the part of prelates wrought their inevitable result. The Dean and Chapter gradually encroached upon the prerogatives and powers of a man who was never on the spot to look after either his own interests or their duties. One by one *they* absorbed them all; and finally the sanction of the Pope was purchased, as usual, to legalize their usurpation. Thus at last it came to pass, that a Bishop was as much a stranger in his own Cathedral as he was to his diocese at large. It was often years before he was consecrated, unless it were necessary *legally* to enable him to obtain the temporalities. And, when consecrated, it was often years before he went down to his diocese to be enthroned in his Cathredral; after which he was off again. It was no wonder that the Dean thus came to be in fact the Bishop of the Cathedral, while the Bishop himself, except on certain set occasions, might have the doors of his own Cathedral shut in his face, and have no redress against the legalized insubordination of his own official,

The Reformation in England mended many—very many—matters which had gone abominably out of the way before, both in faith and practice. The Cathedrals, however, received no benefit except on paper. They were all well plundered to begin with. They received in return amended sets of statutes, which recognized all the chief purposes (with one exception) for which they had originally been so magnificently designed. These were the constant daily singing of the public service of God in the most solemn and beautiful manner, by a competent Chapter of clergy well trained in divinity and sacred music, and with a competent choir; the delivery of sermons and lectures more diligently and attractively than in any other Church; the keeping a competent School, in which the singing-boys should be trained in all good learning, and thence forwarded to the Universities so that they should be in due time admitted to Holy Orders; for which latter purpose, also, Divinity lectureships were to be maintained at the Cathedral. In addition to which provision was made for the maintenance of a certain number of veteran soldiers, who had been wounded or maimed in the King's wars. There are beautiful things about these old Cathedral statutes, which show a thorough comprehension of their original intent, and their great power for good; and the weight of these obligations was bound down likewise upon the consciences of Deans and Chapters, with sanctions as solemn as the Latin language was capable of expressing. But one mockery and one omission spoiled all. The *mockery* was the confirming to the Dean and Chapter their old right of *electing* the Bishop of the Diocese; while at the same time by the ingenious contrivance of a Letter missive sent with the *Congé d'élire*, backed by the statute of Præmunire, they were sure to have their goods confiscated, and be themselves banished the realm, if they dared to choose any person as Bishop except the one whom the king himself recommended to their mechanical suffrages. This enormous abuse continues to the present day, and has been the chief cause, perhaps, why such a great gulf often exists between an English Bishop and his diocese. The mockery of an election was made worse by the *omission* to restore to the Bishop his ancient powers in his own Cathedral. The Dean and Chapter were left in undisturbed possession of that abnormal independence which had been so corruptly acquired during the

Middle Ages through the usurpation and venality of the Popes, the ambitions of Deans, and the unprincipled indifference of the Bishops. The consequence of which is, that most English Bishops have even *now* as little power in their own Churches as their predecessors had before the Reformation. They appear there to be enthroned, and on certain set occasions ; and they have the legal power of *Visitors :* but as to the practical conduct of its affairs, or the regulations of its services, the Bishop has in most cases no more to say than the humblest Deacon in his diocese. Nor has he any power in the nomination of even his own Dean ; nor yet, in some cases, of even a single member of his Chapter. These dignitaries are generally appointed by the Crown—like himself ; and generally, too, from political considerations. And with such utter indifference to the original purposes of the foundation have these nominations often been made, that although all the Cathedral clergy are bound to sing their part in the choral service, men are not unfrequently appointed who cannot tell one note of music from another, or who perhaps never even tried whether they could hum a tune or not until after they received their appointment. It became customary therefore to get a set of second-class clergy to do the singing, while the first-class dignitaries took the fat incomes ; the Minor Canons being kept on starvation salaries, I suppose, because empty vessels are best for sound.

With Dean and Chapter thus appointed and thus exercising the duties of their office, it is no wonder that great decay and demoralization have attended these magnificent foundations. The Great Rebellion put them all through another extensive plundering, besides great dilapidations of their fabrics as well as their fortunes. As the prices of property rose and the value of money fell, however, the remnants of the old estates yet left began to yield rich incomes once more ; whereupon the Deans and Canons, who held supreme control over the corporation purse-strings, took care to keep the poor Minor Canons and choristers and choir-boys and organist and schoolmaster, all down to the original number of shillings and pence ; while they shared among *themselves* the multiplying thousands of pounds of annual income. The poor old soldiers soon disappeared, and have never been heard of since. The preachings became few and far between, and of the prosiest specimens of thoroughly educated dulness and classic orthodoxy. The divinity lectures have hardly even been heard of, time out of mind. The schools have dwindled miserably, and in some Cathedrals exist only in name. The choir-boys are often contemptibly few in number, undisciplined and scandalous in their demeanor and irregular in their attendance. What wonder is it that, with a cathedral system so utterly perverted as this, the worship should become a dull, lifeless, listless routine, often executed with such mercenary eye-service, such heartless indifference, and such shameless slovenliness, if not profanity, as to alienate wholly the affections of the people, if it did not drive them in sheer disgust to the dissenting chapel, or the Wesleyan field-preaching, or *anywhere* in fact, where there seemed to be something like earnestness in preaching the gospel and something like heart-worship in singing the praises of God. The only wonder is, that so many generations of these unconnected abuses have not altogether swept the Cathedral system from the English Church. There have been several premonitory warnings, indeed, of this ultimate result, if the Deans and Canons do not repent and do their first works. And we are happy to say that there are many decided symptoms, within the last few years, that they will at last wake to something like a sense of their duty. Whether or no it will come in time to prevent their magnificent foundations from being hopelessly ruined by the result of their past sins, yet remains to be seen.

We need hardly say, after this sketch of the Cathedral System in England, that we are no advocates for the transplanting of that corrupt system, or anything like it, to the soil of these United States. Indeed the thing would be impossible, because so many of its greatest abuses are intimately bound up with the existing connection between the Church and State there—a connection which, thank Providence, is utterly out of the question here. But, nevertheless, we *have* inherited not a few of the evil results of the English system, and these are they which produce the visible and undeniable practical anomalies of which we complain. The disjointed and shambling way of getting through the manifold business of a great diocese is a direct inheritance from the Church of England of the last and deadest century. In many respects, indeed, we have, from circumstances, much amended our pattern. In others, we seem to be in danger of acting like the Chinese tailor and making the unsightly patch to be an essential feature in our idea of a new coat. Thus the very common and very popular notion that a Bishop must have no church of his own, but must spend all his time in the visiting, or in the direct service of his Diocese, is founded on two errors. The first is, that a Bishop having a church of his own (that is, a Cathedral) must perform in it precisely the same duties that an ordinary priest performs in his parish. The second is, that a Bishop ought to have a diocese so large that it will take him all the time, from one year's end to the other, to get round all his parishes ; whereas, the Bishop's Church is for essentially different objects from those of ordinary parish churches, as we shall presently show. And our Bishops— especially if, as is our almost universal practice, they are to be married men, ought to be allowed to remain at home a sufficient portion of the year to rule their own houses well and to exercise that hospitality which is one of the indispensable duties of their office, but which they cannot well exercise when they are constantly away from home.

No. In this respect, as well as in many others, it is our bounden duty to go back to the *primitive system of the Church* and take our pattern thence ; and we shall thus find that what is earliest and purest, has likewise most of true power for the furtherance of God's work in the Church, because freshest from the hands of those who had the *wisdom of the serpent* as well as the harmlessness of the dove ; and who left, upon the whole of the fabric, whose foundations they laid so wonderfully well, the most unquestionable proofs of their extraordinary clear-sightedness, and common sense.

Let us then briefly sketch what the Cathedral system *ought* to be here in New York—a city of which it may truly be said that there was never before seen anywhere in Christendom so great a city as this is, *without* its Cathedral. And in making our estimate for its wants, we will not ask it to rank higher than some second- or third-rate provincial town in the Middle Ages, with its fifteen or twenty thousand inhabitants.

In the first place there should be a Church—the Bishop's Cathedral Church—cruciform in its plan, with area far larger than any other Church in the diocese. It ought to be able to accommodate on great occasions—perhaps with the aid of a light, movable iron gallery, and also of its *triforia*—at least eight to ten thousand worshippers ; with a chancel capable, when well filled, of holding five hundred—Bishops, clergy, choristers, and choir-boys. This should be the Church in which all Diocesan Conventions should meet, all regular ordinations be held, all consecrations of Bishops performed (when in this city), as well as all great anniversaries of Church societies, and all great general celebrations of Ecclesiastical occasions. The vast area of its nave and transepts should be forever free from the pollutions of bargain and sale. Its lofty walls should never re-echo to the sound of the auctioneer's hammer. Here in daily Morning and Evening Service should be celebrated, with all that the loving care and zeal of men and human art can do, to make it measurably worthy of being regarded as a sacrifice unto the most High God : and having, therefore, also a sweet savor among men. On Sundays and Festivals there should be additional services, in the early morning, and later in the evening, or at such other hours as shall be found most convenient for those who cannot attend at the more ordinary times. At least from twelve to twenty-four Priests and Deacons should be appointed to the stated service of this great Church, all, or nearly all, of whom must be competent to take their part in the choral service. These should form the great body of city missionaries, each two having their peculiar district assigned them, in which they should daily visit from house to house. The *Four Principal Persons* —as they were called in the old cathedral foundations—might be married men, of greater age and experience, in receipt of larger income, and more permanently attached to the Cathedral than the rest. These four were the *Dean*, the *Precentor*, the *Chancellor*, and the *Treasurer*. The *Dean*, under the Bishop, held the chief rule, and the cure of souls of all within the precinct. The *Precentor* held charge over the Musical service. The *Chancellor* was the lecturer in Divinity—the principal instructor of the Candidates for Holy Orders. The *Treasurer* administered the temporalities, and took care of the Fabric, for which purpose it was needful that he be well skilled in architecture. In smaller cathedrals, some of these different offices might be combined in one person ; but in the larger, the four should be filled, each by a man of full ability and energy. These four, whose permanence is necessary to the best interests of the institution, should have sufficient income for the maintenance of wife and family ; but the remainder of the Cathedral Clergy should be young men and unmarried, living in common, in a common house, and at a common table. The term of their service should have a limit as a *minimum*—say two or three years ; after which, whether as Priests or Deacons, they might be transferred to parish duty, and be free to marry, if they pleased. This plan would insure a constant succession of younger and more energetic life in the service of the Cathedral, at the most moderate expense, and with a certainty that the institution could never sink down into being *only* a receptacle for aged and dignified drones. It would also keep up a constant circulation of clerical life from the centre to the whole body of the diocese ; and the mode of celebrating Divine Service would, before many years, become so homogeneous, that, on great religious gatherings, when thronging crowds came together in the Cathedral from all the parishes, one heart and one voice would animate the whole mass, and the praises of God would be sung so lustily and with such good courage, as the whole of Christendom has hardly known for more than a thousand years.

To supply this ministry with abundant members, there should be a thorough system of education connected, as of old, with this Cathedral. The boys' school should be open only to such boys as had approved voices, and were sufficiently well-behaved to be employed in the stated service of the House of God. To such, a competent maintenance should be afforded, with thorough instruction, not only in Church music, but in all the other branches needed for a full theological education thereafter. By the time their voices began to break, they should be ready for admission to college ; and the Cathedral should have at its disposal scholarships sufficient to carry through all who should possess requisite ability, and disposition toward the ministry. On graduating, by which time their voices as men would be settled, and once more at disposal for regular service, they would be admitted as Candidates for Holy Orders, and at the same time take their places as men-choristers in the Cathedral choir. The ancient cloisters should be so far modified as to supply sufficient rooms and accommodations for these students, while preparing their theological studies preparatory to the Diaconate. Into this Order they should be admitted at the end of their first year, and then at once begin, under the charge of Priests, their proper apprenticeships, in the originally intended work of the order of Deacons ; not rising to the Priesthood ordinarily until they have fulfilled for at least three years this humbler service. Then, after one or two years' service as Priests also, they would be ready, if they so desired, for matrimony and a parish.

All this while they would be in more or less of close contact with the Bishop. He could watch the development of the character of each from boyhood, knowing well what was his temper and ability, what he was good for, and where he would be likely to serve the Church best. And the Clergy would thus learn to know and love their Bishop with a warmth of personal attachment which is now impossible. For, in our ordinary system, a candidate in a large Diocese like this, commonly meets his Bishop for a few minutes at the time he applies to be received as a candidate, and also at his examination and ordination, and after that only at a Visitation, Convocation, or Convention ; neither party having really any chance worth talking of to become truly acquainted

with, or attached to the other.   Upon our proposed plan, these younger
clergymen would not be overworked at the scribbling of one or two
wishy-washy sermons in a week, while they have no time left them to
practise the true essence of the pastoral function—the going in person
after the wandering sheep, through the streets and lanes, among the
poor and destitute, the sick and the dying—which will teach them more
of true spiritual growth in a month, than the writing of sermons will
in a year.   Nor would it be necessary for poor people, when in want
of a clergyman, to hunt him up among boarding-houses down-town, or
indistinguishable rows of brick or brown stone uptown.   No !   There
this house full of clergy would reside, on the Cathedral grounds ; none
of them would be allowed more than one month's absence during the
year, and not more than two to be absent at once at any one time from
the city ; nor ever less than two or three left in attendance at the house
at any hour of the day or night, and this house of residence would be
perpetual and unchanging, so that once known it could be found again
with ease.

But it must not be supposed that this Cathedral will stand, like old
Trinity on Broadway, with nothing but graves beside it, solitary, amidst
the noises of this huge business Babel.   Nowhere should this great
Church abut upon the open street.   But it should stand in the centre
of a large inclosed ground ; protected by a complete *entourage* of other
buildings, from the dust and noises of the street ; approached by its
four gates, and the green grass and quiet trees filling the space—as
large a space as could be gotten—between the great church, and its
surrounding buildings.   Nor should these surrounding buildings in-
close anything except what is needed for the service of the Cathedral,
or the diocese of which it should be the mother-church—the very heart
and centre.   First there should be the Bishop's house—plain, though
large and liberal, and of superior dignity to any other in the group.
Next to him should be the houses of the four principal persons, followed by the common residence of the rest of the cathedral clergy.
Then there should be a house for the head of the cathedral school, and
school-rooms, and common rooms and dormitories for the choir-boys.
The organist should have his own house also, and there should be
others for the vergers or sextons and their families.   Beside these
there should be the chapter house.   There would the House of Bishops
meet and sit during General Convention or in council, while the Lower
House occupied an adjoining transept.   In the great surrounding circle
of buildings there should be a church hospital, a sisterhood house,
a dispensary, an infirmary, an asylum for superannuated and infirm
clergy, where they could live upon the Church they had served during
their lives, and daily attend her cathedral worship, and pray for her
when they were too old to do anything else in her behalf.   There should
also be the cathedral library—the chief collection of books which could
be found anywhere in the country ; and the muniment room, where the
archives of the American Church should be kept safely, instead of in a
tin box in a private residence, subject to all the chances of fire.   There
should be the diocesan treasury, and there the offices of every one of

the Church societies, whether diocesan or general—the more prominent position being of course assigned to the latter. The *cloisters* we have already mentioned as devoted to the accommodation of the candidates for the diaconate. Thus there would be gathered within one great circuit, every part and parcel of that which is needed for the general life and organic operations of the Church, together with a portion, at least, of that which is necessary for her work anywhere, even down to the least detail. And this complex variety of institutions, thus clustering around the base of the great Mother-Church, would furnish of itself—even without any aid from elsewhere—a large and devout and constant congregation of the faithful for the daily service and the weekly Eucharist, and for every other function which constitutes, or ought to constitute, any part of the Church's life. Who is there who would not rejoice to see such a sight as this?

But it may be asked, even by those who would approve and admire so glorious a scheme as we have rudely sketched—where could it be possible to get the means for realizing it?

To this I reply, that *we have already all,* or nearly all, *the means lying ready to our hand now in our very midst, only we do not see them.* Or, if we have not enough to complete, we have at least enough to begin, and begin well, with the confidence that by the time the work is ready for completion, the additional means will come by the process of natural and inevitable increase.

[He goes on to specify these elements of his plan : the estates of Trinity forming a basis, at least sufficient, without hurting their present use, for " a fair start." He speaks of that corporation as an immense money power, which may work with the Bishop, and may not ; but which if it does work with the Bishop should in some way do so on account of his Order, and not because pleased with the Bishop personally.

The G. T. S. ought to be brought into the Cathedral close, and thus its lack of a proper chapel could be met by the Cathedral Choir, and its library safely housed. The Episcopal Residence owned then by the Diocese, if sold, would furnish abundant means for the erection of a better one in the Close. *Trinity School* would be the basis of a full Cathedral School. *Columbia College* would furnish the full education spoken of, the Trinity School already having a large number of scholarships in the same. The *Society for the Promotion of Religion and Learning* would help candidates for Orders. The *City Mission Society* would have abundance of means, when once revived with active zeal. By its Charter it may hold unlimited amounts of property, and on this Charter full provision could be made for the support of the Cathedral Clergy, should no other mode be feasible. The Sisterhood House was already in existence in New York and St. Luke's Hospital and Dispensary and Infirmary were just rising into existence. The other Societies were in New York, too.]

What, then, is wanting? The ground is covered with confused heaps of stone, all cut and squared, of timber measured and shaped, and all manner of materials for the erection of a mightier and more beautiful fabric, material and spiritual, than has ever yet been seen on this American Continent. We want nothing but *The Architect*—the wise Master Builder—who can see clearly when each fits into each, whose hand is cunning enough to bring together the parts already prepared for one another ; who can, in other words, simply pick up and put together the admirable and abundant materials that now lie scattered in chaotic confusion all round him on every side. Let this be once done, and the head of the Diocese will be no longer head only in *name*, while the substance of power and influence is in other hands.

The visible array of the Church will be no longer dispersed in such wise as to be almost invisible to the world around. But after the long eclipse of her primitive and powerful system, she will once more " look forth as the morning." Not dimmed and hidden by the petty jealousies and suspicions, the cowardly fears and misbelieving apprehensions, which men are forever conjuring up to cloud the very light of day ; but once more " clear as the sun." Not split into disjointed fragments ; not left at sixes and sevens, as if hap-hazard were the only law of the Church's growth ; not lying in such pertinacious confusions that it was impossible that any two pieces of the Church system could ever be made to hang together ; not like an undisciplined, disorderly mob, so scattered and mixed up among the superior members of the foe as to be almost imperceptible ; but once more a compact Body, in goodly order and close array, each several man gaining strength from his union with all the others, marshalled side by side under lawful command and in perfect discipline ; and through the gathering clouds that foretell the approach of earth's greatest battle and her last, flashing in bold and peerless beauty, full upon the sight of her innumerable enemies, " terrible as an army with banners."

The spectacle presented in these later days of Columbia College, St. Luke's Hospital, and the already rising walls of the Cathedral of St. John the Divine, show how true was the outlook of Hopkins when, in 1855, he pictured this very combination of great corporations near the Cathedral Church.

24

LETTERS.

"**JULY 27, 1891.**

"DEAR S——: Writing grows harder and harder for me, especially when there is nothing to say, except to thank you for your kind letters. . . .

"As to myself, there are so many others in the world who have more to suffer than I have that I *can't help* being patient. It gives me neither thought nor trouble. I am only *thankful* that it is no worse. I can yet *read* with entire comfort, and hardly move from my seat from morning till night. I read and doze and doze until it is time to go to bed; and there you know my whole life except when—very rarely—I write a few brief letters. Your items of news about friends are *always* welcome.

"Ever yours,
"H. (ENRY)."

"TROY, N. Y., August 14, 1891.

"DEAR MISS HALL: Our dear friend passed away in his sleep shortly after midnight.

"That his end should be so free from suffering, at the last, was a great comfort.

"His death took place at my place near Hudson, and I am in Troy arranging for the funeral. . . .

"Faithfully yours,
"E. D. FERGUSON."

TO THE SAME.

"AUGUST 22, 1891.

"We have returned from conveying the body of our dear friend to its last resting place at Rock Point, and knowing the long friendship that had existed between you, I felt that you would be interested in the events at the close of his life.

"By what may seem almost providential means—or at least by escaping constantly threatened dangers, his life extended much further than I anticipated, by at least more than a year.

"It had been his dread, and my expectation, that he would be absolutely helpless for a time preceding his dissolution, for during all this time there was a loss of strength, and he had for a long time required occasional assistance.

"He was able, however, to occupy his time in reading and conver-

sation, though during certain feverish attacks to which he was liable
he would be very sleepy for two or three days at a time.

" On Monday and Tuesday preceding his death he had one of these
attacks, but on Wednesday and Thursday he was bright ; read all the
time when not talking, and was as comfortable as could be expected.

" He was unable to lie long in one position, and the night before his
death he had been rather more restless than usual, so that I went to
his assistance quite frequently to get him up, and to aid him in lying
down again.

" The night of his death (Thursday night) he asked to go to bed
quite early, and I had one of my family sit up in an adjoining room to
go in and watch him.

" He went readily to sleep, and lay perfectly quiet, until soon after
midnight, the watcher, noticing that he did not for a few minutes make
his usual noise in breathing, called me, and I found he had just passed
away without a motion—without a struggle—from sleep to *sleep*.
Knowing that you would take an interest in it all I send you this brief
account of his passage from this life to life eternal.

" Sincerely,
" E. D. FERGUSON."

FROM THE SAME. TO THE SAME.

" I will supplement my letter by a brief note.

" I may say that he was not only brave but cheerful to the end. Only
for a few times did the peevishness of invalidism show itself toward
the end, and even that which might be called peevishness in him would
in the average invalid have passed for good humor.

" He left no special messages to anyone. All of that seemed to have
been arranged. Last year, when it seemed he might soon pass away,
he left some suggestions to me concerning you.

" The end stole on him so that there was no time for messages—and
his last words were ' that will do, dear,' as I turned him and arranged
him in bed. He often spoke to me of you, and I fully understood the
deep interest you took in each other, so I telegraphed you, it being the
only telegram I sent except to his sister, who attended to the rest.

" I do not feel that I need thanks or praise for my care of him. I
was glad to do it, and would do it gladly again ; hence there is no merit
in it.

" Sincerely,
" E. D. FERGUSON."

FROM MRS. FERGUSON TO MISS HALL.

". . . I assure you of dear Dr. Hopkins' unwavering faith until his last
moments. No word of doubt *ever* escaped his lips, and his one remark
when speaking of the future state, and his nearness to it, was, " just as

the Father wills." He frequently spoke of his death as one would
speak of passing from one room to another. There was no evidence
in his daily conversation that he ever had a fear or a doubt of the future
or his Master's infinite love. Could you have seen how perfectly happy
he was you could never have doubted his trust and confidence in God.
The influence of his cheerful resignation and perfect trust has left an
impression on our family that can never be forgotten—in fact it was
felt by all who came to see him.

" Yours very lovingly,
" MARION A. FERGUSON.

" Nov. 13, 1892."

" 233 CLARENDON ST., BOSTON,
" July 15, 1891.

" DEAR DR. HOPKINS : I thank you very much indeed for both your
letters. They give me opportunity to acknowledge your kind and cordial advocacy of my election, and all the chivalrous things you have
said during this prolonged discussion. I have no right to regret the
discussion, prolonged as it has been, since it has led my friends to say
so many friendly words, and has clothed the election with all the significance that could possibly be given to it. Now I shall rejoice indeed
if I can receive strength and wisdom to do a Bishop's duty faithfully
and well.

" I hope that you will come to the consecration ; and with all best
wishes for your health and happiness I am sincerely your friend and
brother,

" PHILLIPS BROOKS."

INDEX.

ADDINGTON PARK, Croydon, 163, 164.
All Saints, Margaret Street, 180, 181.
Altar vessels, designs for, 49–61.
Alms bason, gift of American Church
  to the Church of England, 54–57.
Alumni Lectureship on Evidences,
  220-222.
Anglican Church, compared with Ro-
  man and Eastern Churches, 291–293.
"Athirst for love," 39.

BARKER, BP., 202.
Batterson, Dr. H. G., 203, 204, 216.
Battle against High Churchmen, 78.
Beauvais, cathedral of, 178.
Birth, 1,
Blank Cartridge, The, editorials, 127–
  145.
"Blow on, Thou Mighty Wind," hymn
  for Whitsunday, 65, 66.
Breck, Dr. James, 196.
Briçonnet, Bp., of Meaux, 283, 284.

CADY, DR. PHILANDER K., 223.
Canterbury, 167–169.
Capel, Mgr., controversy with, 217.
Carey, Rev. Arthur, 21, 22.
Caricatures, 34, 35.
Cathedral System in the City, 359–369.
Characteristics of parents, 2–5.
Chester, 150.
Church Journal, 83.
"Church, as it is," editorial, editorials,
  95–104.
Church, in the face of Civil War, 105–
  108.
Church Music, 61–72.
Clarkson, Bp., anecdote of, 216.
Clerical life of the elder Hopkins, 5–7.
Colenso, Bp., 146, 147.
Controversy about Ritualism, 187–190.
Courtney, Dr. F., 199.

DANA, CHARLES A., 36.
Death of Bp. Hopkins, 183.
Death of Dr. Hopkins, 231.
Decline and Fall of the Low Church
  Party, Appendix, 295–358.

Defeat of movement to divide diocese
  of Central Pennsylvania, 208.
Defence of Low Churchmen, 191, 192.
Designs, 49–61.
Diaconate, Dr. Hopkins on the, 85–87.
Dieppe, 173.
Diocese of Springfield, 198.
Dix, Dr. Morgan, 61, 146, 213.
"Dream of a Child," 231–234.
Durham, cathedral of, 151, 152.

ECCLESIOLOGICAL SOCIETY OF NEW
  YORK, 49, 61.
Election of Dr. Phillips Brooks to the
  Episcopate, 198, 372.
Elliott, Bp. of Georgia, 21.

FAILURE of Bp. Hopkins, 13–15.
Family prayers, collects for, 250.
Family school, 8–10.
Fearlessness, 91, 94, 192.
Ferguson, Dr. E. D., 186, 223, 224.
Fredericksburg, Va., 201, 202.

GALLICANISM, 179.
General Convention, 216, 218.
General Theological Seminary, 21, 22,
  45–49, 93, 94, 206–209, 220–223.
Goethe, translation of, 36.
Graduated Representation, 239–242.
Graduates from University of Vermont,
  12.
"Gregorians vs. Anglicans," an inci-
  dent, 63, 64.

HOFFMAN, DR. E. A., 161, 210, 222,
  223.
Home-making, 18–21.
"Huckleberry Pudding," editorial,
  112–114.
Huguenots, 289–291.
Hymnal; the right to use an unauthor-
  ized, 69, 70.

ICONOCLASM, 223, 228.
Illinois, Province of, 199, 200.
Illness, 223–225, 231, 235.
Innovations, 110, 111.

"JERUSALEM, my home," hymn, 67, 68.

LAMBETH CONFERENCE, 147–149, 167–171.
Laon, cathedral of, 177, 178.
"Law of Ritualism," by Bp. Hopkins, 126.
Lay Element in England and America (from Contemporary Review) 258–280.
Letters, 15, 18, 21–38, 196–217, 220–228, 370–372.
Liberty and Constitutional Law, 115–118.
Liddon, Dr., 205.
Lincoln, cathedral of, 154, 155.
Littledale, Dr., letters from, 280, 282.
London, 158, 159, 162, 163.

MACKONOCHIE, REV. A. H., 162.
Mahan, Dr. Milo, 61, 83, 93, 103.
Marriage of his parents, 3.
McVickar, Dr. John, 61, 84.
Montluc, Bp. of Valence, 287.
Mother of Dr. Hopkins, 1–5.
Murder of President Lincoln, 108.
"My life is like a freighted barque," 37, 38.

NORWICH, cathedral of, 157, 158.

ORDINATION, Deacon, 73 ; Priest, 186.
Oxford, Colleges of, 164–167.
Oxford Tracts, Bishop Hopkins on the, 36.

PARIS, 174, 175, 179.
Parliament House, 160.
Pastoral staff for Bp. Howe, 58–61.
Pennsylvania, Federate Council of, 205–207, 211–213, 215.
Perry, Rev. T. W., 159, 165.
Personal customs of Dr. Hopkins, 115.
Peterborough, cathedral of, 155.
Plattsburgh, 183–193.
Policy of Church Journal, 84.
"Print-Colorer's Lament," 43, 44.
Province of Illinois, 223–225, 231, 235.
Provincial system, 252–257.
Pusey, Dr., 165–167.

RACINE COLLEGE, 199.
Reunion of Christendom, 218–220.
Review of the history of the Church, 74–81.
Rheims, cathedral of, 175, 176.
Ritualism, birth of, 49.
"Ritualism, what is," 119–126.
Rock Point, 18.
Roman Church, changes in, 225–227.
Rouen, cathedral of, 174.
Russian Liturgy in Trinity Chapel, New York, 109.

SALE of the Church Journal, 184.
Savannah, tutor at, 21.
"Scholars and Gentlemen," editorials, 87–90.
Seals, 49, 50.
Sermons, 244.
Seymour, Bp., 82, 84, 198, 231.
"Sparrows in Winter," 189, 190.
St. Alban's, Holborn, 160, 161.
St. Alban's, New York, 110.
St. Alban's, Peale, Pa., 214.
St. George the Martyr, 211, 249.
"Stuffed Tiger," editorial, 101.
Sweet, Rev. C. F., 223, 228.

"TENACITY of purpose" on part of Rome, 100, 101.
Thompson, Bp. H. M., 236, 237.

VERGENNES, 185.
Vermont, Dr. Hopkins' father Bp. of, 11.
Vermont Drawing-book, 42.
Vermont Episcopal Institute, 11, 12.

WALKER, BP. W. D., 168, 211.
Walter, W. H., Mus. Doc., 63.
Ward, Rev. Julius H., 184.
Westminster Abbey, 158, 159.
"We three Kings of Orient are," carol, with music, 71, 72.
Whitehead, Bp., 201.
Williamsport, 193–195.
"Wooden Turk," editorial, 103.
Wordsworth, Bp. Chr. (also Archdeacon), 56, 57, 228.

YORK, 152, 153.